The
Canadians

The Canadians

☙☙☙

Andrew H. Malcolm

St. Martin's Press
New York

For Connie, eh?

THE CANADIANS. Copyright © 1985 by Andrew Malcolm. Cover photos © 1985 by Image Finders Photo Agency, Vancouver, Canada. All inside photos copyright © 1985 by Andrew Malcolm, except that of the Toronto Skyline, which is reproduced courtesy of the Toronto Convention and Visitors Association. All rights reserved. Printed in the United States of America. No part of this book may be used or reproduced in any manner whatsoever without written permission except in the case of brief quotations embodied in critical articles or reviews. For information, address St. Martin's Press, 175 Fifth Avenue, New York, N.Y. 10010.

Library of Congress Cataloging-in-Publication Data

Malcolm, Andrew H.
  The Canadians / Andrew H. Malcolm
     p.   cm.
  Includes bibliographical references and index.
  ISBN 0-312-06921-9
  1. Canada—Civilization.   2. National characteristics, Canadian.
  3. Canada—Description and travel.   4. Canada—Economic
conditions—1945-   5. Canada—Relations—United States.   6. United
States—Relations—Canada.   I. Title.
  F1021.M37   1992
  971—dc20   91-35865
                                                                   CIP

First published in the United States by Times Books. Second edition published by Bantam Books.

Third U.S. Edition: February 1992
10 9 8 7 6 5 4 3 2 1

ACKNOWLEDGMENTS

I owe a great debt of gratitude to many people involved in this book, even when it wasn't really a book. First, I must thank Doris Adler, my assistant in the Toronto Bureau of *The New York Times*, researcher par excellence and good friend, who spent countless hours pursuing the big and little details that make a story of this scope come alive. I want to thank A. M. Rosenthal, Seymour Topping, Craig Whitney, Robert Semple, Jr., John Lee, Mike Levitas, Mike Sterne, and other editors at *The Times* for the assignment to and assignments in Canada and for allowing me to pursue so many projects there, even when they may have seemed somewhat unorthodox. Far too many Canadians to name here helped with the myriad pieces of this work, showing me their communities, explaining their lives and work, sharing their dreams and sadnesses and trust with a strange Yank always asking so many questions. I should also like to thank C. Conway Smith for his friendship, Arthur G. Hughes for his love of words, Jonathan Segal and Julian Bach for their guidance and encouragement, Martin Lynch for his keen eye and mind, J. M. S. Careless for his perspective and patience, and Ralph and Beatrice Malcolm, who taught me more about Canada and life than I will ever realize. I have appreciated the patience, company, support, and insights of our children, Christopher, Spencer, and Emily, during our long joint journey of discovery in Canada and elsewhere. And most of all, I thank my wife, Connie, for the idea of this book, for her research and editing assistance, for her encouragements, and for so many more special things that had nothing—and everything—to do with this book.

A. H. M.

v

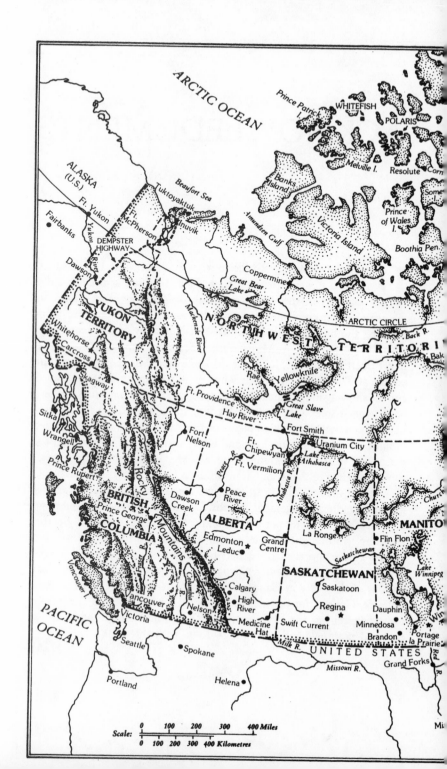

ARCTIC OCEAN

Prince Patrick I.

WHITEFISH

POLARIS

Melville I.   Resolute   Corn

Banks Island

Prince of Wales I.

Some I.

Boothia Pen.

ALASKA (U.S.)

Beaufort Sea

Tuktoyaktuk

Ft. Yukon

Ft. McPherson   Inuvik

Fairbanks

Amundsen Gulf

Victoria Island

DEMPSTER HIGHWAY

Dawson

Coppermine

Great Bear Lake

ARCTIC CIRCLE

YUKON TERRITORY

Whitehorse

Carcross

Mackenzie River

N O R T H W E S T   T E R R I T O R I

Back R.

Bak

Skagway

Ft. Providence

Rae   Yellowknife

Sitka

Hay River

Great Slave Lake

Wrangell

Fort Nelson

Ft. Chipewyan

Fort Smith

Uranium City

Prince Rupert

Rocky

Peace R.

Ft. Vermilion

Lake Athabasca

Churc

BRITISH

Prince George

Dawson Creek

Peace River

Athabasca R.

La Ronge

MANITO

COLUMBIA

Mountains

ALBERTA

Flin Flon

Edmonton   Grand
Leduc   Centre

Vancouver I.

Columbia R.

SASKATCHEWAN

Saskatchewan R.

Lake Winnipeg

Calgary

Saskatoon

Vancouver

High River

PACIFIC OCEAN

Victoria

Nelson

Regina

Dauphin

Win

Seattle

Medicine Hat

Swift Current

Minnedosa

Portage la Prairie

Spokane

Milk R.   UNITED STATES

Brandon

Grand Forks

Red R.

Portland

Helena

Missouri R.

Mi

Scale:

0   100   200   300   400 Miles

0   100   200   300   400 Kilometres

Don Pitcher

CONTENTS

FOREWORD

Pierre Berton, the prolific and perceptive Canadian writer, once defined a Canadian as someone who could make love in a canoe. So precariously afloat on unmanageable waters surely headed for rapids ahead, so torn by conflicting forces inspired by nature and man, so at the mercy of unseen awesome powers, Canada, at only slightly more than half the age of the United States, has long felt it lacked control over its own destiny. And rightly so really. It had to develop a most keen sense of balance and propriety just to survive.

The second-largest country in the world, Canada was created by another foreign power for reasons of its own that had little to do with Canadian desires and nothing to do with natural geographical boundaries. And so, beset by political handicaps, a harsh climate, and a divisive geography, a disparate Canada, with one-tenth as many people as its American neighbor in 110 percent of the space, set out to build a modern, independent country in the economic, military, and cultural shadow of the world's two superpowers, the United States and the Soviet Union, both next door. The fact that it accomplished this task at all without a military revolution, without a civil war, and without the overthrow of any government denotes an impressive amount of skill and grace. But it was also accomplished without much attention even within Canada.

Throughout its history Canada, what President Ulysses S. Grant once called "this semi-independent and irresponsible agency," has been many things to Americans, including a puzzlement. It has been friendly neighbor, ally, vacation playground, enemy, investment paradise, provider of raw materials, electricity, and numerous inventions, refugee haven, guerrilla base camp, rumrunner, military buffer, hostage rescuer, prime trading partner, practice bombing range, and recalcitrant cousin. It has also been taken for granted. But one thing Canada has never been to Americans is understood.

What is this place and its people "up there" who beneath a thin veneer of similarity are simultaneously somehow so different? What is the depth of the unique relationship that links—and divides—these cousin countries along the world's longest undefended border in the world's most massive trading relationship? (It is a most unusual relationship between two independent countries, one which Paul Robinson, one American ambassador in Ottawa, illustrated with a story about some questions he asked American intelligence officials before he first departed for Canada. First, he said, he asked, "Do we spy on Canadians?" The reply was "No." Next he asked if Canadians spy on Americans. "No," the spy chiefs said, "but they do spy on the people we would use if we did spy on them.")

What is it in Canada's history and character that explains its superior inferiority complex which has colored—until recently—so much of what it does and how it thinks? What is happening to a new generation within this overlooked land that threatens to disrupt its internal harmony and force dramatic changes in its relationship with an unaware United States? Canada, the Eagle Scout of nations, that rescues American hostages in Iran and then openly discriminates against American companies. Canada, the familiar but quaint character, that gets so angry when Americans ignore it and then so uncomfortable when they praise it. Canada, whose people, financed by a fraternal phalanx of national banks, visit the United States by the millions and quietly continue to accumulate greater economic power there by the billions. Where has Canada come from, where is it going, and what are the ramifications for the United States? In short, what do Americans need to know to understand accurately, for once, that puzzling collection of frequently feuding fiefdoms called Canada? And for Canadians, who are always so curious to know what others are saying about them especially if it's negative, what is it about their own land that strikes others as so vital, so promising?

After an absence of two decades and the expiration of my dual American-Canadian citizenship, I returned to Canada full of such questions about a country I had known affectionately and intimately as a youth. Canada had been a second home for me and a first home for both my parents and all my relatives. From Canada and Canadians, I believe, came much of the values and attitudes I carried with me to many other places and then back to a different Canada, a Canada changing so drastically yet so quietly from within that even many Canadians didn't seem to realize it. I think this gave me a unique perspective to step back from the fables and foibles and favored clichés of both lands and write from an intimate and human, yet professionally detached, viewpoint about the intertwined lives of these two lands. I saw that for two countries living so close to each other there was a truly awesome ignorance in each about each. Neither country genuinely appreciated the other. The Americans usually seek to see superficially what is the same between them and Canadians, while Canadians usually look, the easy way, only for what is different and wrong and, hopefully, both. It seemed to me that Canada, one of the world's best-kept secrets, was an exciting place of new beginnings next door to an aging nation full of fear for its decay.

For four years I wandered the vast expanse of Canada's real estate from top to bottom and side to side, by car and motorbike, jet plane and crop duster, helicopter and ski-plane, four-wheel-drive van, and on foot, even by dogsled and canoe. But what began as the professional travels of the Toronto bureau chief of *The New York Times* soon became also a voyage of personal discovery for a not so young man. Just as I found my assigned country changing, I discovered myself changing, too.

This is the story of those adventures and that journey.

Andrew H. Malcolm
Toronto, July 1984

INTRODUCTION

Canada and the United States remain puzzling places for each other's myriad peoples.

The differences between the two are obvious to subtle Canadians and subtle to obvious Americans. With an increasingly confident generation of increasingly diverse Canadians coming to business, political, and cultural power as Canada passed its 125th birthday, this increasingly intimate relationship between the two countries requires not less but even more attentive nurturing. This is not just for the altruistic motives of harmony among neighbors. This is for reasons of blatant self-interest, economic and political, for both sides.

First, the economic: In 1989, after years of sometimes grumpy negotiations and petulant posturing, Canada and the United States began implementing a new free-trade agreement governing the massive commerce that flows between the two lands around the clock around the calendar. By 1999, unless one country takes the drastic step of implementing escape clauses, virtually all duties and tariffs will be eliminated between the two countries. Within months of its formal beginning, officials on both sides agreed to speed up implementation in many areas.

Already, this commerce totals around $200 billion per year, by far the largest bilateral economic relationship in the world. The United States, in fact, trades more with the single province of Ontario than it does with the entire nation of Japan. And the province of Quebec, by itself, is the United States' ninth largest trading partner.

The free trade agreement, which was proposed by Canadian leaders, stands as a done-deal in the American mind, a good-faith symbol of the

United States' episodic interest in and dedication to its best friend. But free trade remains a potentially volatile issue in Canada, where bashing Americans and playing on a waning national inferiority complex has often been a popular political ploy by desperate campaigners. Many Canadian sectors have long resented their proximity to and dependence upon American markets, American decisions, and the unintended and sometimes thoughtless turbulence that can wash up onto any land caught in the economic wake of a country as large, powerful, and cumbersome as the United States.

To further complicate matters, in 1991, Canada and the United States, two modern, affluent, industrialized economies, began lengthy talks with the far-less-developed land of Mexico to create a truly continental free trade zone of some 350 million consumers. This is necessary, in the eyes of many, for North America to compete in an increasingly global economy where so many other immense and powerful economic blocs are emerging in Europe and around the Pacific Rim. But even the partial economic integration of a country as culturally, politically, and economically different as Mexico is bound to place many unanticipated strains on the relations of the other two, which often share their own divergent needs and fears.

Now, the political: In the 1980s, both Canada and the United States experienced a shift to the conservative side of the political spectrum (although Americans must always remind themselves that Canada's conservatives are more liberal than many liberal Americans).

And Canada has been going through another one of the unpredictable but familiar cycles of French-English animosity that erupt every now and then atop the northern half of North America and spew out invisible ill feelings the way sunspots spit out radiation. The 1980 provincial referendum in Quebec saw the defeat, for a time, of a proposal for that province to begin a form of separation from Canada. But the fearsome debate of that time, its continuing echoes, and the growth in both power and self-confidence of Quebec's business community in subsequent years has made the departure of the largest province from the Canadian Confederation seem somewhat less unthinkable in the minds of many staunch Canadians.

Many in Canada's majority English-speaking sectors have long grumbled about Quebec's regular demands for new special treatments. But a majority of the country seemed prepared to make extra protective accommodations for the French speakers as part of an unspoken agreement among Canadians to give each other an enormous amount of room to be different. Canadians have shown an extraordinary skill at compromising their diverse interests over the decades. Implicit in this cross-cultural relationship was the belief that the majority of French speakers within Quebec would display the same special concern toward that province's minority of English speakers.

But as that special northern land moved toward the twenty-first century, there were growing signs of impatience by both sides within both places. The French, projecting their declining birth rate into the future and fearing the eventual dissipation of their ancient culture, sought their own immigration policies to attract newcomers and took aggressive steps within Quebec to protect French, long the majority language there. Some of these steps, like banning outdoor signs in English, were less important for their linguistic effects than for their emotional impact on English speakers outside Quebec, who felt a violation of Quebec's unspoken English protection policy. As one result, many prominent Canadians, who had long regarded the physical splintering of their country as unthinkable, were, in fact, privately contemplating the inevitability of such an event.

Culturally, there seems little question that a semi- or completely independent Quebec could survive; it already has done far more than survive for over two centuries as a flourishing French-speaking island of art, music, and literature adrift on an English-speaking continent.

Economically, however, the debate continues within Canada. Within the United States, the consequences of another, possibly economically unviable country suddenly emerging on the Americans' northern flank, remain publicly ignored for fear of worsening the delicate situation. (Although with tongues only partly in cheek, some might suggest that the best way to unify Canadians is for Americans to come barging in with their own ideas about solving the Quebec problem.) But the prospect of partitioning its largest trading partner (and the only country that physically separates the United States from the Soviet Union) with all the accompanying potential for instability and its weakening impact on the larger Canada is hardly reason for delight in Washington and elsewhere.

It seems clear, then, that the United States and Canada are embarking on a new phase in their dynamic and surprisingly delicate relationship. No one can predict where this will ultimately lead. But it certainly requires a much greater understanding of the underlying cultural, political, and economic forces that form the foundations of these two countries.

As the only child of two Canadians, I grew up in both countries. As a correspondent for *The New York Times*, I have spent most of my quarter-century career covering these two countries, wandering back and forth across these two vast lands, communing with their peoples, their politicians, and their places. They are special places, indeed, made even more special by their largely unappreciated juxtaposition. It is my hope that, within this new light, this new edition of *The Canadians*, with its examination of the cycles in their national lives and the forces behind them, will help promote a little better understanding of both sides by both sides.

Andrew H. Malcolm
Creston, British Columbia
August, 1991.

The Canadians

ONE

❦❦❦

Geography

❦❦❦

It sits atop the Western Hemisphere, a brooding geographic colossus, immense, hostile, forbidding, and unforgiving of those who ignore its natural rules of survival. Canada's population of more than 25 million is puny by most international standards. The wild country Canadians inhabit is not. It is the second-largest in the world, a distorted parallelogram of almost 4 million square miles of land and water stretching far beyond the average citizen's scale of belief. East to west, it spans 4,545 miles and one-quarter of the world's time zones. Scattered across this area like a few specks of pepper on a huge freezer-room floor are the people, huddling together along the porous border with the United States. Looking to the south, always the south, Canadians rarely see or even think of what lies behind their thin line of population. But like some unseen, dark, powerful presence in a midnight dream, it is felt.

Americans look north toward their Canadian cousins and are often puzzled and perplexed by a people who can simultaneously seem so similar yet somehow strangely different. Occasionally then Americans spot something dim looming behind that neighbor's friendly front fence. It goes at least to the distant horizon one can see, and probably a ways farther. Pretty big, all right. But big is too small. South to north, Canada stretches almost 3,000 miles, farther than New York City to Los Angeles. Regular passenger jets soar above southern Canada heading north. They touch down six hours later still 800 miles from the end. They pass over land almost the entire time and hardly see a community of more than a few hundred hardy souls. They pass over city suburbs where bands of coyotes threaten household pets, over lakes and bays larger than entire states, and over a forest six times the size of France. They pass over herds of wild caribou so numerous they take a day to pass one rock. They pass over, if anyone has ever counted them all, more than a million lakes, streams, and rivers carefully containing 30 percent of the globe's entire freshwater supply. They pass over immense weather systems spawning storms which a week later rage out of the sky to paralyze American cities and entire regions. They pass over long lines of marauding thunderstorms that rumble across the countryside for days and never soak a human. They pass over towering waterfalls frozen in mid-plummet, a score of mountains more than two miles tall, and spectacularly scenic sites that go nameless and unseen. And then their airplane, looking somehow smaller than it did at takeoff, lands in a desolate, forever-frozen place called Resolute in territories constituting 40 percent of Canada that remain largely unexplored, untamed, and unincorporated 118 years after the country's birth. It is Canada's North, one and a quarter times larger than India with fewer people than a New York Yankees baseball game.

The North is but one of the many distinct geographical regions that have made Canada what it is today—and kept it from being more. "Canadian history largely records a struggle to build a nation in the face of stern geographic difficulties," according to J. M. S. Careless, one of Canada's most respected historians.[1] "We have this vast country to overcome," a Task Force on Canadian Unity heard from one witness a few years ago, "the spaces and the people to bring together." Canada's awesome geography and its accompanying harsh climates share a palpable power that shapes the life, the work, the thinking, and the values of every soul on its broad landscape. It is a threat to some, a challenge to others, and an excuse for many.

Americans and other nationalities can look up at the skies on clear, dark nights and feel humbled, for a moment, by a distant universe of stars. Canadians can feel that within their own country without looking up. The shared hardship of their geography is one of the few national bonds within this newly intriguing and rapidly developing land that has come to play, unnoticed by most, such a deep, far-ranging, and growing role in the life of the United States in everything from real estate, books, and movies to beer, banks, railcars, and even the space shuttle's vital "arm." If their frontier-taming experience convinced Americans that anything was possible, the geography of Canada taught its captives true skepticism, that everything, especially themselves, has its limits. Until now at least.

There is a revealing expression in Inuktitut, the simple but insightful language of Canada's northern peoples. It is *ionamut.* It means "It can't be helped," a strongly fatalistic saying which, interestingly, has direct parallel expressions in other Asian tongues, like Japanese. For scores of centuries and still today *ionamut* has enabled these hardy Canadians to accept, with a relieving shrug, the impact of those inexorable and extreme geographic and climatic forces—the shifting ice, the barren tundra often so empty of game, the bitter, battering winds, the killer blizzards, the piercing cold, the hard luck of the hunt—that are so far beyond their control and still shape their daily lives. Southern Canadians do not have that expression, in English or French. But they often have had the same attitude, a kind of "Why bother?" mental shrug which helps them cope with harsh realities or forces seemingly beyond their control, even when others perceive those forces as eminently controllable if they are given some determination, imaginative effort, and a game gamble or two.

It took the United States more than a century to conquer fully its continent and develop as an integral nation. And as Canada moves through its twelfth decade as a separate and very different North American country plagued by a pendulum of divisions, there are mounting signs that it too is on the brink of a newfound maturity in a number of sectors. Economically Canadian businessmen and bankers have pretty much developed their domestic markets to the fullest and are throwing off the mental bindings that have largely confined their efforts solely to Canada. They are aggressively thrusting their products, companies, and philosophies into the much larger United States arena with a scale of energy, imagination, and skill that requires considerable adjustments by Americans accustomed to a more complacent Canada.

In the turbulent, iceberg-ridden sea off its East Coast and across its resource-rich West, a new generation of young Canadian entrepreneurs, at times goaded by a nationalist government, is carving out new empires, fueled by fossil and human energy resources that have surprised their own countrymen. From the flat, broad prairies Canada's family farms turn out millions of tons of grain to feed many other countries of the world, help Canada's perpetual balance of payments problems, and overload the country's limited rail transport system. From Vancouver, the largest port on the West Coast of North America, Canadian companies are moving to exploit the burgeoning markets of the Pacific rim's rapidly developing countries. In the North, that vast, hostile void that stayed frozen so long in the back of the Canadian mind, domestic resource hunters devise, design, and forge complete new computer-run technologies of drilling, mining, exploring, extracting, and surviving. On the drawing boards are ambitious plans for icebreaker and even submarine tankers that would, after more than four centuries of hoping, finally bring to reality the fabled idea of a year-round Northwest Passage.

Lined up along the banks of the St. Lawrence River and Lakes Ontario and Erie, central Canada watches with envy as its dominant controlling role is diluted by these new historic shifts of power to other regions, much as the neighboring northeastern United States watched its dominance wane in the bright glare of the emerging Sun Belt in the 1970's. Halifax, once the major seaport on the East Coast, finds itself presiding now instead over Canada's poor Appalachia and hoping, along with two cities named for St. John, for some bountiful spin-offs from offshore oil and gas discoveries.

Ottawa, the plain, cold old canal town chosen as the nation's compromise capital by a queen named Victoria who never saw the country, remains a cold, old canal town with hourly flights to Canada's other real centers of power, a would-be huddle of electronics companies and one old industry, a frustrated federal government isolated from the country by geography and its own sense of self-importance.

Montreal, once the premier city in North America, remains a delightful bilingual destination for visitors seeking delicious dining and Old World charm with New World convenience. But thanks to economic and political-linguistic forces beyond its control, it has, like Boston after its heyday, seen its national importance dwindle to regional prominence. Even its winning hockey tradition, no small measure of civic stature in Canada, has moved west to new arenas in upstart towns with names like Edmonton and Calgary, where a new moneyed class in cowboy hats buys the season tickets, near mid-rink on the blue line. No longer is Montreal Canada's largest city, the center of finance and national commerce.

There are, in fact, many new major centers of population and commerce developing to handle the more diverse needs and interests of Canada's 25 million-plus citizens. Once a single city dominated the entire land; now there are many, each specializing in some sectors, each rapidly growing in importance, and each quick to protect jealously its newfound strengths even if the threat is only perceived.

Still presiding over this geographically fragmented scene, but increasingly wary of its wily challengers for national power, sits Toronto, the old Indian winter camp whose muddy lanes are lined now with sprawling underground malls and eye-catching steel and glass skyscrapers housing many of the huge corporations that control Canada's economy. Toronto, a 244-square-mile metropolis once called York like its troubled American counterpart, remains home to one of every eight Canadians and is still the preeminent center of Canadian business, finance, culture, fashion, publishing, and communications. It is also the symbol for Canadians of the Ontario Octopus, that hated complex of power networks that seems for so long to have controlled all of Canada's geographic regions for the benefit of one, itself in the center.

Canada can be divided into an almost infinite number of regions, subregions, and subsubregions, from the rain forests and deserts of British Columbia in the West across three or more ranges of mountains to Alberta's rolling rangelands, the tabletop-smooth wheat fields of Saskatchewan and Manitoba, and the forests and bush country of northern Ontario, to the rocky river-bottom land of Quebec. The scrub country of New Brunswick, the petite potato patches of scenic Prince Edward Island, the lush valleys of Nova Scotia, and the rugged island wilderness of Newfoundland and its mainland rump called Labrador. To the north, of course, lie the Arctic taiga and tundra, the frozen fjords, forests, waters, and ice cliffs of Canada's third seashore, giving it the world's longest coastline and a unique frontier potential among industrialized nations.

As Canada's political leaders long ago discovered whenever they tried to fashion a single national policy on any issue from oil to the wording of the national anthem, these varied, sprawling, separate kingdoms have few things in common with each other save their dogged determination to remain separate and their abiding suspicion of each other.

Spanning half the country in a semi-sterile swath splattered across Quebec, Northern Ontario, Manitoba, and Saskatchewan and into the Northwest Territories lies the Canadian Shield, the 700-million-year-old mass of elemental bedrock that serves as Canada's geological foundation, its most prominent geographical feature, and a stark reminder to Canadians of their geography's hostile, brooding presence. As E. J. Pratt, the poet, described the Shield, it is "too old for death, too old for life." For many hundreds of thousands of years two massive ice sheets several miles thick pressed and scraped their way across much of what was to become Canada, crushing an entire mountain range before withdrawing to the north in a glacial retreat that lasted 6,000 years.

These marauding ice fields left behind only sparse pockets of arable soil, thousands of lakes, muskeg bogs, and bug-laden swamps that constitute, in effect, a 1,000-mile-wide corridor of inhospitable wilderness severing Canada's East from West. It was the rock-strewn specter of this Shield which prompted Jacques Cartier, the French explorer, to note in his diary in 1534: "I am rather inclined to believe that this is the land God gave to Cain." For decades its somnolent bogs swallowed train roadbed after train roadbed, at times even some locomotives. Its wilderness expanse was free of any through highway until 1943. And even forty years after that, long parts of the transcontinental road remained rugged and two-laned.

In some respects, though, the Shield is a blessing. For while it limits much about Canada physically and mentally, it has also provided over the years a treasure trove of resources, albeit a trove that first required the mining of foreign capital. The Shield's lakes and environs yield a bonanza of furs, a multimillion-dollar industry to this day. The same waters formed a crude waterway for the canoes of early traders and, at certain bug-free times of the year now, an isolated playground to attract the wallets and checkbooks of fishermen, swimmers, campers, and other tourists, many of them foreigners eager to flee their lives in more southerly civilizations for a spell. The Shield's ground yields a plethora of minerals (40 percent of Canada's production) as well as abundant woods for lumber, firewood, and pulp for the world's paper industry. By themselves, the Shield's waters give Canada access to vast amounts of cheap hydroelectricity, which provides some 70 percent of Canada's electrical power and an increasingly popular export to power-hungry, less blessed states nearby.

Novelist Hugh MacLennan has written eloquently of Canada's two solitudes—the English and the French—simultaneously living together yet apart within the same land. In reality it is Canada's geography which has made it less a homogeneous nation with a common identity and more a conservative collection of regional solitudes separated from each other by formidable natural barriers and from their natural American neighbors by artificial political boundaries.

For Canada, distance and size are among the most serious geographical barriers. The country is so big and so empty—less population density, for instance, than Saudi Arabia—that its federal government spends $135 million a year just investigating reports of people lost or in trouble in planes and boats. The country's political units—the ten provinces and two northern territories—are simply huge in area, possibly unmanageable despite their relatively compact populations. At its widest point, for instance, the single province of Quebec stretches as far as from New York City to Omaha. It takes thirty-six solid hours of driving to move from Toronto to the next large Canadian city to the west, Winnipeg. Eight American states touch the Great Lakes across from one single province, Ontario, which continues eastward almost to Vermont. The smallest Canadian province, Prince Edward Island, is still almost twice as large as the smallest American state, Rhode Island, while Texas, the largest of the forty-eight contiguous states, would easily fit inside just Quebec with enough room left over for Connecticut and Delaware. There is room for four Great Britains in British Columbia and almost three Frances in Quebec. Nearly three Japans would fit inside Ontario, which has fewer people than Tokyo. And Canada's two northern territories, which have yet to be organized and fully incorporated into the country as provinces, are by themselves larger than West Germany, France, Britain, Italy, Egypt, Austria, Spain, Portugal, and all the New England and Middle Atlantic states put together.

There is very little sense among Canadians of their geographic whole. "The fundamental question in English Canada," said Northrop Frye, a prominent Canadian scholar, "is not 'Who am I?' But 'Where is here?' "[2] Canadians know their city and their corner of their province, probably the adjacent American territory a little, and the through route to the American Sun Belt. But much of the rest of their own country remains a very large blur imprisoned in derogatory stereotypes perpetuated by geography, indifference, ignorance, and media which, with irregular exceptions, provide column after column of coverage of the United States but only episodic glimpses of elsewhere in Canada. Thus, in the popular mind, Canada is populated by stuffy, Calvinist Torontonians, French-speaking lumberjacks in plaid shirts, drunk Indians, hay-sucking farmers, maniac Montreal drivers, meat-and-potatoes immigrants from Central Europe, faddish British Columbians in hot tubs and blue-eyed Albertan "sheikhs," newly rich from oil. When Canadians tell ethnic jokes, they don't reach for Poland or Italy; it's their own Newfoundland. (Did you hear about the elderly Newfie woman who took birth control pills because she didn't want any more grandchildren?)

Most of Canada's regions one after another were settled directly from abroad and not by any massive waves of second- or third-generation Canadians moving inexorably across a fertile landscape and becoming ever more aware of their new land with each passing day and mile. "This pattern of settlement sharply differentiated the Canadian experience from the American," according to Cole Harris, a historian at the University of British Columbia. "[In the United States] the land was perceived as a garden as readily as wilderness, and it attracted far more settlers, and focussed European dreams. . . . As different streams from the initial settlements along the colonial seaboard, augmented by newcomers from Europe, moved west across the Appalachians, different ways met and substantially merged. . . . The American occupation of an essentially welcoming land had the capacity to mold different peoples into a relatively homogeneous culture as it spread them over an astonishing area. In Canada, all of this was checked by the land's ineluctable niggardliness."[3]

As one result, more often than not Canada's new scattered communities maintained stronger ties with the old country or another distant Canadian point, leapfrogging the vast geographical and psychological area in between. Even today eastern Canadians will drive their children all over New England and western Canadians will show their offspring the famed American West, and then both sets of parents will say they hope someday to get to see Canada's capital in Ontario. The gap in understanding grew so wide at one point that Canada's federal government sponsored a foreign student exchange program—between children in neighboring provinces.

In between the two large islands, Newfoundland and Vancouver, which bracket Canada from sea to sea, east to west, the country's geography has discouraged a sense of nation and encouraged, instead, deep intercourse with neighboring, more easily accessible American areas. This has created some startling anomalies; there is, for instance, a Canadian beer, Moosehead Lager, which many Canadians have never heard of and can't buy. Brewed in New Brunswick, Moosehead, the Canadian beer that is among the top ten imported beers in the United States, was available in fifty American states—but only four Canadian provinces.

In the east, in Canada's Maritime Provinces, which were at first largely populated by Loyalist refugees fleeing by ship from the advancing democratic rabble of General George Washington, New England is still referred to as the Boston States.

The Maritimes and Atlantic provinces—Nova Scotia, New Brunswick, Prince Edward Island, and Newfoundland—rarely seem to fit into Canada. The first three opposed the country's formation in 1867. Nine years later, many decades before Quebec garnered global attention for its efforts to seek separation, Nova Scotia's legislature passed a resolution to secede from the country.

Such political grumbling is endemic in Canada. But Nova Scotia's step, unfulfilled as events developed, was symbolic of the region's antipathies toward the country. For the Maritimes, becoming a part of Canada carried few apparent tangible benefits and many immediate minuses. It meant severing or curbing many of the deep economic and emotional ties they had with New England, where thousands of Maritimers and Quebecers went to seek work when times were tough in the north.

Taken together, the four Atlantic provinces are about six times the size of Maine in area. Although they comprise 40 percent of the country's provinces, they contain only 10 percent of the country's population and 6 percent of Canada's area. They do have, however, a much larger proportion of its problems, primarily economic. Rural, rustic, rolling, and proud, these provinces have withered at Canada's back door as a chronic center of high unemployment, a roughhewn, resource-based economy far from major markets struggling in a mass modern, technological era.

Times were good in the beginning. Halifax, Nova Scotia, was a major seaport. The area's tall, sturdy trees held aloft for decades the sails of the Royal Navy, and even when prosperity's winds weakened with the coming of steam power, Nova Scotia had its undersea coal mines. It was the first North American landfall for westbound traffic braving the storms of the North Atlantic and the most convenient jumping-off point for eastbound ships, even as late as World War II, when the supply convoys congregated at Halifax for the dash to Britain.

Fish, of course, were the original attraction. The island of Newfoundland, Great Britain's first overseas colony and a British protectorate that didn't join Canada until 1949, was originally just an offshore fishing platform for the European fleets that arrived with the good weather and left with the bad and holds full of cod, haddock, and the area's other abundant sea life. Traditionally the first officer of the first ship each year governed the town or region for that season.

The principal city of St. John's, named for the feast day of St. John the Baptist (June 24), the supposed date in 1497 when John Cabot came upon this newfound land, is one of the oldest settlements in North America and at the hands of Guglielmo Marconi was the reception point in 1901 for the world's first transatlantic wireless message. With its distinctive Irish-flavored English—for instance, the word "here" comes out "hair"—Newfoundland was trading with the American colonies as early as 1641.

But Newfoundland, with the country's highest unemployment rate and the smallest per capita income, remains apart from Canada, an isolated, Tennessee-size island at sea slightly closer to Liverpool, England, than to Toronto. In Newfoundland, which is separated from the Canadian main-land by stormy, icy straits and two islands—St. Pierre and Miquelon, still overseas territories of France—everything is shaped by the certainty of uncertainty that accompanies life still controlled by such powerful natural forces as the Arctic and the sea. With its own dialect, frequent insulating fogs, its own diverse traditions, and even its own time zone, thirty minutes off everyone else's, Newfoundland is connected to the mainland by air-planes that are often crippled by the thick fog, by storm-tossed ferries that must also be icebreakers to dodge icebergs like the one that sank the *Titanic* nearby, and by the political paper that, formally at least, made it a part of Canada. The result is that more than three decades later, when a St. John's company wants to hire someone locally, it often must advertise in a newspaper in distant Toronto, where hundreds of Newfoundlanders have been forced to move to seek some work. And there in Toronto a college-educated television reporter can tell a foreign acquaintance, seri-ously, "Oh, I'm not Canadian either. I'm from Newfoundland."

The Atlantic Provinces, primarily Nova Scotia and Newfoundland, had hopeful visions of a new prosperity dawn on them in recent years. The escalating world price of oil and natural gas finally brought within eco-nomic reach their treacherous offshore depths. And the dangerous energy hunt with encouraging initial finds and all its potential for bust as well as boom seized the areas. It was an economic hopefulness the region had known before, when a refinery, an auto factory, and other products of the technological age were launched with great optimism only to sink ig-nominiously by the docks in the face of intimidating economic and geographic realities. And it was enough to make even a hopeful Newfoundlander think of that old island saying "Nofty was forty when he lost the pork." The expression, seemingly incomprehensible and literally untranslatable, refers to the score of a Newfoundland card game but is also a warning that the uncertainties of a brief life and a harsh land must always be kept in mind to temper any sudden hopes for anything better.

To the west of the Maritimes just up the wide St. Lawrence River, which is frozen shut one-third of the time, is Quebec, the largest province. There, clustered along the broad, rocky river bottom land and around the weathered spires of each little community's Roman Catholic church, is where Canadian settlement actually began on farm fields drawn narrow to maximize the number of families with riverfront access. It is also home for most of the country's French-speaking Canadians, one-quarter of the country's population, and for the province's two principal cities—Quebec and Montreal—which are where they are solely for geographic reasons: The river was narrow and full of rapids there, and the ships had to stop. Upstate New York's system of lakes and rivers also gave Montreal's early commercial interests, the American colonies, and the British army and their Indian allies an efficient means of transportation and, at times, an invasion route toward one another.

To the north, almost immediately upon leaving both cities, travelers are plunged into the wilderness of the massive Shield, rich in minerals and ores and flowing fresh water to generate inexpensively massive amounts of what eastern Canadians call hydro, or electricity. There the roads are few or nonexistent, and the country remains untamed by the straight lines and cement of civilization.

The same country flows farther west into the empty woods and leaky mines of northern Ontario, where lonely trains slowly winding through forests bent low beneath the weight of heavy snows still stop along the way for trappers and anyone else who flags them down from trackside. On the other hand, southern Ontario, dipping down into the American heartland atop the Great Lakes, is another world of tidy, lush green farms neatly linked to scores of industrial communities, some not so tidy, that produce fully half of Canada's manufacturing. Economic and family links with the United States' huge, adjacent markets have always been close there; indeed, crossing southern Ontario was, and is, the shortest route from New York and Buffalo to the American West through Detroit and

Chicago, a geographical fact that both the pioneers in covered wagons and modern truckers in their tandem trailers have appreciated.

From Ontario, the aging heart of the Canadian Confederation, drawing the raw materials from its distant limbs and pumping back the finished goods, the rest of English-speaking Canada can appear to be a fairly solid, similar mass. But from anywhere else in the country, Canada comes into a clearer focus as a diverse collection of English-speaking peoples with a common unease about and distaste for the center.

There is no midwestern Corn Belt in Canada. Ontario's crowded croplands come the closest. But to the west, beginning at the distant, distinct Ontario border as if someone had taken a colossal pencil to the countryside and erased anything taller than a bush, are the Canadian prairies—flat, fairly fertile, and ferociously uncompromising. These broad, semiarid plains atop the American Dakotas span the two provinces of Manitoba (a combination of Sioux and Assiniboine words meaning "prairie water") and Saskatchewan (a corruption of the Cree word *kisiskatchewan* or "swift-flowing").

There, grains and trains dominate life, the former because those crops can use the strong sun but don't require frequent moisture, the latter because Canadian geography is not blessed with the same massive inland river system whose vital veins drain the water, crops, and goods of the interior United States. Instead, many of Canada's major rivers, frequently frozen, flow north toward more ice and away from markets. So the bulky wheat, rye, barley, and oilseeds must be moved, at least initially, by Canada's overstressed, underfinanced rail system.

Sitting in an overheated observation dome car, grinding along the shiny rails on moonlit winter nights, I am always impressed with the natural forces silently at work outside the smudged glass. Wild winds whip the dry snow into the lighted arcs of the lone lights burning in every farmyard. Leafless trees, a feeble attempt to build windbreaks, bend and sway in communities with names like Griswold, Moosomin, Boharm, and Summerberry. Towering above trackside in virtually every town is at least one mammoth grain elevator, standing like some darkened prairie cathedral at midnight. Inevitably, two or three rusting boxcars rest nearby with their rippled doors ajar and the snow blowing into those dark slits. Beyond the railroad crossing guard, clanging to empty streets, parked pickup trucks dot the icy lanes, while little patches of yellow warmth seep out some windows stapled shut with plastic sheets until springtime.

Being so open to unpredictable, uncontrollable elements, when hailstones, insects, wind, rot, or interest rates can wipe out a year's work in minutes or hours, is a harsh conditioning lot. Today heated bricks warming feet in horse-drawn sleighs may have been gone forty-five years and the tractor cabs may be air-conditioned, but humbling hardship remains a familiar figure in the fields. It differs only in degree from earlier days this century, when the American frontier was finally settled and the Canadian government sought American and European settlers with advertisements for the "last best West." Prairie family life is still smoke-cured with a caution that remembers too vividly the days of the "dirty thirties" and twenties, when sawdust sold for more than wheat and a child's chores included breaking the morning ice on the washbasin and selling milk door to door to help make ends meet.

It is a life whose political geography at times has seen sincere searches for some sudden radical solutions to stubborn problems, perhaps with a violent general strike or the regular election of unorthodox political parties, including now the spread to the West for the first time of political groupings dedicated to separatism.

In the north of both provinces and spilling over into neighboring Alberta to the West, far beyond the reach of standard roads and phone lines, runs the Shield again like some geographical theme uniting Canada's regions in adversity. Some of these communities are former frontier forts, where furs changed hands for knives. Some are disposable towns, there to mine the ground while the price is right in Germany or Japan, and then to disappear. Others are mere outposts, just camps, where residents get extra isolation pay and wily wolves eat unwary pets. There, frozen rivers become local roadways. Airplanes are the only reliable link to the "outside." And trackless trains of bulldozers dragging huge skidding sleds of fuel and food to distant settlements crunch their way through the long winters and woods and frozen swamps at four or five miles an hour.

Little more than a half century ago officials needed trains of pack mules to penetrate Alberta's northern Peace River country to take the census. Riders killed their own food as they went or ate in the kitchens of the isolated cabins they came upon. Occasionally circuit-riding preachers passed through. Today the circuit riders are judges of the provincial court, arriving in chartered airplanes or cars with tape decks to dispense justice from the basements of ice rinks and fire halls.

Alberta is changing rapidly. Named for a daughter of Queen Victoria, the province, from its rugged northern wilderness, where bushy buffalo still roam freely, to its southern rolling rangelands along Montana's boundary, has been a dusty, rural backwater specializing in the production of cattle, grains, and breathtaking Rocky Mountain scenery to be recorded by millions of clicking Instamatics every summer. In many places on many days Alberta remains the same. But its future—and the economic and power makeup of Canada—began changing on a blustery February afternoon in 1947 in those pale, waning moments of twilight that come early during northern North American winters.

A curious crowd had gathered in a field near Edmonton about 170 miles north of Calgary, one of a handful of poverty-stricken provincial population centers scattered like shriveled corn across Canada's prairie provinces where the dusty taste of the Depression still hung in the air. Everyone was looking at the tower when the rumbling began. "Here she comes!" a man cried. There was an intense pause. And then, suddenly, violently, as if held back for far too long, the future of Canada's neglected West came blasting out of the ground. "It's oil!" the crowd screamed as it gushed forth. After 133 dry holes, on what was the last scheduled attempt, Vernon Hunter's Imperial Oil drilling crew had struck it big. So big, in fact, that Imperial Leduc No. 1 and thousands of subsequent wells tapping the vast riches beneath the western provinces ignited an economic boom that is changing the basic balance of power within the Canadian Confederation.

Ironically, in a quintessentially Canadian way, these lucrative riches with their accompanying growth and prosperity did not become bonds of good fortune and affluence offering unbounded opportunities for present and unborn generations of Canadians. Instead, they became genuine threats to the fragile foundations of Canada's national unity. They were fuel for the kinds of fierce federal feuds that frequently erupt in Canada, pitting one geographic region against another to the detriment of all. Thanks to their 80 percent energy self-reliance and a politically ingenious pricing scheme, Canadians across their land long enjoyed petroleum prices less than half that of the rest of the world. And the rate they burned up their energy, combined with their severe climate and grand distances, quickly made Canada the greatest per capita consumer of energy in the industrialized world.

But under Canada's federal system, the provinces control their own resources onshore, requiring price negotiations between the provincial and federal governments. This pitted Albertans, whose petroleum revenues enabled them to eliminate all sales taxes and still have gasoline at two-thirds the price of other provinces, against the other energy-consuming regions, which enjoyed a bargain by any other country's standards but still were jealous of the Canadian West's good fortune and its push for higher oil and gas prices closer to world levels.

The fact that Edmonton, Alberta's capital, and Calgary, Canada's energy capital, witnessed building and employment booms, with construction cranes reeling over mounting battalions of modern skyscrapers, only served as a heightened symbol of the new West's increasingly assertive—and increasingly resented—demands for a realignment of national political and economic power. "It's the West's time in Confederation," said Peter Lougheed, Alberta's premier, "and it's about time."

The remaining link in the resource-rich West is British Columbia, a varied, self-contained economic and social empire 1.3 times larger than Texas. Divided from the rest of Canada by mountains, a desert, a moderate coastal climate, a time zone, and an air of genial superiority, British Columbia was the first Canadian region to consider independence. But in that last quarter of the nineteenth century the British saw British Columbia as the crucial last link in their much-desired safe land route to India. So British Columbia was promised a transcontinental railroad to link it to the East.

Those rails are one of the few national bonds for British Columbia, an area where landslides, snows, and rampaging rivers can still cut off rail access from the rest of the country for days at a time. Physically the province is largely a westward-facing wilderness that is, in the 1980's, still forging surface transportation systems to open its northern interior for the first time to economic development. Two-thirds covered by trees, which it saws and chips and ships to hungry markets in the United States and Asia, B.C., as it is inevitably called, is also endowed with gas, coal, some oil, bountiful fish, and orchards. Its unique political tradition accords no role whatsoever to Canada's two major political parties—the Progressive Conservatives and the Liberals—preferring instead its own brand of conservative and socialist local politicians. And the province routinely looks past Canada for its opportunities, preferring to develop and service the larger American market just down the flat coastline and the burgeoning markets of the developing countries around the Pacific rim, especially Japan. As one result, Vancouver, which is 350 miles closer to Tokyo than it is to Halifax, ships most of Canada's export coal, 93 percent of it, to Japan. And the city is the office home for scores of American companies, which employ fully one of every five workers in the province.

As elsewhere throughout Canada, British Columbia's population is clustered in pockets largely along the southern border with the United States, making Canada, despite its immense size, into a kind of thin, horizontal Chile. But to the north, stretching fully across the width of all ten provinces covering everything between Alaska and Greenland, are Canada's two territories—the Yukon and the Northwest Territories, which, despite its formal plural name, is really only one. "The North," a northern Canadian judge had warned me, "it bites you, and you want to return."

Britain did not turn over its North American Arctic holdings to Canada until several years after Canada's independence in 1867. Once little more than a frigid fur farm for the Hudson's Bay Company and its competitors, Canada's northern territories still constitute four-tenths of the country's land area, even after the prairie provinces were carved from them around the turn of the century. They are special, addictive places with a colossal size that expands the mind. In these territories people are still intruders, and animal tracks from the 1960's remain frozen fresh in the sometimes soft soil. The territories remain largely unexplored but are estimated to hold within their frigid, forbidding frontiers fully 40 percent of the country's nonrenewable resources: 13 percent of Canada's gold, 20 percent of its silver, 44 percent of its lead, 100 percent of its tungsten, not to mention untotaled amounts of uranium, oil, and gas.

From time to time there have been episodic eruptions of national interest in that vast void—during the Klondike gold rush, for instance, or the Northern Vision of one political campaign by the late Prime Minister John Diefenbaker or when the question of national sovereignty emerged during the pioneering 1968 voyage of the Americans' icebreaker-tanker SS *Manhattan* from Atlantic to Pacific through Canada's Arctic waters. But until recent years Canada's Arctic and its opportunities have lain largely frozen in a mental permafrost, much as the Americans don't think of Guam. It's there. It could be useful someday. Meanwhile—yawn—

there are more important matters afoot. And Ottawa continues to rule its North as a distant, silent colony, a nineteenth-century anachronism atop North America.

There are signs, however, that in many minds this attitude toward one of Canada's unique geographical areas is changing, like the Arctic spring that comes by June so slowly, so imperceptibly that only the most astute note any change in the cold until one day, suddenly, the ice cracks and by mid-morning is flushed away by chill summer currents.

Shaped like a backward capital letter *L*, the Yukon (from *yucoo*, an Indian word meaning "clear water") contains enough room for almost five Pennsylvanias, twenty-one mountains more than 2 miles high, fewer people (23,000) than several city blocks, and 2,726 miles of road, only 119 of them paved. From its southern settlements in the woods on lakes where steamers and homemade rafts once hauled gold seekers north and poor men back south, the Yukon stretches north alongside its turbulent namesake river past copper mines and gold mines and abandoned sheds and a large log cabin owned by a young New Jersey couple determined to make their way in the wilderness.

Its dirt roads wind through woods where Arctic owls perch idly on overhanging branches to watch cars zip by in the dust toward historic, decaying old Dawson, nestled in the forested hills served only by steamboats until the 1950's. Dawson, where the old hotels used to advertise "Rooms $1.50, with Bed $2," is where the yellow riches of two local creeks gave the English language new meanings for the words "Klondike" and "bonanza" and the pen of a bank teller named Robert Service gave English literature such memorable characters as Dangerous Dan McGrew and such memorable phrases about the Canadian North as "the unharnessed big land" with the "silence that bludgeons you dumb."

Today Dawson is a muddy pothole at the end of the rainbow. With the lazy smoke of wood fires still hanging in the nippy air of a midsummer's midnight, Dawson lives on its fabled past with Diamond Tooth Gertie's, long Canada's only legal gambling casino, and some new buildings built to look old, some old buildings restored to look old, and some old buildings just looking old. Every year the chance to rub hubcaps with the ghosts of greedy gold seekers, most of them Americans, draws some 70,000 tourists, most of them Americans, to Dawson, whose 350 year-round residents make it Canada's smallest city and a mere memory of the 30,000 who once lived there.

The Yukon's other northernmost communities, such as Old Crow, are still not reachable by land, and modern-day Mounties in fur hats, some of them now women, are still the only sign of government sovereignty. In fact, it wasn't until 1979, after $97 million in costs and twenty-two years of sporadic effort by civilians and maneuvering military units, that the first public road, the 460-mile-long Dempster Highway, was completed to connect the Yukon to its next-door-neighbor territory.

The "highway," actually a dirt lane subject to washouts, landslides, and potholes, begins near Dawson, winds through a series of lush valleys, across the Ogilvie Mountains to a chain of ridges on the elevated Eagle Plains, across the Arctic Circle, over the snow-swept Richardson Mountains, across the Arctic Red and Mackenzie rivers on ferries by summer and ice bridges in winter, and through the dusty delta to Inuvik in the Northwest Territories.

In the winter daring truck convoys, carrying their own bulldozers and survival gear, may take two weeks to drive the Dempster, buried in twenty-four-hour darkness. In the summer it is a spectacular two-day adventure across barren moonscapes through dense forests to a sunny summit flush with ripe blueberries and bright purple fireweed down a cloudy incline to an overcast valley where soft rain falls in rippling folds resembling a twelve-mile-long theater curtain. In an instant a stone path becomes a swollen golden stream, while nearby a roadside pond lies still as glass, perfectly reflecting the sky and surrounding evergreens until a family of ducks, practicing for the fall's migration, shatter the calm with their gentle V-shaped wakes.

On one day's drive my sons and I saw only ten other vehicles in nine hours. We crossed empty valleys twelve miles wide to reach a ridge that gave a view of other vast valleys as far as the eye could see in all directions. There were no man-made structures for hundreds of miles.

One summer midnight I stood alone on the Eagle Plains and watched in the east an immense thunderstorm, full of roiling blue-gray clouds silently hurling Y-shaped bolts of yellow lightning at some distant nameless peak. Then I turned to the west to see simultaneously a spectacular sunset bursting with moving fingers of clouds and pastels that changed tones every second.

Geography

Stormy sunsets. Daylight after midnight. Flowers in the Arctic. Sunshine in storms. Property with no fences. Snow in July. A highway without traffic. No buildings after hours of driving. And then live professional football on a lonely motel's satellite television. Individually all the sights are familiar enough. But they come on a grander scale and are assembled differently in Canada's North. And they hint at something special there.

The Northwest Territories make up one-third of Canada's mass. It is actually a collection of isolated regions so large that residents of Inuvik in the western end traveling to Baffin Island on the eastern side need at least two days to fly there and end up one-eighth of the way around the world. As one result, domestic airlines making "local" flights in the Northwest Territories require special union dispensations because such jet trips, even with only two or three stops, cover such huge distances that they exceed the flight crews' contract provisions for a maximum twelve-hour workday.

The regions vary from the flat scrubland around Yellowknife, the territorial capital where the trees can take several generations of brief summers to grow as thick as a man's arm, to the groaning green ice of the Arctic Ocean, where schoolteachers pass leaves around their classrooms so Inuit children can touch what southern Canadians must rake, to the Scandinavian-type fjords of Baffin Island, where the waters lead to the world's northernmost national park, Auyuittuq (EYE-you-eetuck, or "Place That Never Melts").

The park is an 8,290-square-mile panorama of ice sheets, snow-covered rocks, and 6,000-foot mountains astride the Arctic Circle. The water, as smooth as the ice it usually is, lies dark blue or black under the low, sullen clouds that impale themselves on the mountaintops, allowing only a little yellow sunshine to seep through.

One of the most striking things about Canada's Arctic is what it is not. It is not warm, not friendly, not colorful, not crowded, not inviting. All the elements of life are reduced—a few people, a few animals, a few basic colors, and a few basic instincts like hunger, fear, survival, and awe at the overpowering physical presence of the geography.

As an open boat churned its way north with Mosesee Tautuakjuk at the tiller, sheer brown 400-foot cliffs crowded the fjord's smooth water ever narrower toward the park's entrance, a mile-long jumbled tongue of rocks several hundred feet thick pushed ahead a few inches every few decades

23

by the unseen mass of a shining glacier looming in the distance far up the valley.

Despite the attractions of hiking and climbing and skiing on snows still virgin years after they storm ashore off the North Atlantic, not many tourists venture into Auyuittuq National Park past the special shelters alongside the food caches by the rescue radios. One recent year 312 people went into the park. But only 311 came out. The 312th visitor stayed behind, on the inaccessible, towering ledge where he had landed as another victim of Canada's geography.

Canada's economic geography generally reflects its physical geography. Where conditions are harshest—within the inhospitable Shield, for instance, or farther north in the frozen Arctic—economic activity beyond simple sustenance is at a minimum, clustered in far-flung population pockets and largely based on local resources, both human and natural. Transportation into and out of such limited markets, where feasible, is costly and, until the more recent times of mushrooming resource values, often uneconomical and requiring government subsidies of various kinds. To this day many of Newfoundland's picturesque little fishing villages, the so-called outports, remain physically isolated with no roads going beyond the berry-picking patches on the edge of town. The only public connection to Canada or the world is a government-owned boat taxi that, when weather permits, plies from cove to cove with the mail and supplies and visitors. Yet in the face of rising costs the federal government was seeking to cut back even that flimsy link. Most of the fish, which eventually will be eaten in Europe and the United States, go elsewhere for processing.

Where conditions are more geographically and climatically temperate —for example, farther south along the long border with the United States and its vast, hungry markets served by ice-free waterways and well-serviced highways—attractive opportunities have been proportionately magnified. And so have the population and its successes.

Immense economic disparities are thus physically built into Canada's regional city-states. Other significant disparities, both good and bad, wash back and forth across this varied geographic scene. Some changes are controlled by the seasons, world demand, or one year's fluctuating commodity prices, while other shifts are timed more in terms of generations.

For instance, the nineteenth-century prosperity of Canada's eastern provinces was beached, possibly permanently, when steel steamships came to dominate the seas, undercutting global demand for Maritime timber. Today, as the supply of ore thins out beneath one northern town, founded simply to serve the mine, the mine shuts down—and so does the disposable community, becoming, in effect, a modern-day ghost town in the bush while its residents ship their belongings out to the next mine site on barges by summer or, in winter, on hazardous ice highways across frozen lakes and rivers. Conversely, as the mounting postwar demand for, and later the ballooning price of, oil and gas fueled the wide-ranging hunt for more isolated basins of petroleum resources and brought them within economic reach, the gritty image of hard-luck Alberta, down in the dust and dependent on cows, changed to that of a booming energy capital. Jobs, if not gold, filled the streets still littered with clumps of mud from the latest construction site. And officials laid grandiose petrochemical plans for the next generation of prosperity.

As a collection of regions, physically and psychologically separate, Canada is unusually ill-equipped to cope with such extreme disparities, which can have serious ramifications for governing the country as a whole. In other regionally varied lands, such as the United States, for example, where there are 60 people per square mile, natural market forces have played a significant balancing role in smoothing out such economic inequalities. Unemployed eastern factory workers had a wide selection of large, hospitable alternate cities to live and work in across 3,000 miles of developed nation. West Virginia miners needed to travel only a couple of hundred miles to the beckoning rubber plants of Akron or the tool and die shops of Cleveland. Laid-off auto workers could drive onto an expressway in suburban Detroit and, without encountering so much as one stoplight or a single dirt road, carry their skills to a new employer in Houston's energy industry.

But in Canada, where there are only six people per square mile, there is nowhere near the selection of cities or the scale of industries or jobs. A 200-mile move wouldn't even get a driver into the next province in a country where the distance across, say, just Ontario is the same as that between Dallas and Los Angeles. Because skills have been tied so closely to the unique individual economies of a home region, fewer of them in Canada seem immediately portable; there are not many lobsters for a Nova Scotian to catch in Saskatchewan—and there has been great reluctance to try a new area. With one's identity closely linked to a region and its culture, a move to another province can be much like a move to a foreign country—a different geography, a different climate, a different culture, different political parties, different job qualifications, different taxes, in Canada even different languages. French-speaking residents of New Brunswick, Manitoba, or Quebec leaving their home province have no guarantee they will encounter French, French movies, French journals, French news, or French music anywhere outside Canadian airports, which are operated by the officially bilingual federal government. English-speaking Canadians moving into Quebec, an occurrence that doesn't happen all that much anymore, have had no choice about what language school their children attend; it has been French.

But despite new constitutional provisions to the contrary, there are also strong legal impediments to Canadians' mobility. Every province has thrown up a defensive network of legislation and regulations to make it difficult for newcomers to move in, even temporarily. For instance, the Alberta Law Society, which controls that province's legal profession, has a rule forbidding its 3,300 resident members from practicing law in partnerships with attorneys from outside the province, effectively banning non-Alberta law firms from opening branches in the province. If a Manitoba auto mechanic moves next door to Ontario, he cannot legally get a job in his trade for six months, thereby effectively limiting such moves to very rich auto mechanics.

Alberta oil workers can't get jobs in Newfoundland, which chronically has Canada's highest unemployment rate, because that province has a registry of local workers who must get first preference on all jobs associated with Newfoundland's offshore oil explorations. No one from outside little Prince Edward Island—and all but 110,000 Canadians are from outside Prince Edward Island—can buy waterfront property there; it is illegal, according to the Prince Edward Island Real Property Act. If a Quebec company bids to sell computers or buses in British Columbia, it will surely lose the competition unless its bid is more than 10 percent under the local competition's. Even within a region there are such rules. When the Northwest Territories held a recent vote, it tried to set a three-year residency requirement for all voters, thereby effectively disenfranchising thousands of newcomers, many on standard two-year government assignments. And Quebec's government requires that all bids for its construction contracts be restricted to companies with headquarters in the region of the work site.

Geography

In part because of the failure of natural market forces to provide a balance of economic opportunities within the country, Canadians throughout their history have remained basically suspicious of a laissez-faire marketplace and basically receptive to the kinds of deep government intervention in many aspects of life that would be labeled "interference" in other democratic societies.

Thus, an integral part of the history of Canada's federal government is a long series of attempts, both fruitful and fruitless, to overcome the geographic and economic disparities that plague that land. From the official beginning in 1867, a foundation stone of the Canadian Confederation has been the government's professed desire and goal to equalize the different legacies of the land. One of the first such efforts was the new country's promise to British Columbia to overcome its physical separation from the rest of Canada by building a transcontinental railroad through the formidable Rocky Mountains; a century later Pierre Elliott Trudeau, campaigning to become prime minister again, was seeking western Canadian votes by promising to double-track the same single rail line through the same mountains.

Some of the government's other efforts to equalize the geography were successful on a specific programmatic basis by, for instance, helping a particular company or indigenous industry with seed capital, product research grants, export encouragements, and salary subsidies. In 1982 the Trudeau government even proposed $50,000-a-year subsidies to individual newspapers to encourage them to open news bureaus in other regions, hoping to increase the flow of news and improve communications between Canada's regions.

Through a complex—and costly—system of laws, traditions, regulations, policies, and fiscal formulas, Canada's federal government has given mounting volumes of financial aid, often called transfer payments, to the provinces. Whether for needs such as education, government health insurance plans, welfare support, subsidies to lower extreme fuel costs in isolated areas, or wilderness bonuses to attract qualified teachers and civil servants to distant outposts, such assistance is designed to reinforce what is called the social contract of Confederation. The goal is to smooth out the country's geographic and accompanying economic inequities and create in the process the crucial sense that all Canadians can gain from being participants in the same national enterprise regardless of where they happen to live.

The provinces also follow a parallel process to even out the regional disparities within themselves. Through direct spending or via government-owned corporations, such as telephone and electric companies, they seek to stimulate new economic growth or often simply to support or replace existing private enterprises. In the 1980's, for example, Quebec's government forced its own pension plan to invest heavily in some private resource companies, and it created a new government asbestos company, intending to support existing industries and to help create new processing jobs. When economic stimulus was necessary and affordable, Quebec had its giant electric utility launch new phases of a massive wilderness power project; when the economy grew too hot and interest rates soared, it backed off the throttle.

One result, however, was a widely accepted, growing government role in the economy. In some years government spending in the broadest sense accounted for an estimated 86 percent of all economic activity in the poor Atlantic provinces. Even in more developed and more prosperous Ontario the rate was 41 percent. One out of every five federal dollars is spent by simply being transferred to a provincial government, an act that provided fully half the total revenues of some provincial governments.

This creates ever-mounting pressures for new federal revenues and borrowing, often from abroad. It creates an ongoing, rancorous focus for federal-provincial negotiations on allocation formulas. But there are few signs that this aid has had a beneficial impact on the poor regions' basic economic structure, enough to begin to generate healthy, self-perpetuating growth. In fact, economic growth in the Atlantic provinces has stayed below the national average, while Ontario in the middle has remained about average and the West, fueled by an energy boom, has enjoyed buoyant growth, all of which combined, in effect, actually to widen the country's regional economic gaps.

There is evidence that this well-intentioned equalization effort of federal generosity (the provinces would call it stinginess) actually helps create a kind of creeping provincial welfare dependency worrisome to many. It has, to be sure, helped support or modestly improve some material living standards. But it has also allowed a basic poverty cycle to continue and created a long-term economic and psychological dependency on governments of all kinds, which may not always have the fiscal means or political will to apply such costly short-term economic Band-Aids. And the raging infection of high unemployment—upward of 50 percent in some communities—holds its own or continues a cancerous spread with its accompanying family and social distress.

The future implications of all this are obviously unpredictable in any society. They can appear especially ominous in a society with national bonds as fragile as Canada's, where latent centrifugal forces built into the geography have always been awakened by economic uncertainty. Canada, it has been said, is not so much a country as magnificent raw material for a country. It is, one prime minister observed, geographically impossible and politically ridiculous. Its vast, intimidating geography and its uncompromising climates have been constants throughout its history, prompting one early-twentieth-century lecturer to title his talks on Canada "The Landless Man and Manless Land."

But without a civil war the country has hung together as a single, though far-flung, entity through a century of quarrels, grumblings, and misunderstandings, accidental and intentional. With some notable latter-day exceptions such as hopeless, half-breed insurrections and bombs in curbside Montreal mailboxes, Canada's violence has been more verbal than violent.

And the spirit of its people, operating as individuals often in isolation, produced and continues to produce a long series of little-noticed triumphs. These victories over a forbidding landscape are especially little noticed by Canadians, who have, without recognizing it, come to know and use and exploit their northern environment with a keen talent honed from the need to survive. Canadians don't want to talk about these achievements, and by and large, they don't even want to hear about them. Canadians may be simultaneously too close and too far from their country to realize some of their own accomplishments. But the number is legion. And they are perhaps more visible to visitors, whose fresh eyes do not peer through lenses of preconceived native notions.

Canadians, I believe because of their divisive, overpowering geography, tend to shrink from grand continental concepts like the national adventure of Americans taming their wild West or Australians conquering the outback or Brazilians wrestling with the uncivilized riches of the Amazon. Canadians are taming and conquering and wrestling with their own undeveloped country. They have been from the beginning. And unlike many other industrialized lands, they continue to do so today, most often in the

Far North, which Canadians find so easy to ignore. But they are doing it in so many little pieces and ways, and there is, for reasons already described, no strong national perspective to pull all the singulars together into a collective achievement.

In my long travels up and down and back and forth across Canada, I kept stumbling over Canadian success stories, ways that these understated peoples had whipped the land, had adapted their life, machines or thinking to it, or had put its powers to their own use, serious and fickle, good and bad. Of all Canadians, the Eskimos, who prefer now to be called Inuit ("the people"), have developed—and, more important, have maintained —perhaps the closest relationship with the geography. They have a saying: "Our land is our life." Recognizing they are but one of the land's many elements—and certainly not the most important—the Inuit use the harsh geography to survive, as an astute judo student turns the momentum of an onrushing attacker to his own advantage. The Inuit language is full of fond and familial references to the geography and nature that so dominate their existence. The giant polar ice cap, for instance, the vast mass that is always there, is called mother ice.

The Inuit knew nothing of home economics classes, sex education, formal psychology training, or modern marriage counselors. But given the vital need for intimate teamwork within a family struggling to survive in the Arctic, they have long permitted and even encouraged trial marriages among young couples, often in a parents' home. If the arrangement does not work, it is terminated by mutual agreement before the young family is out on its own. If it seems to work, then a formal marriage takes place. And if that matrimony appears to falter at a later date, the troubled couple can be sent out alone together on the ice to cope together for a few weeks and to let the great geography teach them what matters truly matter in life and death.

In the South a handful of innovative new schools have emerged to use Canada's wilderness areas as outdoor classrooms to teach self-reliance, self-confidence, and stress management. Called wilderness seminars, these programs use mountain climbing, natural obstacle courses, long hikes, and survival training as methods to teach urban businessmen how to get along better with colleagues, trust co-workers more, and pace themselves physically and emotionally, whether the challenge be a sheer rock face or a long series of labor negotiations.

Using a network of communications satellites positioned over the Equator, Canada has linked its most distant outposts with its largest cities by telephone and television. Some radiophone numbers may sound unconventional (Rat Pass JL 25889 is the phone number of the Eagle Plains Lodge on the long, lonely Dempster Highway). Likewise, the ubiquitous northern white satellite dishes, always aimed low toward the distant southern horizon, draw in television broadcasts, bringing live football or hockey games and pirated American satellite entertainment to Arctic drilling platforms, mining camps, or little communities where fresh seal carcasses lie chilling on the front doorstep and household refrigerators are placed outdoors in the cold to help the mechanical cooling units. It always struck me as so wonderfully Canadian that anyone in Pangnirtung on distant Baffin Island could pick up a regular phone and dial a number in Ottawa almost 3,000 miles away. In order for these Canadians to talk, however, the signal had to travel somewhere else, to a point 22,300 miles in space over the Equator and another 22,300 miles back. But it does help link individual Canadians in a land without many natural links.

One town, Igloolik, voted down the installation of any television equipment for fear it would adversely affect local life-styles and values. But most other communities eagerly embraced the electronic link. And the tube became the filler of many idle hours and the focus of much social activity, especially during the long winter nights that last all day. Couples or entire families in their mukluk skin boots might shuffle down the icy streets to a neighbor's to watch TV, sip tea, and exchange tales. In many homes the television is left on around the clock, like a farmyard light providing some mental reassurance of another world out there. Besides news, weather, and sports, the Northern Service of the Canadian Broadcasting Corporation (CBC) dishes out Canadian dramas, Hollywood situation comedies, old TV reruns, and documentaries on subjects such as horse raising in Spain, the relevance of which to Canadian Arctic life is at best distant.

Some southern teachers on assignment in the North were disturbed by the unorganized assault of television, as the powerful symbol of urban Canadian life, on the developing minds of Inuit children. "They come in from the simple struggle of a nomadic life on the tundra," one worried high school teacher told me in a cafeteria serving hot dogs, hamburgers, and a strange delicacy called carrots to children reared on seal and caribou, "and they are exposed without any preparation to jiggling bosoms, talking horses, and colossal spaceship struggles for galactic dominance. If you're brought up with it, you can weed out the garbage. But if everything is a fantasy, how do you discern what is real and what values to embrace? It's terribly disorienting for these kids." Like many modern societies containing significant undeveloped sectors, Canada had not yet learned how to bridge effectively the cross-cultural gaps, frictions, misunderstandings, and jarring confrontations that can erupt when a modern welfare state with satellites comes in contact with an ancient, established society whose culture had to be portable enough to fit on a sled. But the modern state had at least introduced itself and launched an educational process certain to take several generations.

Other teachers like Kathleen Purchase in Resolute near the top of Canadian Arctic settlement use television as a tool to teach verbal skills. Knowing full well that the lack of discipline in most Inuit homes allows even young children to stay up until predawn hours, often watching TV, Mrs. Purchase launches daily discussions on the previous night's visual fare. She teaches new words to youngsters who speak English only in school. She helps them analyze social situations in shows like *Three's Company,* inane though she finds them. One day she launched a discussion on white man's humor by asking, "Now why was it so funny when Jack said that?"

Mike Pembroke, her principal and one of the school's three full-time teachers for its fifty-three students, has also adjusted to the demands of his isolated school. Each northern school can schedule its 190 days of instruction whenever it wants because local traditions and hunting patterns vary by community. So with the agreement of the town's 177 residents, Mr. Pembroke's school year runs from late August, the Arctic's fall, until late May, Resolute's spring. To keep parents informed of their children's academic progress, as he would in a southern school, he once scheduled an evening at the school for parent-teacher conferences. Three people showed up, all teachers not as shy as local residents. So now after every report card period Mr. Pembroke and his teachers and an interpreter troop around the settlement from house to house, calling on each child's family to pass the time of day or night, sip the ubiquitous tea, which is made at the slightest excuse in Canada's Arctic, and slip in some comments here and there on the student's schoolwork. "They don't seem to care much about the grades," Mr. Pembroke told me during a long chat one dark afternoon, "but they are very interested in their child's behavior.

And there is a marked improvement for a couple of weeks after every meeting."

Each winter Mr. Pembroke hires some local men for a week or two to take his older male students out "onto the land," as the Inuit put it. It is a fond phrase spoken proudly that always made me think of "going home." The aging men, who are performing informal survival instruction routinely provided by fathers until the recent disintegration of their authority role, teach the youths how to make igloos, a lifesaving knack in sudden Arctic storms. They teach them sled making, how to tell directions by the way the snow blows, where to find seal air holes, how to tell what lies over the horizon by reading reflections in the clouds, and, important, which ice is old enough to be free of salt and safe to melt for drinking. One day these old instructors let Mr. Pembroke and his students learn the hard way about Arctic tides when they spent hours drilling through six feet of ice for a fishing hole only to discover just rocks below, the tide having gone out in the meantime.

And from time to time during each school year Mr. Pembroke must cancel recess because of polar bears. The huge, powerful animals with the large teeth and foul breath wander around town whenever they like, attracted by the smells of food, dogs, and people and the generally curious sight of other creatures also trying to scratch out an existence on the barren tundra. In some more accessible Canadian communities the bears' urban meanderings have been turned into a tourist attraction. But in Resolute an airport sign warns: ATTENTION! THE HAND THAT FEEDS COULD GET EATEN. And there is a large picture of a large polar bear who bears no resemblance whatsoever to his southern cousin, Smokey. BEARS ARE DANGEROUS, the sign says. THEY ARE BIGGER AND FASTER THAN YOU ARE. DON'T FEED THEM. Not long ago the bears did get hungry. So they caught, killed, and ate five of Resolute's pet dogs. "But they haven't been too bad this year," I was assured by Raymond Girard, one resident who thought Arctic life was not too bad compared to the two years he spent in a Chinese prison camp during the Korean War.

The bears, like many human residents of northern Canada, live on the ice, an integral element dominating life up there like dirt on a farm or concrete in a city. For 99.74 percent of Canada's population, ice is something to drop in a drink or sprinkle salt on in the driveway several months a year. But for the 63,000 other Canadians, ice is a brutal geographical fact of life—and death. No rarity are tales of Canadians like the man in Fort Chipewyan in northern Alberta who set out one winter evening, perhaps a tad tipsy and certainly fairly foolhardy, to walk the half mile across a frozen lake to town. They found him midway the next day, his body frozen in its death throes. He was thawed and buried in the spring.

The frozen surface of the Arctic Ocean, one and a half times the size of the United States, forms natural highways and bridges for wildlife to migrate and humans to follow. It forms hunting grounds everywhere, playgrounds in Resolute, racetracks for cars, trucks, and snowmobiles in Pangnirtung, airfields all over, work platforms in the Beaufort Sea. It carries drifting scientific outposts north of Alert, a pseudosecret military post listening in on the Soviet Union. And its harsh, empty surface, bouncing the sun's weak heat off its glaring surface, helps shape the climate that dominates North America.

Cut in certain ways by skilled hands, northern Canadians have long since learned, Arctic ice makes a handy, homemade refrigerator to hold fresh-killed game frozen solid until spring. If no ice is handy, the catch may be covered with stones and water poured over it. The new ice not only preserves the meat but locks the stones in place against thieves of the human or animal variety.

Ice may also become a lifesaving shelter against the vicious winds that can freeze flesh in moments, a danger I discovered one bitter March day when a partially exposed cheekbone went numb, despite a stocking cap, face mask, and parka hood properly tied to hide the face in a tunnel of fur and feathers. I had gone outdoors for perhaps ten minutes to walk over to a nearby airport. I leaned into the wind, carefully breathing through my nose, squinting against the brilliant glare and blowing snow, and beginning to puff as if I'd been climbing a steep hill. Indoors the front of my face stocking with the eye holes was frozen solid, my breath having provided sufficient moisture to freeze the wool the instant the air left my body. My mustache was a horizontal icicle. Invigorating, all right, until minutes later my right cheek began to sting and then burn like a fire. In the mirror it glowed brilliantly red; in those few moments the flesh had been frozen, unknown to me, and the graying skin was to peel off like a bad sunburn for many days. A minor, major lesson.

Yet very quickly these same winds and unseen, still uncharted currents in the Arctic waters beneath the ice can seize that frozen surface that offered a safe route home across its smooth, snow-covered expanses. Within moments they can turn it into a twisted, impassable jumble of pressure ridges and insurmountable minimountains riven by open lanes of water or thin layers of white snow treacherously masking hidden chasms of saltwater slush that swallow unsuspecting victims in seconds. The huge ice plates, as they bend and battle and fracture in constant movement, even seem to talk, emitting low, groaning sounds or moans that are truly haunting in the open Arctic void when land or anything living seems so many miles away.

"The great constant up here," a voice from within a nearby parka hood told me one biting cold day, "is the ice, that marvelous menace that is so lethal and so helpful and so predictable in its unpredictability, all at the same time." The nearby parka was wrapped around Dr. Joseph B. MacInnis, a Toronto physician who is one of a relatively few Canadians who see their vast North as a unique environmental heritage requiring far greater attention and study for two basic reasons: because it is there and forms such an integral part of the country's physical identity and because immense, unpredictable economic developments drastically affecting its future are coming or looming, depending on your personal viewpoint.

Many Canadians are uncomfortable paying attention to or celebrating their unique northernness or hearing others do so. Every time I was planning a northern trip, I ran an unscientific test. I would describe my plans to friends. Inevitably, Americans would bombard me with jealous protestations and offers to serve as luggage bearers while my Canadian friends and neighbors would simply say, "Whyever would you want to go up there?"

"It's true," said Dr. MacInnis, who has encountered similar reactions in his international lectures. "The farther from the Arctic you are, the more fascinating it seems." As one informal measure, whenever I would write a travel article for *The New York Times* about some northern Canadian attraction, Canadian newspapers often bought the piece for publication. Without fail, however, promoters told me later that the mail and telephone inquiries were overwhelmingly American.

Canadians too have an image of the world's image of Canada as a land full of Mounties and Inuit existing only on snowy panoramas with maple leaf backdrops. Of course, neither Canadian image is correct. Any land, especially one as large as Canada, is far more diverse than any single image. But the expressed concern for perpetuating a partial cliché is actually a straw man often used to explain away Canadians' attitude, or rather the lack of one, toward their North. As the late prime minister Louis St. Laurent once put it, Canadians deal with their North "in fits of absentmindedness."

"We have to learn to cope with the ice and North better," Dr. MacInnis added, "and to use them both better." We were standing in pale sunshine on top of 340 feet of water and 64 inches of pale green ice about a mile offshore from Beechey Island in the Northwest Territories. We had flown out there in a tiny Twin Otter, Canada's ten-passenger wilderness workhorse that uses wheels, floats, or metal skis to set down anywhere. Circling low once to appraise the ice, the pilot brought our craft down with a scraping thump.

As soon as the motors were shut down, the cold began to intrude. Even in Inuktitut, the Inuit's language, the single word "cold" *(iki)* is inadequate to describe truly the temperature in Canada's North. Arctic cold is big-league cold for keeps. Like a knife, it pierces the best boots. It freezes up pens in seconds. Numbs noses. Jams machinery. Joins metal plane skis to snow like glue.

It is so cold so much in the Arctic that no one bothers with the minus before temperature readings. Thus, there is no incongruity to watching someone don two pairs of long underwear, wool trousers, three layers of socks, three shirts, a sweater, two pairs of gloves, a mask, immense rubber boots, a scarf, and a parka to go out when the temperature reads "40." That is 40 degrees *below* zero, which with a modest local breeze of, say, thirty miles an hour, produces a wind-chill factor of minus 65. That is actually too cold to snow, so Canada's Arctic is a desert with very little precipitation. It snows only a few inches every year, but the same few inches, driven by vicious winds, blow back and forth for nine months, forming huge drifts against any obstacle (and even providing a little natural insulation for buildings).

It was only "35" as Dr. MacInnis and I walked across the shore-fast collar of ice around Beechey Island, whose 700-foot sheer cliffs were once an ancient sea floor pushed skyward by unknown forces a few million years age. The snow underfoot sounded like broken glass. Twin tuna fish sandwiches, which had frozen solid after being unloaded a half hour before, were thawing thanks to body heat inside our down-filled coats. From the rim of the ice, we watched the currents of Wellington Channel twist and turn and torture the floes before us. We saw a huge, house-size pan of ice six feet thick forced out of the green water like a lumbering whale breaching for air and then slipping back to refreeze instantly atop a neighboring chunk, now twice as thick.

Dr. MacInnis, who preaches the Arctic to his countrymen with a missionary zeal, has made scores of dives beneath the ice, including the North Pole. "There are more than five million square miles of Arctic Ocean," he said with excitement. "It's a whole continent of ice! And man has seen only a few city blocks under it."

Drawn by the lure of resource riches, however, a new generation of Canadians and Canadian companies is quietly launching scores of unheralded research and some actual operational programs that are laying the scientific foundations and setting the ground rules for the future exploitation and perhaps simultaneous preservation of Canada's northern wilds. Dr. MacInnis and I were joined on the ice that chilly noon hour by Peter Jess, one of Canada's emerging troop of ice experts. His employer, Dome Petroleum, perhaps the most active private explorer for Arctic oil and gas, must contend with the region's geography daily. "In the Arctic," said Dr. MacInnis, "everything is something to overcome. For man up here it's not just getting the answers to questions. It's learning what questions to ask in the first place and how to get the answers on nature's own terms."

When, for instance, can an oil company fight the elements successfully —keeping its drillship on site while a sprawling ice floe approaches? And when can it employ the elements for its own purposes—using the cold to freeze huge cement caissons in place around an exploration well? What kinds of man-made obstacles on the shorelines of artificial drilling islands best deflect the gnawing forces of the shifting pack ice? What kinds of equipment, metal, and materials work best in the climatic extremes when drills go from subterranean heats and frictions to sub-zero colds? What kinds of personalities, personnel policies, physical amenities, and even foods work best in the globe's harshest environment?

What is known now really is how little is known. There are no definitive formal studies, for example, correlating the surface traits of the ice to what lies beneath. Are there predictable dynamics or characteristics in the ice that would enable the captain of an icebreaker-tanker like those currently under design to find the weakest ice to break through? What kind of life goes on in and under the ice? What made the large troughs that show up on some pictures from the Arctic Ocean bottom? Were they man-made, perhaps from the anchors of early explorer ships a century ago, or were they natural from the dragging "feet" of mammoth icebergs? The answers have important practical applications since the icebergs could easily sever an underwater oil pipeline. And what would be the awesome consequences for the Arctic, its ice, its wildlife, and even the world's other oceans should there be a massive oil spill or well blowout someday, leaving the gas or oil to spread slowly under the ice just six feet below helpless cleanup crews?

The alternative system that Canadians are devising to transport the vast amounts of gas and lesser oil deposits uncovered so far is a fleet of liquefied natural gas icebreaker-tankers or even ice-strengthened submarines carrying their costly compressed cargoes to the world's waiting energy-hungry markets.

But no one knows yet what impact such regular maritime movements will have on the Arctic's harsh but delicate environment, where summer-time footprints or tire marks on the tundra can last for decades. Constant cracking open of the ice would destroy many traditional "highways" for human and animal movements, perhaps blocking the way of animal herds migrating to less severe wintering spots, exposing them to harsher ele-ments or draining their physical energies through longer forced hunts for a migration detour. Beyond this, what would be the long-term impact on the water temperature and its fragile ecosystems since each fracturing of the ice cover exposes the water to more heat loss? It is an unresolved controversy similar to one waged over longer shipping seasons on the Great Lakes, but with global environmental and climatological conse-quences.

Modern man arrived in Canada's North basically just twenty-five years ago, but it has only been in much more recent times that the higher-priced economics of increasingly scarce resources have brought the Arctic's riches within practical reach. And in this short time much has already been learned and accomplished. Canadians now often use the ice rather than fight it. The wilderness Dempster Highway, North America's only public road crossing the Arctic Circle, is open year round only because workers, laboring in sub-zero temperatures, combine crossed logs and water spray guns to build ice bridges across the Mackenzie and Arctic Red rivers. Special new steam guns now can carve precise holes in thick ice or steam free frozen objects without the destructive force, danger, and cost of explosives.

The study of ice dynamics and the judicious use of some portable steel minibridges have enabled transport companies annually to build a six-week winter road across forty-three miles of northern Saskatchewan's frozen Lake Athabasca, the only land link for some isolated mining communities. The trucks, weighing some 74,000 pounds, creep their way across the cracking ice, feeling the hard lake surface bend and roll beneath their gigantic rigs. Sometimes the growling diesels also feel the ice break beneath them. That happened to Eli Sherstobetoff twice in one day in 1978. The first time his truck sank, the driver was able to leap onto a nearby ice chunk. A fellow trucker picked him up moments later, sent the wet Mr. Sherstobetoff on ahead in his warm truck, and stayed behind to warn others. A mile later Mr. Sherstobetoff and the second truck went through the ice, and again he barely escaped.

Another driver, Fred Oberg, spent an interminable minute on the lake bottom one day, waiting while the icy water seeped into his cabin slowly up to his neck, enough to ease the pressure and let him open the door. He came up under the ice and happened to find the hole. As he headed for land on the surface, his clothes froze. "It was just like I was in a cast," he recalled. But Mr. Oberg was back at work the next day.

"Up here," Mr. Jess, Dome Petroleum's ice expert, said as we strolled on the Arctic Ocean, constantly wiggling our toes for warmth, "you've got to think of ice in a different way. Think of ice not holding things up, but floating things up. It's not the floor of a house. It's an immense raft."

When a likely ocean oil or gas site is spotted seismically, a small shaft is drilled through the ice, and a pump placed over it. A steady, small stream of seawater is drawn up from the ocean and for many days allowed to seep in tiny ripples across perhaps a square mile of ice surface in temperatures hovering around minus 40. The thin layers of water gradually freeze atop each other, eventually creating a mammoth upside-down dome of ice twenty-five feet thick with, not enough strength, but enough buoyancy to carry a 5.5-million-pound drilling rig.

The gangly rigs come in out of the sky. Spike Sheret brings them, piece by piece, laborious load after laborious load, aboard his C-130 Hercules cargo plane. Wearing a turtleneck sweater and a blue jump suit and always chewing his cigar, Captain Sheret and the other Arctic charter pilots of Pacific Western and Northwest Territorial fly into the night through the night as long as the winter and ice hold up.

"Are we ready?" he said over the crackling intercom one midnight as I stood behind this pilot's seat. The huge propeller plane sat at the end of the runway, straining at its brakes. The roar of its four powerful engines billowed out across the tundra. Its strong wing lights sparkled off the blowing snow and frozen mud stretching for more than a mile ahead.

"Yo," came the reply of the copilot, Bob Bridge. And with a jerk, 141,000 pounds of men, machine, volatile fuel, and one pinup photo began rolling down Runway Three Five at the Resolute airport. Some 4,000 feet later someone said, "Rotate," and we arced into the bitter Arctic night. Around the clock these giant craft struggle down crude runways, ferrying their freight—fuel, food, men, supplies—to distant dots of light on the ice, landing on even cruder runways marked by a series of 100-watt bulbs, and turning around to do it all over again.

With names like Cisco, Sculpin, Cape Mamen, and Whitefish, these little drilling communities of fifty or so people are huddled on the open sea in trailer types of housing against winds and snows and a wind-chill factor of minus 80 that can seal them off from the world for days at a time. Their drills first pierce the 25 feet of ice and then glide through perhaps 500 feet of black water to grind their way through 2 or 3 miles of rock, probing for pockets of oil and gas that might heat southern homes or run distant engines in a decade or so.

The thirty-six-year-old Spike Sheret (nobody dares call him Andrew) has worked for Pacific Western for fourteen years, flying businessmen, babies, and baggage to Toronto and Hawaii. But he prefers the more independent, less predictable, perhaps more boisterous life of a "Herc rat," two weeks on and two weeks off of twelve-hour days. "You get to spend fourteen lovely days with your dear loved ones," Captain Sheret noted to a bunch of relaxing flight crew members eager for the punch line, "and then you have to go home to your families." He wheels his lumbering plane all over the world wherever there are heavy or outsize cargoes to move. "One time," he told me, "we flew a sailboat, caviar, and thousands of goldfish to some sheikh's birthday party in Oman. And we flew a load of green peppers to Sweden and some very heavy 'farm equipment' from France to Algeria. Well, tonight we're flying gasoline to an oil rig. We took in the rig itself three weeks ago, a hundred twenty-five loads it was."

He got his orders by company radio at 8 o'clock that night: Take 5,300 gallons of fuel, enough to run an oil rig for one day, from the steel tanks of Resolute's fuel depot, which had been filled by a tanker the previous summer, and fly it to a rubber bladder out on the ice at a rig named Whitefish, 254 miles to the northwest. "Yes sir," he said on the intercom, "it's a bee-ooot-iful night in the sky tonight." We were climbing into a cloudless sky, and Captain Sheret announced it to the world. "Attention, air traffic," he said to no one in particular and everyone in general, "Pacific Western three-eight-three departing Resolute climbing northwest through two [thousand] en route to twenty [thousand] and Whitefish." An Arctic code, the opposite of big-city etiquette encouraging people to ignore each other, requires everyone to announce to everyone where he is, where he is going and how. This helps avoid collisions in the absence of a complex air traffic control network. More important, it sets a route and arrival time which, if unmet, launches immediate rescue efforts. It also reinforces the fraternity of Arctic pilotdom whose radio voices, if never the faces, become so familiar in the long dark hours four miles above the ice where the engines run more efficiently. Sometimes Captain Sheret even chats with his stepson, Darren, also an Arctic pilot, down below.

Captain Sheret, who never takes off in the Arctic without several alternate airfields in mind, has learned many little tricks flying over Canada's northern geography. "Every Arctic season has its own special thrill for you," he says as he points out all the plane wrecks left along the way. In winter there is ice fog, tiny drops of ice hanging suspended in the bitter air. Summer has pea soup fog, sometimes predictably. The hard dirt runways can become mush overnight. Altimeters don't work well in the bitter cold. And compasses whirl uselessly so close to the magnetic North Pole.

Sometimes in the spring, despite the worried urgings of impatient pilots, oil drillers cut it a little close on timing their rigs' complicated disassembly and removal to an island for summer storage or drilling there. Captain Sheret told me a story of landing his large cargo craft on the ice one spring day. While his loadmaster and rig operators muscled another twenty tons of gear into the plane, the pilot went for a coffee in the nearby dining hall. Minutes later came the terrifying cry "The ice is going!"

"I ran out of the trailer," Captain Sheret recalled, "and sure enough, you could see the water moving over the ice toward us at a pretty good clip. We headed for the plane at a pretty good clip, too, jumped in. When we got the engines going, it was a very informal taxi. We just took off and got the hell out of there fast. The water was coming over the wheels when we lifted off." The ice wasn't sinking; it was settling, losing some of its buoyancy. So the rest of the rig was quickly removed from the ice by trucks splashing through hubcap-deep seawater.

Another danger of Arctic flying is looking out the window too much. "It's tempting," Captain Sheret said as we cruised along at 22,000 feet. "It's so beautiful up here. Those stars look like diamonds, don't they? That's Saturn, Mars, and Jupiter all in a row. Down South, you've got city lights and other landmarks to give you bearings. But up here there are no visual guides, nothing, just the black hole out there? Do you see a horizon? You could be ten miles high or ten feet. It's like flying into a colossal inkwell. You look out there much without using your instruments, and you're gonna find yourself in some trouble."

A real boon for Arctic fliers was the development, thanks to the American space program, of the inertial navigation system, which measures the plane's every movement in every direction. Tucked into the cluttered cockpit by Captain Sheret's knee, the system keeps track of its own latitude and longitude, the winds outside, the ground speed of the craft, its decreasing weight as fuel is consumed, and the latitude and longitude of its programmed destination. He removed some charts, did a few calculations, and punched numbers into the computer. "At this speed with this wind," he announced in a few minutes, "it would take us nine hours and twenty-three minutes to fly to your house."

Then he uttered the hallowed cockpit cry for help: "Coffee! Coffee! Coffee!" And Second Officer Dave Graham arrived with the hot liquid that is consumed like engine fuel. Switching on the radio, Captain Sheret announced to the world that he was descending. Outside, there was no sign of anything. But the navigation system told him it was time. The oil rig, little more than 700 miles from the top of the world, warned it had some ice fog. Captain Sheret shrugged.

"Whitefish!" shouted Mr. Graham, pointing ahead into a black void. One minute later a twin stream of faint lights became barely visible. And the crew began its monosyllabic exchange.

"Gear?"

"Down."

"Lights?"

"On."

At about 140 miles an hour Captain Sheret was roaring down toward the improvised strip, trying to land 42,612 pounds of flammable fuel between two rows of light bulbs on an ocean of sheer ice sprinkled with patches of fog and ravaged by 35-mile-an-hour crosswinds. "C'mon, girl," he said. The cigar was not moving.

With a jolt, the scoured ice ripped the balloon tires into instant high speed. Lights flashed past. The propeller pitch changed. The engines roared. Huge swirls of snow blew about. The plane slowed. There were no visible ice cracks. The temperature was minus 38. "Welcome to the Arctic Ocean," said Captain Sheret. "Six feet under us is five hundred feet of water that'll kill you in one minute." He stuffed the cigar back in his mouth and turned to a visitor. "Boring," he said, "isn't it?"

Within thirty-five minutes John Sproat, the loadmaster, would have Pacific Western 383 unloaded. And the lightened Hercules would be lumbering back into the black sky again. Spike Sheret makes four runs most nights. On that night's first ride home Captain Sheret would point out a lone dim glow of yellow seeping through some clouds far below. "That's Polaris," he said.

After all my years of flying, it seemed strange to be startled by lights down below. But they didn't seem to belong. As I gazed down on little Cornwallis Island in that broad, bitter darkness, it did look like a brilliant single star. But up close, beneath the clouds and ice fog and blowing snow, the single light became a cluster and then a whole human complex emerging on the barren moonscape. It was the pioneering, new Polaris lead-zinc mine, the northernmost base-metal operation in the world and the guiding star for the resource development of Canada's Arctic. Many resource projects have been planned there. Many more are on the drawing boards. And surveyors and seismologists and drillers are finding new deposits regularly. But Polaris is already taking out the riches.

The attraction of resources has always been the historical driving force behind Canada's economic development. First there was fish. Then came furs. Gold and copper led many to the Yukon. Uranium brought some to northern Saskatchewan and Ontario. Asbestos was the attraction in northern Quebec. Heavy oil sands awaited exploitation in northern Alberta.

And the cheap electrical generating potential of all the freshwater resources in Labrador—indeed, across the whole top of Canada—has drawn the bulldozers ever northward over the years. Quebec's $16 billion hydroelectric project in James Bay alone will take more than a decade to build, involving a series of dams, powerhouses, and at least one generating room the size of five football fields carved from solid granite 450 feet underground. Rerouting large rivers and creating Quebec's largest lake, the project at times employed 16,000 workers and even required the careful relocation of 1,500 beavers to safer waters.

Nearly 2,000 miles away, most of them to the north, sits the Polaris mine. Designed to produce 187,000 metric tons of zinc and 42,000 metric tons of lead a year, the mine was a $150 million gamble for its Canadian owners, Cominco Ltd., one of the mining arms of the sprawling Canadian Pacific business empire. The physical, engineering, and economic challenge was to build a massive underground mining operation well north of the Arctic Circle, supply it, and keep it running efficiently year-round—regardless of weather and geographic isolation—and then ship a year's supplies in and a year's production out by freighters during a narrow forty-two-day ice-free period.

The collection of lights at the mine, which even has its own postal code and swimming pool (indoors, not surprisingly), is home to 200 men, 26 women, and 5 dogs—all, except the Canine Polar Bear Patrol, living in snug luxury while carving out a new deep mine and a niche in business history. "It's home," Sam Luciani told me when I entered his isolated homestead. A gruff, gray-haired fifty-seven-year-old mine manager, Mr. Luciani has worked on northern mining operations across Canada for much of his life. "In 1942," he said during a long evening's conversation, "I spent a month in Goose Bay, Labrador, waiting for a connecting flight. I haven't spent much time down South since."

He and his energy-efficient little town inhabit a three-story complex of 200 comfortable rooms and apartments interspersed with offices and storerooms to hold a year's supply of foods, including such items as Korean mushrooms, African pineapples, and Chinese apples. Fresh produce, dairy products, and some meats come in on infrequent Hercules flights. They are eagerly unloaded while pilots like Spike Sheret take a quick dip in the swimming pool with a broad picture-window view of the blustery tundra just 825 miles from the North Pole. Polaris also has a gymnasium, two saunas, a small library, and a battalion of easy chairs to hold weary workers while they watch a better array of satellite TV programs than their citified cousins in southern Canada. Just down the hill, a thirty-second bus ride away through winds that can reach 70 miles an hour, is the complete mill, a building larger than a football field that was constructed on a barge in Quebec, floated some 3,000 miles down rivers, across gulfs, and through straits to be run aground here for the next quarter century or so. Its empty hull now holds fuel oil.

And just under the hill George Casavant and his mining crews, dressed in orange coveralls like some James Bond movie assault team, are nearing the 1,000-foot level. To the subterranean thunder of huge diesel machines, they drill, blast, and scoop away the rich shafts of permafrost, thaw the sparkling rocks for the first time in a few million years, and crush them to fist-size nuggets for the conveyor-belt ride to the mill, a storehouse, and eventually European smelters. The ore is chemically treated to float off first the lead and then the zinc. With heat from the mine's diesel generator exhausts, the metal powders are dried and carried on belts to an adjacent but unheated storage shed. En route they lose their heat in the constant sub-zero weather and often touch off indoor snow flurries that cling and accumulate softly on any surface in lovely crystalline shapes so fragile that the slightest movement of air sends them flying in the light. Tailings go into a nearby, biologically dead lake.

"This is why we are here," Bob Owen, a metallurgist, said as he handed me a clump of cold ground about 90 percent lead. Not all of the mine's 23 million metric ton reserve, which oil prospectors stumbled upon in 1960, is that rich. But miners like Jean-Paul Brazeau, who earns $40,000 a year, regularly send up 60 percent ore. In more civilized parts of the world, Cominco is delighted with 6 percent ore.

The lode had to be so rich to support all the extra expenses of operations in such distant, hostile surroundings. One corporate burden, of course, is no cash flow for forty-six weeks a year. Additionally, employees work six twelve-hour days for ten weeks, earning overtime after each week's first forty-four hours. Then the company flies them out for two weeks' vacation. Workers also get free room and board and a special northern isolation bonus of 50 percent of their pay. Understandably, perhaps, the mine has a waiting list of 3,000 job applicants. But in winter months, when darkness is total for twenty-four hours a day, employee turnover is a significant and costly 12 percent. For many winter weeks at a time there can be no outside activities. Sometimes the wind and snow are so strong that the bus can't even safely drive the 100 yards between the dormitories and the mine, so one group of workers has to take a double shift until the weather eases.

Besides the extra pay and vacations, Canadian companies have devised a number of methods to combat northern morale problems. They have designed open, brightly colored living areas with lots of private spaces (maximum two persons per room). There are movies, many TV sets, sports leagues, and recreation rooms, and because mealtimes take on such a vital socializing role, breaking the monotony of work and foul weather, there are unlimited quantities of delicious food and pastries. Married working couples get hiring preference for their desired emotional stability. "Up here," said Lyn Luciani, one of the twenty-four working wives there when I visited, "I miss the restaurants and shops and having my hair done. But down there I miss the peace and quiet of up here."

"When you get cabin fever," noted Sam Luciani, her father-in-law, "you get very grumpy. Of course, I don't. But one of the worst is my wife, Kay. You know, people living in the Arctic are a funny but wonderful breed. They may be mighty quiet at times. But you'll find no better, stronger friends anywhere ever. When the chips are down, they'll literally kill themselves trying to help. Because up here everyone knows they could need help themselves any minute and we're all in this, the North, together. For me, it's a big attraction of the North."

"Everything is harder to do in the North," added Mr. Owen, the thirty-five-year-old father of one. "Where something would take you four hours down South, up here it takes eight hours. Everything is more intense —your work, your friendships, the climate, and your frustrations. It's hard to get used to."

There are many other adjustments required for northern life. In the cold, door handles just break off in people's hands. Vehicles are left running from October to May. Even then, the oil needs an antifreeze. "Try surveying in the Arctic dark," Mike DeGruyter told me as he donned full outdoor gear. "It gets a little frosty out there." But inside the mine itself, any warm area must be refrigerated because the permafrost holds up the walls.

Cominco has also undertaken to hire Inuit, about 10 percent of the workers so far. This, however, requires vocational as well as cultural training for supervisors and native people whose nomadic lives have not always been built around punch clocks, yelling foremen, and hamburgers. So Rick Luciani, the personnel manager, Sam's son and Lyn's husband, makes public relations trips to Inuit towns. And he also keeps a lot of seal meat and caribou on hand for snacking. Inuit workers are also allowed to go on vacation after only six weeks' work so they can get in some regular food hunting for their families.

There were, however, some stubborn problems in establishing a business 625 miles north of the Arctic Circle, where the ice is at least seven feet thick by May. For one thing, the mine's pool table wouldn't fit through the game room door. And the palm trees for the swimming pool took many months to arrive.

Except for supplies on the annual food freighter, everything else must be flown in by planes, mostly Twin Otters. They are piloted by men like Brian Duncan, who visits the Polaris mine so often that he is a regular on the volleyball team. When the weather permits, he brings in the mail, some perishable foods, odd machine parts, company directives, and refreshed miners. When the weather permits, he takes out the mail, company documents, miners needing refreshment, and the odd, perishable journalist whose normal duties do not include flying in small planes in raging Arctic blizzards.

But the weather would not permit. When we had put on our hardhats, battery latterns, safety belts, big rubber boots, and bright-colored overalls to go deep in the lead mine that March morning, it had been a beautiful, sunny day—39 degrees below zero, but sunny nonetheless. When we emerged ninety minutes later, the winds had come, picking up last December's snow and moving it around so swiftly that visibility was less than 100 feet. Outdoor conversations are short in that kind of weather, with all voices muffled by hoods and masks. People must turn their entire bodies to aim their parkas at a listener. Even the leased huskies, the Canine Polar Bear Patrol, were padding around in a group for safety.

Brian Duncan, the pilot, was packed and ready to go, but he wouldn't because he couldn't see the runway. "I'm going for some lunch," he told a group of would-be passengers by the front door. "We'll take another look in an hour." An hour later he took another look. "Nope," he said.

The passengers dozed in the lobby. Finally, after another hour had passed, the word came: "Maybe."

Ten people and their luggage were hustled outside for the fifteen-second bus ride to the runway. According to the special Arctic dashboard gauge, the vehicle, a standard-looking school bus, had been running for 3,189 out of the previous 3,300 hours.

The gale winds had moderated to only thirty-five miles an hour, so the plane was loaded. Mr. Duncan removed the custom blankets from the engine cowlings. He unplugged the craft's electric engine heaters. And then he gave the signal: He waved to us. One by one, we piled out of the bus, stepped up onto the flimsy metal step hanging out, squeezed into the cramped craft, and adjusted the seat belt buckles that felt as frigid as ice cubes against the stomach. "I said," he said, "we may give it a try in a few minutes." Mr. Duncan thought things were clearing.

The engines were started. And the rattling little plane sat there. Mr. Duncan, a prudent pilot, likes to be able to see at least three lights, or 600 feet, down the runway before taking off. Only one light was visible. The plane continued to rattle and sit. Ten minutes later, as he had suspected, a small patch cleared. With a sudden jerk the Twin Otter leaned into the wind and tottered off down the stony runway. As if on a string, it bounced into the turbulent sky, where all its cabin windows quickly frosted over.

Within seconds we burst through the thin storm and into the same sunny sky that had reigned that morning. When we descended into Resolute, thirty minutes and countless air pockets later, there was no storm. There also was no commercial Jet Liner. Arctic schedules being what they are, that is, theoretical sketchings to satisfy the bureaucratic paper demands of another world far from the all-powerful, unpredictable forces of geography and climate, the stubby 737 jet was waiting elsewhere for another storm to clear. It might try to get us later that day, a Friday, or it might not and we could wait for the next plane to Montreal—on Tuesday. We might hear later.

More waiting. More dozing. More chatting. More thinking. Such customary inconveniences, it seemed to me, can sometimes overshadow the many minor and major achievements within Canada's geography. They are far too numerous for any comprehensive listing. Just building and running so many outpost airports linking so many Canadian communities are notable accomplishments. Elsewhere Canadians continuously monitor by air and study thousands of square miles of ice floes. They have designed and built special airborne water bombers to combat the many isolated forest fires that rage across Canada annually; the large planes have belly scoops enabling them to reload on the fly from any nearby lake.

Individual Canadian entrepreneurs are trying to utilize their geography profitably, whether it's Jacques Van Pelt launching a wildlife-watching business in Fort Smith, Northwest Territories, or some small-scale farmers in Yellowknife, Northwest Territories, employing their twenty-four-hour summer sunshine to grow melons, or scientists in a nickel mine deep beneath Sudbury, Ontario, utilizing the earth's steady 55-degree temperature to grow vegetables with artificial light. The Mistassini band of Cree Indians in Quebec open some isolated fishing camps for urban customers. The Northwest Territories' government plans the Inuits' first university, an open university concept using radios, satellites, and computers. In the high Arctic, scientists ride the drifting polar ice cap searching for clues to the history of the Alpha Ridge, an 800-mile-long mountain range that is as large as Europe's Alps but totally covered by water. The federal government has financed cheaper water transport for distant communities by funding a network of supply barge operations to navigate wilderness rivers like the Mackenzie, which is 300 miles longer than the Mississippi River. A business arm of the Inuit community is investing native funds in northern resource development projects. Engineers are designing and building underwater "windmills" and other ingenious devices to harness the vast electrical generating potential of Canada's tidal basins, much of it as electrical exports to American markets. Others devise plans to bury society's unwanted spent nuclear fuel in chambers excavated in the solid rock of the inhospitable Canadian Shield. And Rangar Jonsson, an eighty-four-year-old trapper who lives alone in a tepee in the wilds of northern Manitoba, can visit Winnipeg for the first time in six decades and marvel at the pace of modern traffic while noting that, living in the woods, he hasn't had a headache for a little more than a half century now.

To link several of Ontario's recreational waterways flowing on different levels, authorities built a large inclined railway just to lift pleasure boats from the water and haul them to the next level. Copying old Inuit travelers, Arctic navigators have learned to read iceblink, the reflected glare of ice beyond the horizon on clouds within view, and water sky, the reverse, when the iceblink is broken by dark spaces foretelling the pres-

ence of open water beyond view of the naked eye. At the University of
Manitoba, H. Leonard Sawatzky, a geographer, has teamed with Walde-
mar H. Lehn, a computer colleague, to develop a new theory that could
change the standard explanation for how North America was discovered.

One widely accepted theory holds that storms blew Norse seamen
across the North Atlantic about A.D. 1000. But these two Canadians are
using childhood reminiscences, Canadian geography, computers, and
translations of ancient Norse legends to amass evidence that the historic
discovery may have actually resulted from a series of island-hopping voy-
ages by Norsemen following an Arctic mirage, a visual phenomenon of the
higher latitudes that enables travelers to "see" beyond the horizon. Arctic
mirages differ from their desert cousins in that they reflect something that
actually exists, although not where it seems to be. Thus, a driver in the
desert "sees" a lake that does not, in fact, exist. But under certain conditions a child on a wintry walk to school on the Canadian prairies can see
on the horizon recognizable buildings of a town forty miles away, far
beyond the curved horizon that limits normal vision. Arctic temperature
conditions can bend light rays around the earth's curve, placing a real
image on an elevated, seemingly real horizon. Beyond its historical interest, it is a misleading phenomenon that carries great import, for instance,
for Arctic fliers, who might try landing on a runway that is not where it
appears.

My reverie was ended that threatening afternoon at the airport by the
appearance on the horizon of a jet plane that really did exist. It was less
than two hours late. While the people came out the back, tons of cargo,
including a Toyota, came out the front. In such planes seats can be
removed or added, and the forward cabin wall is movable to allow for
varying loads of humans and bulk. It was about half and half that night
as we lifted off for the five-hour flight toward the South. By the time we
were climbing over frozen Beechey Island, the drink orders were in and
the chicken liver canapés were warming in the rear kitchen.

Down below, invisible now, the ice floes were grinding and groaning
their way toward spring extinction. Spike Sheret was suiting up for another long night of hauling fuel out onto the glistening ocean ice. Mike
Pembroke was grading spelling papers to the radio sound of the news first
in Inuktitut and then in English. Several Inuit hunters were preparing
their snowmobiles and high-powered rifles for a week's business trip away

from home. Ray Girard was stopping by the bar after closing his general store. A company of Canadian soldiers was cooking its canned dinner over heaters on a long survival-training trek. The night shift still had several more hours to go underground at the Polaris mine, where concepts like day and night and Saturday and Sunday are irrelevant. The mine's overnight shift was sound asleep in rooms marked "ZZZZZZZ." And after a beef dinner and apple pie, the day shift was relaxing, watching basketball from an Atlanta television station on a giant wall screen. Brian Duncan had already returned to the mine with the mail and left again (no volleyball game scheduled that night). Sam Luciani was talking via satellite with his distant daughter a sixth of the way around the world, while the boys on the Whitefish oil rig were secretly testing for gas at the 2,000-foot level.

It was long since dark down there. Up in the sky nearly seven miles high, it was late afternoon. The sun was setting to the south, a mixture of pale blues and pinks and faint yellows. There was nothing warm or hot about it. The sunset lasted for one hour, right through dinner.

Below, there was nothing human or humane. The empty white wilds stretched on for hour after hour. This is where North America's winter storms breed and grow before blasting southward. Typically these cold high-pressure zones—American weathermen always seem to call them Canadian cold fronts—squat over northern Canada for days, building pressures higher and higher while temperatures plummet lower and lower —to minus 81 Fahrenheit once, Canada's lowest, in the Yukon. Rising up to ten miles in the air, these bitter-cold domes eventually collapse on themselves, squirting long streams of icy fingers and fronts toward the south and west. There, they clash with warm southern air, igniting chains of storms that come barreling in off the Great Lakes, newly laden with tons of warm moisture capable of dumping several inches of snow an hour on the Canadian South and the American Midwest. Seen from above, these weather systems look like some giant continental coffee cup with white storms, some of them 150 miles long, swirling about like milk being stirred in.

But the sky was clear above and below that night as darkness reached our high-flying plane. In the full moonlight the whiteness beneath was broken only occasionally, as we inched southward, by the jagged gray cracks of open water where winds had moved ice plates apart. We cut across Hudson Bay, an ocean inlet that is tiny by Canadian standards but is nearly five times the size of Michigan. We cut into northern Quebec, the white still unmarred.

Slowly, almost surreptitiously, some scrubby trees began to dot the sharp white. The sky was a deep, dark blue sparkling with the bright, crisp lights of thousands of stars that faded toward the horizon as the bands of blue grew paler and paler before merging with the ground without any distinct horizon line. Another half hour, and the patches of scrawny forest grew thicker, and huge, unmarked lakes dotted the lonely landscape with clumps of clean white.

Nowhere was there any sign of life or civilization. One hour. Then another. And another. No lights. No straight roads. No smoke. Just the silent chilled mass as far as anyone could want to see. Peering out the windows, some travel companions and I sat silently in awe as the hours passed. It was hypnotic in a way and frightening in a sense. I couldn't turn my eyes away from the vast emptiness of it all, watching closely for even some little sign of humanity or civilization, yet strangely exhilarated when none came. I felt vulnerable, too, and terribly tiny.

And then it happened: A sudden glow loomed below, lighting the whole landscape. It was Montreal and the thin mass of urbanized southern Canada packed there. Lights. Many lights. Streets. Straight streets. Cars. Lines of them creeping along. Factories. Haze. Trucks. Parking lots. Billboards flashing past. Fences. Colored paint. Blinking signs. Lines. Bushes. Crowds. We landed then in another world. And Canada's North seemed very, very far away.

TWO

⁂

The
People

⁂

About 100 parents had eagerly assembled in the little Toronto school auditorium one night when their fourth-grade offspring raised the curtain on the homemade cardboard stage. The youngsters were to present a show using puppets they had made in class and a script entirely written by the Canadian pupils themselves. "Good evening," said the master of ceremonies, a puppet bearing a certain resemblance to Bert Parks. "Tonight we are going to talk with the finalists in our beauty pageant."

"My name is Betty Lou Jones," said the first contestant in that fraudulent accent that Canadians think sounds like the American South, "and I'm from Durham, North Carolina."

"Hello," said the next young lady puppet, "my name is Amy Sue Barker. And I'm from Little Rock, Arkansas."

The last puppet finalist spoke very softly, and the chuckling parents hushed and strained to hear. "My name is Roberta Mackenzie, and I'm from Canada," she said. "But I don't know what that is." The immediate, knowing outburst of parental laughter ignited prolonged applause that required extra bows all around. Somehow, with their natural openness and honesty, those nine-year-olds had struck a key chord in the Canadian personality. Statistics can show where Canadians come from, where they live now, when they marry and give birth and divorce and die, how they earn a living and spend their time and money. But after more than 360 years of settlement and after nearly one and a quarter centuries of independence, no one—least of all, Canadians themselves—has been able to tell Canadians who they are.

For Americans, perhaps the most surprising discovery about Canada is that a land so rich in so many ways, still so pure in so many places, with a people so obviously intelligent, hardy, warm, and so insistent on who they are not, still suffers such anguish over its national identity. Americans are basically ignorant about most aspects of Canada, but at least they see it as one country. Canadians, instead, mostly see their land in a wide assortment of pieces with large gaps in between.

They are always looking so hard for their identity, perhaps too hard, in monthly magazines, weekly supplements, daily newspapers, on radio and television, and in intellectual discussions. I remember in my military training for night fighting the sergeant, a Korean War combat veteran, told us that hard-to-see things could be spotted in the darkness if we did not look right at them. We were to look off to the side and rely on our peripheral vision and our sixth sense. You didn't have to stare at something nose to nose to know it was there, he said. He was telling us there are other levels of knowing that are just as good, something that despite their impressive growth and maturity in other areas, Canadians have not fully sensed or are afraid to believe. I began to think during my years in Canada, chatting, overhearing, and reading, that for many Canadians perhaps their unfortunate identity was to search forever for an identity, a Sisyphean task guaranteed to ensure eternal angst. The search itself had become the identity because Canadians were always staring so hard straight ahead in the dark woods, intensely looking for it. If they ever sat down and relaxed and pretended not to care about it for a moment, they would suddenly find that elusive sense of self-comfort lurking just out of the corners of their eyes, back where the pale light from the campfire merges with the edge of the deep forest. It would be fuzzy and indistinct, to be sure, but nonetheless reassuring.

American schoolchildren and perhaps even their parents might have a tough time identifying exactly what an American is. They might lapse into the past, pulling up names like Paul Revere, George Washington, Abraham Lincoln, Daniel Boone, Davy Crockett, and others from the nation's colorful history. They might talk about the Revolution or the Civil War or Pearl Harbor or how their great-grandparents came from Italy speaking no English and carrying only a suitcase and a burning desire to become an American. And an American child could talk about these things regardless of where he or she grew up or went to school. More important, perhaps, Americans with their peripheral vision assume they know who they are.

Not in Canada, where it seems some Canadians are also uncertain of even where it is. Leo Doucet of New Brunswick tells the not uncommon story of moving to Whitehorse, the capital of the Yukon Territory, a few years ago. He wrote to his Canadian insurance company to change his policy address and was promptly notified that it was canceling the policy because that company insured only drivers in Canada.

There was no Revolution in Canada, no Civil War, no broad mythology of national heroes for Canadians to share, however subconsciously, across their broad, geographically fragmented land. The first prime minister of Canada, for instance, was Sir John A. Macdonald, a dour Scot and alcoholic whose name is often misspelled and whose birthday (January 11, 1815) is unobserved these days. Canadians do, however, celebrate religiously the May birthday of Queen Victoria, the British sovereign whose birthday passes unnoticed now in her own nation. Possibly the only "hero" of national stature most Canadians might know is Louis Riel, an Indian half-breed whose late-nineteenth-century western rebellion actually symbolized the bitter French-English linguistic divisions that still plague Canada. He was hanged.

Canada was launched as a country by the British with as much thought to the domestic consequences of this within the new land as they showed when, a century later, they freed their African colonies with artificial boundaries drawn by foreigners far from the tribal and geographical realities of the continent. By their official departure in 1867, the British, as they had in their other foreign colonies, had instilled magnificently in Canadians an inferiority mindset from the start. One Canadian comedian, noting how Britain did not always dispatch its finest folk to people new colonies, described the difference between two such colonies, Australia and Canada. He noted Australia was populated by British convicts. In Canada, he said, they were never caught.

One bright January morning in Toronto I drove to the Moore Park area of the city for a long visit with John Hirsch, one of millions of immigrants to Canada now leavening that conservative land with his own considerable aspirations and ambitions. While squirrels bounced across the bright snow in the ravine out back, he shared his analysis of the situation. "Canada's inferiority complex," he said, "stems from a colonial mentality. Successful colonization consists of convincing the natives that whatever they have or can produce is a priori inferior to the culture, skill, and standards of the colonial power. The British were masters at this. They managed with brutal charm and incredible arrogance to walk into many colonies of older culture and convince them they weren't worth anything. The Scots were dumped on as the poor white trash at home, so they came over here to dump on someone else and pass on this terrible repression. The Americans were smart and got out of that. But I can never understand here how a country, even before it starts, accepts that it is not as good as the guy next door. When I was little back in Hungary, we were taught that the world is God's hat and Hungary is the bouquet on it. That's a pile of BS, of course. It's flowers mixed with weeds, but you're taught to believe you are special. You are here on earth to do something and take pleasure and pride in doing it the best you can. You don't start off being spiritually and psychically retarded, believing you are less than everyone else. If I had enough money, I'd send Canada to a good shrink for twenty years." Instead, Mr. Hirsch became the artistic director for the famed Stratford Festival, further enhancing, despite considerable frustrations from his countrymen, one of Canada's few internationally recognized symbols of excellence.

"American students have been conditioned from infancy," said Northrop Frye, who has taught many Americans at the University of Toronto, "to think of themselves as citizens of one of the world's great powers. Canadians are conditioned from infancy to think of themselves as citizens of a country of uncertain identity, a confusing past and a hazardous future."[1] And he notes some distinct historical differences. "The pattern of Canadian history has been almost the opposite of the pattern of American history. The United States had a War of Independence against a European power in the 18th Century, and a civil war on its own soil a century later. Canada had a civil war of European powers on its own soil in the 18th Century, and a movement of independence against its American partner in the 19th."[2]

Historian J. M. S. Careless traces this conditioning to a "loser syndrome," created by the rigors of pioneering a northern land, and to the many political and social defeats that conditioned Canada's immigrants before they fled to their new land. It is, of course, impossible to generalize about all immigrants' motives. But the sense one gets is that many immigrants went to the United States with a specific goal to do something they could not do elsewhere—to practice a particular religion, for example, like the Pilgrims. Many of Canada's immigrants were simply fleeing something—the Irish potato famine, the Highland clearances in Scotland, persecution against Indians in Kenya, or, in the case of some English nobility, a somewhat sullied reputation back home. The latter were called remittance men because they were not trying to create much of a new life in Canada; they lived, instead, off remittances from home.

"Americans," Professor Careless told me over lunch one day, "cannot conceive of losing unless there's a conspiracy somewhere. Canadians, constrained by climate, distance, and history, see no reason to expect victory." In fact, they are suspicious of it. Some years ago Nordair, a small regional airline and perpetual underdog in the scramble for business, suddenly began offering a free limousine ride or one-day car rental to all its passengers on the busy Montreal–Toronto route. Within days the Canadian Transportation Commission, which licenses airlines, ordered a halt to the promotion. As Dick Smythe, a radio commentator, analyzed it, "It's not Canadian to be competitive and imaginative. You have to watch out. You might reward the tough competitor, the guy who comes up with the different, imaginative way of doing things." Upon returning from a round of international competitions, one of Canada's emerging new breed of stellar amateur athletes remarked on the difference between Canadians and Americans. Her countrymen, she said, would congratulate a Canadian on winning tenth place; the Americans would tell their returning competitors, "Fifth place? Tough luck. You'll do better next time." Donald Sutherland, a Canadian who left his country to excel elsewhere, once described Canadians as being like the children who press their noses against the window of life, secretly suspecting they are missing all the fun that their rambunctious American neighbors have but too worried to try it themselves lest they fail.

At the same time, however, there are numerous indications of change emerging from the safe gray of old Canada. There are many more signs of an eagerness to compete aggressively in a variety of international arenas from the America's Cup yachting races to the World Cup skiing championships, where the new downhill daring of the Canadians earned them the nickname of Kamikaze Kids. This new attitude among a growing minority was even apparent on the neighborhood athletic level, where

Canadians like Mike Tzekas, one of our son's football coaches, organized and trained his own club of teenagers so well that they usually destroyed their opponents. Their reward was to be expelled from the club league as too good. "This country," said the young Mr. Tzekas, who had several thousand of his own dollars tied up in equipment for "my boys," "is so afraid of competition. But if they think they can get me down, they're so wrong." He soon attracted other similar-minded coaches. They began forming their own league and were swamped by boys eager for excellence.

Canadians have grown up in the only British Commonwealth country forced to develop in the towering shadow of a superpower. They are bombarded daily by the overpowering cultural, economic, political, and even athletic influence of a dynamic and sometimes boorish United States, which has blithely drawn away much of the best in Canadian society—its inventors and inventions, TV celebrities, singers, businessmen, athletes—to repackage and market internationally as a kind of homogenized human. It doesn't matter to the world if the discoverer of insulin or Alexander Graham Bell or the actor famous for portraying Abraham Lincoln or the inventor of basketball was Canadian, as all of them were. But deep down it does seem to matter to Canadians, who desperately would like their due recognition yet feel an equal distress when they get it.

Canadians rarely praise themselves or each other. About as effusive as they get about themselves was an editorial in the *Toronto Globe and Mail* on January 2, 1984, marking the country's population passing a historic level: "At 25 million we are still a handful of souls rattling around in a great empty country, yet so tightly packed into our cities that only a few farmers, trappers and truck drivers have a real feel for the emptiness. We are a long way from realizing our full potential, but still doing quite nicely, thank you, in comparison with most other nations in the world, whether we measure by bellies filled or freedoms enjoyed." In their hearts, a growing number of Canadians know when something is good or excellent. But it seems the recognition, the confirmation of suspected excellence must come from somewhere else. "Phlegmatic Canadians are suspicious of adulation," Allan Fotheringham, a popular columnist, wrote, "but Americans love heroes; their system depends on them." He was writing about how Americans lionized Canadian Ambassador Kenneth Taylor for rescuing some U.S. hostages in Iran and how uncomfortable Canadians felt then. Yet when a Canadian wants to show how good some Canadian athlete, broadcaster, or actor is, he will note how that person has turned down many lucrative offers from the United States. Oh, he must be good then! The American offers confirm the quality; his rejection of them makes everyone feel better, especially those who never get such offers.

But even success can make friends or associates maliciously envious at home, as some Canadian writers successful abroad have discovered to their dismay. Canada, many have noted, is a country of debunkers uncomfortable with celebrity. "This being a small country," Charles Gordon of the *Ottawa Citizen* wrote, "everybody's an insider. Everybody knows somebody who knows how flawed some famous person really is. And, failing that, virtue can be its own punishment, as in: 'Wayne Gretzky? He's just . . . well, he's just too perfect.' "[3] There was in recent years a popular Canadian prairie drama. Its title touched on the problem: *If You're So Good, What Are You Doing in Saskatoon?*

Canadians were originally conditioned by a harsh climate, a heritage of international shyness, an entirely different history of immigration from their fellow North Americans, and a considerable fear of failure to expect the worst in any situation. If failure came, they knew it all along. If it didn't come, that proved no one paid any attention to Canada. And if success somehow erupted, there must be something wrong somewhere— perhaps it was a bogus victory or the victor wasn't very Canadian anymore. "It's simple," Pat Muelle, a moving van operator, explained to me on one of my last days in Canada. "You Americans are much more confident than we Canadians. You are taught that from birth. And so are we." And there is the stubborn story in Canada about the elderly woman at a party when word came that Prime Minister Lester Pearson had won the Nobel Peace Prize. "Just who does he think he is?" the matron demanded.

The Royal Canadian Air Farce, the perceptive comedy troupe, captures this feeling in many of its radio and TV sketches. In one, for instance, Canada launches its first astronauts, two winos who are already sky-high, and the hurtling satellite, named Beaver, achieves an altitude of only fifty feet. In another, the troupe suggests that Canada form a drama company that will perform Shakespearean plays using Donald Duck-style voices. This, they claim, will finally make Canada "a leader." In some scenarios, an Air Farce member compares a segment of society in Canada to the United States, an instinctive act in Canada even if a more appropriate comparison would involve another region of Canada. The character notes, "Americans say, 'we have nothing to fear but fear itself.' A Canadian says, 'Things are going to get a whole lot worse before they go bad.' "

Individually the Canadian people strike visitors as among the world's friendliest, the most open and reasonable and least dogmatic, and now among the most economically aggressive and imaginative. In the populated parts of the land, the cities look tidy but familiar, the houses well kept but not all that dissimilar from those lining the residential streets of other North American cities. But every once in a while there comes a detail, usually minor, that is somehow different, mildly jarring and usually intriguing, to alert the astute observer that he is in a foreign land.

The baseball game looks the same, but it starts with two national anthems, and fans in the stands are drinking hot chocolate even in July. The football game looks familiar, but the field is larger, the point system more complex, and the offense has only three downs to move ten yards. There are children safely by themselves at these events as young as ten. The television screens carry multilingual shows, and not just on Sunday mornings. There are no liquor stores on every corner, but there are streetcar stops and in some city sections street signs in English and French or Chinese. The architecture is not unusual, but it is a different blend of new and plots of savored old. In season, boulevard median strips contain lighted fountains gushing their beautiful sounds through downtown, and thousands of tulips blossom undisturbed by anything other than cool breezes. Sunday newspapers are so thin as to border on inconsequence; Saturday's bulge enough to wrench the back of an unwary reader. There are familiar holidays at Christmas and Easter, but the fireworks displays come in May, and Thanksgiving in October.

Of course, none of this was apparent 450 years ago on one of those typical Canadian autumn days, windy and brisk despite a strong sun, that foretell the wan winter weeks ahead. But Jacques Cartier, a tough Breton sailor, might well have sensed something different in the scale of the place as he slowly worked his way up a massive river without a name. By the size of the body of water, Cartier thought it was a bay, for like many before and since that day, he had come to Canada on the way to somewhere else.

He was seeking the Northwest Passage, the fabled water route to the equally fabled riches of the Orient. Others looked to the North and were awed, and often killed, by the weather and the geography they found there. But King Francis I was seeking a New France, new settlements, new treasures, and new sailing routes to match the New Spain his European neighbor was carving from the southern New World. So Cartier tried the middle, sailing through the forbidding fog and the rugged rocks of the northern North American coast into a broad bay to a peninsula now called Gaspé. There in 1534 he erected a thirty-foot wooden cross and pronounced a new French sovereignty over that North American land. It was a pronouncement to be echoed in the late twentieth century as his descendants in Quebec sought independence from Canada to erect, finally, that new French society Cartier had envisioned.

The next year Cartier returned, sailed past the weathering cross and on into the powerful waterway he hoped would lead to open sea not far ahead. But the waters grew narrower and narrower, and, finally, at a spot later to be known as Quebec City, he went ashore to talk with some Indians. What does one call this place? Cartier is believed to have asked in French, probably sweeping his arm across the horizon. The local Indians, apparently thinking he meant their town, naturally replied, *"Kanata."* It was the Huron-Iroquois word for "a settlement." Cartier returned to France to announce the discovery of a new land with a strange, hard name. Thus, conceived in bilingual misunderstanding, did the country get its name forever, Canada.

It was a suitably symbolic beginning for Canada, misnamed, misunderstood, and mistaken for somewhere else. The country would have other names suggested later: Britannia, Albionara, Norland, Transatlantia, Superior, Borealia, Hochelaga, and, my favorite, Tuponia. But whatever it was called, it was not India. The land was rich all right, but not with diamonds and jewels and spices. And while peacefully conversing, two of the many cultures to populate the new land were both speaking earnestly and honestly but talking right past each other. There would be many other *kanatas* in Canada's history.

A few years later the French tried to colonize Canada, once again sailing up the river Cartier named St. Lawrence for the third-century Christian saint. But after a single Canadian winter, the settlers packed up and went home. Canada, not for the last time in its history, would have to wait to get the world's attention and understanding. It would be another seventy-five years before white settlement actually began, again near Quebec City.

In the meantime, British explorers showed their flag and monarch's interest in the area, adding to the existing ethnic mix. Martin Frobisher's crews peeked into the icy void of the Arctic in 1576, 1577, and 1578, leaving five of their number to be buried in frigid graves after clashes with natives. In 1610, Henry Hudson pushed west through the ice until a mutinous crew, fearful of continuing farther into the depths of Canada's harsh elements, set him adrift to perish in the vast bay that later carried his name.

But the French and British were not the real pioneers in Canada. The first Canadians came several thousand years before Cartier. They came not from across the Atlantic but from the Pacific at its narrowest point. They were the Eskimos and Indians, who wandered across the Bering Strait to Alaska, a distance of only fifty miles today. Accomplished hunters, they probably came in animal-skin boats, possibly lured by the prolific colonies of seabirds that nest on the Diomede Islands in the strait. Drawn by the attraction of new animal resources, these natives discovered Canada on their way to new hunting grounds.

Once in North America, they meandered over the centuries and the landscape down the coast and inland, where they developed the languages and skills and patience and cooperative social structure so suitable for survival in their harsh environment. For instance, Canada's Eskimos, later to be called Inuit, had 100 words for different kinds of "snow," but no words for "war"; they were too busy fighting the Canadian climate to face off against each other. It wasn't until these arriving bands of immigrants dispersed over the more temperate areas of what was to become the United States that they had the inclination to spend time fighting among themselves. But then Canadians have always known that Americans are more violent.

Confronted with the differing demands of Canada's overwhelming geography, however, these northern groups, some containing only a few hundred members, did drift off into distinct, distant bands with their own customs, spirits, and unwritten dialects incomprehensible even to neighboring nomads. To survive, the ancestors of today's Canadians had no time for any frills. While they had rules (a primary one being the obligation to share everything with everyone), they had no concept of and no word for art. Even writing would have to wait for the twentieth century, and then it was imposed by white men from other countries. And so these nomads created the first of the many kingdoms of Canada that were to proliferate over the years.

Fueled by immigrants and based on culture or language or native country or occupation or home province or political party or economic needs or race, these separate allegiances grew over the centuries like hundreds of separate stalagmites in an immense continental cavern. Some were large. Others were small. Some merged and flowed together. Others stood stubbornly separate. Each stalagmite, each kingdom, was beautiful and could stand by itself, and when viewed together by visitors from afar, they presented a fascinating, colorful panorama of diversity. But up close in one country with virtually no national bonds of significance, these kingdoms turned Canada into a land-based archipelago of jealousies and suspicions.

The immigration of millions of people has played a large role in shaping Canada's modern personality, as it has in many lands. Chances are for the first few generations they came from a British background probably speaking with an aristocratic accent, acknowledging the importance of government, authority, and, of course, the king or queen. (In Canada the government does not "release" budgets or programs, it "hands them down," a revealing image placing authorities, often referred to in the press as Mandarins, on a higher level than the citizens they presumably work for in a democracy.) In fact, the largest initial influx to Canada came during and after the American Revolution when thousands of Loyalists fled the emerging democratic rabble by sea and land to Canada. They came not because that land was a challenging new frontier or because it offered a new promise for tomorrow, with spices and riches and golden opportunities beyond anyone's imagination. They came simply because Canada was less awful than where they were, a key conditioner to Canada's generally conservative personality that puzzles its friends. As Scott Symons, the Canadian novelist, once wrote, "Canadians are, after all, simply romantics who lost the courage of their hopes."

Later waves of immigrants changed the whole character of Canada's population so that by 1984 one of every eight Canadians had been born in another country. They arrived after Canada's big immigration liberalization in the early 1960's with many not speaking English or French. And they likely still don't. One 1983 survey of Vancouver's public schools revealed that almost half the students have a first language other than

English, and of those, two-thirds speak mainly Chinese, Italian, or an East Indian language. Many of the immigrants concentrated in Toronto, Canada's New York without the reputation for filth, and a city where at least one study showed that four out of every ten residents had been born outside Canada. These newcomers live in urban ethnic enclaves, where they can wear the same old shawls to their ethnic grocery store to speak the same old patois with friends from across the sea while buying the familiar vegetables to make the familiar dishes from the old country, a phrase that in my family referred to Scotland and ran through family conversations for a century after my great-great-grandfather's arrival in Canada in the early 1800's. You see, being Canadian usually means also maintaining a simultaneous strong emotional tie to another country. You may not intend to go back, but you don't have to forsake the old country to embrace the new one if it's Canada. That is one reason, besides Canadians' basic abhorrence of the Vietnam War, that they could so easily accept that era's American draft dodgers and deserters. In fact, Canada has a special immigration status called Landed Immigrant, which means one can live there as a citizen without actually becoming one and without giving up a previous nationality.

This all makes for a delightful and delicious ethnic diversity which attracts many tourists but which is fast disappearing in the urban United States as the nationalities are absorbed into the larger American personality. And this underlines one of the major differences between Canada and the United States. The United States believes it believes in the great melting pot, many influences coming together, each making its own contribution and each adding its own distinctive flavor to the larger whole. But Canadians believe they believe more in a mosaic of separate pieces with each chunk becoming part of the whole physically but retaining its own separate color and identity. This certainly makes for an interesting mix, and it provides Canadians with an identity peg, one major way they can differentiate themselves from Americans, as they must.

But when combined with Canada's spread, it also makes for considerable difficulty in governing, resulting in decentralization and a weak federal system with political provinces closer to the people and wielding far more power than American states. The most obvious example within Canada is Quebec, once a colony of France, where the people and their politicians have clung with official encouragement to their separate ethnic diversity with a stubbornness that spans almost three centuries and has made them one-quarter of Canada's population.

In many ways Quebec's culture is the most vibrant in Canada, with music, art, drama, and literature sprouting naturally and speaking to the hopes and needs of Quebecers that remain unfathomed by English-speaking Canadians, who can live next door physically but in another world culturally. It is novelist Hugh MacLennan's old "two solitudes" of Canada. Earlier, back in 1837, Lord Durham, the British statesman dispatched to Canada, made a similar finding: "I found two nations warring within the bosom of a single state; I found a struggle, not of principles, but of races." And to this day Canada's French recall the Quebec historic discrimination and humiliation with a potent little slogan on their license plates: *Je me souviens* ("I remember").

But actually there are many solitudes across Canada, smaller perhaps but just as separate. Inuit in the eastern Arctic. Inuit in the western Arctic. Indians from above the tree line. Indians from below the tree line. Full-blood Indians and half-breeds. English-speaking Canadians in a French-speaking sea of Quebec. French-speaking Canadians in an English-speaking sea of Winnipeg. Germans in Alberta. Ukrainians in Manitoba. Chinese, Pakistanis, and Indians in Vancouver and Toronto. Former Prime Minister Pierre Elliott Trudeau, a staunch believer in Canadian unity, used to draw derisive laughter in parts of western Canada with his talk about the country's two peoples, Anglophones and Francophones. Many elderly citizens of Alberta, for instance, have never known any French-speaking Canadians, who in their province are far outnumbered by German-speaking Canadians and Chinese-speaking Canadians. One Toronto radio station broadcasts in thirty languages, including announcements on arrival delays for flights from "back home." There is a Toronto TV station that survives simply by broadcasting programs in a multiplicity of languages aimed at specific ethnic communities, including movies in Urdu (with English subtitles). That city's municipal government must prepare its annual property tax notices in six languages: English, French, Chinese, Italian, Greek, and Portuguese.

In some cases, such as various forms of subsidies or specific legislation, the governments actually help perpetuate such ethnic blocs or divisions. As long ago as 1774 with the Quebec Act, the British Parliament entrenched the separation of Canada's two language communities by guaranteeing religious freedom to Roman Catholic French-Canadians and by instituting French civil law for French-Canadians in Canadian court-rooms. Among other things, this created a major difference with the Americans, strong government financial support for parochial school systems, which in Canada, honestly enough, are called Separate Schools. Begun as French institutions, they were meant to be separate. All this has prompted some people to warn that an individual's ethnic heritage is as sacred as his personal identity in Canada and should be free of any state involvement. It also caused me, one of those perennially suspicious Yank reporters who so annoy Canadian journalists, to wonder if these divisions were perhaps being subsidized to keep the newcomers in a category of hyphenated Canadians and thus politically divided and tame.

These differences are also overlaid by a strong historical sense of regionalism, with many people identifying much more closely with their province or territory than with the larger, ill-defined country. Back in 1907 Henri Bourassa lamented, "There is Ontario patriotism, Quebec patriotism or western patriotism, each based on the hope that it may swallow up the others, but there is no Canadian patriotism." In fact, there were street riots in Canada over military conscription in World War II. A couple of years ago, as the scheduled stock car races were about to get under way one evening in Calgary, the bustling symbol of Canada's energy-rich West, the track announcer asked everyone to rise for the playing of "O Canada," the national anthem. Everyone rose. The recorded music began. Five seconds later with a wrenching scratch the record was terminated. "You all know the rest," said the announcer. And the cars' engines roared to life.

Insulated from one another by geography, language, culture, and economic self-interest, Canadians go on about their daily business happily affluent in the main but strangely susceptible to constant sniping and regional bickering. Bruce Rankin, one of Canada's most outspoken and experienced ambassadors, got into a lot of political trouble some years ago when he called his countrymen among the world's most "negative, parochial and balkanized people." Some Canadians said he should not have said it, but no one disputed his analysis. There have been no permanently national political parties to help define a Canadian and a Canadian interest, to smooth over these misunderstandings and grievances and to help parcel out compromises to everyone. There have been, instead, basically two regional parties—the Liberals and the Progressive Conservatives—

who made forays into each other's strongholds, plus the socialist New Democrats, an ideological minority.

As one result, Canadians can agree on a very few things: perhaps the vital importance of hockey in the world, the belief that Canada's Rocky Mountains are prettier than the Americans' Rockies, and the efficacy of leaving Canada at least once every winter for the warm sunshine of the American South or tropical islands. Canadians, however, can always agree on who they are not—namely, Americans. This is an essentially negative definition of a country and one which does nothing to counteract the centrifugal forces that always blow over Canada and gain such added strength during times of economic uncertainty.

Until now bowing to the queen and knowing who they are not have, to over-simplify, seemed sufficient to hold together, however tenuously, the forever feuding fiefdoms of Canada. "Imagine a Canadian dream, which implied that everybody in the world ought to share it!" Hugh Hood, a Montreal novelist, once wrote, "Imagine a Committee on Un-Canadian Activities! You can't. Un-Canadianism is almost the very definition of Canadianism." But Canada need not try to reshape the world for there to be strong internal forces at work today quietly and noisily setting the stage for some vital adjustments in its economics, its politics, and its culture. "In Canada," said Mordecai Richler, the noted author of *Joshua Then and Now* and *The Apprenticeship of Duddy Kravitz*, "there's a tradition evolving at last and it's worth defending." In short, more Canadians are becoming more comfortable with themselves. "For all our complaints," Mr. Richler added, "as we come of age, we're realizing we're Americans too."

In many ways, despite its age and its colossal neighbor's well-established pattern of life, Canada remains a developing country, with many traditions and patterns still to be shaped. Politically the country, after 115 years of independence and a half century of internal wrangling, finally crafted its own Constitution and Charter of Rights and Freedoms, a major event in Canadian history. No longer must Canada go to the British Parliament to alter its legislative foundation, the old British North America Act. And the new document, the product, as always in Canada, of compromises between semiautonomous regions, has significantly altered the fundamental rules of the land in ways that will become apparent only as the years pass.

At the same time as Canada's federal government has grown more powerful in recent years, so, too, have the already powerful provinces, which control the country's educational systems and all their own natural resources, among other things. The rising values of many of these resources, such as oil and natural gas, have given some of the poorer provinces the prospect of one day getting off the federal dole that has kept them economically afloat and psychologically on a leash to a distant capital. It has given others, such as Alberta, a multibillion-dollar nest egg to reshape and build its own economy and, in so doing, to create the lure of new work that has drawn thousands of Canadians into a migratory job market, further breaking down traditional barriers within the country. Eventually these population shifts and their accompanying legislative reapportionments will also be reflected in a political realignment of national scope, giving new regions a greater share of the political clout that has traditionally been Ontario's and Quebec's alone to share.

One of the fruits of a Quiet Revolution, which is considered so important in Quebec history that these words are inevitably capitalized, was a change in attitudes and ambitions that crept through Quebec in the 1960's. Such changes saw a decline in the Catholic Church's influence and a growth in assertiveness that fueled the stunning election of the province's Parti Québecois in 1976. The party of Premier René Lévesque, a chain-smoking former broadcaster whose popular French nickname translates as "Little Hair," continues its cunning populist drive for separation from Canada. And now the PQ is organizing to present its candidates in federal elections, too. The PQ lost a 1980 referendum seeking authorization to negotiate a new sovereignty association status with the rest of Canada. The party never fully defined how much sovereignty and how much association it envisioned in that new relationship. But the powerful dreams of a democratic people for a new status within an old land are unlikely to be forever dimmed or confined by such a nonbinding referendum. And the issue of a new political entity emerging along the United States' undefended northern border is certain to rise again, as it has throughout Canadian history.

Canada's West too feels aggrieved, angry, and alienated over its continued treatment as a political colony of central Canada—so much so that in the 1980 election, the one that saw Canada's first western-born prime minister, Joe Clark, ousted after a brief nine-month political reign, not one of Trudeau's Liberal party members was elected in that entire region west of Winnipeg. In the 1984 elections Liberal strength crumbled in Quebec, its traditional stronghold, while only one Liberal, then Prime Minister John Turner, was elected in the West. Some western areas saw the emergence of separatist movements, whose political goals may be unrealistic but whose political emotions (and racial animosity toward Francophones) are potent. While the federal government led by a Quebecer devoted billions of dollars and much effort to assuaging Quebec's acknowledged grievances within the Canadian Confederation, it dubbed as "hysterical" similar western grievances. The West, peopled by swash-buckling bands of free-swinging entrepreneurs with a brash touch of Texas and a can-do attitude about anything, has built new economic empires to threaten the historical dominance of Ontario's aging manufacturing. While this struggle is less apparent without the language barrier, the process of Canada's adjustments to this new regional reality will be a long, painful, and probably bitter one, threatening to jeopardize the future of the country at least as much as its much publicized language divisions.

Other language divisions come together with regional frictions and cultural gaps in Canada's northlands, that vast stretch of continent reaching toward the North Pole and populated by many times more caribou than people, all trying to scratch out a living in a beautifully forsaken area. These vast Northwest Territories have voted for a territorial division along ethnic lines to split the 24,000 Inuit and the 10,000 Indians.

These peoples are divided by language from each other. But they are united in their growing quiet militancy to change their status within Canada and assume more self-control. In a symbolic gesture paralleling the recent terminology change from "Negro" to "black" in the United States, Canada's northern natives now shun the words "Indians" and "Eskimo" (literally "eater of raw meat") in favor of "Dene" and "Inuit," respectively. Both words mean "the people." They want their territorial name changed to Nunavit. They already hold a majority on the advisory elected territorial council. They are organizing their own television system to span the immense distances between communities. They have won minor victories, such as forcing northern airlines to print their schedules in the Inuit syllabary, Inuktitut. And negotiations continued here and there over government compensation for native land claims, never settled by treaty.

Despite all its idealistic talk about separate ethnic communities operating as equals within a larger Canada, Ottawa has ruled its northern territories as Canadian colonies. Though comprising nearly half the country's landmass, the North has been frozen in the back of the public imagination as a distant, perhaps romantic void visited by migrating birds, government bureaucrats on special expense accounts, and hardy travelers seeking isolation.

Until the 1950's the Canadian government virtually ignored the North. Inuit were referred to by government-assigned numbers, not their one-word native names like Pitseolak, which the white men found hard to pronounce. But coloring—in many cases corroding—all such contacts between southern government officials and shy northern natives is a complex network of cultural differences, something which Canadians claim as a benefit but which they have often systematically, if inadvertently, tried to erase. Canadians claim, with some justification, to have handled their native "problem" better than the violent Americans have. By this, they mean there were not so many large-scale slaughters of prairie Indians. But despite government welfare, Indian poverty is widespread today, and an element of racism does definitely exist. During World War II thousands of Japanese-Canadians were carted off to inland internment camps, as they were in the United States. Canada, although it was the ultimate destination of runaway American slaves on the famous pre-Civil War Underground Railroad, has not until recently had the large concentrations of racial minorities to be the focus of white animosities. But there have been racial incidents in Vancouver and Toronto involving blacks, often from the Caribbean, Chinese, and turbaned Sikhs, whose religious and political frictions erupt within their own communities at times, too. It is not uncommon in Canada to hear racial comments. I was talking with a Mountie in Frobisher Bay in the Northwest Territories one day when he said, "The Inuit are good, good people, but they are so lazy."

These attitudes are complicated in the North by differing views of the land. For whites on a two-year assignment there, for which they receive a northern hardship allowance, the Arctic land and climate are things to be conquered briskly by roads, radar, radio beacons, machines, and determination. Canadian whites think it natural to gather the once-nomadic Inuit into formal communities, as they have. This certainly has improved health care and education.

But for the Inuit, the land is a special, almost holy place, the source of all life, a natural home with predictable rules and consequences and familiar creatures, of which mankind is only one. It rewards patience, not haste. If a ten-day storm halts all outdoor activity, including hunting, a traditional Inuit will shrug and stay indoors to sip tea. When springtime, unaware of the white man's school calendar, calls Inuit families from their artificial, trash-strewn towns back to their distant tent sites, the whole family must go. "To be on the land again," explained John Amagoalik, whose Inuit family was moved several hundred miles into a formal town, "is to rediscover reality, to feel small, to keep a proper perspective on your importance to the world." For one group, the whites, change is the norm. "It's what makes life interesting," one federal officer told me in Frobisher Bay, a town of 2,000 just below the Arctic Circle. For another group, the Inuit, change is new, and the transformation from dogsleds to jet planes in a short time has been bewildering and frightening to those accustomed to following traditional ways. The idea was to give the natives a decent living and the ability to cope in a modern wage economy. But things have not always worked out the way the planners planned. "What we've done here," Bryan Pearson, Frobisher's mayor, said over dinner as the wind howled in off the frozen bay, "is to build a pseudosouthern Canadian town with many of the faults and few of the pluses." And so, at Mayor Pearson's general store, you can see an Inuit woman, with fresh seal meat at home, buying boxes of frozen pizza and licorice.

Federal police in the North are constantly frustrated by an apparent lack of parental discipline, which they blame for the many break-ins and vandalism. Native children wander the streets at all hours, entering the homes of other band members at will, sleeping through school at times, and skipping meals. But this actually stems from a native sense of timelessness, an Asian type of indulgence of children, and a desire to avoid open conflicts, such as those between angry parent and misbehaving child. Bureaucrats, assigned to promote native democratic development, grow impatient with long, wandering Inuit discussions that produce a consensus but no formal vote for the bureaucratic record (and also no formal "winners" and "losers," preserving the element of "face").

Canadian government hunting regulations stipulate that certain game birds may be killed only in the fall, when they just happen to be absent from the North and just happen to be flying over southern Canada. But for centuries hunting has been a year-round way of life for the Inuit, who

73

are even prohibited, for conservation's sake, from gathering wild birds' eggs. Chicken eggs are, however, available at the white man's store for around $3 a dozen. "But who would take more than one egg from a nest?" one Inuit elder asked me.

Regional schools illustrate the typical corrosive cultural problem. To fulfill the government's mandate for equal education at an affordable cost, it takes Inuit high school students from home settlements for hundreds of miles around and for ten months a year generously feeds them and teaches them modern courses at a central high school, at no financial cost to the parents. In so doing, however, the schools undermine the Inuit family's self-sufficiency and the father's traditional role as chief provider and teacher of all-important hunting and survival skills. They introduce the young to town life and television, where they can see strange things from another world, like scantily clad females, trees, and tall buildings on streets full of people who ride in confining boxes called elevators. They habituate the Inuit young to a life of freedom, often making a return to the structured, hierarchical family unit unappealing. Values can become skewed. Students will spend $4 of their government stipend on a taxi ride to make a $1.25 purchase at the general store. One resident counselor in Frobisher Bay, where the students live in the former barracks of U.S. Air Force tanker crews, told me of an incident in the cafeteria line where an Inuit high school girl fell into a noisy temper tantrum upon discovering that the day's supply of airfreighted carrots was gone. "But I want some!" she screamed. "I want some!"

Despite their best efforts, the schools often leave the youths ill-equipped to cope in either their own traditional native economy or in the modern local urban economy, where jobs are few. The same goes for adults who don't need to find animals to hunt anymore but can't find the modern skills that are the key to employment in a wage economy. As one result, alcoholism, drug abuse, and suicide among young and old Inuit are common. I vividly remember my shock one late-autumn night as I waited in a drafty vestibule near the Frobisher high school. Casually I read the bulletin board and then noticed some graffiti etched in the wall about teenager-tall. The words seemed to scream out from the wood: "I wish I kill myself like hell."

"I knew my Dad as a proud and independent hunter, the master of his own destiny and ours," said Mr. Amagoalik, then a thirty-one-year-old native rights leader, "but a few years after we were moved, I saw alcohol, the resource exploration boom, and town life reduce these proud people to beggars outside a bar. We can't shut the doors to the outside world. We just want to be self-sustaining again, to have our language and traditions of equal importance, and to have more local control over decisions that affect us." It is not such an abnormal or revolutionary goal in a democratic society. But given the geographic, economic, and cultural setting, given the same kinds of conflicting demands from a wide array of Canada's many other kingdoms with different priorities, and given the range of inadvertent pressures from the large neighbor to the south, the simple goal can very easily become a very difficult task for Canadians to handle, let alone control.

Who are these people?

For one thing, according to a variety of statistics I collected as a minor hobby during my time in Canada, there are about 8.5 million Canadian households containing around 25.2 million people and more than 4 million pets, dogs being by far the most popular, followed by cats. Canada's population included about 200,000 Indians when the white man first arrived, a number that was cut in half by 1900 but that has now climbed to 290,000 plus 300,000 métis, or mixed bloods.

Today 3 out of every 4 Canadians live in a city, 2 out of 3 own their own homes, and 1 out of every 7 houses is heated by a wood stove. About half the country's water usage goes down the drain to flush toilets. But for now there is enough to go around; 8 billion metric tons of moisture fall on Canada each year, producing a large enough river flow to fill every bathtub in the country every ten seconds, although few Canadians bathe that often.

The average Canadian today is 33.7 years old. But more than 2 million Canadians are over age 65, an indication of the graying of the country's population; when the postwar baby boom generation retires in thirty years, the elderly population will triple, placing a heavy financial burden on all the hallowed government aid programs at a time when the working population contributing some earnings will be declining. When Canada's oldest citizen, David Trumble, celebrated his birthday some time ago, he made a frank observation to his party guests. "When you're a hundred and fourteen," he said, "you're stepping on the gas to heaven."

Canadians are buying more diamond engagement rings per capita these days than are residents of any other country, but 4 out of every 10 Canadian marriages will end in divorce (20 percent of them after twenty years). More marriages seem to last in the island province of Newfoundland, while far more seem to founder on the rocks of Canada's other coast, in British Columbia. In recent years around 13 percent of all brides and grooms have been married before. But 1 out of every 10 Canadians over eighteen is living with a member of the opposite sex without being married.

Canadians are having fewer children; the average woman now has 1.7 babies compared with 3.4 four decades ago. Every tenth mother is less than twenty years old herself, accounting for a large part of the 600,000 Canadian households headed by a single parent. In 1945, 1 out of every 20 babies died before its first birthday; today the rate is 1 in every 100, one of the world's best survival rates and two-tenths of a point better than the United States'.

Canada's diverse regions are reflected in provincial family sizes from the 4 persons in the average family in rural Newfoundland to the 3.3 in British Columbia and 3.4 in Ontario, both with large urbanized areas. This carries obvious import for the housing industry. Fewer than 1 of every 10 families has 4 or more children now; this not only affects school enrollments, teaching careers, and clothing manufacturers but also means that couples will spend many more years alone after their children leave home, a matter of considerable interest to travel and leisure time industries as well as health care planners. (The Canadian government already pays 75 cents of every health care dollar, compared with the United States' 43 cents, a fact reflected in Canada's much higher taxes.) As one result of better health care, the average Canadian male can now expect to live through 72 hockey seasons, 7 more than a World War II baby and 1.2 years more than a male football fan in the United States. The average woman can expect to live until 79, 10.5 years longer than her World War II mother and eight-tenths of a year longer than an American woman.

The greatest killer of male and female Canadians at the age of twenty-five is motor vehicle accidents, followed by suicides in second place. Canadian women appear to be safer swimmers than men or they don't swim as much: Drowning is the number three male killer; strokes are third for women. At age forty-five, heart attack is the top male killer, followed by lung cancer and cirrhosis of the liver; for women it's breast cancer, heart attack, and strokes. At sixty-five, men and women are equally likely to die of a heart attack with lung cancer the number two male killer. For women, number two is stroke and number three intestinal cancer.

At the end of World War II more than half of all Canadians had no more than eighth-grade educations. Now more than 80 percent have gone at least through ninth grade, while the number with postsecondary education has climbed from 1 in 30 to 1 in 3, one of the major reasons behind the massive growth in audiences for all aspects of Canadian culture.

Canada has not been accustomed to such rapid social change. In recent years an average 58 English-speaking Canadians per day have left Quebec to start a new life elsewhere. Throughout Canada there has also been a dramatic movement away from multifamily households, with 6.7 percent of all households containing more than one family in 1951 and only 1.3 percent recently.

In the work force only 24 percent of all women worked in 1945; today half do, and two-thirds of them are married. Most of them still earn less than their male peers. Farm jobs have fallen from 21 to 4 percent while clerical jobs climbed from 9 to 17 percent. A typical Canadian worker spends fewer than 40 hours a week at work and more than 50 hours in leisure time activities, with 100 percent watching television, 83 percent reading a newspaper or listening to the radio, and nearly half the population participating in some sport. The average employee will miss 4.5 days of work a year because of illness. On the average workday more than 400,000 Canadians in a labor force exceeding 11 million members are absent for some reason, a loss to the country's economy of more than $20 million a day.

Together Canadians spend upward of $6 billion a year on their vacations. "Vacation travel," one Tourism Department study concluded, "is clearly regarded as a necessity by Canadians, rather than a discretionary activity and expenditure." Canadians spend an estimated $8 billion a year on another kind of trip, illegal drugs, which is one-third more than they spend on legal liquor purchases. In fact, the beer industry alone accounts for nearly 2 percent of the gross national product, a fact that helps contribute to the country's population of nearly 650,000 alcoholics.

Albertans rank near the top of Canada's alcohol consumers, with each man, woman, and child downing 23 gallons a year, according to statistics.

But the same residents also lead Canada in per capita milk consumption with 30.2 gallons. Canadians are the world's third-greatest soft-drink drinkers, too, behind only the United States and the leader, Mexico. Recently Canadians were buying more pork, around 65 pounds per capita per year, and less beef (88 pounds). For unknown reasons, they were also consuming fewer tranquilizers.

Half of all Canadian children try a cigarette before they are twelve years old, but only around 40 percent of the adult population smokes now. Those Canadians who do smoke, however, apparently puff up quite a storm, enough to rank Canada fourth in the world in daily per capita cigarette consumption, behind only Cyprus, Greece, and Turkey. (The United States trails badly, or nicely, depending on your habit.)·With more Canadians working, they are earning more and saving more, nearly 14 percent of all earnings. In fact, there are 3 million more bank savings accounts in Canada than there are people.

Canada is also one of the most heavily wired countries in the world. There is 1 telephone for every 1.74 people. Together Canadians all make around 23 billion telephone calls per year, or nearly 1,000 each for every man, woman, and child in Canada. What is the day of the year that they talk the most on the phone? Not surprisingly it is Christmas. The second busiest talking time for Canadians? Calling Mom on Mother's Day. And when it comes time to pay for all this, Canadians, the world's most heavily insured population, prefer to pay cash much more than do credit card-carrying Americans. Much of that money is spent now in restaurants, several hundred million more dollars than Canadians spend on defense.

It is one measure of the country's affluence that Canadians who own radios (98 percent) and televisions (97.8 percent) can turn off their FM sets (82 percent) and jump in their cars (79 percent), their boats (14 percent), or one of their other cars (25 percent) and head off to work in one of their 11.5 million motor vehicles, grumbling about the economy. With the highest oil self-sufficiency rating of any of the seven major industrialized nations (producing nearly 90 percent of the oil Canada needs and more than 150 percent of its required natural gas), Canadians can still complain about the cost of energy, which is the lowest of the same seven.

Of course, not all Canadians are happy with their lot in life. They shop-lift on the average more than $1 million a day in merchandise. Despite having 2.3 police officers for every 1,000 citizens, they still manage to commit around 2,600 crimes per 100,000 citizens a year, with the largest number by far being crimes against property. In a typical twelve months Canadians kill fewer than 600 of their countrymen in homicides, which is about one-third the number of New York City residents who die violently in the same time. In a typical year Montreal, the North American bank-robbing champion, experiences about 2.5 bank holdups every day, a third more than New York and twice as many as Los Angeles. Despite Canadians' reputation as law-abiding, a special committee on sexual abuse recently estimated that 1 boy in 10 and 1 girl in 4 under the age of sixteen have been sexually assaulted. As one result, more than 21,000 Canadians now reside in prisons (compared with 454,000 Americans).

Still on a weekend, law-abiding Canadians can drive their snowmobiles (owned by 10 percent of the population), put on their skis (20 percent), or get out their bicycles (41 percent), motorcycles (5 percent), or camping gear (24 percent). Those who stay at home can watch cable TV (47 percent), play their pianos (12 percent), watch their other TVs (34 percent), or start up their electric lawn mowers (51 percent). Those with even less ambition can take hot baths (98 percent) or raid their electric refrigerators (99.4 percent).

But as in any land, behind the statistics are a myriad of people whose personalities, taken together over time, mingle to leave a lasting image of the land and the nation it is fast becoming. The most memorable Canadian for me is a man named Napoleon Snowbird Martin. He was seventy-seven when my son Spencer, then seven, and I met him early on a bright March morning on the outskirts of Fort Chipewyan. Fort Chip, as it is known, is the oldest community in Alberta, a gathering of 1,400 souls around a Hudson's Bay trading post in northeastern Alberta hard by the Northwest Territories. It is 800 miles by frozen trail from the outside world. The barges come regularly on the Athabasca River in summer. The planes come a couple of times a week, weather permitting.

Snowbird (he never uses any other name; everyone in his world knows who he is) came to town reluctantly that winter. His wife was ill. Physically he stood about five feet tall in his caribou-skin boots. His hands were dark and wide, the skin thick like leather, showing, as I remember my grandfather's hands had shown, the collected strength and scars of many years in the open. Snowbird's face, heavily lined, was free of expression as it peered from under the peak of a battered baseball cap. It was a sport he had never heard of. But the old eyes, even behind bifocals, were sharp and clear. Snowbird has lived in the Canadian bush, in cabins, behind lean-tos, on mattresses of boughs, and under buffalo robe blankets and the crisp stars ever since Theodore Roosevelt was President of the United States. Snowbird is unable to read words on paper. But he can read tracks and blood on the snow and branches broken certain ways, and sounds in the air. He knows the colors of good clouds and bad clouds and the sunsets and different winds that presage tomorrow's weather. He knows tales as timeless as their morals. He has some theories on modern problems. And he can speak four languages—Cree, English, Chipewyan, and dog— sometimes in the same sentence. "I'm seventy-seven years old," he told us. "I'm just beginning to grow."

Through that special invisible bond that links the very old and the very young, my son Spencer knew instantly about Snowbird. "He's neat," he said. It took me, stymied by the old man's initial silence, an hour longer to fall under his spell. And by the end of our first day on the trail with him, when the wind was banging the tent walls and the dogs were howling back at a wolf they would never see, the two city residents who had come to discover dogsleds and the Canadian wilderness were also discovering the unusually strong presence of a man who is old only in terms of years.

Snowbird is one of a few Canadian natives who still run dogs. Most have changed to modern snowmobiles, which can go farther faster across the frozen lakes, down the frozen rivers, and through the frigid forests of their countryside. Snowmobiles don't get sick with worms or fight each other, but snowmobile spark plugs can easily foul a very long way from help. And there aren't too many gas stations in the woods. Snowbird's sled dogs, no purebreds they, have never let him down, never turned on him, never even nipped him. All they want are a couple of frozen fish a day to crunch up whole, frequent mouthfuls of snow along the route, and the chance to hear through much of the day his reassuring tone of voice behind them as the wooden sled whispers its way across the snow.

As a married couple after years of living together come to read each other's moods and meanings through little signs, movements, and inflec- tions, Snowbird reads his dogs. He knows their tail signals, what a cocked ear or wiggled nose means, the instincts behind certain howls or growls, when a fight is about to erupt. "Dogs can't live without love," according to Snowbird's philosophy. "All my dogs are friendly, except that last one. He's borrowed and doesn't know my rules yet."

In turn the animals, all males with no names, learn Snowbird's little signals—what "click-click," "hup," and "jah" mean; when and where they can expect to eat. They know that two or three of them trying to grab a mouthful of snow on the run prompts Snowbird to call a rest stop for a longer "drink" of snow. They know it means trouble when Snowbird breaks off a handy branch and strides forward, muttering. But they read, too, the abiding affection in Snowbird's voice, regardless of the words. "This dog something you call dumb," he said, smiling, as he lifted one misplaced leg back into harness. The dog gave Snowbird a lick of appreciation.

"Okay, boys," he said, "click-click hup now jah" (translation: "let's go, get going now to the left"). Even when the trail is obvious down a frozen riverbed, Snowbird continues a nonstop bilingual banter. "They like to hear me here," he said, omitting how much he liked it, too. Then, addressing the dogs, he whistled and said, "Hapsiko hup chee chee let's go, don't get crazy, boys, watch out I kill you and eat you click keep quiet you." We were to spend many hours like this, my son in my lap, half sitting atop the soft sleeping bags, feeling the gentle nonrhythmic rocking of the oaken sled bending its way over hills and mounds and through woods. The six animals had their accustomed trotting pace, hauling their 600-pound sled along at four or five miles an hour, softly panting while turning their heads to the right and left and waving their snouts about in olfactory observations of the surrounding wilds. Canine chaos erupted one time when a tiny field mouse darted across the trail beneath the padding feet of our band of dogs. Instantly six mouths reached for the intruder, and, for a moment, running and the sled were forgotten. It took several minutes to untangle twenty-four feet and a thirty-seven-foot-long leather harness and proceed on our way.

The warming March sun tanned our faces inside parka hoods while Snowbird addressed the dogs and us, sometimes in the same breath, issuing orders or observations or memories or tidbits of bush knowledge. "See that Y-shaped birch?" he said once. "That makes a good natural vice."

"A wolf came through here last night. A big one."

"And that blood over there was his breakfast. It was deer."

"I wish I keep you one month in the bush. Boy, I show you how to live pretty good for sure."

The old man took little Spencer in tow, dubbing him Little Snowbird, assigning him camp chores and lessons, and seemingly inadvertently giving little lectures, passing on the same knowledge he had heard from his father seven decades before. "Animals are like garden," the veteran trapper told the wide-eyed boy. "You treat them right, and they grow right. You treat them bad, and they don't grow right." One time Spencer stepped off the trail of packed snow and promptly sank up to his waist in powder. Snowbird strapped a pair of snowshoes on the boy, and the youngster ker-flumfed off across the drifts. He taught us how to harness the dogs, how to feed them (whole frozen fish tossed from a distance), and how to start morning fires when the wood is damp ("pine cones always stay dry"), and he passed on a modicum of Cree vocabulary: *dahnsi* ("hello"), *atim* ("dog"), *peahtik* ("look out"), *hay-hay* ("yes"), *nehmoyeh* ("no"), *kaynana-skoh-mitten* ("thank you"), *etahtomskahgan* ("goodbye"), and, Snowbird's favorite phrase, *aygotah* ("right on, brother").

The voyage into the northern wilderness with Snowbird is one of a growing number of such excursions organized by Canadian groups to utilize their wilderness resource and to pump needed money into the native economy there. It is not a luxury trip where guests are pampered or waited on. There is wood to be cut, snow to be melted for tea, food to be prepared, and countless other chores. The bathroom is the great outdoors. There are no such things as showers. We spent two nights on cabin floors and one in a tent. The temperature was around 20 below, Fahrenheit. Usually we were up by 7:00 A.M., and the sled was under way a couple of hours later. We stopped for lunch at midafternoon, when the spring sun starts to make the snow sticky for sleds, then resumed our travels by 5:00, when the night chill has tightened the snow and made the pull easier for the dogs.

The dogs seemed to love their work, as long as the temperature didn't climb too close to freezing, when the "heat" starts to affect them. They would jump up and down and bark excitedly every morning as we emerged to start our day's travels. The alleged objective of visitors to that backcountry is a tour through the Wood Buffalo National Park; at 17,000 square miles of woods, swamp, and lake, it is North America's largest park. It is also the wild home for nesting whooping cranes in summer and, all year, for around 5,500 wood buffalo, the larger, shaggier cousins of the American Plains buffalo.

But beyond the sights, I found the experience of the Canadian wilderness had a profound effect on me. I found similar awe and respect and a thirst for such scenes later in reading the unpublished memoirs of my grandfather, who wandered much the same regions of Canada back before they were provinces, when roads were marked by slash marks on trees and doors were locked with short lengths of string. But on this trip I also found it necessary to make some important mental adjustments. "Two cultures, two worlds meet in this park," I had been warned by Jacques Van Pelt, a tall, determined Dutch immigrant who seemed to have several careers simmering from his round home built into a hillside at Fort Smith, in the Northwest Territories, some 200 miles north of our park trek. With an outgoing enthusiasm not usually associated with Canadians, he is the matchmaker for the travelers and their Indian guide through his Subarctic Wilderness Tours Ltd. He does office work for the Royal Canadian Mounted Police. Wearing his long stocking cap atop his towering frame, he runs his own tours of the landscape and nesting grounds around Fort Smith on skis, by bus, and in rafts. And he raises rabbits commercially as a cheap source of meat for his family and customers.

One adjustment that Mr. Van Pelt and everyone else must make in such areas is stretching the concept of time, erasing such confining things as minutes and even hours, which require gadgets like watches to measure. Snowbird and his friends deal in seasons or periods of sunlight and darkness; that makes eminent sense, there being little need for trappers to punch a time clock going to work. In that society, time is something to be spent, not conserved. There is always tomorrow or the next day. It is not laziness, I don't believe, although it can appear so superficially. It seems more a conservation of energy and personal resources, just in case, a sense of the looming unexpected out there somewhere, a natural sense of foreboding that is often warranted, as it was to be later on our journey. City folk carry a spare tire in the car trunk; Snowbird takes extra food on his sled.

In this life, mechanical timepieces strike Snowbird as unnecessary, just as newly arrived visitors find it hard to comprehend the need for eight Indian words for different kinds of ice. Thus, the first day Spencer and

Snowbird and I were to have begun our trip from Fort Chipewyan at 8:00 A.M., we actually left at 12:30 P.M. And the first afternoon Snowbird, the man now in charge of everything, including our lives, asked me, "How long we stay out?"

"Uh," I replied, about to escalate my level of concern, "until Friday."

"Okay," he said cheerily. "Today Monday, right?"

"No, it's Tuesday."

"Okay."

Except for the last night, when we got in trouble, we stopped for the night around seven. Snowbird has an aversion to dogsledding in the dark, having once helplessly watched a traveling companion die after spearing himself on a protruding branch. Being his latest traveling companions, we were willing to avoid that fate, too.

The tasty meals were prepared in wood stoves by oil lanterns. We had snacked all day on chunks of dried caribou in a paper bag and impromptu sandwiches at a rest stop. But at night there was duck, rabbit, and buffalo with instant potatoes, powdered drinks, and muffins. In March, food is kept frozen by being put just outside the door. After dinner Snowbird would scratch his head through his green cap and inevitably comment, "Good food. Now I have power for two days."

These were also the times when Snowbird, if coaxed, would sit on the buffalo robes that made his bed, sip his tea, and talk a little about his life on the land. He talked of simple joys like muskrats. "You trap some rats," he said, "and skin them and build a little fire and roast the rats. It's nice, I tell you." He talked about his personal philosophy of life, although he would never package it that grandly. It is more a collection of observations on life that he would pass down to his children, an amalgam of thought from his elders plus what he himself had seen. He believes the important elements of life include respect for nature, for being part of nature, not an intruder. He will cut down a tree for wood and hunt animals for food, but never for fun. Having a wife is important, and picking the right one is even more so. Snowbird had moved into Fort Chipewyan (population 1,400) that winter for the first time because he had to, but he didn't like it. "Too many people," he said. If he were hunting for a wife now, Snowbird said, he would go to a city. Women seem more adventurous nowadays, he said. And of course, mothers must nurse their babies naturally. He has seen too many sad cases of children and animals that were not nursed by their mothers and then grew up to be plain, mean creatures.

He remembers when he and his friends spent all summer getting ready for winter and all winter trapping and hunting and cutting wood to earn money and food to spend all summer getting ready for winter and all winter trapping and hunting and cutting wood. "In old days," he said as we crunched along a frozen river in our sled, "people live all down this river in sheds and tents. They fish and hunt and trap. All Cree. Now all gone. They don't move to town. They move down into ground. All dead. Some sick. Some get funny, you know. Some just die. I sick once. They say flu, something like that. Long time ago. I don't remember what time that is."

But things have changed in the wild now. "Today," said Snowbird, "young people go in bush, they get lost. They don't listen to fathers, and fathers don't try teach. Always drinking and stuff like that. Now buy everything from store. I don't know why—crazy or lazy, I guess." As one example, he told us about an older friend who had left the bush to move near town. They had found him two days before our visit out on the lake ice, a solid frozen block, the victim likely of a meandering drunken stroll at midnight. Snowbird's point was that this would never have happened in the bush, where everyone knew the rules and watched over each other.

Then, as the fire died down and the dogs outside noisily chewed on some bones they had discovered, he told us a tale that Cree grandfathers have told for the 9,000 years since the glaciers left those northern boreal plains pocked and open as one of the world's richest fur grounds. It is the story of an old Indian, blind and unable to hunt for his own food, a terrible fate. He was sitting sadly by the lake when a loon approached. " 'Hang onto my neck like this and come swim with me,' " Snowbird said the bird said. And the old man did. Three times the bird dived under the water. And three times the man opened his eyes there. And when they surfaced the third time, the Canadian waters had done their healing job, and the forces of nature, the hunter and the hunted, were back in balance. The man could see. "He could hunt once more his own food," said Snowbird. "It is a true story." And he got no contradiction from either of his wide-eyed listeners.

We wandered through the bush for more than 100 miles together (the Indians pay no attention to metrics yet). We saw one wilderness settlement, Snowbird's little community where perhaps twenty-five people—and a seemingly equal number of dogs—lived atop a steep bank on the Athabasca River. The river had moved 100 feet, Snowbird said. When he was young, it was over there. So they simply moved the town, too, hauling the handful of cabins back farther into the woods.

A hundred yards from the last cabin, there was no sign of human life. It was wilderness, hundreds of miles of it, beautiful and humbling and provoking silence in case you somehow marred it. Like being at sea on land. It reminded me of staring out over the water from the stern of an ocean liner in mid-Atlantic; there was a sense of privilege in being there, but also a feeling of silent humility as if you should bow to some unseen force lest you suddenly be deemed an unwelcome intruder. We saw many tracks and signs of life, wildlife anyway. There was wolf, fox, rabbit, lynx, field mice, and muskrat. "Hey look!" Spencer exclaimed at one trapper's camp, pointing at a piece of natural refuse, "Somebody's foot!"

One time Snowbird stopped the sled and wandered off the trail a ways, examining Christmas tree-size balsams. He cut one down, slicing out a five-inch section of the slim trunk that had one long, thin branch protruding. That night he whittled it, peeled off all the bark and needles, and let it dry. Then he presented us with our own weather forecaster. When the little branch turns up, good weather is coming. When it's down, that's bad. Today Snowbird's balsam is predicting good weather.

The third day out we lunched at Ernie Courtorielle's tent to hear news of about 200 buffalo grazing on a nearby frozen swamp. These are the shaggy descendants of a herd of buffalo, which, nearing extinction, were assembled in 1922 in a new park; for fairness's sake, the government promised that all Indians living there then and their descendants could still live and trap on the parklands. There, despite wolves and anthrax, the buffalo have multiplied.

After two hours' travel along Beaver Ass Creek we reached Hilda Lake. There in the distance we could spot huge, dark shapes. It is difficult for six dogs, two men, a little boy, and a sledful of gear to creep across an open field of ice without being scented or seen. And the buffalo herd has not grown by standing about curiously awaiting the arrival of strange shapes on the horizon. So within minutes we could see the dark forms bounding away. Twenty minutes later we observed the devastation of their flight upon the grass, bushes, and fields of snow. Unaware of the adventure ahead, we headed for Archie Cardinal's cabin on the Hay River, there to spend our last night.

At 6:00 P.M. we reached it, but the structure was empty, boarded, and locked. Wilderness protocol discouraged an unarranged break-in. Darkness was approaching. The temperature was plummeting. Faced with a night in the open wind or another three hours' journey to the nearest cabin, we downed some granola bars and dried caribou, closed up our parkas, wrapped the buffalo robes around ourselves, and set off.

The air was brisk. The eastern sky was darkening. Even after the day's twenty-five miles the dogs loped along well. Our spirits were high. Over our shoulders we watched the sun set, leaving behind bright pastel bands of pinks, blues, and yellows. We swung around bend after bend of the Prairie River, and soon we emerged onto Mamawi Lake, a twelve-mile crossing. In the east, some stars were starting to twinkle and so were my toes. Our legs were a little cramped. Sticking out of the robes, my right knee was feeling chilled, even with three layers of clothing. But the growing beauty of darkness, the animals' rhythmic soft panting, and the exhilaration of the wilderness kept us alert.

Lying on his back, Spencer was counting stars. I was discovering areas of exposed skin stinging. And Snowbird had become unusually quiet. But the moon was out, bleaching the snow and throwing long, strange shadows of tall, doglike monsters off to our left. The night was just as dark, the sky just as star-speckled as before, and the snow still serene.

Then, it happened. We coursed off the lake onto the Chenal des Quatre Fourche River. Suddenly bewildered by an array of snow paths scattering in all directions, the new lead dog hesitated. All the dogs began stepping high. And the crunching began. "Overflow!" shouted Snowbird.

It is a treachery of the North's early spring. Shining on the river, the daytime sun melts some snow. The weight pushes the ice down in the river, forcing water over the ice's edge to sandwich the ice between layers of freezing water. All this, however, remains hidden beneath a misleading cover of benign white snow.

Incredibly in all that cold, the night was full of gurgling sounds while the rear of the sled began sinking. Then it tilted sideways, apparently threatening to capsize us all into several feet of freezing slush. My hand shot out to the side. "Don't move," said Snowbird. And then he talked to the animals. He spoke to them softly but firmly, giving them directions around the worst visible water gaps ahead. Splashing and struggling, the dogs strained in the wet dark. But the rookie leader had never seen such a variety of path choices, left by snowmobiles and other sleds scurrying out of danger before us. And the dog was slow to grasp Snowbird's left and right directions. For a spell the Indian sloshed his way through the thigh-high mush to hand-lead the confused animals closer to the river-bank.

For two miles it went on like this, the sled moving well on solid snow, then a crunching sound, the too-familiar gurgling and splashing, and a sense of floating in slush. With each such soaking and then prompt freezing, the sled grew heavier with ice. "This is great," said Spencer.

"I'm glad you like it," said his father.

"No danger," claimed Snowbird.

The threat, it seems, is not so much from drowning in slush and being entombed until spring. It is from being soaked and then exposed to freezing air. But Snowbird knew the cabin was just ahead. So, too, apparently did the dogs, which turned it on for a dash around one last bend toward a chimney that would soon be smoking and sparking from a warming fire within.

There, despite temperatures of minus 20, the animals could thaw their paws with warm licks under the eerie green shapes of the Northern Lights overhead. We all sipped hot chocolate while Snowbird thawed his pants, which had frozen like cardboard. Then he chipped off an inch-thick ring of ice from his ankles. We fed the dogs extra grub that night. Then, at 1:00 A.M., after feeding himself and checking the animals one more time (they had become large balls of curled fur in the blowing snow, noses buried in their tails for the night's snooze), Snowbird went to bed on the floor. Sometime before 6:00 A.M. he was back outside, chopping down a tree. "We needed wood," he explained.

The next day, leaving the bush, would be a long one. Because the Friday plane had been canceled, we faced a 200-mile drive out from Fort Chipewyan to Fort Smith. There being no road, just a rough trail frozen into usefulness only during nighttime's biting cold and some frozen streams and rivers probably not yet thawed enough to be hazardous, we drove the distance in Mr. Van Pelt's van. It was to be an eight-hour ride through woods and along rivers. We saw no other humans. And we arrived just before dawn, in time for a two-hour jet flight back to another form of civilization. That last day with Snowbird, we naturally joined in to help

chip off more than 100 pounds of ice caked on the sled. After breakfast
we covered the last eight miles into town, where it was time for parting.
"*Etahtohmskahgan,*" said Little Snowbird.

"*Kaynana-skoh-mitten,*" said his father.

"Good-bye," said Snowbird.

After the Soviet freighter *Stanislavsky* had tied up in Toronto with a
load of tractors one chill fall day, Captain Yuri Surnin ordered the ship's
red carpet rolled out when he saw a crowd of officials, police officers, and
reporters waiting on the pier. That was the Russians' second mistake.

The first mistake occurred when the Soviet Embassy in Canada failed
to pay Wallace Edwards for a $26,000 printing job it had commissioned.
With a stubbornness, persistence, and single-mindedness that added a
whole dimension to Soviet-Canadian relations, the fifty-four-year-old Edwards spent thirteen years trying to force a foreign government to pay its
bill. "No one," said the feisty Canadian, "not even some big-shot foreign
government, should be above our laws."

By having a $13 million Russian ship seized as legal hostage, Mr.
Edwards finally succeeded in getting his money, plus $10,000 interest.
Not only that, but he also insisted on and got the Russians to pay for a
hotel meeting room, a case of vodka, and an ample supply of Russian
caviar so that he could toast himself before a crowd—and give the Russians a taste of some crow.

Mr. Edwards is not a Canadian of the old school, quiet, unassuming,
seemingly plodding. He saw a wrong. He determined what to do. He acted
on that. He faced numerous setbacks, including a number thrown in his
way by his own government. But he persisted, somewhat flamboyantly.
And in the end he won.

It began in 1967, when a Russian Embassy official refused to pay for
some magazines Mr. Edwards printed for the embassy for distribution at
Expo 67 in Montreal. "That really burned my, uh, dignity," said Mr.
Edwards. He was further annoyed when the same Russian returned to
Moscow and kept sending him "Peace on Earth" cards. The Russian
Embassy in Ottawa continued to refuse to pay. And Mr. Edwards found
his own government reluctant to pursue the case. "They told me the
Russians had immunity," he recalled. "I asked them what kind of immu-
nity I'd have if I went to Moscow and violated some of their laws."

So Mr. Edwards decided to use the tools of his democracy. He went to court. He thought about trying to impound the skates of the Russian hockey team or some animals from the Russian circus. Then he settled on a Soviet airliner. He got the right court papers. But the sheriff got nervous about creating an international incident. So he sought advice from Ontario's attorney general, who sought advice from Ottawa's Department of External Affairs, which told the attorney general to tell the sheriff to tell Mr. Edwards to forget it. The Russians had immunity.

Mr. Edwards sued the sheriff.

The government cut off his legal aid. Mr. Edwards found a law firm intrigued by the legal issue and not intimidated by the authorities arrayed against it. "Our position," said Ron Manes, the Toronto attorney and a transplanted Ohioan, "was that if a country descends to participate in our capitalist system, it must play by the same rules as everyone else and pay its just debts."

Mr. Edwards phrased it somewhat more bluntly. "I want my money," he said, "not one penny more and not one penny less."

But he found many of his Canadian friends saying he was "too American," meaning he had become brash and demanding and no longer reluctant to force a confrontation. "Too many of us are starched Canadians with cemented minds," he said. "We've let ourselves be suppressed by the system instead of using it as a tool for the people. We're too afraid to fail, so we too often don't even try." Legal appeal followed legal appeal until finally in 1980 Sheriff Joseph Bremmer appeared at Toronto's Pier 51 to greet the *Stanislavsky,* slap a warrant on its mast, and station officers on board. There were some shoving incidents and a door was jimmied open after the crew had secretly changed the ship's locks, incidents that *Pravda,* the Soviet Communist party newspaper, later charged were provoked by "police thugs acting like medieval pirates."

The shipping line threatened a long legal fight by suggesting that the Soviet government did not own the ship. So Mr. Edwards moved on the Russian Embassy's bank accounts and had them frozen. It was then that lawyers for the Russians suggested a possible out-of-court settlement. They agreed to pay the debt plus interest plus Mr. Edwards's legal fees plus the sheriff's costs and pier charges. "By the way," Mr. Edwards added, "I want some caviar and vodka, too."

Then, in a downtown hotel room festooned with no fewer than twelve Canadian flags, Mr. Edwards savored his victory and vodka. He gave his lawyers pewter mugs inscribed with their names followed by the score—his side 1, Soviet Union 0. And Mr. Edwards hired three armed guards to watch over his cash award, $36,000, which he had demanded in $1 bills. "I've touched them all," he said, "and I've even ripped one. You've got to have a little fun in life."

But Mr. Edwards, Anti-Hero of the Soviet Union, had started something he did not expect. Also attending the celebration and in a markedly less joyous mood was a Canadian woman who identified herself as Diane Mellor. She said she was once an employee of Mr. Edwards's defunct printing firm. She said her last paycheck had bounced. And she wanted to know what Mr. Edwards was going to do about it. "He fought his fight on a matter of principle," she said, "so I think I will, too."

Justice comes to Grand Centre, Alberta, every Wednesday and sometimes on Friday. His name is Marshall Hopkins. He is one of sixteen Alberta provincial judges who still ride the circuit as in the old days (another ninety-two judges, including three women, preside in a regular courtroom). Today the circuit riders don't travel on horses; they use planes or vehicles with tape decks and cruise controls. Other judges do the same in the northern portions of other provinces. They hold court in ice rinks, police stations, and fire halls. With rural Alberta undergoing the pressures of a modern resource boom, the judges hear cases on everything from narcotics dealing and armed robbery to littering and poorly placed moose tags. Calgary and Edmonton, the two largest cities in a province that is five times the size of New York State yet still just one telephone area code (and the same code—403—covers the Yukon and Northwest Territories), were expected to double in population to 1 million each by 2000. Rural towns that once were shriveling now overflow with people drawn to Canada's most promising province for the lucrative search for and extraction of the vast volumes of oil and gas hidden beneath the prairie, the woods and rangelands, and the buffalo grass. New bedroom towns are emerging. Three weeks of each month such communities are populated by children and working mothers. One week each month the fathers return to rest and spend money earned on oil rigs as distant as the Arctic and the North Sea. Family life in this pattern often means trouble with juveniles and domestic disputes.

One certain trouble spot is Judge Hopkins's circuit, an area of 5,000 square miles and, when I visited him, 26,000 people centered on Grand Centre. In Alberta a provincial judge is considered to have a full docket if he presides over 3,500 cases a year. Judge Hopkins regularly handles 6,500 cases, some days sitting from 9:00 A.M. to 9:00 P.M. and traveling through blizzards of snow and bugs for an annual salary around $36,000. "Frankly," the six-foot four-inch judge told me as we cruised down the frozen, deserted highway to the day's trials, "I love this work, talking to the people, listening to them. I can't imagine any job anywhere I'd rather do. Bar none!"

The fifty-seven-year-old son of a pioneer who surveyed the area of northeastern Alberta that is now his son's judicial circuit, Judge Hopkins is the great-great-grandson of a captain in the Welsh Fusiliers who came to Canada to fight the Americans in the War of 1812. He was captured and then ransomed by the British. He returned to Canada to settle near Hamilton, Ontario, to rear seven sons, four of whom ended up as American cowboys. Judge Hopkins's mother was a Quebecer who spent part of her life in New England whenever the job situation in Canada was too bad. His father was a British land surveyor, and the judge grew up thinking that every child naturally spoke English to his father and French to his mother.

Judge Hopkins remembers going barefoot in the Alberta summers and how his father bargained with Indians to buy his family handmade moccasins each fall. Like many western Canadians, including my own father, the Depression, the "dirty thirties," left a searing impression on that generation's mind. Judge Hopkins recalls how his family was so poor it could not afford gasoline for its Model T. So his father removed the engine and hitched up his horses to the bumper to have a metal buggy. Little Marshall would sit facing backward, hanging his legs over the back to draw designs in the dust with his toes. He left home as a teenager and spent the first seventeen years of his working life as a Mountie. Another job took him into construction work in eastern Canada. But he missed the broad skies of the West and working daily with legal intricacies. So he studied law on his own, and before the law required a bar exam, he was appointed a provincial judge, a post where he earned a reputation as stern but understanding.

A sensitive man, he recalls with fondness his many assignments as a member of the Royal Canadian Mounted Police (RCMP), and with sadness the linguistic prejudice he often encountered in Quebec as the hated symbol of federal (read, English) authority. "We'd be out on a patrol," he said, "and stop at a farmhouse to ask for a glass of water. They'd say, '*Non.*' "

By eight each winter morning now, Marshall Hopkins, wearing a business suit, western boots, and a parka, begins the two-hour drive to his distant courtroom to become the Honorable Judge Marshall Hopkins of the Provincial Court in and of the province of Alberta. His courtroom often is rented for $100 a day in a former dance hall balcony over a coffee shop. "It pays our propane bill," noted Judy Sjerven, the owner. In one day he heard forty-four cases, including eight nonjury trials and eighteen matters adjourned to a later date. He ordered three people arrested for not answering summonses. "I'm very tough on respect for the courts," said the judge. "When that goes, so does the whole fabric of our society." Fourteen defendants pleaded guilty and were fined more than $1,600 in total, the majority for alcohol-related offenses. Aware of the tape recorder monitoring every statement in the room, Judge Hopkins runs the court briskly and firmly and at times offering stern warnings. "The next time I see you here for drinking too much," he told one offender, "you've got four months in the slammer, and if that doesn't motivate you, tough." Perhaps remembering his own four children, including an adopted Indian teenager, and his own teenage brush with the law when an understanding Mountie steered him straight to a firm father's spanking, Judge Hopkins is usually more fatherly with juveniles, offering first offenders advice and probation instead of punishment. "Eighty-five percent of these kids we'll never see again," he said. "Why make it harder?"

Drumming his fingers in sequence on his chair arm, he manages to remain calm, on the surface, all the time. But he admits that for assaults on children, he intentionally calls an adjournment during the hearing to let himself cool down inside and remember that the application of the law, not his own anger, is the key. Such brief adjournments are taken over a cup of coffee around a table of the Burger Inn in Grand Centre, a town of 3,000 hard by an isolated area where the air forces of NATO countries roar and soar overhead in military maneuvers. Around these tables attorneys for the Crown and the defense, men who make the rounds of the rural justice circuit themselves, gossip and work out the plea bargains that save court time. "It's a hard life up here," said Pierre Michel Dube, the

Crown attorney, who escaped eastern civilization on a motorcycle with his wife to ride to a new life in Canada's West. "People live hard here, and they play hard here."

Judge Hopkins is philosophical about the crimes he's routinely exposed to. "I don't get depressed over what people do to each other," he said. "It's disturbing, of course. People don't seem to ask themselves, 'What's right?' anymore. They just say, 'How much can I get from this other fellow?' You can't let it get to you, I guess. That's futile. This has gone on for thousands of years before and will for thousands of years more. I sit back and observe. Here's man acting out a game. We practice self-deception so much to create an image of humans as so humane while we're denying our animalistic instincts. We're far from perfect, all of us."

Then, by late afternoon or early evening, after several defendants have changed their pleas to guilty in conferences with the Crown attorney, Judge Hopkins adjourns court and heads home in the dark to his wife, Toni, across the snow-covered countryside, where the stunning nighttime silences are still broken by a coyote chorus. Wildlife remains a prominent part of the Canadian countryside and a nearby neighbor for most Canadians, even in cities like Toronto, where the extensive, meandering park system is home to thousands of raccoons. These furry, audacious bandits routinely appear in backyards and on city sidewalks and inside unsecured garbage cans. In the summer the Alberta provincial government even plants crops in scattered fields and then leaves them unharvested to nourish the food chain of rabbits, herons, ducks, geese, moose, eagles, deer, and weasels, the province's nontaxpaying population.

It is at such pensive times, when a music tape is playing softly and the cruise control is holding the car right at the legal sixty-two-mile-an-hour (100 kilometer-an-hour) speed limit, that Judge Hopkins ponders some of his own doings. "One day, you know, when I was a lot younger," he told me, "I saw a coyote in a field far from the road. To scare him, I fired my pistol in the air. And you know, even at that distance, he fell. I went over there, and both his back legs were broken, and I just stood there. I had to put him out of his misery. I was so stupid, you know. Just fooling around and he paid for it. A beautiful animal he was. He had a right to live, too. Oh, me, I've thought about that so many times over the years. I guess we all make mistakes. That's why I'm in business as a judge."

*   *   *

The first sound a deeply sleepy Reid Tait heard that winter day in those black minutes before 6:00 A.M. was a cheery little jingle for *Sesame Street,* seeping into his bedroom from the TV and the Canadian satellite hovering 22,000 miles above the Equator. It had been a long previous day, or rather a short night. There had been another traffic accident out on the dirt highway, which is what almost all roads are in the Yukon. And as the sole representative of the Queen, the government, and the law in his assigned 5,000 square miles of territory, Corporal Tait of the Royal Canadian Mounted Police had climbed into his dark blue van with the little minijail cage in back and the familiar gold insignia on the door (a crown with the motto *"Maintiens le droit"* or "Uphold the right"). At 2:00 A.M. then, he had driven out to oversee the cleanup, the ticket writing, the towing away, and the care of injuries. It hadn't been a bad wreck, as wilderness wrecks go—no deaths; no fire sixty miles from help; no fighting; no pieces of bodies frozen to the road surface. The big black ravens sitting vigilantly high in the trees as nature's cleanup crew would go hungry that morning. And Corporal Tait could be back in bed by 4:30.

Corporal Tait is one of 18,000 members of the mounted police, the unique Canadian agency that combines elements of an FBI, a highway patrol, a city police, a secret service, and a park ranger division. In recent years the force, as its members call it, has come under attack for authoritarianism and abuse of its considerable powers. But in the Yukon, where forty Mounties cover an area twenty-five times the size of Massachusetts, there are few discouraging words for the men in blue who have a reputation for wearing scarlet.

"We do everything that police do everywhere," said Chief Superintendent Harry Nixon, Corporal Tait's boss. "We just don't have the volume they do. In the old days, by the time you heard about a crime, got there, did the investigation, found the culprit, and got a circuit judge in, it could take two years. Now it's more like days." Thanks to computers, Superintendent Nixon can tell immediately that the Yukon's 23,000 residents report around 12,000 offenses annually, everything from trespassing to murder. Thanks to computers and satellites, he can inform all of North America's law enforcement agencies that he is seeking someone; that is how a state trooper in Florida not long ago discovered that a speeder there was wanted for murder in the Yukon.

Thanks to computers and satellites and radio repeaters atop a score of windblown mountains, Superintendent Nixon can talk with any of his men anytime anywhere; that is why Michael Macy, a lone cross-country skier from New Jersey, is alive today. Alerted by friends that he was overdue, Superintendent Nixon radioed Corporal Tait to begin a search. And after hours of flying over countless valleys rarely visited by humans, Corporal Tait found the young man, lost, frostbitten, and starving. "It was a good feeling," said the corporal. "He drew a heart in the snow for thanks."

The son of a prairie farmer, Corporal Tait joined the force sixteen years ago at the age of 19. Counting seven months basic training, he has had fifteen assignments all over Canada, including a stint with the RCMP's touring horse show—the only time he has ridden a horse or worn the famous flat-brimmed hat. "They're so cumbersome," he said, preferring the peakless fur jobs with the fold-down earflaps.

Thanks in part to the attractiveness of Nelson Eddy crooning "Indian Love Call," in uniform to a smiling Jeanette MacDonald in some Hollywood woods in *Rose Marie*, the Mounties are one of three things that Americans think they know about Canada (the other two being Eskimos, who aren't called that anymore, and the queen, who never has lived there). In view of Canadians' more reverential attitudes toward authority, the Mountie has played a special role in Canadian history, especially locally. Over the years he has always been chief law enforcement agent, but in the provinces that contract for the RCMP to be provincial and local police, he also became an unofficial judge, mediator, father confessor, and quiet uncle. He might short-circuit his own investigation of a youth, knowing of the boy's troubled family, and substitute his own regular counseling. He might help organize basketball games, pat little boys on the head, turn a gaggle of little girls into soft giggles by actually bending over to talk to them, or address awestruck kindergarteners about bicycle safety. He'd have to make many appearances, in uniform, to lend a federal presence to important and not so important local celebrations, a diplomat from that faraway place called Ottawa, acknowledging by his esteemed presence the import of that day in Flin Flon, Manitoba. At not so friendly times he might act as a social mediator; it is instinctive for feuding Canadians to turn to federal authorities as allegedly disinterested compromise forgers. There was a time when the vigilant Mounties even served as immigration officers, for lack of any other authorities. They'd encamp in tents atop the rugged mountain pass entrances to the Yukon and there hold court, interviewing the American gold rushers, screening out those without finances or supplies or character sufficient for a full year's stay.

Historically, outside the cities and Quebec, where the Mounties are to the French what the British are to the Irish, there always seems to be a Gary Cooper aura around the Mountie—tall; principled; slow to anger; lonely; appealingly vulnerable in a strong way. He would be young and vibrant, a real catch in any daughter's mother's eye. But in the old days, before seeking a woman's hand in marriage, a Mountie would first have to propose it to a senior officer for permission.

Times have changed now. And Corporal Tait is a thoroughly modern Mountie. When I visited him for a few days, he lived in the tiny Yukon crossroads town of Carcross in a double house trailer with his wife, Bonnie, and their three children, including a six-year-old girl named Heather, who had some definite thoughts on keeping Daddy safe. After the *Sesame Street* reveille, Corporal Tait's day could include a court appearance in distant Whitehorse, investigating an illegal moose kill, registering a boat, checking the cargo of an arriving American plane, completing his budget estimate for next year, befriending a disturbed Indian youth, breaking up a violent family fight, chatting, apparently idly, with local residents, writing a report on his activities, taking another walk around town to be seen, and trying once more to train his dog, Smokey, to come when called. "The only thing I never do around here," he said, "is give out a parking ticket."

For his work Corporal Tait receives around $24,000 a year plus a cost-of-living allowance. His office was his home, his hours irregular, and his duties all-encompassing. "Reid loves his work so much that I try to hide my worries," said his wife, who has been trained to run the office and radio in his absence. "I have big plans for later, when we're not policemen anymore, but I know that deep down he'll never change. And I tell myself that if you're going to get blown away, you're going to get blown away. We had some friends killed at a stop sign. So worrying doesn't help. And all the moving is getting easier. We have friends all over now. And we promised each other we wouldn't say we didn't like a place before we got there."

Corporal Tait, who has never fired his gun on duty, belittles the dangers except when responding to family fights and while on his frequent wilderness patrols, which are still seen in part as demonstrating sovereignty over remote areas. "This country doesn't forgive mistakes," he said. "You never know what you'll find out there. But when people see you out and about regularly, they tend to keep their horns in."

In the morning Corporal Tait might wander down to the local coffee shop, not because he likes coffee but because he likes to chat and keep in touch with the regulars. He warns one local driver about his broken taillight. "In town," says the corporal, "I'd give him a ticket. Out here I might let an occasional little thing slide. It's a small town. Everybody knows everybody. And someday he might tell me something I need to know."

He talks with Johnny Johns, a local Indian guide since 1917. "I tell you things have changed in the hunt," says the Indian. "We used to go out for two months at a time, shoot only the best. If we didn't see anything special, we didn't shoot anything. No hard feelings. I had an Austrian count or something here once. 'Johnny,' he says, 'I'd like to see some trapping.' I says, 'You got to wait for snow to trap.' 'Okay,' he says. So he waits two months and we go out. Now it's six to ten days out, shoot quick and get out."

Corporal Tait listens intently, like a politician. "I got lots of friends in the U.S.," Mr. Johns continues. "They say, 'Come on down, Johnny, and retire.' They got places six miles wide and twenty-eight miles long. But I tell you that's not enough room for me. I been all over, but I never seen any place better than here." Corporal Tait agrees. Speaking of animals, he complains about his dog. Everybody laughs. He asks about the condition of some trails in the mountains. He mentions, by the way, has everybody heard about the new gun regulations? No, no, no one had, as a matter of fact. So Reid, their neighbor with the disobedient dog, fills them in. And everybody nods. The information exchange is over. They all have reaffirmed their friendship. And Reid hasn't come on too strong. He's still one of the boys.

Outside he dons his helmet, checks his .38, makes sure that others know his itinerary, and packs extra supplies and fuel for one of the snowmobiles that the Mounties have used since 1969 instead of more expensive dogs. "Trouble is," Corporal Tait says, "if you're stuck out there, you can't eat a carburetor." He also ties himself to a clip on the snowmobile; should he somehow fall off, his body would pull out a pin and halt the machine, his ticket to safety, in its tracks.

To bridge any ethnic gaps, the corporal is often accompanied by Richard Baker, an Indian and one of the force's new category of native constables. The first stop several miles down a frozen lake was the Harder residence. There the Mountie checked on the logging family's health, delivered messages from town, and inquired about events in the area, anything suspicious or unusual, anyone overdue anywhere, strangers seen around. "In the cities," the corporal explained, "no one wants to see a policeman, but out here, they're insulted if you don't stop."

He moved on across the lakes, up some hills, through dense woods, and into immense meadows, where he was just a minute dot on the landscape. On Lime Lake the supply sled crashed through the snow cover, miring its runners in a foot of freezing slush. After freeing the gear, the corporal visited the Eastwick couple, talked about dogs, the weather, and any strangers about, then moved on to the day's destination, the log cabin of Art Smith and Lloyd Reid, two trappers. He accompanied them as they checked their traps. The Mountie brought news, companionship, a few jokes, and, as a polite wilderness guest, some fresh food.

After a dinner of corn, instant potatoes, and moose steaks cooked on a wood-burning stove, he helped with the chores, hauling water from the lake, cleaning dishes, and clearing snowmobile treads of ice and snow for his morning departure. Around the table, under a row of squirrel pelts hung to dry, he listened to and told tales of Yukon life. Oh, by the way, he said, there were some new firearms regulations coming out, and he explained them as a favor. Art Smith, it seemed, was pretty fed up with all these government regulations on everything. Time was you could do what you thought best, long as it didn't hurt nobody else. You know my uncle? Up north of Whitehorse? Well, he pioneered this country, and now some government bureaucrat comes along and tells him he can't build his new cabin on account of he's got the wrong wiring or something. "All these rules and regulations," said Mr. Smith, a lifelong Yukoner, "they seem small, all a part of life and right small things, too. But there are good, hardworking people it's hard on. They're used to doing what they want when they want. Everything's changing so fast. Used to be you could travel these roads and not see anyone for days, and if you did, you'd stop and pass the time of day. Now people are all over the place, and you could be lying in the middle of the road bleeding and no one would stop. They'd drive right around you."

Drinking tea, the men talked and played cards into the evening, pausing once for a stroll into the zero-degree air to gaze silently at the moonlit snow, the thousands of crisp stars, the stark frozen trees creaking, and the powerful mountains looming overhead. The moon bathed the area in an eerie blue semidaylight. But thousands of stars were still visible in the chill air above, where a strange, muffled roar thundered across the valley as the wind tore through a gorge far away and carried its snow high over the lake to fall in a silent white curtain. "My God, I love it here," said Mr. Reid, the trapper. After a final hand of hearts the guest's bed, a sleeping bag atop the plank table, was prepared. Corporal Tait pushed a button on the radio in his hand. There was a click as an unmanned relay station twenty miles away turned itself on. Three more buttons. A ringing sound and an answer: "RCMP Carcross." It was Bonnie Tait. Her husband, the traveling policeman, was checking in from the wilderness thirty miles away. The trappers pretended not to listen. Then little Heather got on the radio to tuck her father in for the night across the hills. "Hi, Daddy. Are you warm enough out there?"

"Yes, I am, Heather."

"Well, you cover up. And be careful, Daddy. I love you."

Corporal Tait smiled. The Mountie's daughter had got her man.

For many years Warren Hughes labored as a food chemist, a soap salesman, and an advertising account representative pushing products such as Pepsodent, Pablum, and Rothman's cigarettes. They were straightforward jobs, respectable, demanding, and ever so normal. Then, some say, one stormy night a wizard disguised as a friend came to Mr. Hughes with a strange message: A small business down the street was getting so small its creditors were about to foreclose. Why didn't Mr. Hughes take it on? In the blink of an eye and the wave of a wand, Mr. Hughes had joined Canada's vast, vital ranks of small-business men. "My business," he said, "is the business of fantasy." Mr. Hughes rents costumes.

By figuring out who conservative Canadians really want to be, or at least who they really want to be for an evening, in little more than a decade of fun and surprises, Mr. Hughes has turned a dying business into one with revenues in excess of $350,000 a year. It draws customers to his Toronto shop from all over Canada as well as the northeastern United

States. With his infectious enthusiasm, a flair for marketing, a floorful of fabric, and a respect for dreams, Mr. Hughes has built a fantasy land that draws giggles, guffaws, and "Oh, my's" from delighted customers pretending to be someone else.

Mr. Hughes and his small business are crucial cogs in the Canadian economy precisely because their operation is small. For every Seagram's, Brascan, or Canadian Pacific in Canada, there are thousands of small-business men, a total of more than 1.2 million companies with 85 percent having fewer than twenty employees. In fact, in Canada small businesses employ about 50 percent of the nongovernment work force. The streets of Toronto, among others, are lined not with the chains or branch stores that are so dominant elsewhere but, instead, with thousands of mom-and-pop outlets, where a bell on the front door still announces a customer's entrance.

The fifty-five-year-old Mr. Hughes is a mustachioed wizard who has created fifteen new jobs with his success as well as constructed a job he can't wait to go to every morning. "I so love it," he told me as we toured a score of costumed aisles. Frequently he would interrupt himself to whistle or exclaim, "Oh, wait here, you've got to see this one." Then he would grab a hanger, disappear to the next aisle for a moment, and return as a new character, complete wiz, how you say, ze accent. One customer he steered away from some expensive makeup because a cheaper brand would do just as well for one evening's masquerade. "I figure I'm going to meet everybody at least two times," he said, "so I behave accordingly."

Mr. Hughes, whose wife, Jean, did the company's books for many years, has no idea how many costumes he owns. Each one breaks down into many different pieces so that it can be reassembled to fit another, different dream. There are also uncounted bins of bonnets and cupboards of caps. But he does know that he has five children. And he knows what to do when the phone rings early one morning and a customer says, "Quick, I need twenty-six Mounties by ten A.M." And he knows, too, that in his business, age is irrelevant. "You are only as old as you behave," he said, "and I have no intention of growing up."

Mr. Hughes has learned a lot about his countrymen over the years. He learned that the real disposable incomes are downtown, so he moved Costume House there. He has learned that Canadian women, seeking a costume, routinely exaggerate their bust measurements while Canadian men routinely underestimate their waist measurements. So he always remeasures every client with the end of the tape measure out of their sight. He won't contradict their quoted dimensions, but he won't embarrass them by producing an ill-fitting outfit either. He keeps the Santa Claus clothes out of sight "in case some youngsters come in." He will never tell customers their idea is dumb, and he will never try to rent any man anything called tights. "Here," Mr. Hughes said with a smile, "we call them 'body socks.' " Likewise, the loose-hanging garb in a Roman soldier's costume is never called a skirt. In Canada, it is a kilt. When one horizontally large lady wanted a Queen Victoria dress, he had his doubts but obliged. The next year she came back. She said she liked being another person so much that she had decided to diet and become one. She had lost 100 pounds, and that year she rented the Cleopatra costume. "A knockout," said Mr. Hughes, approvingly.

Some costumes, like bunnies and Superman, are so popular they require reservations months in advance (Halloween, which in Canada is usually spelled Hallowe'en, is the busiest time, followed closely by Christmas; New Year's business is down in recent years). And Mr. Hughes keeps flow charts on many outfits to make sure they are out earning their keep the maximum number of days or nights. When Prince Edward Island had a festival to celebrate its agricultural produce, Mr. Hughes had to produce several dozen different vegetable costumes. To break the winter monotony, some northern Canadian communities plan a masquerade ball and order a couple of hundred costumes by mail. Knowing Canadians' penchant for exaggerating measurements up or down, he adds two to four inches on men's waist sizes and takes off a couple of inches on women's bust sizes. "It works out well," said Mr. Hughes, "but according to their measurements, most people up there have a head only three inches tall."

Sometimes, he says, he thinks some American customers are already wearing costumes when they come in to shop at the Costume House. But Canadians, he says, are a more reserved people who dress conservatively, normally. But when they rent costumes, they want to become, for a time, outlandish in a socially acceptable way. "They tiptoe in here, some nice man, usually by himself, and he says, softly, 'I want to be Zorro.' Superheroes are big items for Canadians, especially policemen. And gorillas are great, too. Canadians love to run down the street carrying a bunch of bananas and acting silly. With the mask on you can't tell who they are, see?"

Nowadays, Mr. Hughes said, donning a wizard's pointed cap to scan his memory, he's getting more men who want to dress up as women, and more women seem to be into leather. There are, of course, some practical problems to warn customers about. "You cannot make a cool furry animal costume," he said, "and it's hard to drive a car to a party wearing a suit of armor." Sometimes one woman's idea of a fairy goddess is considerably more revealing than Mr. Hughes's idea of the same magic creature. "And what's a witch?" asked Mr. Hughes. "To me, it's a nun with a pointed hat and a broom. To one woman it was a silver lamé gown with not much of a front and a slit in the skirt up to her broom."

There are always special requests to honor: the woman who wanted to go to the party as a head of lettuce with two bunches of leaves on her breasts. "Her boyfriend went as a rabbit," recalled Mr. Hughes. "These are the parts of the business you never dream of at the start."

For men, the most consistent costume moneymakers, after striped vests and straw hats, are wizards, Zorro, and the Three Musketeers. Women customers, who are much more certain of what they want, most often go for Playboy bunny costumes, pregnant nuns, and harem girls ("We've got see-through pants or not, according to taste"). Mermaids are always unpopular, though. "Too hard to walk," said Mr. Hughes, "even though we put a zipper in the tailfin." And he is having technical problems with the kangaroo outfit.

"People have definite images about what they are and what they want to be," said Mr. Hughes. "You have to be very careful about contradicting them. Some fat fellow you might try to steer away from Superman. But what's the difference between him and some shy little thing who wants to be a western dancehall girl? It's my business, but it's their fantasy."

Johnny Bryk was in pretty fair shape for groceries, so his shopping list included only thirty dozen eggs, twenty-two loaves of bread, sixty pounds of beef, sixty-five pounds of chicken, fifty pounds of potatoes, eighteen heads of lettuce, twenty pounds of tomatoes, and a dozen boxes of a dozen different breakfast cereals. It is not that Mr. Bryk eats a lot, although he does; it is just that he has 200 or more guests stop by for three meals a day every day.

Johnny Bryk is a railroad chef, a disappearing breed that for decades has enabled millions of Canadian train passengers to spend days eating their way across North America in style and comfort amid the breathtaking scenery that Canadians so take for granted. Trains have always been vital to Canadian history, their ties stitching the diverse land together and held there by the rails' steel bonds. Some recent federal administrations, whose officials carve careers by dashing back and forth across Canada on government airline passes, have systematically cut Canada's passenger rail service, citing budgetary considerations. The airlines may zip passengers coast to coast in six hours and give them two foil-wrapped, portion-controlled, reheated meals served with metal tongs from an insulated box on wheels. But the railroad dining car cook is a trade with special skills on the remaining Canadian long-haul trains. These culinary vagabonds may not use coal stoves anymore. They need not cut up a swaying side of beef in a giant refrigerator room. And the silver service is stainless steel nowadays.

But it remains a career that is more a way of life than a job, and there aren't many of these left. Thirty-five times a year Johnny Bryk, the son of a railroad man, leaves his home in central Ontario, boards the train in Toronto's Union Station at midnight, and works his way to Winnipeg, thirty-six hours and five meals away. He lays over there for six hours, then cooks his way home again on a returning train. He has cooked his way along routes all over the continent ("I remember in '62 in Chicago I went into a bar, and all I had was Canadian money, and they threw me out, thought it was some kind of pretend money, they said"). When I met him, Mr. Bryk had lived forty of his fifty-five years on the rails. "It kind of gets in your blood," he said. "You know what I mean? You see guys retire, and then you see them back hanging around the station."

For a chef like Mr. Bryk, a cross-country trip takes four breakfasts, three lunches, three dinners, countless snacks, and several large batches of the special fish chowder that is never made the same way twice. Not to mention the roast beef, the pork, the omelets, the spaghetti, and the handmade chicken pot pies. All of these must be prepared in a nine-by-fifteen-foot kitchen wobbling along at forty-five miles an hour. Mr. Bryk needs to know not only how to cook but also where he can cook what. "Time was," he recalled while he made dinner one morning, "when you made custards or pies, you'd have to wait for a certain smooth portion of track or else you'd lose it." On other parts, the soup pot had better not be too full. In his gravelly voice and with his paper hat pushed way back on his head, Mr. Bryk told of one fellow chef who knew what milepost the train was passing by the bumps he felt in the track. "Amazing," growled Mr. Bryk, "course, he went nuts later."

Mr. Bryk's workday begins around 5:00 A.M., when he and perhaps Mike Wolfe, an assistant chef, and a cook named Chico Wong light the propane stove and prepare the oatmeal and coffee and rolls and eggs for the 200 or more passengers still snoozing between the crisp white sheets in their compartments. The lake and woods passing by outside are frozen solid in winter, but the kitchen is warm and the banter lively. By the time the chief steward, someone like Dansil Braithwaite, shows the day's first customer to his seat to write out his own breakfast order, the kitchen is steaming and smells strangely of turkey. Mr. Bryk, who believes in slow cooking and light seasoning, is preparing dinner. On one trip I took with him, he secretly prepared a special meal, not on the menu, for my wife, Connie, and me, on our honeymoon. When we first boarded and entered our compartment that time, there sat a large platter of exquisite hors d'oeuvres, compliments of someone special in the dining car up ahead.

The cramped kitchen there places a premium on efficient movement and use of space. Waiters bark out orders. Eggs and bacon start to sizzle. The kitchen crewmen may travel together for years, spending more time with each other than with their own families. "You're glad to get home," Mr. Bryk said gruffly, "and you're glad to get away. And sometimes home seems like away and away seems like home."

The basic menu on the train, which connects Toronto and Montreal to Vancouver, changes only three or four times a year. But there is always roast beef to prepare, and the chicken pies. One day Mr. Bryk guessed passengers would buy fourteen of them; he actually sold twelve. And the fish soup must simmer. VIA Rail, the Canadian government's passenger train company, has a book of official recipes, but veterans like Mr. Bryk tend to follow their own preferences. Of the soup, for instance, he said, "I throw in anything I can get my hands on—a little of this, a little of that, and a dash of cream later. I don't know. I got to be doing it to know what I do. You might be a carrot short one time or a potato ahead next time. But if I went by precise recipes, nobody would ever get anything to eat around here."

Then he laughed. "We had no cooking schools. You watch the other guys, and over all the years you develop a style of your own. That's all." My wife asked him once how he knew how much pasta to cook for spaghetti. "I don't know," he said. "You just grab a handful like this and throw it in." When the passengers have eaten, Mr. Bryk must feed the twenty or so train crew members, who praise his fare. So he cooks all day. "The only time I don't cook," he said, "is payday, when my wife lets me take her out." During his absences his family eats the meals he prepares while at home. His favorite dish: "After forty years of cooking, it don't make no difference. I like to throw a steak on the grill. My wife, she likes fish."

On the train the hours are long; rarely is he finished before 10:00 P.M. The feet can hurt. The scenery is less exciting the six-hundredth time. It is far from home, and other cities can be lonely places during brief stopovers. In the summer, kitchen temperatures can reach 140 degrees. But there are some special rewards to wandering his country on a train schedule. Mr. Bryk pulls a bulging wallet from under his stained apron. From deep inside he produces a tiny, yellowing photograph of a smiling child. It is a machine-made photo of Diane, who was ten when she ate in his dining car back in 1965. She had walked straight into the kitchen that day and handed the chef her picture. "She said she liked my cooking," said Mr. Bryk, who has carried it everywhere ever since.

Nancy Sorg was in her kitchen in Moose Creek one day cleaning up a muddy smear and a lot of spilled sugar she thought her husband had left behind. Out of the corner of her eye she saw someone pass by the window, and she went to the door to greet him with some disparaging remark. Instead, she met a growling six-foot black bear returning for the rest of his dessert. She closed the door rather promptly. "That doesn't happen all that much in New Jersey," she said.

Bears are just one of the hazards of housekeeping that a newlywed immigrant couple from the Garden State must endure when they decide to exchange the wilds of New Jersey for the civilized ways of the Yukon and carve out their own new life in their isolated corner of Canada. In their case, town was 233 miles down the dirt road. Over the years millions of Canadians and Americans, my father among them, have exchanged countries for personal, political, or even profitable reasons. Most often they enriched their new land, bringing fresh eyes to old problems that seem to them as new challenges. The American immigrants I came across in Canada, many years after the anguish of the Vietnam era draft dodgers, were excited and enthusiastic and comfortable in their new surroundings; it almost seemed as if they had come home to their new country. What gave the Sorgs away was when my son Christopher spotted and inquired after an American flag they had flying next to the maple leaf flag over their cabin in the Yukon.

Chris Sorg, then twenty-six, had been working at his family's Eighth Avenue financial printing house in New York City. Nancy Sorg, then twenty-one, was a student at the Parsons School of Design. And the thought of running the Moose Creek Lodge—and, in fact, constituting the entire human population of Moose Creek—was as distant as, well, northwestern Canada. In retrospect, it seems fate led the Sorgs to Moose Creek. When they were returning along the Klondike (dirt) Highway one day from a vacation in Alaska, their car died as it coasted into the driveway of the lodge, then owned by Mike and Shirley MacKinnon. The Sorgs, who were not yet married then, stayed for several days, exchanging their labor around the buildings and land for room and board.

Then, with an open invitation to return anytime, it was back to the New York area, where Nancy continued her studies and Chris commuted to Manhattan on the bus and train from Ridgewood, New Jersey. "I wasn't all that keen on that life," he recalled between turns on the hand-powered gasoline pump out front, "and I just loved this place right off." A couple months later he took a leave of absence from work and returned to Moose Creek. He laid sod on a cabin roof. He pumped gas and helped cut the twenty-three cords of wood necessary for each winter's heat. And then one day Mr. MacKinnon announced he wanted to sell. The asking price—$70,000 for 5.5 acres, the large log house, and restaurant-gas business—was dickered down to $50,000. Mr. Sorg promptly left for home and two days later walked in on his surprised family. To his father he proposed a loan. To Nancy he proposed marriage. Both parties accepted.

Mr. Sorg returned to work at the printing shop for a few months. In the spring Nancy was graduated from Parsons. Five days later they were married. Four days later they got their Canadian visas. And then they left on a 4,300-mile honeymoon drive to Moose Creek. Their home is a large three-level log cabin lighted by propane gas lanterns. The water comes from a creek, which seems nearby only to those who don't have to haul the water wagon to the house tank. The mail comes 50 miles from Mayo, whenever someone thinks to bring it. All supplies come from Whitehorse, more than a four-hour drive down the two-lane dirt road. Telephone calls come from nowhere—which is to say, they don't come at all. That's because there's no phone. But customers come from all over. "You meet more interesting people in this place," said Mr. Sorg, who was so into his rugged new life that he sported a new beard to match it. "There are miners, trappers, tourists from Florida, Germany, all over. And it's funny. Up here it's so quiet you can hear people coming a couple of miles away."

Customers can find a wide assortment of sourdough pancakes served all day. There are cold and hot drinks, cinnamon buns, chocolate chip cookies, homemade breads, and, of course, gasoline served up to thirsty vehicles through a pump made in 1912 with a serial number of 599. "There's all sorts of things you can do with a place like this," said Mrs. Sorg with the enthusiasm of a young bride. "There aren't that many places in the Yukon that look like you'd expect a Yukon place to look." They started building small overnight log cabins and a hiking trail. In the fall they shoot a moose and get more than 1,000 pounds of meat at a crack. Mr. Sorg does some prospecting. Mrs. Sorg presses Arctic wild flowers and makes craft souvenirs. They can cut down their own Christmas tree just outside the door. They can smoke their own salmon. And they plan on starting a mail-order business selling Yukon gold pans from their Moose Creek address. "Oh, there's so much to do," said Mrs. Sorg.

They will do much of this during the long winters when temperatures plummet to minus 40 degrees and a fire must be lighted in the garage five hours before they try starting the car. The battery must be removed to the house every night. "Actually," said Mrs. Sorg, "the summers are the rough time. Up at six A.M. We don't get to bed until after midnight. That's when I think I wasn't planning on being a frontier wife. But in the winters we'll just put on a pot of soup all day and relax."

"We made full use of New York," her husband said, pausing between evening chores. "But you find once you get involved locally, there's plenty of bustle right here. New York seems a long ways away. You seem to help each other more out here. There's so much room. So little that's threatening. Canada and the Yukon are lands of opportunity the way the United States used to be." But, his wife added, "We're not in this to make a fortune. We just want to make a living. And the benefits are great. One night we spent three hours out front just watching the Northern Lights."

They also felt a certain soothing sense of isolation from having no idea about current events until they were history. Just then a hitchhiker entered the new immigrants' old shop and walked across the creaking wooden floor to ask when the next bus south was due past. "Let's see," said Mr. Sorg, "what day is this?"

It was a chilled Tuesday when I first drove into High River, Alberta, between Calgary and the American border. The Marathon gas station hadn't sold a fishing license in many weeks. The fortune-telling machine at the Centre Café was spewing out the same futures for everyone. Heated car exhausts rose straight up in steamy plumes like flags behind their tailpipes. The snow, which creaked loudly underfoot, was powdery and terrible for packing snowballs as the muffled youngsters wandered home from another of the 2,000 or 3,000 days they would attend in their school life.

Charles Clark was puffing a pipe in his living room, watching the silent street scene through his window and, once again, admiring the neat rows of giant fir trees that were not planted yesterday. The first settlers put them in about eighty-five years ago. A lot of them were Americans, creaking along the Macleod Trail on wooden wheels from Montana to the government-promised land in Canadian territory. The people of High River liked the trees then. They still do. Only someone from outside High River would think of widening the Macleod Trail and chopping down the firs. And he'd have a bit of a scrap on his hands.

High River is not a typical Canadian town. I don't think there is one, frankly. The little communities in western Ontario and eastern Quebec and southern Alberta look rather alike, except for the churches, of course: the grand edifices of the Catholics with the high spires and all the steps so both families can line up for the happy wedding picture afterward, the little boxy clapboard churches of the Protestants out West, and the shiny gold domes of the Eastern sects in Manitoba. In Quebec towns inevitably the tallest structure is a steeple. In Alberta the tallest point is always a grain elevator, green and red and gray and windowless and right by the tracks, where trains seem never to pass while I'm around.

"Sedate" is the first word that comes to mind in these places. And tidy. The farm fields are shaped differently—broad and square out West, long and skinny in Quebec. But the work is still governed by the seasons.

Success seems to depend so much on faraway factors. And the penetrating frost still squeezes up a goodly crop of new rocks by spring each year.

From this soil, three-quarters of a century ago, also sprang Charles Clark's generation. That was back in a time when horseback riders were the only travelers and the only road signs were marks on tree trunks. My grandfather wandered through these areas, spending all summer in the bush to count a few dozen hardy souls for the census of 1911. Mr. Clark and his playmates then were frontier youngsters who didn't know they were living history at the time. And now that they are aware of the different times, they think perhaps the old ways were the better ways. Some of the settlers were British, second and third sons who were forced into adventure by not getting the main inheritance at home like their elder brothers. But for many years many of these towns and families flew the flags of both Canada and the United States. Many of the settlers, including Mr. Clark's wife, Grace, had come from the States. And so the towns had two Thanksgivings each year (in October for the Canadians and in November with the Pilgrims for the Americans) and two July independence festivals—on the first for Canada and on the fourth for the States. It was natural and not laden with anything beyond celebration.

Everyone worked in or around town. A person's reputation then depended on his or her word. Everyone knew everybody. High River was smaller than its current 4,000 population. People would sit on the veranda of a summer evening and talk about the day and work and what they had heard. Much of those details and news items made their way into Mr. Clark's newspaper, the *High River Times*. "We were settled by people who came to stay," said Mr. Clark. "They weren't coming to make a fortune and move on.

"I knew the original settlers," he said. "They didn't seem so special then, but they do now. They were very sturdy, independent folk. On the weekends my boys and I would go tramping around in the bush and the foothills camping, and you'd happen on them. Some came to town maybe twice a year to pay bills and get supplies. And the stores had harnesses and shoes hanging from the ceiling and big cheeses on the counter." The communities were built on cooperation. Everyone pitched in to rebuild a neighbor's burned barn. If someone had fallen on hard times, a friend would create an occasion to barter and purposely agree to an exchange much in the stricken person's favor; perhaps the friend said he needed a hired hand for a couple of days' hard work, but sorry, all he could pay was a hog. Thus, he got the work done, and the man in tight straits got more than his due, but he could maintain his dignity. No handouts, no charity. And without words, the gesture was understood. It would also be reciprocated somehow someday.

Mr. Clark, who was to become something of a prominent local elder statesman in High River with his newspaper and many other civic activities, traces the beginnings of change to the Depression, when everyone was long-stricken and suffering and hopes died stillborn. "Canada lost a whole generation in those years," he said. "They were living, but not alive. Just when things could have gotten better, and the country take off, everyone's worst possible fears were fulfilled. It set the country back a long ways.

"At one time here," Mr. Clark continued, puffing on his pipe, "you'd never think of going to a government for aid. You'd do it yourself or go to a neighbor. If you needed a culvert dug by the road, well, you'd dig it yourself and take it off your next tax bill. Today there are a dozen committees and bodies you've got to go through, and that drains people's independence and initiative. And of course, someone is always opposed to anything. Life is getting all cluttered up with rules and regulations. It's changed the whole character of our society." Once society's links seemed to run between people. But today, he said, they run from each person to some government body. "Now," he added, "people by necessity have to look out for their own interests. Selfishness has taken over. Youth expects to be handed everything on a platter. Each community, small and large, becomes fragmented by all these competing interests. And you have not got compromise anymore but confrontations all the time. Canada wasn't started by confrontations. You must have compromise and cooperation to build anything new here. But those people in Ottawa are bent on confrontation, and they act so damn busy they don't remember what the real Canada is. The simple times as we knew them are gone forever. And every field has a NO TRESPASSING sign."

Nonetheless, the Clarks went on about their simple but busy retired life, he doing his errands and going to hospital board meetings in a little pickup truck, she tidying up their house with all the living room pictures of their grandchildren ("We could do with a few more grandchildren, but you know, daughters-in-law these days have their minds set on a different career"). And Mrs. Clark always kept a radio on to catch all the latest news. "We seem to have so many problems without solutions," she said, "but I don't want to miss any excitement."

Her husband added, "I could miss some of it." One of their sons even suggested they get a new appliance. "Joe has this idea that we should get modern and get a dishwasher," said Mrs. Clark. "I was afraid they'd give us one for Christmas. Last year they gave us a microwave oven. I think Charles used it once or twice, but I haven't. I'm not used to it, and I need directions just to open the door. So we listen to all their talk, and then we go our own way."

One year they went on a vacation to Europe, which they enjoyed. "We were just folks there," Mrs. Clark said. "Our name is so wonderfully common no one recognized us."

But they found they could not do without their life in their little home on the Macleod Trail. "I can never understand," said Mr. Clark, "why some people wear themselves to pieces in the city to earn enough money to go back home again where they came from." The elderly Mr. Clark never left where he came from. And when it was time to go forever, the old pioneer died upstairs in the same old bedroom where he had been born. His sons, Joe and Peter, had been born there, too. But when they got the news about their father, Peter was in Calgary, and Joe, the former prime minister, was in Ottawa, leading their new lives. And one more piece of Canada's past was gone.

There is a calming comfort and a crushing oppression to the routine of life in Canada's resource towns. They are scattered all across Canada. And there are thousands of men like Reggie Bouffard who have spent most of their lives pulling things from the ground for employers in distant places. One day many years ago a youthful Mr. Bouffard came home from his Quebec school to learn that his thirty-three-year-old father had died around the 1,000-foot level of the asbestos mine down the street in Thetford Mines. A rock the size of a truck had fallen from the ceiling. A few days later a teenaged Mr. Bouffard dutifully honored the request of his impoverished mother: He left school and went to work in the mines. "To get the money," he recalled, "you need to work, no?" More than three decades later he is still there.

Ever since the nineteenth century, when residents of northeastern

Quebec found the fuzzy fibers in the ground and began weaving them into clothing, asbestos has been the economic focus of Thetford (pronounced TET-ferd), a community of 28,595, where 27,870 speak French and just about everyone has something to do with the area's many mines. Here sons like Reggie Bouffard and Denis Lessard grow up to follow fathers and grandfathers into the pits and the shafts. There they work their long hours in the dusty darkness for the honest paycheck and the vacation in Maine or at the lake. They blast the rock loose, carry it, crush it, and haul the refuse and pebbles to man-made mountain ranges of tailings that sprawl in most directions. They sort the little asbestos fibers into ninety-five grades, bag them, and load them on trucks and ships bound for unpronounceable foreign sites. And the work brings in around $650 million a year to Canada.

There are strikes, at times bitter ones. There are also promotions and raises and weddings. Some try, halfheartedly after some large layoffs, to break away and find work elsewhere. But the relatives mail them the newspaper want ads each week, and if there's something, anything, interesting, they and their lonesome wives will usually jump at the chance to come "back home." Some of the men die violently. Some die years later, complaining of the short breath that everyone simply associated with old age. Others like Mr. Lessard have no intention of dying before spending many more years of scotches and beers and songs and laughs and storytelling sessions with their growing grandchildren. That has been the natural order of things for generations. And that is all that Mr. Lessard and Mr. Bouffard have known, although they have had inklings of more somewhere else.

Now past fifty, both men entered the mines as teenagers. Mr. Lessard recalled, before the huge mechanical rock crushers came along, swinging his eight-pound sledgehammer for eight hours, crushing rocks in a dusty shaft where men could not see each other fifteen feet away. "I went in at seventeen like everyone else," said Mr. Lessard in French, "for the job security, for sure. You go in there once, and you can spend a whole life there." They were paid around $26 for their forty-eight-hour workweeks. They could keep $2 for themselves; the rest went to support their parents and siblings. Today, they average $11 an hour with a cost of living bonus every ninety days.

They brought up large families on those wages. The girls likely married miners. Some of the boys went straight into the mines. Others like Luc Bouffard tried to labor elsewhere. He spent several years in a good machinist's job with Pratt & Whitney in Montreal, which is a three-hour drive away for normal drivers, a little over two for Quebec drivers. But after five years his wife missed Thetford too much, and so the young escapees returned to the mine town, and Luc Bouffard became a floor sweeper in the asbestos plant. And he was happy to get that. There is less work around the mines nowadays, the result of soft world markets for the fuzzy fireproof fibers that work so well in brake linings and cement but tend to accumulate in human lungs and stand accused of causing a slow, breathless death by asbestosis.

Elsewhere in the world there are multimillion-dollar liability lawsuits, asbestos cleanups, and bans on its use. The mines and mills are run more cleanly now, too, thanks to powerful vacuums and fans that suck the stuff safely away. Now and then some older friend, usually in his fifties, falls victim to the condition. But asbestos is such a part of the town's life, so familiar, so beneficial for so many families, that it is not a villain. "Why are people so afraid of asbestos?" asked Mr. Bouffard. "No, I was not afraid in the old days. I had no choice to be afraid, you see? You have to earn money to live, no? It's like going to war, but war is dangerous. Maybe you get sick, maybe not. If it comes, it comes. If it doesn't, it doesn't. What the hell, eh? Today you can get afraid of anything. You can get cancer from soup."

The miners look at these deadly diseases the way American city dwellers view muggings. It happens, though not as often as most of the world imagines. Everyone knows someone it has happened to. But no one believes it will happen to him. And the more familiar the subject, the more distant seems the threat. "If I had a better education, I might have gone elsewhere. Who knows?" said Mr. Lessard, who went into the mines after the seventh grade but still taught himself English so he could listen to American radio stations and follow his beloved New York Yankees. "But the biggest problem here is not cancer. It is the shift changes. You work one week of nights, then one week of days, then one week of evenings. That is more dangerous 'cause you get all turned around, don't eat right, sleep right, all mixed up." It is a crushing routine for some, but a familiar one. The sons still follow their fathers, and the wives still produce sons to follow their fathers. The miners note that their mine started in 1950 at the 650-foot level. Today they are mining the 1,000-foot level while crews develop the 1,500-foot level, following the gray, dusty veins of asbestos that run under the region for 100 miles or more. "We know this one deposit is good for twenty-five more years," said one miner. "After that, nobody cares."

"I don't believe in violence because I'm a female and I'm small," said Audrey Jewett. She is living proof that there is no Sergeant Preston of the Yukon. He's a she, and she's only a constable. When I first met Constable Jewett, she was the newest member of the historic Dawson City detachment of the Royal Canadian Mounted Police. She is also a small part of a revolution creeping its way through one of North America's most famous law enforcement agencies and, indeed, through Canada, which has been somewhat less militant than the rebellious United States in its embrace of the women's movement. According to media legends, the Mounties were rugged individualists who roamed the frontiers on horseback, by dogsled, and on foot, always getting their man, always with their trusty dogs, and always wearing their fur hats and red coats. Until 1975 the Mounties were all male. Now headquarters assigns women to the more distant detachments.

Constable Jewett, the daughter and sister of Mounties, arrived in Dawson after three years of undercover and general police work in British Columbia and after a five-day dirt road drive straight north. As one of the five regular members in Dawson City, which has a population of 700 but a summer census of 3,000, she quickly shouldered her share of accidents, break-ins, robberies, distant patrols, and barroom brawls. "I wanted to be in police work," she said, "because I like to help people and I'm used to moving around a lot." Between her father's transfers and her own moves as a cashier, secretary, and nurse trainee, she estimates she lived in thirty different places in her first twenty-four years. "After two years anywhere," she said, "I want to go."

Police work, she said, is not just a job. "You think police even off duty. I especially enjoy working with teenagers. They're the ones whose ideas we've got to change about the law. Just let 'em know we're as human as they are." But many calls do not involve teenagers. The bars themselves handle a lot of fights, but whenever a disturbance call comes in on her shift, Constable Jewett jumps in her four-wheel-drive van and races to the scene through Dawson's pothole-pocked streets, where people park their vehicles wherever they are when they want to stop. "I don't barge in anywhere," she said, "I radio in where I am, what I'm doing. The idea is to break the two parties apart. I find a lot of them, even when drunk, are so stunned to hear a high, squeaky voice come out of a Mountie's uniform they just do what I say. And I rely a lot on the old you're-not-supposed-to-hit-a-lady law."

Of course, progress is not always smooth even with her colleagues. Constable Jewett said she and her fellow female Mounties have encountered resistance from male colleagues. This might include responding slowly to a female Mountie's distress call, not including a woman member when a shift goes for an after-work beer, or conspicuously accompanying a female officer just to "help out." "There is no question females have to prove themselves more than men," she said with a shrug. She has found that a firm statement of her views defused any problems. But there are also moments of real satisfaction in her work. "Once in a while," she said, "someone thanks you for helping."

When Ross Peyton quit the trading post business and built his own hotel in Pangnirtung, up on Baffin Island, the hard part was picking a name for the new establishment. Mr. Peyton finally settled on Peyton Lodge after his wife, Yvonne, rejected his favorite candidate: Peyton Place. Being the only hotel for 200 miles eliminates most need for advertising, Mr. Peyton feels. So there is no hotel sign.

The thirty-two-room establishment is a long two-story structure overlooking a frigid fjord. Mr. Peyton, a tall, bearded veteran of thirty-five Arctic years, built the place himself by hand. First, he sketched his building plans on an old calendar and had a friend in distant Montreal draft the blueprints for government approval in even more distant Yellowknife, the capital of the Northwest Territories. Bureaucrats there amended some details before returning the approved plans. Then Mr. Peyton, who cannot read blueprints, put those funny-colored papers in a drawer somewhere and got out his old calendar. "There's always so much to do in life," he says. "For ninety percent of my days, twenty-four hours are just not enough."

Mr. Peyton limps a little, the result of a fuel oil fire that ignited his nylon trouser legs one day years ago. He is always reading some new maintenance manual or radio guide. "When the year's supply ship leaves in September," he said, "it's gone for one year. And you are on your own." A tiny commercial plane tries to fly in from Frobisher Bay two or three times a week, blizzards, fog, and Arctic winds permitting. Special notices warn fliers: "Pilots, Do Not Buzz Caribou." All the planes are met by Mr. Peyton, who used to work for the Hudson's Bay Company. For years he traded supplies for furs and skins, traveled to outlying camps on medical calls, and opened the trading post at 3:00 A.M. to greet a customer on a dogsled with hot tea and warm talk. Now, though, as Pangnirtung has become less of an outpost and more of a community with a school and a nurse, his work has become less an unpredictable challenge and more a predictable job with a desk, inventories, and, worst of all, set hours.

He opened his own trading post for a while. He became an airfreight handler. Then he decided to build the hotel, in large part because he had never done it. Reservations there are an informal affair, especially if he forgets to write them down or the previous guests decide to stay longer because the plane hasn't arrived for several days.

"Which room do you want?" a clerk asked on my arrival. I chose 5, which was near the bathroom. It measured perhaps twelve feet square, had two single beds under two wall lamps, a couple of hooks and a nude pinup behind the door. It also had a view across the fjord three miles to the mountains. And the price of $75 a day, including meals, didn't seem too bad, considering the alternative. The dining room has no opening or closing hours. Mr. Peyton likes dinner served at six, lunch at noon, and breakfast "before nine." If you are present, you eat. If not, tough.

Table conversation varies with the clientele. During my stay a construction crew discussed the challenges of erecting the first civic incinerator for Pangnirtung (the name means "gathering place of the bull caribou"). The facility eases the disposal burden on nature at the existing dump, where the 900 residents' garbage and sewage are, well, dumped. Since temperatures do not soar much beyond 40, obnoxious olfactory observations have not been a problem. The town's toilet facilities lean to the practical. "Hey, Dad," said my son Christopher our first night, "it's a bucket." The bucket, lined with a plastic bag, is emptied daily, and the bag put outside to freeze. The hotel showers were clean and simple, and someone usually leaves some soap.

"Once they're up here in the Arctic," Mr. Peyton said, "people seem to put up with things they'd never stand for down south." His different life scratching out a living like the wolves in the nearby mountains may not leave much time to smell the grass; anyway, nothing taller than moss grows north of Quebec. But the different pace and endless winter nights do leave time for reminiscing about the old days or taking a couple of the town's total fifteen vehicles out on the fjord ice for a slippery race or two. The mail may not go out for a few days if the postmistress, Leesee Komoartok, has the flu again. But in the summer there are overnight fishing expeditions to distant lakes unvisited by humans for many years. "I pushed a pencil in an office for a lot of years," said a fifty-nine-year-old Mr. Petyon early one evening, "and then I built this place and started to live."

I met Jacques Potvin in a huge mud puddle by the public phone on a dirt street in beautiful downtown, pothole-filled Dawson City. We took turns feeding coins into that little black box while dodging the waves made by cars and trucks slowly cruising their way down Dawson's flooded thoroughfares. "Well, yes, I know, but . . . ," he said into the phone. "Yes. Well, how about for just one night then? I could . . . Yes, I see. Well, do you know any other place in town?" Jacques Potvin had come to fabled Dawson in the Yukon Territory to find his fortune in gold. But he could not even find a hotel room.

Mr. Potvin was one of many Canadians I came to know who were, both figuratively and literally, looking for something somewhere somehow in their new country. They were uniformly decent folk, friendly, hardworking, willing to chat. But in these talks, casual and formal, brief and lengthy, I kept coming across a sense of their wanting something else, a striving especially among younger Canadians in the West and North. It wasn't so much dissatisfaction as it was ambition. You would encounter this in cities and suburbs and among the many Canadians who had flowed south to seek their fortune in the United States. But this generation planned on going home to Canada eventually, a crucial difference from previous emigrants. Of course, this wave of energy was not for everyone. Canada, like anywhere, has a considerable cadre of comfort-conscious folk who know how many steps it is to the bus stop each morning, who keep their pencils in the same corners of their desk drawers at work, who go back summer after summer to the same cottages at the lake, and who like things just that way, predictable.

But there is a spreading sense in Canada today of striving. It was the same feeling that while reading countless history and frontier adventure books from a rural Ohio library, I had mentally attached to the motives of American pioneers rocking their rickety way across the vast midwestern prairies 100 years ago. Every day and every chapter, it seemed, saw an encounter with something new and exciting. There was a familiar mild but definite sense of striving in these Canadians I encountered, which over the years I had not routinely associated with their countrymen.

There was a man by the wonderful name of Réal Champagne in northern Quebec. He was a construction foreman, a thirty-seven-year-old pioneer in a hardhat, one of thousands of laborers who wash back and forth across Canada building the mammoth projects that are harnessing the vast wealth and power of Canada's riches. He was working on the $16 billion James Bay hydroelectric project, turning the tundra's lazy La Grande River into a power source for cities as far away as New York, 1,300 miles distant. Some of his colleagues dug 120-foot-deep shafts across swamps to fill with cement for power-line pylons. Others bulldozed frozen earth into 80 miles of dikes to help reroute the flow of two rivers.

Mr. Champagne worked underground in a turbine room, five times the size of a football field, which was carved from solid rock. He had two little girls, age six and seven, back in Montreal and a wife who didn't much like it that her husband was absent forty-eight days out of every sixty. "Sometimes I don't like it either," he said over the tumult of construction 450 feet underground. "My wife and I, we have drifted apart some, yes. But I make good money. And she knows it's not forever." He said the Quebec dams would be his last long job away from home, a claim that his many co-workers said they too had made after the Churchill Falls power development and after having erected a nuclear heavy-water plant in the East. And now there was a lot of talk about pipelines out West, and heavy oil plants.

For his 60-hour weeks, Mr. Champagne sent home $425 after taxes. His room and board were free, as were the regular airplane round trips from work to Montreal. "When I first came here two years ago," he recalled, "there was nothing, just rock. Now I've helped build all this. I've got a nice house down South, and I'm paying it off real quick with these wages. I can pay for all we want. I pay cash, no problem. But it's tough to raise kids this way. *Ce n'est pas* fun." And nothing can pay him for Sundays, the only day he might have off. He used to call his children every

Sunday, but he did so less at the time I knew him. They always asked him when he was coming home.

Mr. Potvin, who had just left home, was twenty-four years old when I met him that day in Dawson. He had never heard the admonition "Go West, young man, go West." But he had done it anyway. After five years of careful consideration he had given up an established job as a carpenter in a small Ontario city. He had sold all his tools to finance his bid for something else. He had bought a bus ticket for a five-day journey from Ottawa across the fascinating wilderness of northern Ontario, through the woods and rocks and out onto the flat prairies, through the windy streets of Winnipeg and out toward the wheat tables of Manitoba and Saskatchewan, and then the scrubby woods before the last big city of Edmonton fell behind in the rearview mirror, to be followed by nearly 1,000 miles of dirt roads with flying stones and darting animals to reach Whitehorse, and then another 300-plus miles of woods and hard dirt road to reach Dawson and the Klondike.

"It's like an old western town," he had said as he stepped off the dusty bus with his small brown bowling bag full of hopes. He had an idea he would stake a claim and mine for gold or help someone else do that and earn enough to start his own operation someday. "I hear there are fifteen thousand claims in those hills," said the bespectacled youth in the lightweight Windbreaker, looking up at the heights above town, "and a few years ago there were only nine hundred. I think I should have come out here then."

Then he slowly walked off down the old wooden sidewalk, passing, as he went, an old man going the other way. He was Fred Whitehead, dressed in a flannel shirt, unpressed work pants, and a floppy-brimmed hat shading a face with the lines that come with eighty-eight years. Nearly three-quarters of a century after he had started the same kind of search as Mr. Potvin, Mr. Whitehead reminisced about what it had cost him: all his savings, all his earnings, all his life. "I just keep looking around," said the old prospector, "and someday somehow I'll find something." Canada was forty-three years old when a teenaged Mr. Whitehead started his wanderings. He took the river steamboat into Dawson at first; the road wasn't built until the mid-fifties.

His strength was less now, he said, and the long bush treks in search of a future were for the younger prospectors like the newly arrived Mr.

Potvin. "It can't hurt to try," said the young man. "If there's no gold for me, well, at least I can tell myself I tried." While up on the hillside there, a Vancouver actor named Tom Byrne stood on the porch of an old cabin to build his career by re-creating the bygone days for an audience in the yard. Some of them were even listening as Mr. Byrne, dressed in a western hat, soiled white shirt and black string tie, and old woolen trousers with suspenders, gently set himself down in a creaking chair and talked about "himself," someone named Robert Service.

He was a British immigrant, Robert Service was, who wandered across Canada and ended up in Dawson less than a century ago. He worked by day as a bank teller so he could spend the long, cold nights in this very cabin with his dog, writing verse about his new land. As Mr. Byrne talked, weaving the country's history into the man's writing, the spell began to deepen in the yard. To help maintain the atmosphere, Dawson authorities prohibit vehicular traffic on that street during the recitations. As the sun edged behind the hill and the new summer night settled on the old ground, Mr. Byrne talked of the winters, the fights, the struggles and deaths, and the humor that went on all around.

When he was done, he nodded, picked up his old book, and shuffled back into the cabin. The spectators applauded and went on their own way. Mr. Byrne, the modern-day Mr. Service, emerged soon to mount an old-fashioned bicycle and ride off to dinner. What was he doing putting on a one-man show two and three times a day near the Arctic Circle so far from home and often before an audience that could be counted on one hand? He wanted to see his country, he said, so he learns an area's culture, designs an act, and works his way there and back. What had he learned about his country? I asked him. He opened his Robert Service book to "The Spell of the Yukon" and began to read:

> *It grips you like some kinds of sinning;*
> *It twists you from foe to a friend;*
> *It seems it's been since the beginning;*
> *It seems it will be to the end.*

Most Americans probably know some Canadians, though they may not know them as Canadians. Americans know, or think they know, that the Canadian people have something to do with the British monarch and that they export many natural resources. But other products and people of Canada have had far more impact, though much less fame as Canadian-made. Anthony Burgess, the British author, once put his finger, perhaps inadvertently, on a key point about famous Canadians. "John Kenneth Galbraith," he said, "and Marshall McLuhan are the two greatest modern Canadians the United States has produced." It has often been true, especially to and for Canadians, that though famous in their own country, they did not really ever attain true fame until they had become widely known in the United States, where their fans or followers ignored their Canadianness. Then, by some perverse twist of the psyche, Canadians back home finally accepted them as worthy of note. In fact, their international fame might even be the signal back home for some to start tearing down the new star through some kind of "Venus envy."

This can still happen, with authors, for example, when the message of a writer of the caliber of Margaret Atwood will ignite banks of positive reviews in American and British journals, while her critics back home take a savage, often catty road. It is almost as if some self-destructive strain in the Canadian mind has forced achievers to prove themselves in a bigger arena, to seek their success abroad, and then once the native son or daughter has done this, his or her countrymen deflate the success: Oh, sure, he did that, but he had to go to another country to do it. There is something in the old Canadian mind that doesn't like success—at least the other fellow's. But this has begun to change in some areas—business, for instance, and show business. Dave Broadfoot is one example, a world-class comedian with the straight face of a tall accountant who has consciously chosen to build his career solely before Canadian audiences as a perceptive stand-up comic and as a member of the Royal Canadian Air Farce radio and TV troupe.

Until now it has always been the Canadians who complained about being culturally overwhelmed by their southern neighbor. But here it might be equally revealing for Americans—and perhaps a few Canadians —to realize how important Canadians have become in so many facets of everyday United States life, without seeming to be Canadians. For starters, John Kenneth Galbraith—Spike to his buddies near the family farm in Ontario—has deeply affected American thought for decades through his economic and political writings, his participation in shaping the Kennedy administration's New Frontier and his government war work, his representation of his adopted country as ambassador to India and as a chief political antagonist for William F. Buckley, Jr.

Another side of the political arena has Professor Robert Mundell, the son of a Canadian sergeant major from Kingston, Ontario, who became the pipe-smoking Canadian economist widely considered the prophet of the supply-side economics that was a policy cornerstone of Ronald Reagan's early years as President. There is, too, the late Marshall McLuhan, the tall, lanky University of Toronto phenomenon best remembered for his controversial thought that the predominant medium of an age largely shapes the thought of that age. From his couch in a coach house near the university's downtown campus, Mr. McLuhan dictated the complex thoughts and observations best boiled down into the famous aphorism "The medium is the message."

When the Royal Swedish Academy of Sciences awarded its 1983 Nobel Prize in chemistry, it looked as though the United States had won again. Henry Taube of Stanford University, "one of the most creative contemporary workers in inorganic chemistry," was the winner. But Professor Taube is a Canadian, one of many who could not find work in his homeland in the early post-Depression years and so drifted south to build a career in "the States." Canada even has an effect on non-Canadians: Toronto's York University provided the necessary job-in-exile for a Greek refugee named Andreas Papandreou, who then went on to become his country's prime minister. And there is Dr. Joseph B. MacInnis, Canada's version of Jacques Cousteau, who has led many missions to explore the creatures and the waters and the artifacts of Canada's frozen northern seas and then returned to rivet American and Canadian audiences with his tales of adventure and natural wonders.

In letters, Canadians have appeared on virtually all American literary fronts: Mordecai Richler, Morley Callaghan, Paul Erdman, Arthur Hailey, and Saul Bellow, not to mention Will Durant and Jack Kerouac, the son of French-Canadians whose literary journeys on the road chronicled the lives of the fifties' beat generation. Kenneth Millar grew up from an impoverished childhood to become better known as Ross Macdonald, the mystery writer. William Stephenson was not a writer. He was, instead, a master spy, the subject later of *A Man Called Intrepid*, who organized the West's intelligence defenses during World War II. These activities included helping form the Americans' Office of Strategic Services, forerunner to the Central Intelligence Agency, and training Allied agents at a famous Camp X near Oshawa, Ontario, where Mr. Stephenson once failed a would-be secret agent who admitted he could never shoot a man in cold blood. The flunkout's name: Ian Fleming.

Canadian literary characters have been prominent names, too. Mr. Richler's Duddy Kravitz entered the popular vernacular. Farley Mowat's autobiographical Tyler, who went to live with the wolves in the northern wilderness, came to symbolize an ordinary man trying to understand nature and shed the myths of the past in the popular Walt Disney movie *Never Cry Wolf.* And David L. Johnston, the principal, or president, of Montreal's McGill University (whose alums include Zbigniew Brzezinski, former U.S. national security adviser), is better known to Americans as Davey Johnston, captain of the hockey team in that best-selling, tear-stained saga by Erich Segal called *Love Story.* Mr. Segal and Mr. Johnston were real-life dorm mates at Harvard. (Mr. Johnston, once at thirty-eight Canada's youngest university president, is anxious to correct two fictions in the novel: One, he never cried during the big hockey game, no matter what Chapter 3 says. And secondly, "We never lost to Cornell.")

In 1983 the American Booksellers Association looked to its Canadian counterpart organization to hire a new executive director, Bernie Rath. More than a century before a Canadian named Joseph Medill went south to preside over the birth and growth of the *Chicago Tribune* into one of America's most influential daily newspapers. It was Mr. Medill, whose name lives on in Northwestern University's Medill School of Journalism, who spotted an obscure country lawyer in his adopted state of Illinois and through his newspaper and influence pushed the young man to the forefront of the new Republican party and, eventually, into the presidency. His name: Abraham Lincoln. Two other Canadians from Ontario, William Maxwell Aitken and Roy Thomson, also went to foreign lands to earn fame and power as press barons under their titled names, Lord Beaverbrook and Lord Thomson of Fleet. It was Lord Beaverbrook who, as British minister for aircraft production, saw the potential and early on pushed the production of a nimble little plane that would go down in World War II's combat aircraft annals as the aviation savior of Britain, the Spitfire. It was Lord Thomson's son, Kenneth, who would go on to own more than five dozen United States dailies as well as one of the two largest newspaper chains in Canada.

Canadian musicians and singers over the years have run the gamut of styles and popularity from the wild screaming of Paul Anka's fans (and the wild screaming of Frank Sinatra's fans when he sings "My Way," which Mr. Anka wrote) to the nimble dance followers of Guy Lombardo and the quiet appreciation of Percy Faith's fans, with the sharp finger snappings of Oscar Peterson's followers in between. In classical music there have been Maureen Forrester, Teresa Stratas, Jon Vickers, and Toronto's reclusive Glenn Gould, with the snappy precision of the Canadian Brass and the lyrical strains of Liona Boyd's guitar. The American peace movement, among others, has been audience to the folk tunes of Buffy Sainte-Marie, a Canadian Indian who also won an Oscar for the theme song for the film *An Officer and a Gentleman*. Singer Dan Hill's followers reach far beyond his hometown of Don Mills, Ontario. There were the folk singers Ian and Sylvia, the partially-Canadian group the Mamas and the Papas, and the old fifties "doo-wah" groups of the Diamonds and the Crew Cuts of "Sh-boom" and "Why Do Fools Fall in Love?" fame. There have been Gordon Lightfoot, Gisele MacKenzie, British Columbia's Mimi Hines, Don Williams, Hank Snow, and Anne Murray, the Nova Scotian native whose hits include "Snowbird," the name Floridians give to the many Canadians migrating there each winter.

More recently, however, Canada's popular music makers have seemed less a collection of individuals and more of a wave. There were, of course, Martha and the Muffins, Steppenwolf, and balladeer Murray McLauchlan. But Canada's own recording industry was spawning many internationally famous groups such as The Guess Who, Rough Trade, Loverboy, Prism, and Rush. The Canadian Broadcasting Corporation was even moved to do a prime-time miniseries (titled *Heart of Gold* for the song by Neil Young of Winnipeg) examining the phenomenon of Canada's English-language music influence. "My God," admitted John Bruton, the producer, "I didn't realize that all those people were Canadian."

One of the reasons, of course, for the Canadian music boom has been a variety of federal Canadian content regulations, so called because they require that at least 30 percent of all musical radio programming be written and/or performed by Canadians. On television programs the figure is 60 percent. To some people outside Canada such a format can smack too much of government intervention or Big Brother dictating cultural tastes. But within Canada it has helped create a large enough domestic market to support the country's own fleet of music makers and helped reduce the age-old Canadian debate about artists having to leave their homeland to become a success. "If I stayed in Canada," said David Clayton-Thomas, a Canadian member of Blood, Sweat and Tears, "I could have done very well. But nobody would have noticed." Today, however, Mr. McLauchlan can respond, "There ain't no problem except that it's a big country and the cities are far apart and you can't make as much money as you can in the States. The only ones who see it as a problem are the television interviewers and the newspaper editors."

A strange dark horse galloping down the middle of a railroad track heading for an oncoming locomotive. A woman, binoculars to her eyes, staring out of a painting at the viewer himself. Two of the haunting images produced during nearly five decades by Alex Colville, one of the few visual artists to earn household-word ranking in his own land. Of perhaps more fame for art is Yousuf Karsh, the Armenian immigrant to Ottawa who has built a global reputation for expressiveness over a half century of portrait photography of world leaders and celebrities.

Canadians have played major roles in theater and cinema both in front of the camera and behind from Hume Cronyn to Kate Nelligan and from the slapstick silent comedy of Mack Sennett to the wide-eyed innocence of little Fairuza Balk, the nine-year-old Canadian resident selected from hundreds of candidates to become this generation's Dorothy in the new Disney production of *The Wizard of Oz*. Canadians have played good guys (Walter Pidgeon, Raymond Burr, Glenn Ford) and bad guys (Christopher Plummer, John Colicos, Arthur Hill, Douglas Dumbrille), happy guys (Leslie Nielsen, John Candy, Jack Carson, Tom Chong) and sad guys (Ben Blue, Lou Jacobi, and Gene Lockhart as poor Bob Cratchit). There were cowboys (Rod Cameron, Lorne Greene) and Indians (Jay Silverheels, Chief Dan George), prospectors (Walter Huston, father of John [*The Maltese Falcon*] Huston) and presidents (Raymond Massey, Alexander Knox), and even intergalactic space heroes (William Shatner).

America's Sweetheart (Mary Pickford) was really a Canadian, as were Superman's (Margot Kidder), Henry VIII's (Genevieve Bujold), and Andy Hardy's (Ann Rutherford), Andy's sister (Cecilia Parker), and James Bond's forever thwarted admirer, Miss Moneypenny (Lois Maxwell). It was even a Canadian who broke King Kong's heart (Fay Wray). Others included Yvonne De Carlo, Katherine De Mille, Deanna Durbin, Marie Dressler, Susan Clark, Alexis Smith, Ruby Keeler, Norma Shearer, and Colleen Dewhurst. Today Hollywood is even making movies about Canadians (Dorothy Stratten and Terry Fox) by Canadians (Norman [*Fiddler on the Roof, The Russians Are Coming, Jesus Christ Superstar*] Jewison; David [*Scanners, Videodrome*] Cronenberg; Phillip [*The Grey Fox*] Borsos), following in the cinematic footsteps of two Canadian architects of the Dream Factory, Jack Warner and Louis B. Mayer. "We had to leave to be recognized," observed Arthur Hill. "It was an anomaly. If we stayed, we were nobodies. If we went away and became successes, we were resented."

In television Canadians have had particular success in news (Morley Safer, Peter Kent, Peter Jennings, Robert MacNeil), as producers *(Taxi, The Loveboat, Hee Haw, Carter Country,* and *What's Happening?)*, and especially as comedians. Americans have had their eyes and minds fooled by the magic of Winnipeg's Doug Henning. And they have had their pomposity powerfully punched for years by political satirist Mort Sahl. There have been David Steinberg and Rich Little, the little mimic from Ottawa who has skillfully imitated and mocked everyone from movie stars to movie-star presidents.

For years millions of Americans watched NBC's *Saturday Night Live* (produced by Lorne Michaels, a Canadian) for the latest live antics of its comedic cast, including Dan Aykroyd, a Canadian, and Gilda Radner, both graduates of Toronto's dinner-club Second City (a spin-off of the famous Chicago Second City troupe and one that is now inaccurately named since Toronto's rapid recent growth has made it Canada's First City and Chicago's decline made it number three). After a long successful run on Canadian TV, the *SCTV Network,* an ongoing takeoff of television and its phony foibles, reached millions of Americans via NBC and, later, cable TV, making John Candy, Dave Thomas, and Rick Moranis familiar faces to laugh at. Their portrayal of Bob and Doug McKenzie, the toque-topped, beer-drinking, slang-slinging "hoser" brothers from the Great White North, was so popular that Los Angeles Mayor Tom Bradley had to declare a Bob and Doug McKenzie Day for their contributions to "increasing awareness of Canadian culture."

On a subhuman level there is on American cable TV (HBO) the cuddly cast of *Fraggle Rock,* a coproduction of Canadians and Jim Henson of

Muppet fame. Thousands of Americans too have received prizes from Winnipeg's own Monty Halparin, better known to daytime TV viewers as Monty Hall of *Let's Make a Deal.* Then there is Art Linkletter of Moose Jaw, Saskatchewan. And Ottawa's Lorne Greene, a former CBC newscaster who became the ultimate gray-haired TV patriarch whether he was heading the Cartwright family on *Bonanza* or shepherding a lost civilization to a new life aboard *Battlestar Galactica.*

In the world of popular culture, Canadians now hold their share of earthshaking honors that are perhaps less important for their place in world history than for what they show of a world's increasing awareness of an emerging Canada—and an emerging Canadian willingness and confidence to compete in a variety of international arenas. Karen Dianne Baldwin became Canada's first Miss Universe in 1982. Newfoundland's Shannon Tweed was revealed as a Playmate of the Year. The Marvel comics group launched a new series of comic books by John Byrne, a Canadian, called *Alpha Flight* with a number of superheroes, including Snowbird and Northstar, aimed at a Canadian market. Calgary's Roy Thoreson won the world whistling championship again, while Alfred Sung's cool, crisply sophisticated look was adorning fashion-conscious women all over North America.

Canadian athletes, until recent years, enjoyed only modest successes. For a long while tough, really tough competition was not an integral part of everyone's life. Oh, it occurred at times—in fact, the worst-behaved Little League fathers I've ever encountered are in Toronto—but it wasn't the day in, day out kind of do-your-best, girls-against-the-boys, this-side-of-the-room-against-that-side kind of competition so deeply bred into so many other nationalities. It was more of a have-a-good-time, it's-up-to-you kind of competition, at least outside the hockey rinks that every city erects in parks every winter.

That attitude still prevails in some schools; high school football games in my Toronto neighborhood were often played during the lunch hour and seemed to rouse little interest among students. But elsewhere spirits are rising along with the demand for excellence and the attempts for it. With government financial help, Canada's downhill skiers flashed onto the international scene, renowned for their reckless downhill abandon. Then they got coaches who told them they could win, a jarring thought in many Canadian minds. Then they started to win. And in March 1982 Canada's

Steve Podborski became the first North American to win the men's World Cup downhill ski championship. (It had been a long time since 1947, when Canada's Barbara Ann Scott waltzed her way to the first figure-skating crown ever won by a North American.) The Canadians came on in the 1984 Winter Olympics, too, in speed skating, men's figure skating, skiing, and hockey, being the first in 1984 to puncture the Americans' dreams of repeating their miraculous Olympic gold hockey win of 1980 in Lake Placid.

"Canadian kids in general are spoiled rotten, given too much for little or nothing, so they have no incentive to get out and hustle on the cut-throat international scene. Better to stay home and be top dog against other mediocrities. It's not even a fear of failure. They simply don't want to work that hard. They are content to practice what they know, rather than concentrating on improving weaknesses and adding new skills."[4] That analysis of the Canadian youth tennis scene was made by *Racquets Canada* in 1978 as Josef Brabenec, a Czechoslovakian émigré coach who helped set the scene in his homeland for the rise of the likes of Martina Navratilova, pursued his personal construction of a national tennis program to make Canada a winner. This involved, among many things, creating adequate pressure and competition and support at home so that Canadian parents wouldn't steer their children into the usual pattern: to win an athletic scholarship to a U.S. college, financial assistance not available in Canada. As one result, Glenn Michibata, one of Coach Brabenec's protégés, is now ranked among the world's top seventy-five male players. Carling Bassett, even as a teenager, has climbed into the world's top twenty female players.

More than a half dozen Canadians, including Cathy Sherk, hold cards to play on the Ladies Professional Golf Association tour while Jim Nelford rises on the men's circuit. At times both Canadian major league baseball teams, the Toronto Blue Jays and the Montreal Expos, have led their respective divisions. Susan Nattrass of Edmonton regularly wins the world trapshooting championship. Terry Fox, the twenty-two-year-old one-legged cancer victim, set an example for millions with his courage and determination, running 3,339 miles across Canada to raise money for cancer research before falling victim to the disease. His achievements, which sparked an outpouring of pride, emotion, and money in a country short on heroes, also earned him a spot in the *Guinness Book of World*

Records for having raised the most money on a charity run or walk—more than $24.7 million.

Wayne Gretzky, the boy wonder scorer of hockey goals, earned millions, too, on the way to a series of National Hockey League records. "Hi, Wayne," said my son Spencer, then seven, from his seat on one airplane flight with me.

. "Hi," said the international hockey hero passing in the aisle, "how are you doing?" Minutes later the same smiling face showed up by our seats again to invite Spencer to sit in the back with the rest of the Edmonton Oilers and to offer the little boy a color autographed photo of No. 99. "I don't know if you might want this," he said.

There have been other Canadian athletes of note: Gordie Howe, Bobby Hull, Bobby Orr, and Ken Dryden, among many in hockey; heavyweight boxer George Chuvalo; race car driver Gilles Villeneuve; pitcher Ferguson Jenkins; jockey Ron Turcotte; and football placekickers Roy Gerela and Ed Murray, a British Columbia native playing for the Detroit Lions, whose last-second boot in one all-star game led to my favorite Canadian headline: B.C. KICKER WINS PRO BOWL. While a growing number of Canadian football players were signed by American teams, a steady stream of Americans such as Joe Theismann played first for professional Canadian football teams. (Even Pete Rozelle, commissioner of the National Football League, drafted a Canadian named Carrie to be his wife.) And in 1983 a four-legged Canadian, Sunny's Halo, followed in the footsteps of Northern Dancer to come south and win the prestigious Kentucky Derby.

Canadians have not done spectacularly in professional basketball in recent times, although the National Basketball Association is considering expanding to Toronto. Basketball as a winter sport must compete with hockey for fans and players in Canada. All this is ironic since basketball was invented in 1891 by a Canadian, Dr. James Naismith, who was seeking a safe, energetic game to replace boring calisthenics. Originally there were nine players on a side and the target was a peach bushel basket nailed to a gym's balcony railing. But this was too many players, and the basket's placement let fans reach in to deflect the ball.

Basketball, first played at a YMCA in Springfield, Massachusetts, has enjoyed its greatest popularity in the United States. But there have been many other successful Canadian inventions too. Sandford Fleming was not a basketball or hockey star. He was a Canadian railroad engineer who invented standard time for the world. On November 17, 1883, the day before the world went on standard time for the first time, the clocks of every town were set according to the sun's position there. Thus, at noon in Toronto it was 12:25 in Montreal, 12:08 in Belleville, Ontario, and 11:58 in Hamilton. There were 100 similar time standards in the United States alone. That was fine when travel was by horse, a few minutes not mattering much in a day's ride. But it meant chaos in an era of steam trains, trying to keep to a master schedule. So over considerable opposition to fooling with God's time, Mr. Fleming, the Scottish immigrant later to become Sir Sandford, divided the world into twenty-four time zones, each 15 degrees of longitude wide. Then he began the even harder task of lobbying world governments to agree to set all their clocks on the hour at the same moment. With Scottish tenacity, the red-bearded Canadian engineer succeeded most everywhere, except on the island of Newfoundland, for instance, which later became a part of Canada but to this day insists on setting its clocks one-half hour off standard time. Sir Sandford went on to tackle easier tasks, building his country's first transcontinental railroad and even designing its first postage stamp.

Alexander Graham Bell was not born in Canada either; he was another Scottish immigrant, who died in Canada in 1922 after inventing the telephone and teaching the deaf "visible speech," his father's invention. He also made the world's first long-distance phone call, and in his honor today Canadians have become one of the world's premier champions of chat in terms of phone calls made.

The robot arm in the American space shuttle is Canadian, as was the world's first commercial communications satellite system. A Canadian company also developed the variable pitch propeller. Canadians bred the first Newfoundland dog, and the new Wei T'o method of treating books to preserve their pages for centuries. While Americans and Japanese were perfecting the copying machine, Canadians came up with a paper treatment that renders the page virtually uncopyable; it is a big item among newsletter publishers. In 1908 a Canadian named Peter L. Robertson invented the Robertson screwdriver and screw, which has a square hole in the screw head and a matching screwdriver. The world beyond Canada may not have felt the need for yet another funny-shaped screwdriver to pinion things, but Robertson advocates claim it provides greater torque turning power, cannot slip, and requires only one hand. They also require many different-size Robertson screwdrivers, which is good for the Canadian screwdriver industry but bad for anyone like me outside Canada whose broken washing machine is assembled with these unique little Robertson fellows.

In food, Canadians have invented Pablum (at Toronto's Hospital for Sick Children), the banana split (Alfred J. Russell), the sweet McIntosh apple (John McIntosh himself), the chocolate bar (reputedly by A. D. Ganong), and Canada Dry, the pale nonalcoholic imitation of champagne that J. J. McLaughlin thought up on a turn-of-the-century trip to France. It took him seven years to come up with the right formula. Orange Crush was a Canadian drink, too, until Procter & Gamble bought its American operations. All this might make some interesting cards in the popular board game of Trivial Pursuit, which was invented in a Montreal kitchen in 1979 by two Canadian journalists, Chris Haney and Scott Abbott, and sells at a remarkably Canadian price of $38.

Canadians have also pioneered in medicine, having discovered insulin (Dr. Frederick Banting and Charles Best). They are also pursuing broad areas of research from the detection and treatment of cancer and anorexia nervosa to heart disease and the side effects of radiation therapy. Canadian researchers are in the final testing stages of a vaccine for infants against bacterial meningitis. There have also been advances in implanting artificial joints and curing spinal deformities.

Solving the complex puzzle of cancer and other maladies may prove to come easier than solving some of Canada's other internal problems. But after 115 years of false starts, fruitless talks, and depressing frustrations, Canada in 1982 finally got its own Constitution. Until then it had existed under an act of the British Parliament, the British North America Act, which first established Canada and required the demeaning legislative approval of another country before Canada could take many steps.[5] The stumbling block, as it often is in Canada, was the rule requiring unanimity: All the provinces and the federal government would have to agree on the final document to patriate the Canadian Constitution, not an easy task, as the Royal Canadian Air Farce comedy group pointed up in a hypothetical conversation between Canadian officials.

"Really," said one provincial authority to his federal counterpart, "your attitude is childish and immature."

"It is not."

"It is so."

"It is not."

The politicians got around the unanimity roadblock by ignoring tradition and approving the package, with all the provinces but Quebec in agreement. But to form a Canadian-style compromise, they also wrote in provisions allowing up to three provinces to opt out of certain provisions if they specifically pass their own laws to the contrary and renew them every five years.

The new Constitution and accompanying Charter of Rights and Freedoms enshrined on parchment over Queen Elizabeth's signature many of the democratic rights that Canadians thought they had in full already, although a look at some Canadian history destroys that hopeful myth. In 1937, for instance, the Alberta legislature passed a bill requiring newspapers to reveal their sources and to publish without charge "information" supplied by the government. A 1950's Quebec City bylaw prohibited public distribution in the streets of any book, pamphlet, or tract without the permission of the police chief. And as late as 1984 the Ontario Censor Board, not without controversy, could still legally censor without specific criteria all films shown in that province. It was one sign of the changes creeping through Canadian society finally as a result of the new documents that in the same year the Ontario court of appeal ruled that the censors were operating illegally, although the board could still operate pending appeal. The Canadian Constitution writers also felt the need to write a provision specifically allowing Canadians to move between provinces and find work subject only to the same rules governing work and social welfare eligibility as that province's existing residents.

It was also one measure of the differences between Canadian and American societies that their respective documents had definitely democratic but definitely different tones. The Americans' guarantees the right to "life, liberty, and the pursuit of happiness." The Canadians' guarantees the pursuit of "life, liberty and security of the person." American officials take their oath of office to God and the people; Canadian ministers swear to a foreign monarch, who they claim is theirs, too, and vow eternal secrecy among themselves under severe penalty of law. The limits of Canadian press freedom are tempered by tougher libel laws than in the United States; truth is not an absolute defense. To be sure, there is plenty of carping at officials by Canadian newspapers, but there is relatively less tough scrutiny by reporters. Authorities are not automatically suspect simply by their position. The emphasis is on orderliness. Police can stop cars without probable cause. Pedestrians generally obey traffic lights.

It is appropriate behavior in a country originally populated by thousands of British Loyalists fleeing the chaos of the American Revolution. In Canada the government gave them free land. And students there today learn from history books about the discontented Americans who fomented the revolution against their British sovereign and about some heroes who nonetheless stood firmly loyal to the cause of peace and stability, men of character like Benedict Arnold.[6] A friend, a New Yorker teaching at a Canadian university, confided one day that once or twice a week he felt the need to jaywalk in Canada, just to keep his official defiance level at the proper Yankee pitch. KEEP TORONTO NEAT AND TIDY, litter basket street signs urge the citizens. So they do.

There are, however, other reflections of a country's people—their language and culture, for instance. Canadians speak a variety of tongues. I heard more different ones on the streets of Toronto than I did in Tokyo. There is Inuktitut, of the Inuit, and Slavey, one of many Indian tongues; both are used officially in the Northwest Territories' Assembly. There is French, of course, which is strongest in Quebec and New Brunswick and certain districts around Winnipeg. French is one of the two official languages that must be available in all federal offices and facilities and publications. There is also Newfoundland English, better known affectionately as Newfie. It is a wonderfully rich and evocative tongue with an Irish lilt that can make anyone forget that ocean island's former main claim to international fame, the annual bashing of baby seals out on the sea ice. In Newfie a "bungalow" is a maternity dress, a "fiddler" plays the accordion, "screech" is a local rum, "bazz" is a punch in the face, "blossoms" are big snowflakes, and a "hangashore" is a weak, pitiful person or an idle mischief-maker. I was a "come from away" (or CFA, for short) when I visited that rural province, and several times I hit a "yes-ma'am," a bump in the road.

There are many other tongues in daily use: Chinese, Japanese, Korean, German, Greek, Italian, Portuguese, Vietnamese, Spanish, and a wealth of Caribbean dialects. The language of the vast majority of Canadians, however, is English, although some Americans might accidentally discover enough differences to call it Canadian (pronounced Can-AGE-jen). Canadian English is subject to the conflicting influences of American and British English. It is most often the British spelling ("colour," "neighbour," "defence," "metre") but American slang.

Most of the time to a Yankee's ear Canadian sounds pretty much like American (pronounced MARE-kin). When I returned to Ohio from Canada as a youth, friends instantly knew where I had been (which in Ohio is pronounced "bin" and in Canada is "bean"). The tip-off for Americans is usually the "ou" as in "out" or "house" or "outhouse." An American tends more to "howse," while a Canadian is more of a "whuse" sound. "Again" in Canada is "ah-GAIN." There is also the Canadians' favorite expression, "eh?," which is always pronounced with a question mark and turns statements into interrogatives as in "Going to the store, eh?" I find that Canadian sound much more useful than, say, a Robertson screwdriver.

Americans are much better talkers than they are listeners. So they often miss the many other differences in Canadian (and in Canada, too, for that matter). In the United States it's a "ki-LOM-eter," in Canada it's a "KILL-oh-meter." In Canada "process" comes out "PROH-cess" rather than "PRAH-cess." "Khaki" is more "KAR-key" than "KACK-ey," "lieutenant" becomes "LEF-tenant," "author" has a New England "AH-ther" sound, "Toronto" becomes "TRAH-nah." And "Montreal" to English-speaking Canadians is "MUHN-tree-all" instead of the Americans' "MAHN-tree-all." (To the French, of course, it's "mohn-ree-al." But all three are nice places.)

In Canadian, "schedule" is "SHED-ual," a "policeman" is a "constable," "electricity" is "hydro," and a "bum" has nothing to do with a roadside hobo (it's your "derriere"). In American, the words "shown" and "shone" sound alike, but in Canadian the past tense of "shine" is pronounced "shawn." The Royal Bank once published a pamphlet that fondly advised Canadians how to spot Americans. "Americans are those persons you meet who speak English with a slightly different accent from yours, who say faucet instead of tap and frosting instead of icing, who don't put vinegar on their french fries and who like their beer weak, their cigarettes strong and their tea ice-cold."[7] To my ear the most jarring difference in Canadian was its frequent dropping of the word "the." Nobody is ever hospitalized in Canada. They are "in hospital." And in many uses, "Today, Montreal Expos play Cincinnati Reds in a night game," instead of *the* Montreal Expos play *the* Cincinnati Reds, etc.

To see how Canadians perceive the language differences, I once spent an afternoon comparing the new *Canadian Dictionary for Children* to its U.S. parent book, the *Macmillan Dictionary for Children.* To save publishing costs, the Canadian publisher used 60 percent of the same pages, but on the rest Canadian editors made revealing changes for their countrymen. The United States, for instance, was redefined as "a country that is mainly in North America." All the states were deleted. On an illustration to accompany the definition of "dirigible" the Canadians cut off a tiny American marking. They added a small maple leaf flag to a picture of children wearing a knapsack. In the drawing for "salute," a Mountie was substituted for an American sailor. Toronto's distinctive skyline replaced Manhattan's, and Paul Revere's monument was removed for one of Sir John A. Macdonald, Canada's first prime minister.

The picture of a mule was dropped in favor of mukluk (an animal-skin boot of Canada's northern peoples). "Cariole" (a light sleigh pulled by horses or dogs) was squeezed in between "caribou" and "carnation." The definition for "hockey," Canada's national sport, remains the same, except the Canadian illustration shows Canadian teams and players wearing protective helmets. The Canadian definition of "confederacy" contains no capital letter and no reference to the American South or Civil War. Certain standard Canadian abbreviations were included such as CBC (Canadian Broadcasting Corporation), CPR (Canadian Pacific Railway), and MPP (Member of Provincial Parliament). Many American football references were dropped, and the Canadian editors felt the need to add another meaning to "charging" (an illegal move in hockey).

Other changes were more subtle. For example, many references to "patriots" in the American dictionary were deleted in the Canadian version. In general, English-speaking Canadians find the word slightly jarring, in part because many have a greater sense of regional loyalty than national patriotism and also because such outward protestations of feelings as patriotism and loud bragging are traits Canadians associate more with Americans, not with their own understated selves. But studies have shown that at least in one area the two languages are moving closer together, disregarding any rules or dictionaries. Surveys of adult Canadians have found almost all pronounce the last letter of the alphabet as "zed," the traditional pronunciation in Canada and the one my grandmother, the one-room schoolmarm, diligently tried to drill into my head (rhymes with "zed"). Indeed, "zed" is given on the next to last page of the children's Canadian dictionary. But of those Canadians studied under twelve, fully half pronounced the letter the American-style "zee." Many attribute the change to *Sesame Street,* the fast-paced preschool educational television program that is not listed in either dictionary.

With its location, cultural heritage, and ethnic and linguistic diversity, Canada, it has been said, could have had French culture, American efficiency, and British government. Instead, it got American culture, British efficiency, and French government. It is perfectly symbolic of Canada's historic predicament that anyone, especially English-speaking Canadians, thought they should have anybody's anything. What's the matter with a Canadian culture, Canadian efficiency, and Canadian government consisting of pieces from all over assembled into unique forms? They might not be the best in all three yet or ever, but what country is, especially at the tender age—for a country—of 118? And so what? Characteristics of Canada's English-speaking culture, government, and efficiency might seem familiar to other nationalities, but then few things today are unique. And until recently most Canadians were not consumed by any drive for originality or excellence. Many still aren't. Adequate has been fine, thank you very much. Try too hard, and you might turn into one of those pushy Yanks. You also might, God forbid, fail.

Canada's French-speaking citizens endured generations of discrimination, but because of their language and their heritage, they have always enjoyed a very lively and original culture. Because of their underdog position as the only substantial French-speaking population in North America, they had no problem seeing their uniqueness and value in a sea of surrounding sameness. English-speaking Canadians, uptight, wondering, worrying, looking for nuances that made them special in the same sea, had no such benefit.

One of the most exciting aspects of life in Canada for me was the mounting clash between the old values and the new Canada, the little sprouts of excellence shooting up through the melting snowbanks. English-speaking Canadians often talk about being misunderstood or overlooked by others. But I think the "others," the outside visitors and immigrants, often had a sharper focus on Canada than Canadians. Theirs was cluttered with ingrained inhibitions. One such immigrant, John Hirsch of the Stratford Festival, told me of a bright twenty-five-year-old Canadian he had interviewed and was prepared to hire as an assistant director at the internationally renowned Shakespearean festival. It was part of the adopted Canadian's plan to nurture a generation of Canada's own theatrical directors rather than always hire foreigners with glowing reputations. Mr. Hirsch made the job offer. The young man said, however, that before accepting, he would have to go over Mr. Hirsch's views of the summer's plays to make sure that their artistic impressions, the language, and their views of the settings matched. The job offer was immediately rescinded.

"My God," Mr. Hirsch said later, "just having the credit of six months' assistant directing at Stratford is enough. I've got two hundred letters on file from Americans who want to do anything here. They're not afraid of failing or trying. They're anxious and eager to learn. That young Canadian man was really copping out. He was setting up all kinds of conditions and rules to assure he wouldn't get the job. You see, that protects him against failing once he did get it. He won't get the experience now. But more important for him, he didn't have to try and then face the possibility of failure. Now he can put that failure off on other causes, on the other guy's not picking him. Canada has been just like that as a country." The difference in Canada today is that not too long ago no one would have noticed that young man's sad little psychological game. It seemed normal. And even today, I believe, no one would have noticed it without the fresh blood, fresh energy, and fresh eyes of a new breed of Canadians. It's like asking a fish what water tastes like; if it's never been out of its own native stream, even the foulest liquid there could seem normal. It takes others to say initially that there is another way, or it takes mature Canadians. And a growing number of Canadians seem to have picked up on that lesson.

For decades the Canadian artistic and literary worlds were known for their domination by British and American influences. As James Bacque of Toronto eloquently put it in a letter to the *Globe and Mail* a few years ago, "The trap for journalists in this country is the same as for many others. Lacking real standards or independence, in envy they emulate Americans who may be better or worse, but are certainly richer and momentarily more famous. So their idea of leading Canadians is to follow

Americans, their idea of originality is to be first to copy Americans, their knowledge of Canada is the United States divided by 10. What they desperately want is to be invited to The Big Apple in New York or Washington or Los Angeles, and the pity of it is for them, who needs more second-rate Americans?"

English-speaking Canadians have often written and drawn and acted and painted and rhymed the way they thought others did. It was an original imitation. As Peter C. Newman, an editor, nationalist, and writer, put it once in a conversation, "We have tended too often to judge ourselves by imported values. That is changing, but it is an established way." The result was a culture that for a long while largely aped others. It imitated somebody else's idea of culture because after all, what is there of special interest about Canada or Canadians? Canadians didn't know. No non-Canadian could ever tell them (Canadians wouldn't have listened anyway). And nobody elsewhere would ever know about the Canadian experience unless Canadians told them about it. Canadians, late to the assembly of an industrialized nation and its culture, were too busy telling the globe what the world had already gone through. To turn Mr. Bacque's statement around, who needs or wants a second-rate version of what they already know? Hugh MacLennan, the Canadian novelist and one of the first to break out of this old genre, once put it succinctly, referring to the old Canadian literary scene, "Boy meets girl in Winnipeg, and who cares?" Even Canadians didn't seem to care much. Bookstores, for instance, segregated Canadian books into a separate category. There were real books listed alphabetically, and then there were Canadian books in the back, patronizingly lumped together, where the owner could claim he was promoting them. But the real message, of course, was that there were the big leagues out front, and then there were Canadian books, the specialized kind customers associated with textbooks.

One of the main problems, of course, was the Canadians' strong sense of being surrounded—French-Canadians by the English-Canadians and English-Canadians by Americans. It is a basic predicament for Canadian culture. How can it express and protect its "Canadianness" in the onslaught of mass American culture from across the border—magazines, newspapers, books, movies, television, radio, styles in clothes and hairdos, cars, and politics—that threatens cultural asphyxiation? It has led in many past ways to what Robert Fulford, one of Canada's most perceptive critics, writers, and the editor of *Saturday Night* magazine, has called "Accidental American Imperialism." This is the adoption by Canadians of American ways that the Yanks never intended to export. They just spill into Canada naturally like air and water pollution that recognizes no political boundaries. "They are a gaudy bunch," a publication of the Royal Bank once wrote of Canada's American neighbors, trying to decipher their actions, who are "much given to travel, colourful clothing, gadgets, hand-held foods, and striking metaphoric variations on the English language. They prefer first to second names, and, in conversation, they seem to use yours in every sentence or two. They play and watch a bewildering variety of games. They belong to clubs and lodges named after animals. They talk to strangers on street corners and at lunch counters. As they themselves would put it, they're friendly as hell."

And the Yanks aren't the only threat. When CFCT, the radio station in Tuktoyaktuk in the far northern Northwest Territories, fell on financially troubled times a few years ago, it broadcast a general plea for funds to keep its seven hours of daily local programs in English and Inuktitut on the air. The only response came from Radio Moscow next door, which offered to supply endless hours of English-language programs free. The offer was politely declined after it had sparked embarrassed assistance from several southern Canadian sources.

But all this is changing. And the signs are abundant. A declining number of Canadian customers seem to associate Canadian works with poor quality in bookstores. "We don't have a British fiction section or an American fiction section," notes Jacui Vannelli of Edmonton's Aspen Books, "so why should we have a Canadian section?" There is a dramatic change, too, noted by *Saturday Night* magazine, a vigilant sentry at the gates to the Canadian identity, in Canadians' attitudes toward flashy advertising and blatant publicity. "Taking out ads in the newspapers to tell people how great you were and other forms of blowing your own horn," the magazine recounted, "were considered if not distasteful at least downright un-Canadian. If Canadians did something they thought they should be proud of, they would wait quietly in the corner for the recognition they felt was due them, and if it didn't come, they accepted the neglect as their birthright."[8] The magazine went on to note that this had changed and that now such people "are regarded impatiently as relics of the bad old days when being Canadian meant always having to say you were sorry." As one example, Jack Wetherall, an actor, vowed in one Canadian interview, "Maybe I'll be an actor who can do Shakespeare really well. I believe I can do that now. And if no one's going to give me the opportunity, then I'll damn well go out and do it myself."

Roch Carrier, a leading Quebec playwright and novelist, reminisced a couple of years ago with *Maclean's* magazine: "I remember when my books were first translated [into English]—everybody felt it was a kind of treason, giving my books to the rest of the country. But today everybody wants to be on the other side of the frontier."[9] Now, when Alan Williams, a British actor, says he emigrated to Canada because it is a freer cultural atmosphere, it becomes the main story on the newspaper's entertainment page, and many Canadians nod and believe. "Here," the actor said, "there's a sense of the individual relating directly to the universe while there the individual relates first to his class, then to the universe."[10]

To be sure, Canadian culture has its share of potboilers and talking elevators and movies like *Porky's*, the teenage-boys-peeking-in-the-girls'-shower film epic that earned so much money for its Canadian producers. But like many outside that country, Canadians, who spend more on culture than on spectator sports, recognize Canada's maturing culture as speaking less to one country's parochial life and more to a universal experience. Without being asked, in many ways the world is beating a path to Canada. Toronto is now not only a standard stop on the theater circuit but one where producers seek new works to take elsewhere. The Toronto Film Festival has become prominent, and that city is a standard site for first-run openings. American magazines devote entire issues to Canada. Critics from the United States routinely travel north to sample new musical and dance works or interpretations. Cornell University in Ithaca, New York, with one of hundreds of new Canadian studies programs, holds an eight-month, twenty-six-event festival of Canadian arts. Canadian museums host important exhibitions. Canadian groups tour to standing room only crowds. As Liberace put it, "I've been in show business for thirty years. At last I've arrived—I've been goosed in Toronto."

Although Inuktitut has no word for "art" or "culture" (there being limited time in the northern struggle of life for such apparent "luxuries"), its simple, often crude carvings are being widely accepted as a truly Canadian art form, appearing in New York galleries, Chicago museums, and even on radio advertisements. They were objects that fascinated me, and so I sought out some carvers. For long moments the old man stared at the rock, turning the object around and back and forth, touching the rough surface with his dark, leathery fingers, staring intently at each detail without and within. "I try to sense," Alivuktuk told me through an interpreter, "what kind of spirit is inside trying to get out." Then he went to work.

Within three days the greenish stone had turned into a graceful bird, its beak and body aimed at the heavens. Finally, after all those centuries of imprisonment in stone, the bird's spirit had been freed. Inuit carving is more than a cottage industry now, with dozens of native co-ops across the North buying the works in stone, ivory, or bone that can range from a simple snoozing seal or wallowing walrus to complex village scenes with igloos, dog teams, and slain seals awaiting butchering. Always the objects reflect an intimate knowledge by their maker, the keen eye and accurate hand of someone who has watched these creatures, hunted them, and lived with them for a lifetime, someone who knows how a wild bird looks with its head cocked the moment it hears a hunter. Somehow these works, some crude and blocky, others curving and polished, remain appropriately cold to the touch, even in a southern living room. And it often struck me as appropriate, too, that this indigenous form of culture should be among Canada's first to gain international recognition. The Inuit don't feel surrounded. They seem so much a part of their environment. They know who they are.

And Canadians are sensing more of that themselves. Stéphane Vanne, an expert on Quebec's recording industry, noted that that industry began to flourish only when it stopped imitating foreign works and sought its own roots. Michael Snow, a renowned Canadian artist, commented, "There's less looking to elsewhere [in Canadian artistic circles] than there was in the late fifties and sixties." Dave Broadfoot no longer need confine his humor to parochial Canadian jokes ("I admire the accomplishments of the Chinese," he has said, "a people who have produced one billion people and still insist their favorite pastime is Ping-Pong"). Without consciously trying to create any statement about Canada, Dave Thomas and Rick Moranis created Bob and Doug McKenzie. They are seen in Canada as the ultimate dumb Canadian rubes from the North. But, Mr. Thomas noted with amazement, "Americans think they're just funny. And that's sort of comforting in a way."

Nowadays writers and artists in many fields are being inspired by significant new strains of originality and energy in regions across the country. Committees of actors have written innovative dramas to help illuminate a locality, whether it concerns struggles over a coalfield or running a farm or surviving in an urban ghetto. The strongest effects have been felt by authors such as Rudy Wiebe, an Albertan who explores area history for the sort of human drama that speaks to a universal experience with, for instance, Indians with human frailties confronting the pressures of advancing whites with their own set of fears and failings. "Fiction must be precisely rooted in a particular place in a particular people," he said. "What we need most is material that comes out of our own life here." Margaret Atwood's fiction often explores the clash of sexes, for which she sometimes reaps better reviews abroad than at home. Al Purdy, the poet, focuses on the sheer size of the nation, a familiar strain throughout Canadian history, but in a way that those beyond Canada's borders can understand. Joe Fafard, a Saskatchewan sculptor, portrays in clay from his region's past an army of characters full of telling faces and positions. A flock of small publishing houses spring up to provide outlets for more writers.

"It's like a northern flower," said Paul Thompson, who directed Toronto's Théâtre Passe Muraille during some very innovative years. "It bursts out whenever it can and grows hard and fast with lots of color." His players once transformed ten paintings by Gabriel Dumont, a half-Indian rebel of the late 1880's, into a full-length drama. His actors also spent a summer living with a rural family to portray rural life. Canadians also wrote and performed *Billy Bishop Goes to War*, the true story by John Gray and Eric Peterson of one small-town Ontario boy who went on to become World War I's leading Allied air ace. Mike Nichols took that production to New York City.

"Canadian actors were not using their capacity to observe life around them," added Mr. Thompson. "They were modeling themselves on United States plays and actors. So we build our own plays that strike deeper." And it seems to help. Canada's theater world is lively. Quebec has nearly 300 theater companies employing professional actors. Toronto alone has 42 independent companies. In Calgary, downtown workers clutching their sandwich bags vie for limited seats at lunch-hour performances. In London, England, theatergoers can now enjoy the renewed life of the Old Vic, thanks to Ed Mirvish, a Toronto restaurateur who bought and restored the aging British institution.

As usual in Canada, the government is involved. Federal officials have denied work permits for foreign directors, a controversial step that can seem to place political citizenship above artistic ability. But it is the kind of policy, when deftly handled, that can, in fact, encourage the growth of local talent. Stratford's John Hirsch, for instance, was sought out only after a previous festival choice, a Briton, had been denied entry. It is unlikely a non-Canadian would place the same priority that he does on bringing along Canadian talent, just as it is unlikely that Canadian radio stations would support through their record play lists a vibrant Canadian music industry without government interference requiring minimum Canadian music content. In Vancouver the opera even receives federal funding to create an assistant artistic director post for a Canadian. Brick by brick across the country, the cultural construction continues.

In literature—what Canadian novelist Jane Rule, a transplanted American, calls "part of what makes a country not only a place to go but a place to come from"—writing from the northern half of North America is attracting mounting attention outside its homeland. "We've loved [American] novels, films, and popular culture," said Mordecai Richler. "Obviously, for all our complaints, as we come of age, we're realizing we're Americans too. In Canada, there's a tradition evolving at last and it's worth defending. There's more good, honest writing in Canada now than 20 years ago. We should count our blessings."[11] There may seem to be some disagreement. "In this country," Margaret Atwood writes in *True Stories,* her ninth book of poetry, "you can say what you like because no one will listen to you anyway." Miss Atwood later told one British interviewer that Canada "is quite hard on its artists. It does not admire success in the way Americans do: it prefers safe mediocrity, and is threatened by anyone who is successful, especially outside the country." When New Brunswick's Antonine Maillet, an Acadian, won France's prestigious Prix Goncourt in 1978, it was the highest international honor ever won by a Canadian author. Yet it was virtually ignored in Canada's English media. "National disunity is right there before us in operation," noted *Globe and Mail* columnist William Johnson.

Canadian writers have always had to struggle, usually with the land. They began with their accounts of exploration and moved through time to focus on humans coping with the land (Louis Hémon's classic *Maria Chapdelaine*, an astute portrait of one woman's hard frontier life). A principal concern of Farley Mowat is what he has called "the unity of life" on the land. "You destroy any one part of it and you are in a sense destroying part of yourself," he said. By trying to save animals such as the wolf, he argues, man is also trying to save himself. Even in humor, Canadian writers couldn't help thinking of the land. "It was a wild and stormy night on the West Coast of Scotland," Stephen Leacock wrote in "Gertrude the Governess." "This, however, is immaterial to the present story, as the scene is not laid in the West of Scotland." In nonfiction, Mel Hurtig, a noted nationalist publisher, is even preparing a $10-million 1-million-word *Canadian Encyclopedia* of his land, scheduled for publication in the mid-1980's, while Pierre Berton examines Canadian history for popular lessons and Peter C. Newman turns his fascinating and detailed eye on the structure of Canadian business and society to revolutionize that form of reportage in his land.

One of the weak spots of Canadian writing for youngsters, according to Sheila Egoff, an expert, is children's fantasy. "We aren't great on fantasy in this country," she said. "It's the same problem that we have in film; we're better at documentaries. Our own landscape is too large and anonymous for us to feel comfortable with putting names to it."[12]

But starting around the 1920's, Canadian poets began shifting their attention from nature itself to human nature. The works of men such as E. J. Pratt, A. J. M. Smith, and Leo Kennedy went into the cities, becoming less concerned with melodies and more with meanings. Morley Callaghan, one of the first Canadian writers to cut the colonial ties with Britain, plugged his writing into the international scene. Alice Munro writes about life in small Canadian towns but with what a *Time* magazine critic calls "a melodic line that catches at the heart with freshness." David Adams Richards writes hauntingly like William Faulkner about class distinctions in his region, which just happens to be the Miramichi River area of northern New Brunswick. George Woodcock, the writer and editor, once noted that Al Purdy's works "fit Canada like a glove; you can feel the fingers of the land working through his poems." But in many of his newer works Purdy writes of Mexico, Spain, and Soviet Asia, areas well beyond his homeland that have attracted his attention and pen. Irving Layton, too, addresses themes beyond a simple large land, subjects of more moral than geographic concern: "We live in a time when atrocity's the norm and survival the sole merit."

Rudy Wiebe's short stories, plays, and novels, such as *The Scorched Wood People* and *The Temptations of Big Bear*, deal less with the standard good guy, bad guy western theme and more with the human stupidities, misunderstandings, and failings on all sides. Canadian children's literature is enjoying a boom, too. In some years the industry publishes a new, well-received children's book every sixty hours, finally giving the next generation of adults a common Canadian knowledge, common Canadian myths and rhymes and doggerel, and a range of common Canadian childhood experiences within their fertile minds that has not existed on their rugged soil. Even in Canadian movies, such as *Quest for Fire*, an Academy Award-winning caveman saga with no dialogue, and *The Grey Fox*, Phillip Borsos, the young Vancouver director, reveals how comfortable some maturing Canadians have become with some realities of their existence. He shows two railroad tracks converging as a Mountie is forced to cooperate with American authorities to return the old robber, Bill Miner, to prison.[13]

One of the major reasons for all this is definitely the increase in higher education across Canada and higher standards within that education, especially within the last twenty-five years. More Canadian children are learning more at more schools for longer. Herbert Hoover was the last American President to have been educated in a one-room schoolhouse, a necessity at one time on the American prairies. But at a later time, when he was still President and such American institutions were dying off, my grandmother was being hired to run just such a new school in rural Manitoba. She got extra money if she also lit the fire each morning. Such an education was adequate for the work, for the life, for the times of its students in a pretechnology era ruled by seasons, not by satellites. Now, naturally, Canadian education has moved on to new, more modern forms of Canadian design. Just as inexorably Canadian minds have moved on, too. And their culture has begun to reflect precisely that. "Stories create a people," Mr. Wiebe told me one evening. And Canadians are creating their own stories.

"Nations have a way of whispering the inner truth about themselves," Robertson Davies, Canadian man of letters, writes. "No ghosts in Canada? The country which too vigorously asserts its normality and rationality is like a man who declares that he is without imagination; suddenly the ghosts he has denied may overcome him, and then his imaginative flights make poets stare."

Fueled by the energies of its immigrants, the developing values of its native-born, the innate natural richness of its land, and a growing appreciation of its bounty, Canada's imaginations are taking flight in all directions. There is a price to be paid in divisiveness for such determined diversity. But Canadians believe—they must, in order to maintain the national differentiation they feel so strongly—that the sum of their separate parts will be greater and stronger than any motley mélange could be. Robert Fulford, the prominent editor of the monthly *Saturday Night* and one of his land's most stimulating conversationalists, noted not long ago, "My generation of Canadians grew up believing that, if we were very good or very smart, or both, we would someday graduate from Canada." For today's generations of maturing Canadians, such thoughts seem increasingly strange.

THREE

❦❦❦

The
United States
and
Canada

❦❦❦

*We are not in the same boat, but we are pretty much in the
same waters.*

—Former Prime Minister Arthur Meighen, 1937

Cecille Bechard is a Canadian who visits the United States several dozen times a day—when she goes to the refrigerator or to the back door or to make tea, for instance. To read and sleep, she stays in Canada. And she eats there, too, if she sits at the north end of her kitchen table. Mrs. Bechard's home is in Quebec and Maine at the same time. It sits on the United States-Canada border, that 5,524.5-mile-long frontier drawn in 1842 to separate, artificially in most senses, the former British colonies from Britain's major remaining domains in North America.

The line, which was to develop into the longest undefended border in the world, runs from Maine's Quoddy Head State Park across a narrow strait from New Brunswick's Campobello Island Provincial Park down the St. Croix River, through Mrs. Bechard's kitchen wall and across the sink, splitting the salt and pepper shakers, just missing the stove, and passing through the other wall to sever the Nadeau family's clothesline next door before it cuts off the candy counter in Alfred Sirois's general store and heads toward the middle of the St. Lawrence River and down the middle of four of the Great Lakes.

Crossing the prairies, it snips the tip off the runway at the Piney Pinecreek Binational Airport in Minnesota-Manitoba, then divides Sweetgrass, Montana, from Belmore Schultz's restaurant in Coutts, Alberta, before passing into the mountains, through the forests across Virgil Lane's U.S. mail route that dips into Canada a couple of hundred yards to Joe Bush's house and down again to the sea at a Peace Arch, where parents photograph youngsters playing international catch across the frontier. The same border picks up again farther north between Alaska and British Columbia and the Yukon Territory at a series of nameless crossings where the customs agents' dogs frolic back and forth between countries at will and the frontier closes every October for seven months because no one can get there anyway until spring.

Almost anywhere else in the world Mrs. Bechard might need a passport to take a bath. The parents' cameras could be confiscated. And the dogs would be patrolling instead of gamboling. But the United States-Canadian border is a unique place. Officially it separates, or rather tries to separate, two distinct political entities. Faced with some 70 million border crossings every year along a line covering more than one-fifth of the world's circumference, agents on both sides grow weary and often-times rude, perhaps because of the nearly complete futility of their jobs. Occasionally demanding to see a driver's license or scan a car trunk, they all ask the same questions: Where were you born a citizen of what country how long you been away purchase or receive any goods on your trip anything to declare? Realistically, they say, they may catch 10 percent of any illicit traffic.

Unofficially the line has created a unique third country, a special long lineal culture where nationality matters less than personality, where the currency of each country is acceptable in the other, and where bilingual, binational families with American sons and Canadian daughters, pay-checks in two currencies, and pensions from two governments are so common that any visitor needs a scorecard to keep track of the connections. "Around here," said Maine's Ben Talbot, who goes to Canada for golf and Chinese food, "the border is almost invisible."

But the United States-Canadian border also unites the two countries in a strange way. For in many respects, as a result of geography, climate, and economic and family ties, each region of Canada has much more in common with its American counterpart just beyond the customs booth than it does with any other Canadian region. Manitoba wheat farmers, for instance, are concerned about the price of their grain and fertilizers, the amount of rain, and the possibility of the Red River's flooding again come spring, precisely the same concerns as those of North Dakota's farmers. The same holds true for fishermen in New England and the Maritime Provinces, lumbermen in British Columbia and the Pacific Northwest, cattlemen in Alberta and Montana, and auto workers in Detroit and Windsor.

East-West ties in Canada have been historically weak, while the constant tug of North-South bonds has been so strong at times as to threaten Canada's internal unity; British Columbia seriously considered joining the United States before becoming a Canadian province in 1871, when Ottawa promised to build a transcontinental railroad as an inducement. Separatists in western Canada still talk of joining the United States as a realistic alternative, albeit one with an outlook that dims in the face of political realities just outside their meeting rooms.

On the American side there seems little likelihood, either, of a state's secession to join Canada, although in the nation's early days Vermont, geographically coveted by both New York and New Hampshire, once gave the thought consideration. But over the decades millions of Americans themselves have opted to join Canada, and vice versa. More than 6 million immigrants have flowed peacefully between these two countries, one of the largest, and socially smoothest, mass migrations in history.

Each country has provided an accommodating and familiar safety valve for the discontented of the other. The Vietnam era draft dodgers who went to Canadian soil fleeing the reach of distasteful American laws were only following 110 years later in the fleeing footsteps of the South's runaway slaves, whose destination on the Underground Railroad was a British-controlled Canada where slavery had been abolished in 1841. Later nearly 1 million Americans, who had just missed snapping up the free lands on the United States' disappearing western frontier, gushed north at the official invitation of Canada to help populate and farm the less hospitable lands of Alberta. In 1911, when my grandfather took his packhorses from cabin to cabin in Alberta's isolated Peace River country, he found American family after American family. To this day Alberta has a sizable population of Americans—upward of 40,000 by some estimates—and a distinct Yankee "can-do" gambling flavor to its business world that has historically set it apart from its more conservative peers in other provinces.

The southbound flow has contained doctors dissatisfied with Canada's national health policies, nurses recruited by staff-starved American hospitals, and Prohibition rumrunners serving a thirsty market of Americans with Canadian hooch. In the late 1930's lack of opportunity and jobs in Canada, where the Depression lingered longer than in the United States, sent thousands of eager, skilled Canadian job seekers, including my father, scrambling south to start careers and families and to finish lives.

"The meat of the buffalo tastes the same on both sides of the border," said the Sioux chief Sitting Bull, who visited Canada for a spell after annihilating General George Armstrong Custer. James Earl Ray, the assassin of Martin Luther King, Jr., initially hid in Canada. And six months before he shot Abraham Lincoln, John Wilkes Booth was spotted in Montreal, where, over billiards one evening, he told an acquaintance, "I must post myself in Canuck airs, for some of us devils may have to settle here shortly."

To be sure, bilateral relations have not always been amicable. Booth's visit came as Britain, a loyal customer for Confederate cotton, permitted guerrilla raids by southern forces into New England from Canadian soil. The United States has twice invaded Canada, once during the Revolution, which Canadian history books treat as more of a revolt, and once during the War of 1812. That was when the Americans sacked Toronto, a gesture often overlooked in American history books, which focus more on Britain's retaliatory raid that set Washington, D.C., aflame and on pithy quotes from the Battle of Lake Erie.

In more recent times relations have seemed misleadingly peaceful as the people of both lands pursued prosperity and a continental affluence and security unmatched anywhere in the world. These relations have been likened to the neighborhood (in Canada, it's spelled "neighbourhood") problems of a city council that can in a matter of minutes vote to spend millions of dollars on some housing project yet requires two weeks to debate increasing the dog license fee fifty cents because it, like affairs between the two countries, touches the lives and interests of so many more people so closely. "Canada is such a close neighbor and such a good neighbor," said Lyndon Johnson, "that we always have plenty of problems here. They are kind of like the problems in a hometown." President Johnson also had problems with Canadian names, once referring to Prime Minister Lester Pearson as Prime Minister Wilson. It was the kind of momentary mental lapse that is nothing between strangers but excruciatingly embarrassing between friends.

The intimacy of the Canadian-American relationship is so deep and pervasive, so broad and diverse that it defies even the best-organized efforts by governments to control or even to monitor it. Perhaps of equal importance, this intense, unusual closeness is completely taken for granted by those on both sides of the forty-ninth parallel. The unusual thus becomes the norm. It is an assumption that seems to carry with it a continuing chain of built-in misunderstandings, frictions, and misinterpretations. As any married couple knows, assumptions, well grounded in fact though they might be, can be dangerously corrosive to intimate relationships.

More is expected of close relatives than of mere neighbors, and more is resented when these expectations go unmet or are challenged. A United States citizen, for instance, might have little reaction to a move by, say, Mexico to erect a wall along its long border with the United States; in fact, it might well be the Americans who constructed such an edifice. Mexico is, after all, obviously a foreign country with its own foreign language, its own foreign politics, and its own revolution, and it figures directly in the lives and business affairs of a relatively small number of Americans.

But for Canada, which also has its own languages, its own distinct political and judicial systems, and its own history, to throw up such a wall along the same kind of international boundary would be taken far differently throughout the United States. It would seem a gross affront, whichever side erected the wall.

Most Canadians, including my grandparents, grew up believing it was their sacred birthright come bitter winter weather to spend at least a few weeks in Florida or Arizona or Hawaii, the precise location depending on the handiest north–south interstate route or the cheapest southbound charter flights organized by battalions of Canadian travel agents and charter airlines that specialize in selling the sun to their countrymen.

When Canada's dirty snows pile up and the thermometer hasn't climbed past the freezing mark in months, it is a very easy sale to make. At any one time in winter there are about 1 million Canadians in Florida alone, where they are called Snowbirds. They spend more than $1 billion a year there, a fair portion of it purchasing their own condominium units for investment and retirement purposes. Canadians visiting Florida have even formed groups demanding that American merchants there accept Canadian money, the same way Canadian stores almost anywhere routinely accept United States currency, though at an exchange rate that certainly benefits the home team.

Canadian newspapers, which publish reports on road conditions on southbound American highways along with countless travel articles on

American destinations and far fewer on Canadian sites, dominate some Florida newsstands. Prior Smith, an enterprising radio newsman in Toronto, has built up his own network of more than a score of Florida stations that broadcast his six minutes of Canadian news, sports, and stock reports each morning, beginning with chilly weather reports from home. "That's just to make them feel good down there," Mr. Smith told me one blustery February day. Going south to the American sun is important even for Canadians who can't afford to drive the American interstates or fly the American airways south. So Canada's sun merchants invented a ninety-minute simulated trip to the south, offering two fake flights a day from inside a Toronto shopping mall. For $7, pretend passengers get a bogus boarding pass to enter a mock airplane cabin in a real department store. They hear a real recorded pilot's announcements, eat a genuine airline meal, and see a fashion show and travel film on sunny California (true to Ontario's Sunday blue laws, however, there are no pretend departures on the Sabbath).

Conversely, millions of Americans think as much about crossing the border into Canada for a summer vacation as they do of driving across a state line. American travelers spend more than $2.5 billion a year in Canada. Going fishing or skiing in Canada seems completely normal, as normal as, say, visiting Niagara Falls, which is also mostly in Canada. For baseball fans in Buffalo, the closest place to see the New York Yankees play is Canada, against the Toronto Blue Jays. And each home game weekend, busloads of Buffalonians pour into Toronto's lakefront Exhibition Stadium, which is also the loading site for busloads of National Football League fans from Canada who routinely travel to Buffalo Bills home games. Even as far away as Cleveland, the Browns football team feels the need every year to print a reminder on all ticket order forms that payment must be in U.S. funds. As a lifelong fervent Browns fan, I was surprised at the many fellow Browns supporters I encountered in Toronto, 300 miles from Municipal Stadium. The reason: In the early days of TV the only U.S. pro football available to Torontonians was on Buffalo stations, which broadcast Cleveland games. The allegiance and familiarity stuck.

Like their Canadian counterparts who travel south regularly, thousands of Americans own land in Canada, much of it recreational and much of it now controlled, when sold, by Canadian provincial governments increasingly conscious of the issue of foreign ownership. In Ontario, for instance, an American buyer of land must sign an affidavit that he is a "Canadian resident," which may become technically true if the sale goes through but is rarely so until then. The provision is designed to thwart the kind of real estate speculation by outsiders with big bundles of foreign money that pushed the market value of many properties, such as the tiny outcroppings of rock that pass for vacation islands in Georgian Bay, beyond the reach of average Canadians. (Canadians still cannot deduct mortgage interest from income taxes, although a Liberal government under Pierre Elliott Trudeau did institute such tax breaks for large companies when they borrow money to finance corporate takeovers, steps taken increasingly against foreign-owned firms in recent years.)

In short, going to Canada for Americans is, well, unremarkable. If it weren't for the two nations' flags in the middle of the bridge, the customs agents, and the funny-colored money carrying the picture of a woman (Queen Elizabeth II), it would be hard for many Americans to tell they were in another country. That is why every summer Canada's post offices post notices by the mail slots reminding forgetful patrons, presumably gaggles of camera-toting Americans in station wagons, that United States stamps are not acceptable in Canada, not even on scenic postcards bound for Indiana. Such reminders can get more complicated when they are delivered by a Canadian judge to an American reporter from Maine who crosses into New Brunswick to report on a preliminary court hearing concerning a murder charge. Under Canadian law evidence from such hearings that is defamatory cannot be published until the same material emerges in a later trial. Does Canadian law apply to a publication outside the country? (One judge said yes and levied a $200 contempt fine on the American, sparking a brief international dispute between press associations and the judge, who won.)

The main struts of the two countries' close relationship are political, economic, and security-oriented. Decisions in Washington on interest rates, for example, have an immediate public and private impact across Canada and in Ottawa, where the currency is also called the dollar and is closely pegged to American money. Yet every day Canadians learn of these foreign decisions directly affecting their own lives only in the news as if they were 10,000 miles away. It breeds within them a deep sense of powerlessness—and resentment—which Americans and American policy makers have never really grasped or routinely taken into account.

Likewise, pricing decisions in Canada on newsprint, lumber, nickel, iron ore, natural gas, and other resources suck more dollars from United States coffers, further deepening America's balance of payments deficit. It sometimes appears to Americans as if Canadians, especially when pricing natural gas exports recently, are out to gouge their neighbors. Suffice it to say here that the economic relationship between Canada and the United States is by far the most important for both countries and the closest of any two truly independent lands in the world. Yet rarely does either side acknowledge the special links by paying more than routine or episodic attention, by lavishing the kind of constant nurturing care and understanding that would seem required.

But if the mainstays of the links are political and economic, the rivets holding things together are the countless number of small things, the far-reaching range of personal, business, and family ties that have overlaid the entire relationship right from the beginning, when thirteen of Britain's North American colonies rebelled and two of them did not, both of them units of Canada. Even during the War of 1812, when Britain and the young United States were at war, St. Stephen, New Brunswick, lent gunpowder to its official enemy across the river so that the American residents of Calais, Maine, could properly celebrate the Fourth of July.

In northern Michigan near the popular boundary crossing point of Sault Ste. Marie, Ontario, and Sault Ste. Marie, Michigan, state authorities have thoughtfully translated some mileage signs into kilometers for metric-minded Canadians. At southern Ontario's Cayuga Speedway on summer Sundays, thousands of Canadians wearing Kennedy Space Center and University of Southern California T-shirts and sipping Pepsi-Colas sit in the stands to watch Canadian and American stock car drivers compete; the fans dutifully stand for the playing of both national anthems, although polite Canadian track officials bother to raise only the American flag.

Many Canadians contribute money to the regular fund-raising drives by American Public Broadcasting System stations along the border; in some cities, like Buffalo, two-thirds of the donors to the American station are Canadian. It is widely known that the two lands share a military self-defense pact; Canadian officers serve in the buried headquarters of the North American Air Defense Command underneath Colorado, analyzing data from, among other points, long-range radar posts atop Canada, while

American bomber and fighter crews maneuver and dogfight over Canada's wide-open Arctic and prairies. Renamed to resemble the most likely European battle zones, British Columbia becomes Fantasia, Alberta is Roslovakia, Saskatchewan is Birmany, and Manitoba becomes Nethergium. Back down on earth, special agreements permit local Canadian and American authorities to exchange forest-fighting equipment and crews easily without bothering with formal requests to their federal governments.

In northern Minnesota a visit to Canada is also a simple matter at the Piney Pinecreek Binational Border Airport. The brainchild of Eugene Simmons, the elderly airport manager who designed the field to serve the customs-clearing needs of the growing squadrons of private planes moving across the border, the 3,300-foot grass runway crosses the international border. At the end pilots simply turn left into Canada or go straight to the United States (symbolical directions that could seem apt to a Reagan administration). Thus, the most serious international problems at this forty-nine-acre binational airport are the binational gophers, whose precise nationality is unknown but whose pothole-digging propensities scar the sod.

Dance fans from the northern American prairies can just drive up to see one of the world's best ballets—the Royal Winnipeg. That is the same city where the Washington Redskins, the football team owned by Jack Kent Cooke, a former Torontonian, went to purchase special sports shoes for a recent icy play-off game. In Montana, where it is usually assumed that anyone pulling out a traveler's check is a Canadian, it is not uncommon for rural American schoolchildren to get lessons on wildlife and conservation from a traveling Canadian troupe. Americans, too, win their share of Canada's government lotteries; the tickets can be confiscated if discovered by American customs agents. In Canada it is not illegal to bring home a "foreign" lottery ticket.

From the skies over North America, American satellite television programming streams down on—or is eagerly pirated by—the most isolated Canadian settlements, providing the scores of basketball games, soccer matches, and local news from Atlanta and other municipalities seemingly far-reached and farfetched from Canadian interests. Some Canadian gas station owners offer a free fill-up if their attendant fails to clean a customer's windshield or to volunteer the day's exchange rate on coveted American dollars. In fact, many Canadian gas stations near border crossings post their prices only in U.S. dollars. "That'll be eight dollars," a Canadian attendant told me in Fort Erie, Ontario, one day. ". . . Oh, you're paying in Canadian! Well, let's see, that's, uh, let's see, about ten dollars and twenty-five cents."

When the midwestern governors hold a regular meeting to study consumer and environmental pressures on the Great Lakes, the world's largest body of fresh water, they naturally invite the premier of Ontario, the Canadian province that is so large it sits across the Great Lakes from eight states. Sitting on the spacious veranda of the grand old Grand Hotel overlooking the Straits of Mackinac and the same passing waters that would soon wash Canadian shores, Premier William G. Davis told me, "I feel very much at home here—the people, the issues."

The silver-haired, pipe-smoking Premier Davis, an astute Progressive Conservative and major figure in the creation, finally, of Canada's own Constitution in 1982, is a good example of the kinds of ties that bind Americans and Canadians, officially and personally. Mr. Davis is a devoted Canadian, a politically savvy leader of his country's most populous province, and a tough competitor in the increasing struggle with midwestern states for new factories and their jobs. But this Canadian politician schedules no appointments for the afternoon of the fourth Thursday every November. This puzzled his secretaries in Toronto because the day is not known as a holiday in Canada. But it makes eminent sense to rabid fans of American professional football like Premier Davis. For that day is American Thanksgiving, a time of televised football games, when cheers and whistles seep from a set within the staid Victorian offices of the premier of the province of Ontario in a large green traffic circle in Toronto called Queen's Park.

When Premier Davis's first wife died some years ago, he married an American woman, Kathleen MacKay, from Hinsdale, Illinois, a graduate of the University of Michigan. They regularly vacation in their condominium in Florida or at the Davises' summer bungalow on a tiny island in choppy Georgian Bay off Lake Huron, where a provincial government seaplane bearing official papers in a leather briefcase is an almost daily visitor. Nearby is the summer home of Mrs. Davis's mother, an American who, under the policies of her son-in-law's government, must eventually sell her home to a Canadian.

When the Super Bowl football game was played in Michigan, then

Governor William Milliken naturally invited his next-door political col-league, Bill Davis, to attend the game. And William Brock, President Reagan's special trade representative, naturally invited Edward Lumley, his Canadian counterpart, whose business partners and mother-in-law are American, to sit in the Silverdome, too. With no Canadian teams yet participating in the championship (although two do in baseball), Premier Davis cheered for Cincinnati; it is closer to Toronto than San Francisco, and Premier Davis remembers, too, Paul Brown, a Cincinnati owner whom he knew as the coach years ago at the old Cleveland games that drifted into Canada on TV signals from New York State.

Across the continent the Washington legislature naturally invited Brit-ish Columbia's Premier William Bennett to address a session; the state and the province have much in common. And every February 12 Hugh-ena Matheson, William McCulloch, and the other members of the Abraham Lincoln Fellowship in Hamilton, Ontario, gather to celebrate with dinner and poems the exact birthday of their neighbor nation's sixteenth President; it is a calendared exactitude no longer existing even in that President's homeland.

Alan Dilworth, an industrial consultant in Toronto, is not famous. But his transborder personal and business ties run deep, too. When his daugh-ter Mary was graduated from nurse's training near home, there were no jobs. So she moved to North Carolina, where she worked, married, and now rears her own binational family. "The natural flow is just north–south," he told me over coffee one morning in Toronto's elegantly reno-vated King Edward Hotel. "At work I naturally think of New York and Chicago. But I have to think consciously to check with Regina or Vancou-ver, where I also have a daughter living."

When the Ontario government wanted 20,000 commemorative coins saying, "We're Proud to Be Canadians," it naturally turned to a local manufacturer who in turn naturally turned to a stamping plant in Roches-ter, New York, that could do the rush job quicker. When the filmmakers of the *Superman* series of movies wanted a filming location for the fictional superhero's small-town hometown of Smallville, U.S.A., they naturally looked in Alberta, where Canadian small towns like Blackie and High River looked more American than American small towns. And Calgary's soaring new skyline, which is dramatic but not yet immediately recognizable, became Superman's Metropolis.

Computers link the police from one end of each country to the other. Even without computers, the two countries are linked, as Tim Collins, an escaped Kentucky convict, learned to his dismay. Calgary police grew suspicious looking at the man's Canadian birth certificate but listening to his southern drawl. His "you-alls" suggested his birth certificate was a fraud and led to the discovery of drugs in his possession and his apprehension for American authorities.

When the makers of Sanders western boots wanted to impress Canadians with their product, they sent stores in Canada window advertisements showing Bum Phillips, the National Football League coach, saying, "Sanders Boots. They're mine, too." Mr. Phillips is known as an aficionado of fine boots, but the American coach is also better known in Canada than Canadian coaches are.

The baseball team that draws the allegiance of many northern Vermont residents is actually in Canada (the Montreal Expos). And Canadian networks provide much of the TV news these same Americans receive. In Rochester, Michigan, when Doug Neumann rises each morning, he flicks on his FM radio and shaves to the dignified tones of Canada's CBC Stereo, the national radio network heavily dominated by classical music. When many Michigan advertisers want to reach Detroit consumers, they buy radio ad time on CKLW in Windsor, Ontario; ironically, a number of these ads, such as sandwich specials at McDonald's hamburger stands, broadcast to Americans from Canada, specifically exclude customers at Canadian McDonald's. There was even a minor local flap once over the fact that the first thing seen by a visitor driving into Canada off the Ambassador Bridge from Detroit was a sign for Kentucky Fried Chicken. (The first one seen as you enter Canada at Fort Erie from Buffalo is a sign for Esso, the marketing arm in Canada for Imperial Oil, which is two-thirds owned by the United States' Exxon.)

When Canada's postal rates jumped dramatically in 1982, many of that country's businesses devised an unusual cost-cutting measure that becomes normal in the American-Canadian context. Overnight the Canadian postal service boosted its first-class domestic letter rates from 17 cents to 30 cents. For letters bound for the United States the old 17-cent rate became 35 cents (now 37). So, many high-volume mailers in Canada trucked their letters, even those bound for Canadian addresses, across the border into the United States. There they mailed them for the existing

20-cent rate. Postal trucks then hauled the Canada-bound letters back across the border, where they were routinely delivered. Even with the exchange rate this simple measure saved the mailers more than $5 for every 100 letters headed for Canadian addresses and more than $10 for each 100 pieces bound for American addresses.

During Canada's regular postal strikes many Canadian companies rented postal boxes just across the border in the United States and sent their mail to similar boxes in U.S. cities across the country near the Canadian border, where their colleagues would drive across the boundary to get their mail and send off replies. During nationwide strikes of Canada's handful of airlines Canadians shipped themselves similarly, driving to American airports, flying to American cities near their Canadian destinations, and renting cars to complete the journey. Even in strike-free times, one study revealed, 11 of every *100* Canadian air travelers first voyage to the U.S. to board a cheaper discount flight.

Over the years thousands of Americans traveled to Canada for specialized medical care in the country that discovered insulin and invented Pablum. This was especially true in the area of children's medicine, even to the point, so common that it was hardly remarked upon, that parents of a dying child on one side of the border donated vital organs to an ill infant in the other country, duty-free. And this intimate Canadian-American relationship even touched on sex. When at least one unidentified Toronto couple discovered they could not have children, they signed a $10,000 contract with a married woman, a surrogate American mother in Florida, to be impregnated with the Canadian man's sperm and carry the infant to birth, which took place in a Toronto hospital, making the adopted child a Canadian citizen like his parents.

In public affairs Canadian politicians can almost always expect a warm, hospitable reception from American audiences, which can prove a helpful tool back home. Using a foreign trip for domestic political ends is a tactic many American presidents have used, too, though rarely involving Canada. Oftentimes, when an embattled Prime Minister Trudeau wanted a rousing reception, he would schedule a speech before an American audience, where his maverick and sometimes blunt style could still seem fresh. Typically, in what Canadians would view as a gesture of flaunting nationalism, the few Canadians in the audience would venture to wear a small maple leaf emblem of some sort (Canadian youths at Mr. Trudeau's address to a sea of graduating seniors at Notre Dame University put the leaf symbol on top of their mortarboards). Also typically, Mr. Trudeau would forge his address around foreign affairs, a topic of virtually invisible import at home. The American cheers and even standing ovations would be played to TV news audiences back home, where such American enthusiasm gave even the staunchest Trudeau critics at least momentary pause.

Even within Canada's domestic politics the United States' influence is widely accepted and pervasive, if mostly unintentional. Negotiations with the United States over a fishing treaty become campaign issues in eastern Canada. American monetary policies and inflation have significant and immediate impact on Canadian life. The winter weather in sunny American climes is closely watched by Canadians, who have no Sun Belt and must pay the going international rate for all their winter vegetables and fruits. The American influence is so widespread that American bashing is a frequent and often politically profitable phenomenon in Canada, requiring a certain sophistication that has not always been present among American politicians. They need to know when the tweaking of Uncle Sam's nose or the kicking of another anatomical part requires a response and when, being aired solely for domestic Canadian consumption, it had best be met by a dignified and possibly more powerful silence lest it seem to prove the point of American interference to no American advantage whatsoever. At times the American influence is so pervasive and subtle that domestic American political events become integral parts of the Canadian lexicon. Thus, at a 1980 political rally for then Prime Minister Joe Clark, one Canadian opponent could strike a meaningful protest chord among fellow Canadians by waving a placard that urged, "Send Clark to Iran and Let Kennedy Drive Him." Canadians knew the meaning of Senator Edward Kennedy's fatal car crash at Chappaquiddick as well as Americans did. Canadians vacationed there, had relatives there, did business there, and they followed, on page one of their daily newspapers, the American presidential sweepstakes at least as closely as their prime ministerial jockeying at home.

And this demonstrates perhaps the single most important fact of life in relations between the two countries. "Although it is probably true that one would have to take the United States greatly into account in describing either the Canadian economy or polity, American politics and economics can be explained fairly well without reference to its northern neighbor."[1] That is because nearly eight of every ten Canadians live within 100 miles of the United States with its powerful media, its sprawling culture, and its immense economy and population, fully ten times the size of Canada's. As a result, the United States, although often seen as the land of bilk and money, looms larger than life in the Canadian mind.

As Mr. Trudeau once told an American audience, "Living next to you is in some ways like sleeping with an elephant. No matter how friendly or even-tempered is the beast, if I may call it that, one is affected by every twitch and grunt." Some 70 percent of Canada's imports and exports somehow involve the United States. Three-quarters of all foreign investment in Canada, including some higher percentages in certain sectors, is controlled by Americans.

Yet most Americans live far from Canada. Only about 12 of every 100 Americans live within 100 miles of Canada. "Only" 20 percent of the United States' imports and exports involve Canada. As a result, Canada, which until recently has been little thought of at all, can seem smaller than life, a North American country similar to the United States yet quaintly tinged somehow with the flavor of British tea and biscuits.

This kind of friendly indifference helps account for the frequent confusions of Americans: the tourists who ask where they can see the queen, who lives on the other side of the Atlantic Ocean; the newspapers that dateline Canadian stories "Manitoba, Canada," which is as specific as beginning American dispatches "California, United States"; and the State Department's assigning its Office of Canadian Affairs to its European Bureau, a title only recently changed to include the United States' largest trading partner. "Americans," said the historian J. Bartlet Brebner, "are benevolently ignorant about Canada, while Canadians are malevolently well-informed about the United States."

A few figures reveal the crucial differing perspectives. In recent times the United States Embassy in Ottawa employed 40 professional diplomats and 40 more support staff with 7 consul general offices around the country. Canada, on the other hand, maintained 50 professionals in its Washington embassy, plus upward of 100 support personnel and 14 consuls general around the country. In the Canadian diplomatic service the post of ambassador in Washington is the top professional job. In the United States State Department the Ottawa ambassador's post is generally a political slot, which in recent times has seen the job left vacant for long periods until the professionals can get the President's attention long enough to make an appointment, even if it does turn out to be a man from the ranks of his party's fund raisers.

Canadians keep close track of such doings as a measure of the esteem in which they believe they are held by their southern neighbor. They know that Canadian prime ministers journey to Washington a half dozen times for every formal visit to Ottawa by an American President. And Canadian journalists carefully chronicle and cherish for long years afterward all examples of American ignorance such as a President's mispronouncing a prime minister's name. Canadian journalists can also cause another kind of embarrassment with some enterprise, as they did by their exclusive reports that American planes had bombed a small mental hospital in Grenada during the 1983 conflict there. There is also a category of Canadian humor which could be called "Dumb Yankee Jokes," based on some incidents that may even have happened once. These involve stories of Americans arriving in Canada in July with their skis, of Americans expressing amazement at the tall modern buildings in Canada's cities, of Americans believing Canada is populated mostly by Eskimos and Mounties. Marilyn Monroe, reportedly on the set of a northern movie-in-the-making: "When they said Canada, I thought it would be up in the mountains somewhere." The classic "Dumb Yank" tale is the comment that gangster Al Capone purportedly once made about the United States' neighbor on the North Side: "I don't even know what street Canada is on." (Of course, ignorance can be a bilateral affair, too; until her arrival to live in Washington Sondra Gotlieb, the novelist wife of Canada's ambassador there, admits she did not know that the United States Senate is part of Congress.)

To me, the recounting of Dumb Yankee stories says more about the teller's insecurities than about the object of the gibe. It is true that Canadian pupils study more about United States history than vice versa. But it is also true that some American neglect of Canada has indeed been warranted over the decades, since by dispassionate world standards, Canada's problems, Canada's threat to the United States, and Canada's previous importance to its neighbor have been relatively minor compared to the perceived needs, the pressures, and the threats of events and places elsewhere for a nation with global responsibilities. It may not be right that the squeaky wheel or noisy crisis gets the grease, but it can be an unfortunate, and shortsighted, fact of life.

Too, whatever validity these tales of ignorance once may have had has waned considerably in recent years in the face of burgeoning American attentiveness, not all of it comfortable to its northern neighbor. Beginning in the late 1970's, the journalists of the United States, as well as of West Germany, Japan, and Britain, began showing greater curiosity about that grumbling, increasingly aggressive resource-rich goliath stretching its new-found muscles somewhere between the United States and the Soviet Union. Whereas once news coverage was largely confined to breaking stories in the capital of Ottawa and in old-worldly Montreal, a platoon of foreign correspondents began wandering the rest of the country.

They uncovered during these treks signs of an exciting culture, new business energies and imaginations, a sprawling geography that touched a responsive romantic strain at home, and a scrappy set of politics and federalism whose success or failure carried ramifications beyond Canada's faint borders. Canadian magazines began writing about this phenomenon, while some Canadian newspapers began picking up and publishing, seemingly without embarrassment, these same American reports on Canada. It became obvious to me early in my four-year tour in Canada that this growing band of foreign correspondents was often displaying a greater interest and curiosity in Canada and its workings than their local brethren were. "Why would you ever want to go to the Yukon?" I was often asked. The fact that it is one of the very few remaining undeveloped frontiers in an industrialized society didn't seem to matter in the Canadian mind.

When Dr. Joseph MacInnis, a Toronto doctor with a passion for undersea medicine, sought journalistic interest in his pioneering efforts to deep-sea dive in the Arctic down to the ancient wreck of a sailing ship, he got nowhere in Canada until he had aroused the prompt curiosity of *The New York Times* and two American TV networks. From the beginning much of his financing had to come from the National Geographic Society in Washington, D.C. Then, after several months of consideration, the Canadian Broadcasting Corporation did send a team of television technicians to assess the situation, and CBC Radio sent a lone reporter, a transplanted Briton who was fascinated by the Arctic. No other Canadian news organization was represented.

More important, such reports by American journalists were beginning to receive the kind of routine, day-to-day attention in the United States that was previously accorded only to more distant, exotic climes where exciting revolutions ran rampant. The romantic escapades of a prime minister's errant young wife could always excite the editors of gossip sheets. But now, for instance, a newspaper profile of a new Canadian political leader could become page one news in San Diego. Canadians noticed this, too. Many times during my tenure in Canada I was interviewed for articles on how Americans were paying more attention to their northern neighbor. In the *Toronto Star,* Canada's largest circulation daily and one noted for its nationalist themes, one such piece began: "Curse those Americans. They are talking away one of our great Canadian preoccupations. They are not ignoring us anymore." The tone was almost sad.

This American attention, which was paralleled by European media to an understandably lesser extent, was not a sudden shift but a gradual one perhaps traceable initially to the energy crisis of 1973 and the realization of Canada's oily underground lode. But its momentum was clearly building, fueled by competition between American publications seeking to match or outdo each other.

And it also fed a growing awareness of an emerging Canadian presence in the world at large and across North America in particular. Canadian banks, real estate and insurance firms, cable TV concerns, newspaper publishers, oil companies, and high-profile—and tasty—beers added to a widening sense among Americans, even more so than among Canadians themselves, that this once-silent neighbor was developing into a more mature country with its own peculiar set of diverse dynamics. This was interesting in and of itself because it was coming to play a more direct and important role in American life. There could be questions about the country's tactics, perhaps puzzlement over its different responses, but not about its existence or changing character.

The full ramifications of these major changes were little noted in either country, even in the cloistered confines of the growing number of Canadian studies programs sprouting on American campuses. It was sixty years after Canada's formal independence before the country established its first diplomatic mission abroad (in Washington, of course, in 1927). Since then, the two countries had managed their relations with the formal diplomatic deference of two sovereign countries but with a special series of private and even tacit understandings. These dictated, among other things, that relations be handled mostly by professionals relatively free of politics, that everything be handled quietly on a strictly bilateral basis free of third-party intermediation and free of public statements to the press

that help create, feed, and dramatize so many open confrontations elsewhere. Issues were to be dealt with on a case-by-case basis—in effect, with
each in isolation—free of the sticky linkages to unrelated issues that
involve leverage and gum up the efficient disposition of disputes elsewhere. There was a tacit recognition that linkage of issues between friends
was an inappropriate exercise, an implicit search for advantage unnecessary if issues are treated solely on their merits.

This meant basically that there was no "Canada policy" in the United
States and no "United States policy" in Canada. Such as they were, the
official policies of each country were simply the sum total of the individual
decisions worked out by teams of experts who knew the special rules and
understood the special relationship. Formal summit meetings, for example, were not part of the process to resolve specific matters. They were,
in the words of Allan E. Gotlieb, an erudite and candid Canadian ambassador to Washington, simple gatherings "to set the beacon jointly."

There was one other tacit understanding. It was that one partner
(namely, the United States) was more equal than the other, the precise
proportion depending on the matter at hand. This understanding of
variable superiority remained unstated, unlike the smoldering resentments
it fostered among Canadians, including my relatives. They would monitor
the comparative values of the two countries' dollars like some baseball box
score that had first one country "winning" and then the other. No matter
that most Americans never even knew the "game" existed. Other Canadians might revel over dinner in the predicaments its southern neighbor had
encountered. I once looked up an aging prairie playmate of my father's
in Manitoba and spent a few days in their hometown of Dauphin. My
father left there in the 1930's. This cousin, into his sixties when I met
him, had never left the town. After dinner this man told his houseguest,
"You Yanks are going to freeze in the dark someday, and we're just going
to sit up here all cozy and smile."

But in return for the tacit diplomatic acknowledgment, the United
States traditionally granted Canada a special status, perhaps discriminating in its neighbor's favor in the application of tariffs, tax and immigration
laws, and foreign quotas. American businessmen or academicians, for
instance, can gather for their annual convention in Toronto, Montreal,
or Vancouver and still write off much of their expenses on taxes as if they
had met inside the United States.

The military defenses of Canada and the United States became mutual in a memorandum of understanding at the onset of World War II; no formal treaty was required. It was, after all, Canada and the United States. Their intelligence services and federal police forces exchanged information, and still do. And often one side could secretly help the other; some foreign lands, for example, are less suspicious of capitalist Canadians, as Iranian revolutionaries learned to their dismay when Canada helped smuggle out a handful of Americans who had escaped their hostage dragnet.

For decades this intimate, although sometimes rancorous, relationship was skillfully managed by an old boy network of experienced diplomats who had shared common trials and common triumphs during the Depression and World War II, who knew each other well, possibly from their university days in New England together, and who were instinctively aware and accepting of the implicit "big brother/little brother" relationship that had evolved.

"Lots of times," one State Department officer told me, "you have to remind yourself you are dealing with the representative of another country. I mean, I just pick up this phone, dial an area code like anywhere in the United States, and it's Joe and Bill talking the same issues in the same language. Except it's really Joe from Canada and Bill from the United States."

Canadians have an easier time than Americans remembering there are two separate countries. A major part of their Canadian identity is that they are not Americans. So in any negotiations with the Yanks they usually have a long shopping list of items they simply must achieve to show their constituencies back home that they got the best possible deal from the big guy on the block. "They've always got a jillion little things they have to have," one American negotiator told me. "They have to have this tariff concession for that town and that little goodie for the lumber industry in little Podunk, Quebec. They really nickel and dime you to death."

To the Americans this attitude indicates a certain smallness of vision, a pettiness of self-gain, which, in fact, the Americans are not above seeking either, only in larger packages. Americans try to sell Canadians on $2 billion-plus fighter aircraft purchases; the Canadians try for the rights to make the plane's wings.

In Ottawa at the allied summit meeting in 1981, Canada, as host, provided each country's leaders with a hotel meeting room or two for press officers to hold news briefings. Typically the United States rented its own hotel and helicoptered in from the rural meeting site top administration officials to meet on and off the record with reporters in the kind of high-powered political hustle so familiar in Washington but much lower-keyed in Ottawa. The White House public relations juggernaut, which made transcripts and texts available to the world's press there before the meeting's host, even set up large speakerphones creating a bizarre scene in which the disembodied voices of absent officials replied to a ballroomful of correspondents who posed their questions to an empty podium. Across town Canadian press officers, under a typically tighter restraint, were often left having to admit, "I don't have the answer to that." The Canadian information officers did, however, have tons of brochures to pass out to the world press promoting Canada as a tourist destination.

When the American leader visits the Canadian prime minister, the bilateral schedule includes the usual panorama of glittering social and mundane ceremonial duties (the regular planting of a presidential tree on government grounds has left behind a small woods as well as a painful memory for President John F. Kennedy, who threw out his bad back during his excavation). But unlike his visits to other foreign lands, on a Canadian visit the President's briefing book includes a large section devoted to parochial matters. The Canadians would call them major, and the Americans, who have trouble at times adjusting focus from global matters to neighborhood issues, would think them minor. These have included fights over fishing rights, certain provisions of American tax laws that inadvertently hurt Canadian businesses, truck regulation disputes, Great Lakes pollution, and acid rain, the washing out of polluted air by rains that fall into and contaminate natural streams, lakes, and forests. The latter is an emotional issue in an outdoors-oriented country like Canada which has so much treasured wilderness that it has yet even to count its lakes. But the threat of acid rain can appear less compelling to a southern neighbor which has seen so much development and pollution that some of its rivers have burst into flame.

On the other side, the Americans see a need in the free world's defense for a new generation of cruise missiles and a need to test them over large, unpopulated regions, which Canada has in abundance. Canada agreed to the tests, but only after an emotional national debate involving the morality of helping perfect deadly new weapons and the fear that its land would become a more likely target in the event of war. These may be valid concerns, but they showed that defense priorities do not hold the same level on a ranking of Canadian concerns as they do farther south.

Likewise, to Canadians talk of an underequipped NATO alliance or the Communist threat to Angola can appear so distant that it frustrates the deeply felt American concern and has in the past often prompted Canada to be privately criticized for its penchant for what Americans see as "small change." To the Canadians, whose "smallness" of vision has only enabled them to conquer the world's second-largest country in landmass, constant nickel-and-diming is an effective bargaining technique if you feel outgunned on the large items. The Americans see themselves as envisioning instead the Big Picture and, not coincidentally, the Big Buck. But both countries, after all, call their currency dollars and their coins nickels and dimes.

My favorite example of the two countries' radically differing perspectives on precisely the same issue involves the bilateral maritime squalls that blow up from time to time over fishing rights and resources in East and West Coast ocean areas where the 200-mile territorial claims overlap. Fishing is no small matter in Canada, the world's largest fish exporter, where even some inland water bodies far to the northwest of the Great Lakes are large enough to support commercial fishing efforts. I talked one day in Ottawa with Mark MacGuigan, then the minister of external affairs. With great emphasis and seriousness he said, "The most serious dispute we have with any country is with the United States over fish." I then took the brisk walk across downtown, over the scenic canal to the American Embassy, which is slightly closer to the House of Commons chambers than the prime minister's office is. There, without prompting, a top-ranking embassy official told me with a dismissive tone, "The most serious issue between Canada and us is fish." He said the last word as if he could smell it.

The history of their bilateral relations is replete with examples of these differing priorities. Often it involves free trade. First, one side wants it and the other doesn't. Then vice versa. First, in the 1930's, the United States thought a St. Lawrence Seaway was a swell idea; Canada didn't. Then, in the 1950's, it was Canada that wondered why the Americans were dragging their feet on the seaway. During the reign of Mr. Trudeau, who was not enamored of large military budgets and faced no defense industry lobby, Americans increased the pressures on Canada to boost its defense spending. At some times Canada, a country that borders on three oceans, is lodged between the world's two superpowers, and has the world's longest coastline, did not have one single destroyer in operational readiness. In one naval wardroom I visited, officers had hung a photograph of their prime minister, Mr. Trudeau. It showed him firing a paper clip on a rubber band stretched between thumb and forefinger. The Canadian sailors had labeled the photo "Canada's Defense Policy." (However, Mr. Trudeau, while slowly increasing military spending, could lecture his countrymen during their protests against testing of American cruise missiles over Canadian territory, "It is hardly fair to rely on the Americans to protect the West, but to refuse to lend them a hand when the going gets rough. In that sense, the anti-Americanism of some Canadians verges on hypocrisy. They're eager to take refuge under the American umbrella, but don't want to help hold it.")

At some unnoted time, probably in the late sixties or early seventies, the old system of managing Canadian-American relations began to crumble beneath the accumulating weight and pressures of a rash of nagging problems, a bevy of impatient politicians on both sides, and the continuing retirement of "old boys" on both sides and their replacement by younger diplomats whose adult memories just might reach as far back as the late Eisenhower, early Diefenbaker years. In addition, there was in the Canada of the 1980's a subtly growing sense of self-confidence and self-importance that fueled a creeping assertiveness strongly supported by voters. It was the message, as David L. Johnston, president of Montreal's McGill University, put it, "that Canada is a good neighbor but a different country." This new feeling was not brash and swaggering. It was quiet and determined, if largely unrecognized across Canada. Americans, too, viewing the episodes individually instead of as part of a historical continuum that bore some resemblance to development of an emerging national identity in their own first century and a quarter, missed the overall significance at first.

There have been frequent seesaw cycles in relations between the two countries. Donald Smiley, a historian and Canadian constitutional expert, noted in a conversation once that Canadians have tended to measure themselves constantly against American achievements—or failures—irrational though that may be in view of their separate histories, geographies, cultures, politics, and economies. When the United States is experiencing difficulties such as Watergate, Vietnam, or a sad series of political assassinations, Canada tends to feel a bit smug or superior. "We would never do that" seems to be the feeling, although such self-satisfaction can appear unwarranted in view of the bombings, political kidnappings, assassination, and police skulduggery in Quebec's more recent history, for example. But when Americans seem to be on a successful roll, Canadians can somehow feel threatened, even though few United States citizens, whose national identity has nothing to do with Canada, would ever think of such a connection. Thus, the Americans could overlook it in an assessment of bilateral relations. A similar pattern emerges in times of economic prosperity, when Canadians can feel safer to criticize their southern neighbor, especially if a Canadian election is in the offing. But in times of economic uncertainty, such criticism seems more muted and the provinces scrap among themselves instead.

Beginning in the late 1960's, the bilateral frictions included Canadian opposition to the Vietnam War and then to an American surcharge on imports that rattled Canada's economy. There was a series of sudden economic moves by President Richard M. Nixon which indicated that the "special relationship" with Canada was not his top priority if, indeed, he thought there was one at all. Americans, in turn, were startled by the sudden end of Canada's oil exports to an energy-thirsty United States and annoyed with Canada's trade dealings with Cuba and China and its stance as a haven for American draft resisters. Both the United States and Canada were disturbed with laws and programs to "Buy American" or "Buy Canadian." Canada was also concerned with the environmental fallout from the Garrison Diversion Project, the massive long-range plan to siphon water from the Missouri River into arid farming areas of North Dakota, which would also coincidentally pollute Canada's neighboring Hudson Bay watershed. It was perhaps a forerunner of more serious future disputes over this vital resource.

In a wide-ranging frank discussion on one of those bright early-spring days in Toronto when outdoor life begins resuming, Mr. Gotlieb, the outspoken ambassador from Canada to Washington, said he anticipated there would always be a lengthy shopping list—he counted four dozen that day—of perceived grievances characterizing the most complex and extensive relationship between any two countries in the world.

But the two countries were drifting apart in political philosophy, too. Canada's voters have always permitted, and often expected, their government to be strongly interventionist. In view of the country's scale and diversity, government was often the only body with a national perspective and anywhere near the resources or inclination to take on projects such as a national airline or railroad. That was sometimes the case in the United States, too. But in the last decade the Americans had been leaning more away from an interventionist policy with such moves as deregulation of oil and gas prices and airline routes. New financial arrangements also emerged, blurring the traditional lines among banks, insurance companies, and brokers.

These were reasonable differences that both sides could coexist with in good faith, and often did. But as reporters and readers gazed over the forty-ninth parallel, these differences helped feed a popular perception of two "relatives" increasingly marching to different drummers—one vigorously pursuing its conservative, semilaissez-faire ethic while the other clung to its liberal semisocialist stance. Not only did they see a different —and changing—country on the other side of the border, but they also saw cousins doing things in sharp contrast with previous ways and could at times feel strangely offended or, worse yet, threatened.

At the same time the devastating economic pressures of a stubborn international recession fed protectionist sentiments on both sides and raised suspicions of bad faith in some circles, suspicions that might well have gone stillborn in a more prosperous time. The same kinds of suspicions were being directed at Japan, the United States' second-largest trading partner (and Canada's, too), which seemed to many Americans to be abusing its open access to American markets. The fact that Canadians, who had seemed for so long to be so like the Americans, could be so easily lumped in with such an obviously "foreign" people as the Japanese was a sign of a significant change in American perceptions.

It was, I believe, a vital, if at times painful or distressing, first step in the creation of a new Canadian-American relationship, one based on a more equitable footing. It paralleled, in a way, the changing relationship between a parent and a teenager emerging into adulthood. Both parties know the relationship is changing, although they may not know exactly where it will end. Both parties know the change is natural, inevitable, and a sign of maturity, although they may at times mistrust the new ways and miss the old. Both parties are probably looking forward to the end of a sometimes painful transition. But also there are times when one party or the other is too tired or shortsighted to see beyond the immediate squabble at hand and falls back, resentfully, into the old patterns of behavior, either expecting acquiescence or indulgence. It is, after all, a familiar relationship and was once comfortable and appropriate.

But there can be no going back, as a number of events have showed. First, Canada began exploring the so-called Third Option (the first two options were to withdraw into itself or to seek even tighter economic integration with the Americans). The Third Option involved seeking closer European ties as a counterbalance to the United States' influence. It was no great success, in large part because of distance and the reality that beyond asbestos and a few other resources, Canada had very little to offer Europe, certainly nothing resembling increased military security.

Then, in 1974, Canada, which had always been so eager, so open, and so delighted to accommodate almost any foreign investor that would bring in the vital capital the country has so lacked, founded FIRA (pronounced FEAR-ah), a bureaucratic acronym that stands for Foreign Investment Review Agency. This body would require applications from foreign investors to start new businesses in Canada or to buy out existing ones, even if they were just minor appendages of parent companies being bought out in another land. Operating in secret, it would in its own good time (a time that could easily last a year or so) examine these proposals for their economic benefit to Canada. Those that did not offer some advantage to the host country were rejected, about 10 percent over the years, usually without explanation. Those that did measure up might also be required to promise in writing more hiring later or to meet a certain quota of Canadian purchases or future investment.

By the world's standards of nationalism, standards which in the last twenty years had seen dozens of new countries struggle with business and themselves in establishing their own national economic identities on other continents, FIRA was fairly tame stuff. But it was new and unheard of in Canada, so it raised some eyebrows in foreign business circles, especially American. There were other pieces of nationalist legislation that signaled a new and stronger tack in the North. The government ruled that Canadian companies could no longer deduct as business expenses costs to advertise back to Canadians on American border TV stations. In 1975 the government also moved to require Canadian content in and control of American publications circulated there. The move, called C-58 for the bill's number, also aroused some freedom of the press concerns. It forced changes in the structure of the Canadian *Reader's Digest* and killed the Canadian edition of *Time* magazine, but its assertive message was clear.

Concern over such steps, especially FIRA, was to fester in the United States and emerge as substantial resentments a few years later in 1980, when the real watershed came. Then the Canadian government released its National Energy Program (NEP), a legislative package of nationalist proposals designed to help Canada achieve energy self-sufficiency and domestic ownership of half its oil industry by 1990. The goal was later quietly amended to "in the 1990's." The package was broad-ranging and forged over years through piecemeal legislation, much of it highly technical. But basically it set the government's firm aim as encouraging or forcing, if necessary, greater Canadian ownership of its energy industry.

Through a complex system of grants, tax write-offs, and other economic incentives that mounted temptingly with the degree of Canadian ownership in an oil company, the NEP vigorously encouraged foreign oil companies to embrace Canadian partners, to boost their shares on Canadian stock markets, or simply to sell out to a growing brace of adventurous homegrown entrepreneurs. The program was particularly aimed at oil and gas exploration on Canada's resource frontiers—the desolate but likely rich Arctic lands and its stormy, iceberg-ridden offshore sea bottom, where transportation, hardship, and the elements made the cost of a single risky well many millions of dollars. One of the program's provisions that proved especially alarming to the oil companies and their home governments was the so-called back-in clause, which enabled the federal government to take over up to 25 percent of a well's interest after a find on land leased from the government. (In the Canadian Arctic virtually all land is federally owned.) This could prove a bonanza for the government, which need not put up any money in the chancy drilling stage but could still strike it rich by moving in on only the successful wells.

Foreign oil companies are accustomed to accommodating themselves to the sometimes demanding wishes of a host government. In Canada, where foreign oil concerns with the quantity of capital necessary for big-stakes resource explorations controlled about 72 percent of the energy business by 1980, there had always been rules and regulations to abide by. As nationalistic regulations go, Canada's were mild. No one talked about government nationalization of foreign oil assets there, although some provinces like Saskatchewan and Quebec had moved into direct owner-ship in other resource areas like potash and asbestos. And the Canadian government, which has as many political constituencies to appear to satisfy at home as has any other national government that must face democratic elections every few years, emphasized abroad that its policies were not aimed at any one country—namely, the United States. To think that merely saying that would calm the waters was naïve or worse any-where outside Canada.

So the fear and the talk began to spread. And so did a flurry of billion-dollar deals as French, British, and American oil companies sought to sell off all or part of their Canadian assets to Canadians with access to the NEP's financial breaks.

These were not fire sales by any means; they were, in effect, firebreaks with the intent and result of drawing the line on foreign ownership in an energy sector viewed as vital to national security. It was also aimed at ensuring that future profits stayed in Canada for investment by Canadians and not to boost the foreign ownership numbers in some other industry. Part of the plan worked, some say too well. Within two years the percent-age of foreign ownership had fallen closer to the 65 percent level, although exploration work was near a standstill. The United States with its freer deregulated energy market was a more lucrative playing field, even for many Canadian energy companies, whose drilling rigs by the dozens followed the Americans to the south across the border.

Whether the NEP served Canada's best long-term interests, whether the heavy acquisition-financing burden on the country's banking system and the slide in the Canadian dollar's value were necessary, and whether economically the expenditure of billions of dollars to change the owner-ship of some oil resources without discovering a single new barrel of oil was worth the investment are worthy topics for discussion. There is also the question in some Canadians' minds of whether the NEP and similar nationalist plans were philosophically, let alone practically, sound. "The notion that foreign ownership is bad ownership," said Rowland C. Frazee, chairman of the Royal Bank, Canada's largest, "and that we can penalize it retroactively, as contained in the National Energy Program, is living

1. *Cecille Bechard, a Canadian whose house sits smack on the United States—Canada border, ends another one of her many daily "visits" to the United States and returns to Canada. The 5,524.5-mile-long boundary, the world's longest undefended national frontier, runs through her kitchen and down the hall, leaving her to bathe in American waters but eat on a Canadian table. The special border creates many such unusual situations, often seeming informally to unite the two lands more than separate them.*

2. The northern Canadian community of Resolute, Northwest Territories, where nothing taller than moss grows outdoors and where school teachers import leaves to teach their Inuit pupils about those strange things called trees.

3. One of Napoleon Snowbird's unnamed sled dogs howling back at an unseen wolf during a rest stop in the rugged wilds of northern Alberta one winter's day.

4 & 5. *Transportation plays a vital role in Canada's nation-building experience. Here, during a brief blizzard one March noon, workers at Polaris, the world's northernmost lead-zinc mine, unload supplies from a Twin Otter, Canada's frontier workhorse. Temperature: minus 39. Below, a transcontinental train pauses at Jasper, Alberta, one late December afternoon, on its three-day journey across just part of the country. Temperature: minus 20.*

6. *A local family chills some fresh-killed food by the front door one brisk fall day in Pangnirtung on Baffin Island. The double front door is designed to curb drafts on winter nights, which last all day.*

7. *A familiar rural scene — tall, multi-colored grain elevators towering over railroad sidings to house the land's agricultural bounty until its shipment somewhere else for processing.*

8. *James L. Malcolm, my grandfather, skinning a coyote for winter wear on a hunt near Trochu, Alberta, 1910.*

9. *Grace and Charles Clark, High River, Alberta. "I can never understand why some people wear themselves to pieces in the city to earn enough money to go back home where they came from."*

10. *A lone traveler, lost in the immensity of Canada's geography, makes his dusty way along the Dempster Highway, a dirt road that crosses the Arctic Circle.*

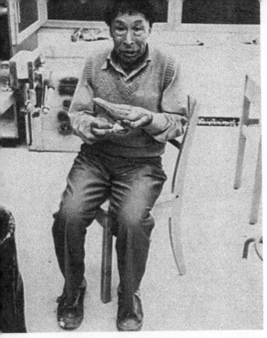

11. After three days' work, Alivuktuk has just finished another soapstone carving, a northern bird preparing to soar. "Now it is free," he said.

12. Some of the more ordinary roadside scenery in the Yukon Territory, where caribou far outnumber humans.

13. *Toronto's ever-changing skyline, dominated by structures built by private companies, banks, government corporations, or governments themselves. An old Indian winter camp once named York, tidy, proper, and prosperous Toronto (pronounced "TRAHN-nah") first became a favored destination for Americans when United States troops sacked the place during the War of 1812, a gesture of respect and friendship reciprocated when the British sailed south and burned Washington, D.C. Courtesy of The Metropolitan Toronto Convention and Visitors Association, Photo by R. Simpson.*

dangerously, damaging Canada's reputation abroad, and fomenting wasteful bickering at home. It must be changed."

What the NEP did do, however, was force the issue of Canadian-American relations into the sustained public spotlight, not favorably in the United States' eyes. Ambassadors were summoned. Notes were exchanged, clarifications sought. Blunt speeches were made on both sides. The Canadian press, always on the alert for alleged American slights, had a field day interviewing American officials, who spoke for attribution in stern tones about Canadian policies. "There is broad, sustained and very deep-seated concern that goes throughout every department of the U.S. government about the current direction of Canadian economic policy," a White House assistant trade representative said.

"I guess you're pretty angry at us," one Canadian official remarked to me, almost gleefully. It signaled the end, if a formal conclusion was needed, of the quiet old boy network of handling bilateral relations.

The feuding was, in fact, most public and widespread. Businessmen spoke out against Canada at U.S. congressional hearings. The Reagan administration worried, aloud, about Canada's doing "irreparable damage" to relations which were "sliding dangerously toward crisis." The administration also wondered, aloud, about barring Canadians and Canadian companies from mineral leaseholds on U.S. federal lands. Writing in an oft-quoted article in *The New York Times,* Paul W. MacAvoy, a Yale economics professor, predicted the certain failure of the Canadian energy policy and said the northern neighbor would be running to the Americans for help by 1990. "Let us not be of assistance," Professor MacAvoy wrote, "given that they've wrecked their markets and expelled efficient United States companies. Let them freeze in the dark."

Writing in *Maclean's* magazine, Canada's newsweekly, Roderick McQueen, a senior editor, responded, "We have been peaceful patsies to every Yankee whim since [the beginning]—an attitude that can only be halted with a Canada-first mentality."

One result was almost a panic selling of Canadian oil stocks by American stockholders, fueled by facts and rumors which, in view of the new context of a more assertive Canada, could be reality but weren't. The truth didn't matter on the emotional stock markets, where share prices of some oil companies dipped to bargain rates, which didn't bother would-be Canadian purchasers.

The souring spilled over publicly into other areas of bilateral concern.

There was talk of retaliatory legislation in Washington as the general awareness of Canada's assertiveness and economic penetration of the United States grew among businessmen and congressmen. It seemed that the series of serious disputes and the new style of open argument threatened what one high State Department official told me in 1978—that is, "The assumption when we talk with Canada is that something will always be worked out."

Relations between the two countries had always been a factor in Canada's domestic politics, but now for the first time on a sustained basis it entered the American political arena, too. New England legislators effectively blocked ratification of a fishing treaty with Canada. And Presidents Carter and Reagan with other legislative fish to fry, so to speak, dropped the matter as too politically costly domestically.

For the Canadians, who believe themselves to be so well informed on the United States, it was a rude lesson in American civics, in the check and balance provisions of the United States governmental system, and in the rising post-Vietnam demands of the legislative branch to participate more in matters of foreign affairs. "I am struck," Ambassador Gotlieb told a reporter in Washington, "by the extent to which important measures that have foreign policy implications actually originate in Congress." In Canada's parliamentary system the legislative majority rules supreme, for better or worse, with the only major check coming at the next nationwide election of the House of Commons, elections which legally can be five years apart. At least one major publication, Maclean's, interpreted the Americans' constitutional checks and balances instead as "symptoms of schizophrenia, often countering with one hand [the Congress] what the other [the White House] is doing."

Canadians, who didn't have their own Constitution until 1982, could perhaps be excused for overlooking a President's constitutional need for treaty ratification in the Senate; an early lesson, the Senate's rejection of President Wilson's League of Nations membership, came eight years before Canada opened its Washington mission. Nonetheless, official Canada vowed henceforth to take its arguments and propositions vigorously and directly to members of Congress like any lobbyist using facts, figures, legal arguments, and the friendly persuasion that occurs so often on Washington tennis courts and in leisure time salon discussions. "I am persuaded," Mr. Gotlieb observed, "that there is an element of public diplomacy to diplomacy and that it is a growing element. There is a need on the part of more than simply the bureaucrats or government officials to understand the point of view and concern of another country like Canada."

Such new tactics and diplomatic characteristics, requiring forthright public stands and even blunt arguments, made some Canadians uncomfortable, although to watch a combative Canadian hockey game, you wouldn't believe that a passion for hard-hitting confrontation wasn't burning in the breast of every Canadian. There is competition in Canada, but not the straight-out, hard-sell, spelling bee, I-won, you-lost atmosphere common throughout many American upbringings. It is the kind of social atmosphere that required some adjustment by my children when they reentered the troubled but generally more competitive and, I believe, more demanding American school system. And it is a social atmosphere that required similar adjustments for Canadian adults in the United States. "In my diplomatic career," one Canadian counselor in Washington said, "I've never done anything like this before." The change in diplomatic style was necessary, if distasteful, in Canada's view. But it represented a further crumbling of the old boy system of dealing with each other quietly and with only a tight-knit cluster of like-thinking cronies.

Americans, of course, have grown up with this blunt style, not always the most subtle or pleasant way of achieving one's ends but one that plays to the nation's perceived strong suit, clout, and ignores the nation's weak suit, diplomatic sophistication. I can recall, not altogether proudly, a roadside confrontation during one of the many childhood months I spent at my grandparents' near Toronto. There was a very brief heated dispute one muggy afternoon between me and another boy from down the road. He made some comment about Yanks and announced that he was fetching a larger friend to take care of me. I did the natural thing for a child of the Cleveland streets about to be outgunned: I bluffed. I suggested he do just that and that I'd wait right there. I did wait, hoping against hope that he would not return. But he did, and the friend was indeed larger. When the larger fellow approached within reach, without warning I belted him one in the nose. And to my amazement, they both ran off.

The ambassador that President Reagan chose to dispatch to Ottawa at the start of this new era of bilateral relations was a model of, uh, frankness, who said, "I didn't come to Canada to pour tea." He was Paul Robinson, a tall, tough-talking Chicago businessman long active in Republican politics and party fund raising. Like many Americans, he had Canadian ties;

his grandparents and great-grandparents were Canadian. Like many American ambassadors to Canada, he had his own direct links to the White House, which Canadians prefer. And like many Americans, he figured, frankly, that if the Canadians wanted to play for big-league stakes, they ought to play by big-league rules. This perhaps meant a special fondness for Canada but little, if any, special treatment.

So from the very beginning of his tour in 1981, he spoke out loud and often on what he thought of a lot of things Canadian, from welfare spending to the metric system, which Mr. Trudeau pushed enthusiastically, to Canada's military spending or, rather, the lack of it. The outspoken Mr. Robinson's statements (he thinks the metric system is "rubbish") aroused indignant articles in Canadian publications, including the *Toronto Star*, the largest newspaper, which one day carried a front-page banner headline on Mr. Robinson's suggestion to one Canadian interrogator to "Shove off!"

Generally dismissing the criticism as "shrapnel" that comes with the job, Mr. Robinson claimed he had been misquoted. He said, for instance, that he had been asked how the United States managed to lower inflation so much more successfully than Canada and that he had replied one way was to lower spending on social welfare. Since high welfare spending is sacred in Canada, this was widely deemed as criticism. But Mr. Robinson said he saw some advantage in all the controversy: It heightened interest in his remarks and he hoped it would speed Canadian recognition that Canada must give more thought to its international commitments. Mr. Robinson said he thought it was "right and proper" for him publicly to raise questions of mutual concern. "I have done this intentionally and with the support of Washington," the ambassador said in an interview, another epitaph to the quiet old days.

The American ambassador's bluntness even came up in Parliament, where Mr. MacGuigan, then the minister for external affairs, with his own reputation for frank speaking, defended Mr. Robinson. "There are some instances which, from time to time, could be considered borderline," Mr. MacGuigan admitted. But he added that giving Mr. Robinson fairly wide latitude to such free speech also enabled Canadian diplomats to exercise the same right in other countries—namely, the United States—a right that Canadians had rarely sought to exercise in previous times. And as Don McGillivray, a Canadian columnist, noted, when Canada's prime minister travels to Philadelphia to denounce American policy in Vietnam, as Mr. Pearson did in 1965, it is frank advice. When an American speaks out in Canada, it is "intolerable interference."

Nonetheless, North American neighborly relations had reached a new level. For the first time in their history the two countries began submitting regularly their disputes to mediation by third parties; the Americans, alleging that Canadian trading practices required by the Foreign Investment Review Agency distorted normal trade flows, took the Canadians before the General Agreement on Tariffs and Trade (GATT) in Geneva. Canada had already filed a complaint there against the United States for its ban on Canadian tuna imports after Canada had seized some American boats in Canadian waters and another against the United States on a complex patent law matter. For the first time both sides had also gone to the World Court in The Hague with their boundary dispute in the Gulf of Maine.

To some people these confrontations signified new heights in American bullying. To others it showed Canada beginning to throw its own considerable economic weight around. As the University of Toronto's Abraham Rotstein, a prominent nationalist, put it, "It's high time Canadians began to interfere in their own internal affairs." To still others these new developments or attitudes threatened a disturbing "descent into ruthlessness" benefiting nobody, according to John W. Holmes, a former Canadian diplomat.

The new tone in relations aroused considerable concern even outside government circles, one measure of the increasing awareness of Canada within the United States and, within Canada, of the need for a changed relationship. As early as the spring of 1982 Columbia University's School of Business and the partners in Touche Ross & Company, an international federation of accountants and management consultants with customers on both sides of the border, were so concerned with the rising frictions and apparent misunderstandings that they held an unusual three-day series of closed seminars in Toronto with prominent citizens from both lands speaking to and interrogating each other.

Presided over by Kingman Brewster, former president of Yale and ambassador to Great Britain, and David Johnston, president of Montreal's McGill University, the sometimes heated sessions brought some insights as participants struggled to define a new relationship. "We're neighbors and we're strangers," said Mr. Brewster. "Both peoples have got to take a longer view of each other."

"The United States is so massive an influence in Canada," said Professor Rotstein, "that anything we do domestically touches American interests immediately somehow."

"Canada seems so much like us," added Sol M. Linowitz, former U.S. ambassador to the Organization of American States, "that we expect Canada to be like us and do like us. And when Canada does differently by recognizing China or Cuba or struggling against us to maintain its independence, we are surprised and can over-react."

"We each get so involved in our own messy problems," said Stanley F. Melloy, president of the Continental Bank of Canada, "and we lose sight of a larger picture and the other fellow's perspective. Some conflict is inevitable. But because of our similarities, we can think that we don't have to work on our relationship. You know, if you like someone, you better tell them occasionally."

There was a consensus that both sides, especially the Americans, should pay greater sustained attention to the other. The problem, said Mr. Brewster, is that "we tend to be more important to any one country than any one country is to us." And there were suggestions, mirrored in other forums in recent years, that new structures were necessary to handle the mounting pressures on the two countries' relationship. Some suggestions involved institutionalization of annual summit meetings between the prime minister and the President to focus the attention of the public and government bureaucracies.

Writing in *Foreign Affairs,* the prestigious quarterly, Marie-Josée Drouin and Harald B. Malmgren noted, "The two governments seem to be on a collision course, in a context that political leaders cannot fully control."[2] They suggested another approach—namely, creation of new bodies to handle bilateral frictions: a joint economic commission to review emerging problems and recommend solutions and a joint Cabinet committee to defuse small disputes threatening to grow. There was a precedent for such bodies; there is, of course, the International Joint Commission that has handled limited water disputes, and there have been occasional informal gatherings of Cabinet officers in certain areas such as energy. But these latter bodies have proved short-lived and of limited effectiveness. At one point the U.S. Senate had before it a measure to consolidate all State Department relations with Canada and Mexico into one North American office. But such new bodies also smacked to Canadian officials of a "creeping institutionalization" that aroused considerable skepticism.

Superficially this rocky period in relations seemed muted as the months wore on. Pushed by the overpowering realities of their complex interwoven economies, both governments made mollifying gestures to the other. Ambassador Robinson softened his criticism, and Canada modified a few of its more nationalistic plans while assuring foreign investors that the concept of the NEP would not be applied to other sectors. In the short run this smoothed the waters, but it could mistakenly lead many to believe that business as usual was sufficient.

It seemed to me, however, that these new frictions between basic partners were warning signs of the need for more fundamental change. Politicians who come and go on both sides could sigh with relief and move on to the next inevitable and rockier crisis period, as they so often do on fiscal matters. Or they could turn these new tensions into a positive force, a kind of growing pain that would force people on *both* sides to realize the need for a more equal and ultimately more mutually beneficial relationship. This would require less attention to mechanisms perhaps and greater attention to new attitudes and principles. It would also require sustained attention on both sides (harder for Americans perhaps), an acceptance of good faith on both sides (perhaps a bit more difficult for suspicious Canadians), and a realization that the relationship is changing drastically anyway and that failure to seize control of the change and forge dynamic new links could lead only to what Professor Stephen Clarkson of the University of Toronto calls, simply, "trouble, big trouble."

For the Americans this new relationship would require an end to the attitude that former Secretary of State Dean Acheson, whose mother was from Canada, once described: "Americans assume Canada to be bestowed as a right and accept this bounty, as they do air, without thought or appreciation." It would require a conscious realization of America's own best interests close to home, that Canada is by far its most important trading partner with nearly twice the dollar volume of its number two trading partner, Japan, and more than the combined American trade with Great Britain, France, West Germany, and Japan. More than that, what country could be more important to the United States in the long run than one so rich, so similar, so basically receptive to friendship and understanding, and, for now, so stable that stretches 5,524.5 miles along its entire northern flank, physically shielding it from the mass of the Soviet Union across the top of the world?

There were some signs that at least a beginning recognition of this was creeping ahead. The criticisms lobbed back and forth seemed to become somewhat more informed, less emotional. It was perhaps no coincidence that this first began after the installation of new men to handle foreign relations in both countries, men who were more professional managers. They were Allan MacEachen in Canada and George Shultz in the United States, two men who just happened to have been classmates together at MIT. And even before Brian Mulroney became prime minister in September 1984, he and fellow conservative Ronald Reagan were joking about two Irishmen running both North American countries.

Canada's newfound economic aggressiveness also kept impinging on the American consciousness in so many new areas that Ambassador Robinson could say that he was mildly offended by Prime Minister Trudeau's story about Canada living next to an elephant and being affected by its every twitch. "I would say now," Mr. Robinson would say, "that the United States and Canada are both elephants." Small, but important, recognition that the shape of things was changing.

Increased and more informed routine American news coverage and expanded Canadian studies programs at American universities offered hope, too, that this change would seep further. Someday perhaps well-meaning Americans, intending a compliment, would notice that now it was only they who kept talking about how alike, how like cousins, these two peoples were. Nothing could ever change the geographical reality, the similar cultural heritage, the pervasive family and economic ties. But Canadians, not always intending any insult to Americans, were increasingly thinking of the Canadianness of their lives and less of their similarity to the United States. This could, if nurtured properly by leaders on both sides, be a positive sign of growing internal strength and need not be turned into some anti-American threat by opportunistic or ignorant leaders on either side.

For the Canadians there was a need not for sustained attention—they already had too much volume in a way—but for a realization that getting their side of any given issue across to Americans, who, unlike many Canadians, were preoccupied with a global agenda, required much more explicit, articulate, and patient explanations to more constituencies. Always to complain about how much American history Canadians studied and how little Americans knew of Canada was to forfeit the match. It had been, bluntly, a cop-out to avoid trying, not unlike the approach of Mr. Hirsch's would-be assistant at Stratford. "The problem is," Ontario's Premier Davis said in a conversation on his vacation veranda one sunny morning, "that some of the multinationals, some of the American companies, have been so used to doing business here just as though they were doing business in the United States that when the policy started to emerge that the government felt there should be greater Canadian involvement or ownership, it came as a great shock. It wasn't handled well. It wasn't explained well."

Canadians, who still seem basically uncomfortable with clout, would have to learn that it does not diminish one's sovereignty to anticipate a new policy's impact beforehand and to seek to explain it clearly and in detail to any number of public sectors, foreign and domestic. And the public and journalists would need to realize that watching intently for any possible slight can become a self-fulfilling fear, feeding unhealthy stereotypes. You will see what you are looking hardest for, even if this perceived slight was never intended.

This new relationship would also require a restatement of the obvious. As Ambassador Gotlieb put it, "We are, after all, different countries." What other two independent countries in the world require that kind of reminder? And with this comes a recognition that despite ongoing reservoirs of goodwill, the interests of these two countries will not always be the same. "The challenge, in managing this massive bilateral relationship of ours," Mr. MacGuigan told a Los Angeles audience, "is to respect our differences as we build on the areas of agreement." Ironically, each country has proved more adept at applying such principles to other more distant and changing lands than to its own next-door neighbor, cousin or not.

"While we would want never to be left alone in the world without America, we would also never want to be left in the world with America alone."

—Dalton Camp, 1980

187

FOUR

❧❧❧

The
Economy

❧❧❧

Geography made us neighbors. History made us friends. And economics has made us partners.

—John F. Kennedy in a speech to Canadians

It is entirely possible today that some average American works in a skyscraper owned by Canadians in a downtown being redesigned by Canadians, processes office forms printed by Canadians, grabs a quick lunch in a restaurant owned by Canadians, buys a Canadian novel in a bookstore owned by Canadians, or watches construction of a new office tower being built by Canadians. After work he jumps on a railcar made by Canadians and powered by electricity from Canada to meet his wife in a car built in Canada from Canadian iron ore to drive on Canadian cement to his home constructed by Canadians with Canadian lumber, underwritten by Canadian financing, and heated by Canadian natural gas to watch Canadian football on a cable TV system owned by Canadians or to read a Canadian-owned magazine or Canadian-owned newspaper printed on Canadian paper.

This fictitious American family, which might well be protected by Canadian insurance companies, could listen to their favorite rock group, all Canadians. They might go out to dinner at a luxurious Canadian-owned hotel and then to a racetrack to watch Canadian Thoroughbreds run. On the weekends, if the weather coming down from Canada is nice, they could take in a Canadian-made movie with Canadian stars like Christopher Plummer, Donald Sutherland, Genevieve Bujold, or Margot Kidder. Or they might prefer to feed the Canada geese that moved into a nearby park or see an American movie about an all-American hero named Superman growing up in a most bucolic midwestern American small town that was really filmed in a Canadian small town. Or they could stay home to watch an American commercial satellite-to-home television service beamed down from a Canadian satellite. They could also take a Canadian-made bus to the seashore to the Canadian-built condominium they rent for a week each year from a Canadian family, there to quaff some Canadian whiskey or Canadian beer hauled south on an American railroad owned by the Canadian government, while their car or jewelry is stolen by Canadian gangsters working the States for a few months.

It is an important measure of the advanced state of economic integration in North America today that no one really pays any attention to this phenomenon, unique in a world just becoming aware of its acute economic interdependence. Two independent countries, each of which began its national life as an English colony and then went its own way politically, have now drifted back together so closely economically that virtually every step any sector takes has some kind of effect on both countries' economies and their different dollars. With a common border, a common culture and language, and a common capitalist tendency for profit, Canada and the United States have forged the closest economic links of any two truly independent countries in the world, exchanging in excess of $120 billion a year in goods, services, and resources. This is the largest bilateral trade on the globe and, for the United States, more than its combined trade with Europe and Japan.

It seemed, finally, to bring to fruition an appeal made three-quarters of a century earlier by President William Howard Taft, who told a midwestern audience, "Canada is at the parting of the ways. Shall she be an isolated country, as much separated from us as if she were across an ocean, or shall her people and our people profit by the proximity that our geography furnishes and stimulate trade across the border?"

But this economic intimacy, new in its intensifying degree, is also an important measure of the advanced unawareness that Americans have—and almost cling to—about the New Canada emerging from the northern half of North America that has seemed so silent so long. It is a factor of its history, geography, economy, and psychological makeup that Canada has been so quiet, so unostentatious, so, well, meek during its first century or so of independence.

Canada's parts were colonies of the United Kingdom that never rebelled. They didn't want to. In fact, Canada had independence forced upon it on July 1, 1867, by a British government anxious to create some kind of political entity to forestall expansion from the south by a well-armed and newly re-United States. That country had successfully cast its territorial eye across the northwestern Canadian wilderness with the purchase of Alaska from Russia agreed to just four months before. Hesitancy, that polite pause that Canadians like to think separates them from the raucous Yankee rabble you-know-where, remains an integral part of the Canadian character in many respects today. But in one major area it has changed, and changed dramatically.

Economically, Canada, the old colonial pussycat, doormat to foreigners plundering resources and profits, is fast becoming a voracious tiger, especially within the North American economic scene. Canadians are starting late from further back. But having fully developed most of the scattered sectors of the domestic market, a new generation of aggressive, savvy, and well-financed Canadian businessmen is confidently buying back large portions of foreign-controlled companies at home and simultaneously marching south with energetic business imagination and cunning into an essentially open United States market ten times the size of Canada's. It has begun moving, too, in other directions overseas.

The speed of this ongoing economic invasion or mobilization varies with the day's or year's changing economic conditions, interest rates, and opportunities. But there is great historical and economic momentum behind it. And such changes will require significant and at times painful business and mental adjustments at home and abroad. Canadians, for their part, hold tenaciously to a comfortable feeling that they are forever doomed to abuse by powers far stronger than they. Robert Morley, the British actor, once noted, "Canadians love to sit in the dark trembling with fear at weather forecasts." Northrop Frye, the Canadian scholar, added, "The Canadian identity is bound up with the feeling that the end of the rainbow never falls on Canada."[1]

Canadians in general still act surprised at each one of their accumulating international business successes, even as the string lengthens in the big-league arena of foreign competition. When the hybrid Canada Development Corporation successfully acquired the Savin Corporation, the American copier company, to get its foot in the office door of the office technology revolution, I was hard pressed to find any Canadian financial analysts who thought it was a good move. Skepticism reigned; it couldn't be too good a deal, they seemed to say, if we could pull it off. American analysts, on the other hand, thought it was an ideal deal, a gamble naturally (what isn't in a shifting modern economy?) but a match made for both sides, if not in heaven. Likewise, many Canadians still feel mentally reassured and nod knowingly when some Canadian entrepreneur gets outfoxed in a foreign deal. It is an attitude that has inhibited imagination there and for many decades chased a good number of Canada's most able and aggressive businessmen, engineers, and even artists to larger ponds in other lands.

The Americans, too, will have to adjust their mindsets. Accustomed to a tame neighbor, they have for decades grown comfortable enjoying easy access to a modest but nearby market while exercising massive economic powers in another country, often at the invitation of Canadians seeking new investments—and jobs. The original attraction was ready resources, of course, and later a safe doorway leading behind the protective wall of Commonwealth tariffs. The last thing these American firms ever envisioned was competition at home—or abroad—from Canadian companies. But we are now quite likely in the most creative and exciting business era in Canadian history since Louis Hebert, a French pharmacist, saw the land's potential and became the country's first white settler in 1617. It is symbolically appropriate for Canada that its first white settler was a foreign businessman.

In a very few short years Canadian interests, funded by a small, well-organized fraternity of sympathetic and ambitious financiers with parallel desires to expand outside their homeland, have poured way more than $13 billion into American holdings, suddenly rocketing Canada from nowhere into at least the third rank of foreign investors, there behind only Britain and the Netherlands. In some sectors, such as metals or machine manufacturing, Canada is already the number one foreign investor. In others, such as food, insurance, and petroleum, it ranks a strong—and growing—second or third.

In actuality Canada's American holdings are probably larger than any official estimates. No precise figures exist, and anyway, they change daily according to millions of independent economic decisions, both major and minor, made on both sides of the open border. The complexity of such an intertwined economic net is so great that neither government could possibly control it, let alone even monitor it. They can estimate open, direct investments but cannot know of the ongoing scale of Canadian purchases financed through American banks, for instance, or purchases of real estate for private use, a major category which saw hundreds of millions of dollars flow into New England and Florida from Canada after the 1976 election of a Quebec provincial government vowing to separate from Canada.

However, using a common seven to one ratio of direct investment to assets, Canadians are likely to control more than $40 billion of assets of companies operating in the United States. To qualify for legal tax savings, higher import-export quotas, or certain money market advantages, other Canadian holdings in the United States are hidden within subsidiaries technically incorporated in other countries, such as the Netherlands.

"Ten years ago all this was unheard of," an American diplomat once told me in Ottawa. "Canadian companies didn't have the economic clout to compete in the U.S. or even with the U.S. Now, one by one, more of them are getting over that image of themselves as too small, too bush league. They find they can compete with the big boys, and compete very well. It's the start of a fundamental change in our relationship."

The United States isn't the only economic target. Billions more are being invested and traded abroad. "It's a big asset to be a Canadian," said Bernard Lamarre, the head of Lavalin Inc., probably Canada's largest engineering company. "When doing business in Africa, for example, we speak both main languages and are masters of North American technology. But we don't have any colonial past to live down. Nobody is afraid of us. We export know-how, not a way of life." Then he noted that Canadians have a good foreign reputation as builders, perhaps because unlike Western Europe and the United States, Canada is still building itself. "There are amazing opportunities for Canadian engineering firms abroad," he added.

According to Bank of Montreal figures, in one recent ten-year period Canadian direct investments flowing into other countries went from $230 million a year to $4.9 billion, an increase of twentyfold. One favorite Canadian target outside North America was the Pacific rim, that elongated and emerging overseas oval of almost three dozen developing nations surrounding the Pacific with about 48 percent of the world's population (1.8 billion souls) and a palpable thirst for heavy industry, raw resources, agricultural produce, consumer goods, and high technology. These Asian economies are growing far more rapidly than those of

Europe, in some cases by three or four times. Americans were beginning to sense this change; in 1982, according to some estimates, for the first time American transpacific trade exceeded transatlantic trade, $121.2 billion to $115.8 billion. But arriving Americans often found Canadian competition already established in such places as China, where Canada, unfettered by a strong pro-Taiwan lobby, had been selling wheat and other items for many years.

Much of Canada's Pacific trade moved through Vancouver, which quietly became the second-busiest port in North America and built a role as the English-speaking jumping-off point for economic adventures in Asia, especially Tokyo (unlike the East Coast, the two cities' time zones, though in different days, do overlap for a few hours of every business day). Vancouver, which is actually 350 miles closer to Tokyo than to Halifax on Canada's East Coast, began attracting foreign bank branches—thirty-six at last count—seeking to share in all the new trade financing.

The United States remained the largest buyer of Vancouver and British Columbia goods, taking more than $6 billion a year. But the percentage of American trade declined to near the 50 percent level as Canada sought to diversify its trade partners and as other countries, such as Japan, boosted their buying—and local investments. Almost half of Vancouver's shipping tonnage in recent years was moving to or from Japan. And when plans for the Alaska gas pipeline across Canada stalled, the Nova Corporation, an Alberta company once better known as the Alberta Gas Trunk Line when it bought up Husky Oil's operations, had one of its subsidiaries carry its pipeline expertise abroad to enter and win a joint pipeline-building venture in Malaysia with two Japanese companies. These were perhaps faint precursors of how Canada's new generation of less passive businessmen might act should American inattention continue in future years.

But it all was typical, too, of the kind of growth that obviously helped western Canada economically and also strengthened British Columbia's independent position in the regional political conflicts that characterize Canadian history. Businessmen in B.C. had always talked of doing business with "the East." But increasingly that meant the Far East.

Often at the behest of the federal and even far-seeing provincial governments (which opened their own trading offices in many lands), Canadian businessmen and officials visit the Koreas, Singapores, and Chinas of the world's largest population region. Sometimes several dozen of Canada's top business executives—friends from high school, graduate business studies in the United States, the boardrooms they meet in together, and the handful of quiet, private clubs they frequent downtown—fly off jointly to tour, say, China. There they all visit senior government leaders, see the obligatory sights and schools, and divide up at times to pursue their own industrial interests and contacts. The same businessmen carry home to their companies a new fervor for international operations. And they play host and reciprocate lavishly when some new foreign friends return the visit. News coverage of such Canadian stays as well as of Canadian business prospects and developments is provided by a growing corps of Asian and European foreign correspondents based in Canada. One daily business publication, Japan's *Nihon Keizai Shimbun,* regularly runs an entire page of Canada news while a typical day sees its Toronto-based Japanese correspondent sending home a half dozen stories on Canadian economic affairs.

At times Canada's prime minister himself even launched his own overseas economic missions, openly ignoring formal diplomacy to make blatant trading forays and boost his country's sales. One particularly effective enticement for the other nations, including Japan, proved to be the prospect of gaining access to some of Canada's bountiful resources with liberal credit terms and notably free of the political and ideological baggage often attached to such deals by the Americans. While remaining inextricably tied to the United States economically, politically, and militarily, Canadians had become skillfully adept at appearing to be separate from the Yanks. It was a kind of honest broker, middleman role that could inflate their meager diplomatic force while once again helping Canadians differentiate themselves from Americans.

There was another edge to this development that affected both Canadians and Americans. Canada's energetic emergence into the international marketplace naturally increased competition. It increased pressures on American branch plants in Canada to help the national economy and create jobs by selling more overseas, a step that could often place them in direct competition with similar international sales efforts by their own home American offices. Canadian government officials and bureaucrats tried to force a looser rein on such branch plant operations with varying success. It was another example of the kind of fundamental subterranean movements under way within Canada's economy and psyche.

In addition, this increased international competition for similar goods (wood, wheat, pulp, coal, communications equipment, for example, and even oil and natural gas) gave other countries a bargaining ploy when it came to determining prices. And these countries' representatives, especially some astute platoons of Japanese business buyers, often tried to whipsaw the two jealous cousins in their separate sales negotiations, attempting to play on their fears of being bested by their neighbor.

But when Canada tried similar tactics to force Japanese automakers to build plants in Canada as well as in the United States, there was much less success. The threat of losing through quotas or other retaliation the tiny Canadian market, which has always preferred larger cars anyway and is barely two-thirds the size of the South Korean market, pales into insignificance next to the hungry commercial chasm that is the United States.

In some Canadian circles doing business outside North America and outside Canada's natural trading partners in the British Commonwealth fairly quickly, if belatedly, became routine, dragging along into the international arena ancillary services like airlines and parts producers as well as new investors. And the intimidation factor of international operations, which had long held Canadians captive to their continent, began to dissipate.

There were times, in fact, when many Canadians wondered where all their businessmen had gone. "There is no shortage of Canadian entrepreneurs," said Rowland C. Frazee of the Royal Bank. "You'll find a lot of them in the United States."

Typically a Canadian operation in the United States began with a small operation or warehouse near the Canadian border in, say, upstate New York and expanded from there later into New England, long an area that drew Canadian immigrants, vacationers, and investors. On the West Coast Canada's swashbuckling investors first moved into adjacent Washington State, buying up vacation homesites with a glee and determination that pleased developers but turned entire projects into little Canadian subdivisions south of their own border. Other attractive regions would be added to the list later as confidence, capital, and consumer demand grew for an increasingly diverse range of Canadian projects and services.

In Connecticut, for example, Canadair poured $6 million into a new facility at Hartford's Bradley International Airport to service and repair its new Canadian executive jet plane, appropriately named the Challenger. Many states advertised in Canadian publications seeking new investments; Kentucky, billing itself as "the 11th province," even noted, accurately, that it is much closer to the major Canadian markets than many Canadian cities. Officials of New Jersey traveled back and forth to Canada to meet with officials and businessmen and to distribute thousands of copies of glossy brochures with titles like *New Jersey & Canada: Partners in Growth.*

Canada's presence in New Jersey, long a vacation destination for sea-seeking Canadians, was typical and soon included a wide range of operations. MacMillan Bloedel, the British Columbia forest products giant, had a New Jersey plant. Scottish & York, the mushrooming Toronto insurance firm, built its new American headquarters in Princeton. Maclean Hunter, a magazine-communications conglomerate based in Toronto, had cornered more than forty-two cable television franchises with more than 100,000 viewers across North Jersey counties. And it wasn't mentioned when President Carter journeyed to New Jersey in the fall of 1980 to open ostentatiously a new $130 million steel plant in Perth Amboy as a symbol of the vigor in American industry, but that steel company, Raritan River Steel, was a subsidiary of Co-Steel International, Inc., a Canadian company.

Olympia & York, the largest and very private building and development company in Canada, became New York City's second-largest commercial landlord, owning more than a dozen major skyscrapers with more than 13.5 million square feet, devising imaginative plans for rejuvenating the dreary Times Square area, winning the bidding for the vast Battery Park apartment-office development and then finding tenants to fill it.

In the $2 billion-plus Battery Park development, which involved land swaps and sales said to be the largest real estate deal since the Louisiana Purchase, Olympia & York also brought to bear some of its Canadian construction innovations, including a dual system of jumbo freight elevators that reduced the average waiting time of construction workers from 3.5 hours per day to 30 minutes, thus increasing productivity, cutting costs, and helping the builders meet their stringent deadlines, as usual. It also set about building its own communications network for tenants, bypassing the regular telephone system.

In Houston, Cadillac Fairview, Canada's largest publicly owned development firm, was developing thirty downtown blocks, part of a rapid foreign expansion that catapulted the share of its multibillion-dollar assets invested in the United States from 8 percent in 1978 to 40 percent five years later. "We've always felt welcomed here," said Martin Seaton, a Cadillac Fairview regional officer. In Dallas, at one point, nine of eleven downtown skyscraper projects were being built by Canadians, prompting one Canadian magazine to headline its article "Dallas in Wonderland."

During Denver's downtown construction boom fully half the eighty-six new buildings under way were owned by Canadians, as were 15 percent of the metropolitan area's apartments. "Canadian investors love Denver," said Michael Brenneman, the Canadian-born manager of a Canadian real estate firm in Colorado. Many projects were financed by Canadian institutions, such as Great-West Life Assurance, a subsidiary of Canada's Power Corporation of Canada, which opened its new American insurance headquarters in Denver, too.

But Canadian real estate investments and speculation in the United States were not confined to corporations. Spurred by their cold climate and for some Quebecers the uncertain political climate of their province, thousands of individual Canadians, including politicians working hard to reduce foreign real estate ownership at home, saved their wages to buy their dream: condominiums in Florida or Arizona or California or Hawaii, where they could visit during "March break," the sacred school vacation, and eventually retire. In fact, on any given winter day about 5 percent of all Canadians are somewhere in Florida.

When Portland, Oregon, wanted an architect to design its new Center for the Performing Arts, the city chose Barton Myers of Toronto from the 60-odd presentations submitted. And when the city fathers of Paris held an international competition to design a new opera house, a Canadian, Carlos Ott, won over 747 other competitors. On one listing of twenty-five major construction projects in Chicago, nine involved Canadian developers, some of whom already controlled substantial holdings in the city and its mushrooming suburban office complexes. Others involved European or Middle Eastern investors who controlled their American investments through subsidiary Canadian holding companies.

Alberta's Oxford Development Group Ltd., which grew up in Alberta and later moved its headquarters to Toronto, also helped revive several blocks of downtown Minneapolis, among other cities, at one time owning 31 percent of the available downtown rental office space. "It's really very simple," explained Gordon E. Arnell, formerly an executive vice-president. "In Canada there are nine population centers with more than five hundred thousand people. In the U.S. there are ninety." In addition, Canadian investors figured prominently in bidding for the rights to buy for redevelopment the Twin Cities' old Metropolitan Stadium; they included David S. Owen, a Torontonian who said the international border between Canada and the United States "is no different than the line between Minnesota and Wisconsin."

After scoring a surprising sales coup by winning a large contract to supply New York City's new subway cars, Bombardier Inc. of Montreal began developing a new generation of diesel locomotives to compete head-on with General Motors, the established goliath of the larger North American market. Flyer Industries of Winnipeg also took on GM in the city bus construction business, successfully underbidding the Michigan company for contracts as large as the one to build 580 new vehicles for Chicago. Flyer even appeared on a list of campaign contributors in Chicago's politics.

Telidon, the Canadian-developed system of video information transmission, was chosen for American use by the late telephone giant AT&T, which, as part of its historic divestiture, founded a new subsidiary to sell phone equipment in Canada. And when television impresario Fred Silverman wanted a fresh, energetic personality to tuck Americans into bed at night with a variety show to challenge the late-night TV dominance of Johnny Carson, he chose Alan Thicke. He is, that's right, Canadian-born. As is Peter Jennings, the ABC-TV news anchorman, and Lynn Williams, a Canadian who became president of the entire United Steelworkers of America, 20 percent of whose 720,000 members are Canadian.

Within just sixty months the eight-hotel chain of Four Seasons, based in Toronto, built or acquired six major luxury hotels across the United States, including New York City's Hotel Pierre. In just ten years the American operations of Northern Telecom, a Montreal concern becoming an increasingly important factor—the second-largest in North America—in the international communications equipment field, grew from a small marketing company in Nashville to a nationwide network of some two dozen American plants, which came to provide nearly 60 percent of the company's revenues and helped finance vast research and development projects that fueled Canada's high-technology drive around Ottawa.

The moves by Northern Telecom also reflected a mounting aggressiveness by the company that owned a majority of its shares, Bell Canada, which is significantly protected against foreign ownership by government policy. "Basically, we entered the U.S. because we had to," said Richard Wertheim, a Northern Telecom spokesman. "Canada was no longer big enough to sustain us, since we already had 70 percent of the Canadian market for our products." Used over the years to carry Canadian exports, the Grand Trunk Railroad, a wholly owned subsidiary of the government-owned Canadian National Railways, has expanded its American rail holdings from its original 60-mile route to more than 2,000 miles, including the Central Vermont Railroad. More recently Grand Trunk made a $400 million bid to buy out the remaining 3,100 miles of the Milwaukee Road's midwestern lines, a step opposed by its American competition. Grand Trunk then swung a deal with Burlington Northern to exchange upward of 100,000 freight-car loadings a year by jointly soliciting freight, offering joint rates, and coordinating operations in the States and Canada.

Retailers and restaurateurs have not lagged behind in the Canadian invasion that quickly came to seem the natural thing to do. Consumers Distributing Company Ltd., Canada's major catalogue-store operation, recently purchased seventy showrooms from St. Louis's May Department Stores Company and planned on opening dozens of others. Immediately unit sales of $2 million-plus per U.S. store outranked their long-established Canadian counterparts. Reitman's, a major Canadian clothier, bought out Worth's, a forty-two-store women's wear chain based in St. Louis, and planned on opening ten to twenty other new stores each year. Coles Book Stores moved into the United States' chain bookstore competition, which dominates American sales. Canadian Tire, the northern chain of hardware and auto supply stores, gained a firm foothold in the prospering American Sun Belt with a bargain-basement purchase of Texas's eighty-one-outlet White Stores, Inc.

Peoples Jewellers of Toronto bought out sixteen stores of White Jewelers in Salt Lake City. "Had we not gone into the U.S., that would have been a major decision," said Peoples' president, Irving Gerstein. Koffler Stores began opening more of its Shoppers Drug Mart outlets in the United States. Canada's Grafton Group bought up Seifert's, Inc., a chain of fifty midwestern women's clothing stores. Loblaw's, one of the supermarket subsidiaries of Toronto's mammoth Weston food conglomerate, which had maintained a small grocery store presence in upstate New York for years, suddenly branched into the Midwest to buy Applebaum's Food Markets of Minneapolis. Loblaw's, which proved successful with its aggressive and imaginative grocery promotions at home, planned on opening many new outlets to avoid the legal nuisances of American antitrust laws. De Havilland was selling commercial aircraft to Air Wisconsin and many other of America's emerging new airlines. The Canadian Broadcasting Corporation was distributing TV and radio programs to eager American outlets, especially the Public Broadcasting System, whose listeners followed the imaginative daily broadcast journalism of such live programs as *As It Happens* and *Sunday Morning.* When the New Chrysler Corporation was locating its new van-making operations, it chose Windsor; executives conceded privately they get better quality from Canadian workers.

In restaurants Canadian names began sprouting all over, though few seemed obviously Canadian to their patrons. In fact, Canadians now are the largest foreign investors in American food services with Swiss Chalet Bar-B-Q chicken, Mother Tucker's, Country Style Donuts, and Pizza Pizza just a few of the entrants. In 1984 Montreal's Imasco Ltd., parent of Shoppers Drug Mart, Canada's leading drugstore chain, spent $320 million to acquire Peoples Drug Store, Inc., one of the United States' ten largest drug retailers. Imasco, which also owns Koffler stores, had already bought the 1,736 restaurants of Hardee's, which, in turn, bought out Burger Chef. Captain Carnival, Inc., a chain of restaurants offering entertainment by robots, began opening units in the eastern United States. And Canadian food service managers became so adept that they even bought out some franchises for American chains in the United States, offering the sight of, say, a fast-food stand selling Kentucky Fried chicken in Florida being run more profitably by Canadians from Ontario.

Pizza Pizza, a large Toronto chain of—this will not come as a major surprise—pizza takeout places, revolutionized the pizza business in Canada with its sophisticated telephone-computer system that has one phone number for an entire city but automatically directs incoming order calls to the Pizza Pizza stand nearest the caller. Pizza Pizza is eyeing both Texas and Vancouver for expansion while it is also selling its technology to American pizza chains. Pizza Delight, an eastern Canadian chain, is also moving into the United States under the Pizza Patio name, but because of some nationalistic taste differences, it is finding profits somewhat lower south of their border. That is because Americans rarely order more than three toppings on their pizzas while Canadians rarely order fewer than seven or eight.

"In Canada, a number of capital sectors are up to capacity," said Kenneth Taylor, the hero of the rescue of some Americans from Iran, whose duties as Canada's consul general in New York were to help facilitate investments between the two countries. "The potential is so extraordinary in the United States."

In the 1970's alone Dominion Bridge (later renamed AMCA International Ltd.), a subsidiary of the old Canadian Pacific Railway empire, Canada's largest corporation in terms of assets, bought out twenty American companies and once moved its headquarters from Montreal across the border into New England. There were strong signs that Canadian Pacific, which was founded with a fledgling Canada and grew up with the country, had now outgrown its homeland. Many of CP's 110-plus companies with names like Cominco and Marathon Realty staged their own forays to the south, spending hundreds of millions of dollars on agribusiness, real estate, and housing developments and by design pushing the percentage of their total assets invested in the United States toward the 25 percent mark. For many other Canadian companies, American revenues came to constitute upward of half their income, the half that was growing the fastest.

In fact, after Canada Cement Lafarge Ltd. had bought out the United States' General Portland Inc. in a nearly $400 million deal, the company decided in 1983 to place its new North American parent concern in the United States, an area that buys one out of every five tons of Canada's cement production. Such moves could help Canadian companies meet the controversial "American" requirements of "Buy American" legislation that grew out of the recession. Under such provisions only American-made cement can be used in federally funded projects, unless domestically produced supplies would raise a project's cost by 25 percent.

Unbeknownst to many, the two countries were also being drawn together by rapidly growing new links in electricity, power sales which experts estimated would be worth $1 billion a year by 1990. The basic rationale is simple and, like most such links between the two lands, economically powerful. The power peaks of both countries are different —the United States needs extra electricity in summers for air conditioners, while Canada needs extra power for winter heat. It is far cheaper to buy extra electricity for the short peaks than to build expensive generators to stand idle much of the time.

The mutual benefit is equally clear. With about one-third of the world's freshwater resources and a sparse, scattered population, Canada has many undeveloped sites, far from environmental protesters, for hydroelectricity, which is cheaper and cleaner than oil- or coal-fired generators. With a signed American sales contract in hand, Canadian utilities can more easily finance the huge projects, which can also be used for cheap domestic power production. And with careful attention to sales agreements, control of the assets remains in Canadian hands.

The sales provide a market for both sides' surplus generation capacity. And Americans get the power from a reliable source at cheaper rates without vast investments in facilities and costly, time-consuming, and environmentally controversial hearings.

The links create some political squabbles within Canada. There are accusations, for instance, that Americans get inexpensive Canadian electricity more cheaply than Canadians, and some Canadians charge that by paying Canadians to produce their electricity, Americans are, in effect, exporting their pollution to Canada. The power links also have ignited complex lawsuits typical of the rancorous rivalries that spring up between provinces. Impoverished Newfoundland, for instance, wanted to build the expensive Churchill Falls power project but needed guaranteed sales to obtain financing. Quebec, the next-door province, bought the power at a very good price and then turned around and sold it to New England utilities at a handsome profit.

The trade in electricity is an old one, with the first transborder line going up in 1901 to link the Canadian Niagara Power Company Ltd. to its American corporate parent. One need not go far to find indications of the serious ramifications these links have for both sides. It was, in fact, the failure of some Canadian relay switches in Ontario that set off the great power blackout of 1965 that crippled most of northeastern North America. Special new high-tension transmission lines are under construction to carry the growing two-way exchange of power that has created greater energy bonds between some Canadian provinces and an American region than exist between neighboring Canadian provinces. Manitoba, for example, sells ten times as much power to American states as it does to Saskatchewan. There are even multibillion-dollar plans, long studied, though not yet beyond the pilot stage, to harness the 10,000-megawatt generating potential of the unusually high tides in the Bay of Fundy between Nova Scotia and New Brunswick. Special ocean gates would trap the high tides and then slowly let the water run out, using the natural flow of the ocean's twice-daily fall to low tide to produce the same power as sixteen nuclear reactors at much less the cost. Typically, Nova Scotia's plan is not backed by its next-door neighbor, New Brunswick. Also typically, the power would be produced not for Nova Scotian customers but for American power companies just to the south in New England, which have signed a $2.5 billion purchase of Quebec electricity for the 1990's and are negotiating to buy more from the New Brunswick Electric Power Commission, which would build one or two nuclear power plants just to supply the Americans (and to keep Canada's own nuclear power plant builders intact).

Americans, of course, had long since turned to Canada for powerful beverages, legal and otherwise. An association of Canada with its liquid refreshments was one of the few things most Americans could make quickly. So much so that Henny Youngman, the American comedian, could draw knowing chuckles with the story about his alcoholic brother: "Somebody told him to drink Canada dry. So he did."

Mr. Youngman did not drink Canada dry, nor did he drink Canada Dry. That famous ginger ale is no longer confined to Canada. Neither are a lot of other bottled liquids. During Prohibition the U.S.-Canada border was predictably porous as trucks and boats delivered much of the alcohol that fueled the illicit bars and the gangsters and even helped forge a family fortune or two in Canada. There has been Canada Dry and Canadian Club, and in 1983 Joseph E. Seagram & Sons, which already owned Paul Masson and Gold Seal Vineyards, bought out Coca-Cola's wine holdings, including the Taylor wine label, to become the United States' second-largest wine seller behind only E. & J. Gallo. And now come the northern beers that have been brewed in Canada for 108 years longer than the United States has been a country.

For decades Canadian breweries simply exported their small surpluses to the United States, where their higher alcoholic content (5 percent versus 3 percent) and fuller taste (Canadian beer uses more natural malt in its fermentation process) attracted a modest audience. At home, in typically Canadian fashion, just three major companies (Labatt's, Molson's, and Carling O'Keefe) controlled 97 percent of Canadian beer sales. This was accomplished by the fact that few companies had the capital necessary to serve such a geographically huge market and by splintering provincial legislation which will not allow a beer to be sold at cheaper "domestic" prices unless it is brewed "domestically" (i.e., in that province).

The provinces also strictly control advertising, with three of them (Saskatchewan, Prince Edward Island, and New Brunswick) banning all radio and TV alcohol advertising. Ontario's Liquor Licensing Board permits advertising but firmly forbids "product endorsement by recognizable personalities." One indignant board official explained, "We can't have Wayne Gretzky telling kids they will play better hockey if they drink Labatt's Blue."

As one result, brewers seek legal publicity by sponsoring countless sports tournaments and teams; the Toronto Blue Jays (baseball), Toronto Argonauts (football), and the Quebec Nordiques and Montreal Canadiens (hockey) all are, along with numerous smaller teams, owned by brewers. For a long time provincial laws even forbade drinking a beer in one's own backyard, and in Ontario it was illegal to drink standing up in a bar.

The standard provincial pricing policy, with all brewers agreeing on the same prices in that province, also effectively eliminated any dangerous threat of competition through a beer price war. In Ontario, for instance, Canadians cannot buy beer at a liquor or grocery store. It must be done at a monopoly beer store, what Canadians call an in and out store because there is one door for "in" and another for "out." The establishment is usually a drab brick box with tired, bored employees putting in their time much like many American post offices. A glass case displays dusty bottles and cans of the available brands. A customer waits in one line to return his empties and get his bottle deposit in change and then carries the coins and himself to wait in another line ten feet away to make a new purchase. In a minute the order comes sliding out of a back room on a noisy conveyor belt of metal wheels, a process that has hardly changed since post-World War II days.

But faced with a maturing domestic market, a budding American thirst for imported brews, and more aggressive Canadian owners, Molson's, Labatt's, and Moosehead lager have gone beyond the provinces and in just a couple years have captured three of the United States' top ten imported beer slots and about 30 percent of all import sales. It was becoming a familiar characteristic of the emerging joint economy of the two countries that one of the Canadian beers, Moosehead from New Brunswick, was better known in the United States, where it was available in all fifty states, than it was in its own homeland, where it was unavailable in eight of the twelve provinces and territories.

In ten years Canadian beer sales in the United States grew tenfold, prompting major capital expansion plans for the Canadians on the sole basis of their American sales. In fact, at present growth rates, within five years Molson's, the leading Canadian beer in the United States, will sell more beer south of the border than at home.

"The U.S.," said Al Farrell, Molson's research director, "is a pretty profitable place to be." The American attractions are also familiar. The United States market is near, fast-growing, and ten times the size of Canada's, which has slower growth rates and tough competition. Add to that strong foreign exchange earnings—in recent years one United States dollar has been converting to $1.17 or more in Canadian currency—and handsome profits resulting from an American willingness to view Canadian beer as an import worthy of a premium price simply because it travels across a bridge from another country.

Canadian brewers work hard to enhance that image. They did their homework and learned that Americans like tall, thin beer bottles, which have been illegal in Canada until recently, that Americans associate green glass with expensive imports, and that Americans will pay more for a beer with a premium import image. So for the American market, Canadian brewers junked the squat brown deposit bottles required at home for tall green throwaway containers. In their advertising, which often is scheduled on border television and radio stations whose signals sprawl efficiently into both countries for the price of one, they emphasize their special, elite origins in the wide-open spaces of the wild, foreign North, full of fresh air, woods, and clean, crisp waters. "Americans have a good image of Canada, and they go for the broad prairies and northern lakes," noted Mr. Farrell, "while for Canadians, that's a bit passé." In Canada, where the same beers have been mass-marketed in identical brown bottles, the "special elite," woodsy premium price aura of the import is dropped to emphasize plain good old friends, who are always young, having good times with just a good beer.

But it seemed that the success of Canadian beers in the United States could lead to some unusual twists that might require a scorecard to keep track of the players. In the United States, Molson's, the best-selling Canadian beer there, became the number two overall best-selling import beer with around 17 percent of import sales. It was behind only Heineken's from the Netherlands, which saw its dominant American import position slip a hair to a still hefty 38 percent. Heineken's then sent in one of its subsidiaries, Amstel Breweries, to compete in Molson's home Canadian market. Then Amstel's decided to try also to take advantage of the Canadian image in the American market. The Dutch subsidiary began test-marketing a new "Canadian" beer called Grizzly specifically for export to the Americans. This not only would give it a piece of both lucrative North American markets, using its Dutch image in Canada and its Canadian image in the United States, but would help hinder Heineken's other Canadian competition in the United States. And it would no doubt help Amstel's meet the Canadian government's requirement to produce new exports, a requirement which Canada's Foreign Investment Review Agency often attaches to its approval of new foreign companies in Canada.

The growing Canadian ownership in numerous other areas developed into a steady flow drawing only routine attention. Hiram Walker, the distillery that had merged with Consumer's Gas and its subsidiary Home Oil, spent $600 million to buy much of the Davis Oil Company in Colorado. Dome Petroleum negotiated a $1.5 billion line of credit for its tender offer for Conoco Inc. Canadian Pacific hotels built the new Franklin Plaza Hotel in Philadelphia. Brascan Ltd., the vast Canadian holding company (Labatt's, Noranda Mines, London Life, Royal Trustco, Canada's largest trust company), owned by a branch of the Bronfman family of Seagram's fame, bought 9 percent of Quaker Oats and then acquired a 24 percent interest in the United States' Scott Paper Company, letting it be known that it hankered for more.

Cineplex, which built a chain of movie houses in a collection of buildings each containing six to a dozen or more small movie theaters, spread its cinematic clusters from its hometown of Toronto to Los Angeles and elsewhere. Harlequin Enterprises, a *Toronto Star* subsidiary that transformed the American paperback book market by introducing packaged goods selling techniques to book sales, reaped large profits by selling its successful romance novels from grocery store shelves like boxes of soap ("Harlequin understands how you feel about love"). It then set up its own American book distribution system and branched out by buying the mail-order division of Miles Kimball in Wisconsin.

Domtar Inc. bought up Mississippi's Delta Brick and Tile Company. Nelson Skalbania bought the Atlanta National Hockey League franchise and moved it to Calgary. Pic 'N Pay retail shoe stores of North Carolina were bought by Bata Industries. Molson's, the brewers, became intrigued with the American market beyond the beer counter and bought into some American specialty chemical firms.

Canadian insurance companies spread their emblems and policies to the south, too, in policy sales and company purchases that became so frequent they garnered little attention. The Imperial Life Assurance Company of Canada spent $24.8 million to buy up Alabama's Loyal American Life Insurance Company. One Canadian insurance officer explained the moves outside Canada very simply: "You can't sell policies to trees."

Using American celebrities in magazine advertisements ("To Ben Vereen, security is being fast on your feet"), Sun Life of Canada, one of the world's twenty largest insurance firms, saw American sales increase a routine 10 percent a year, more than $1.25 billion every twelve months. And then to position itself to take profitable advantage of the growth and development in the United States' rapidly changing financial services industry, Sun bought up the Massachusetts Financial Services Company, which, among other things, manages several mutual funds with total assets around $3.5 billion.

Even Canadian farmers got into the invasion act, putting their expensive equipment to more prolonged, and thus efficient, use by bringing it across the border. Hundreds of Canadian combines and their hardworking crews became common sights every year, following the wheat harvests north from Texas to North Dakota and then back into Canada just as their own wheat was ready, with a goodly sum of worthwhile American dollars in the pockets of their overalls. American farmers who hired them had nothing but praise. "Those Canadians always have such good, clean equipment," Sammy Crissman said in a Kansas kitchen one late fall day. A wheat farmer who hires the Canadians each June, Mr. Crissman added, "Their stuff is always new and in great shape. And they do a very good job. Those Canadians are resourceful, I tell you." The American crews had more negative views of their new competition.

Watching the American stock markets closely from Vancouver, home of Canada's wildest stock exchange, the reclusive Belzberg brothers and their First City Financial Corporation from western Canada made a significant profit assembling more than 11 percent of the stock in New York's Bache Group from holdings once held by the Hunt brothers of Texas. Bache was later acquired by Prudential Insurance to the Belzbergs' profit. The brothers then took their earnings and won control of more banks in California as well as obtained the Bekins Company of Los Angeles, the moving van firm, for around $80 million.

Even K-tel, the music recycler of "solid gold" hits, with the shouting late-night TV commercials which awaken millions of dozing viewers around the world, expanded operations in the United States by opening a headquarters in Minneapolis (just south of its Canadian headquarters in Winnipeg) and by dabbling in some Texas real estate and oil investments. K-tel, which was founded by Philip Kives (the K in "K-tel"), a Canadian turned boardwalk barker in Atlantic City, was also selling its kitchen gadgets and "greatest hits" albums in more than two dozen countries worldwide.

At the same time millions of dollars in Canadian mutual funds poured out of Canada, seeking the best investment spots. By 1980 one out of every four dollars being managed by members of the Investment Funds Institute of Canada was invested abroad. In the next twenty-four months the amount climbed to one out of every three dollars, and this at a time when the Canadian dollar brought only around eighty cents on the dollar in the United States, where most of the funds went. Japan ranked as a distant second.

Using prominent local citizens as their representatives and their many years of cable experience drawing in and distributing American signals to Canadian subscribers, Canadian cable TV companies scored many successes in the competition for urban American franchises. After a long legal fight, Canadian Cablesystems of Toronto, already with thousands of subscribers in Southern California and Portland, Oregon, won the lucrative right to serve the whole city of Minneapolis. But the company learned a lesson, one that American firms long ago had learned in Canada: Play down your foreign affiliation. So Canadian Cablesystems became Rogers

Cablesystems. Likewise, there was no grand stir when Mortimer B. Zuckerman of Montreal stepped in to buy and try to save the financially struggling *Atlantic Monthly* magazine and, later, *U.S. News & World Report.*

For some early Canadian investors, the movement south was simply a reaffirmation by others of business decisions made many years ago. "I think we should be thankful that our present newspaper holdings include sixty-two daily newspapers in the United States," said Kenneth R. Thomson, chairman and president of Thomson Newspapers, Ltd., the publishing monolith bequeathed to him by his father, Roy, the son of a Toronto barber, who went on to own the *Times* of London and be named Lord Thomson of Fleet.

Thomson's American newspaper holdings have grown since then. In the United States the chain favors smaller publications like those serving Middletown, Piqua, and Xenia, Ohio, where it grants large editorial independence but demands strict cost accounting. But in 1983 the International Thomson Organisation, a related Thomson company with vast holdings in North Sea oil, European travel, and North American educational and reference publishing, agreed to buy the *American Banker* and the *Bond Buyer,* the daily newspapers for the United States banking industry and the tax-exempt bond sector.

The reasons for Thomson's interest in the United States were typical and illuminating. "It is interesting to note," Mr. Thomson told an annual company meeting not long ago, "that Canadians now invest more abroad in total than do foreigners in Canada. Political uncertainty and unrealistic wage increases have helped to create this situation, but anti-business attitudes and prejudice against foreign investment have certainly made a considerable and regrettable contribution. Canada can and must put out the welcome mat again." And the Canadian noted, pointedly, that most of his company's profit and productivity growth was coming from its American, not its Canadian, holdings.

As a people Canadians, perhaps as a result of their strong Scottish strains of pragmatism, thrift, and caution, do not tend to think in grandiose, ideological terms. Their constraining geographic and economic position combined with their psychological makeup has not allowed that luxury. As a former university history major in the United States, I have often found myself thinking of the life of a nation as that of a river, flowing ever onward, changing course here and there, overflowing into excess at times and running shallowly and weakly at others, simultaneously drowning and bringing new life, sometimes moving cleanly and sometimes filthily, but always progressing toward an ill-defined somewhere with an unscheduled arrival of sometime in the future, maybe. In Canada, however, I found my thoughts and image of its national life as being contained in a series of unconnected sitting ponds shaped by their locale and unseen fates. Some of the ponds are bigger and many are smaller; some are deep and lasting, and some shallow and threatened with parching; some slowly refresh themselves with subterranean flows of fresh water, and some simply sit there often dormant and aware only reluctantly of life beyond the pond banks. Now with the exciting emergence of the new Canadian entrepreneur outside his homeland, it seemed that many Canadian ponds were overflowing and forming their own ongoing river to somewhere. These flows hadn't yet merged into a single national river, but at least they were reaching out beyond themselves. From water level within these ponds this was hard to see. Life remained familiar and, oh, so comfortable. But from the outside the phenomenon was easier to spot; in some United States areas Americans who thought to look down noticed that the ground was quietly growing moist from new sources.

The Canadian economic expansion outside its borders is not part of a hemispheric vision calling for the conquering of new and exotic realms by a unified nation, such as the Japanese marching around the world in unison to common precepts, values, and goals. It is not a Canadian Manifest Destiny. It is more of a simple businessman's Destiny of Manifests. "Canada is a large market," David Bauer, an economist, told me one day as the Canadian flow of funds heightened, "but the U.S. is an enormous market. As Canadian companies reach maturity, it's only natural to look south. It's close, large, and logical." It is also a market that is familiar, easily accessible, and politically stable, and it provides some good investment values for Canadians, especially when the American dollar has been weak and/or Canadian profits at home have been strong, producing hefty corporate cash collections that cried for investment lest they tempt another company to seek a bargain takeover. Both Canadian and American companies were affected by high inflation rates, which, among other things, often made it far cheaper to seek expansion through takeovers of existing firms and equipment instead of through costly new capital investments. (Typically, with its higher rate of government economic involvement and spending, Canada's steep inflation rate lingered longer.)

According to statistics, the American market also has greater growth potential, a higher return on investment, lower real wages, higher productivity, a less militant labor movement, and, in many, many cases, less government regulation than the Canadian market. But there is another less obvious incentive for Canadians to invest money and reinvest American profits in American holdings such as real estate. They can deduct their carrying costs for loans there against U.S. income, just as American householders can deduct interest costs on their home mortgages. Neither deduction is allowed in Canada.

The eagerness of states and individual American communities to attract new investments of almost any nationality with tax deferments, cheap loans, and other development assistance has not exactly been a hindrance either. Michigan's Chamber of Commerce, like many groups becoming increasingly aware of Canadian economic clout, even organized a state-wide program to encourage towns and businesses to accept Canadian tourists' Canadian dollars at the same value as American money, equal to a minimum 20 percent discount. "Canadians like to spend money," explained Patrick Gagliardi, a state representative. "They are not tight. They're a very good market to get into."

For businessmen the attraction of the United States was strong in contrast with the many rules and regulations found in the government-bound Canadian economy back home, where for a time, for instance, the city of Toronto slapped a forty-five-foot height restriction on all new buildings.

That may have helped control development of the city's skyline into one of the most beautiful, if least recognized, urban lakefront profiles in North America. But such steps were taken at a price. And part of that price was a shifting of developers' attention and dollars away from Canadian investments toward spending in the United States, where such concerns over skyline and downtown access to sunshine would have been appropriate over a quarter century ago but had long since given way to a hunger for new jobs and growth.

One Canadian developer active in Los Angeles cited differences in the two nations' view of foreign ownership. "Americans brag about being so attractive," he told *Saturday Night*, the Canadian monthly. "They are far less xenophobic than Canadians. And there's a pro-business attitude here on the part of the mayor, the council and the civil service. If you're profitable here, you almost become a hero, whereas in many parts of Canada, particularly in the Toronto area, the prejudice is against earning money."

The outspoken chairman of Canadian Pacific Enterprises Ltd., Ian D. Sinclair, put it another way: "We feel there is a growing understanding of the role and requirements of the private sector in the U.S. Rules for business are definitive there. You may not like all the rules, but you can ascertain what they are and adjust to them. The climate there, in my judgment, is good for investing."

Declining American rules and regulations was one major attraction for Canadian oil and gas companies, whose multimillion-pound drilling rigs were disassembled to lumber south in truck convoys in search of more lucrative underground fields. Exploration land was available at what seemed bargain prices to Canadians. American production royalties were smaller.

The United States, in the midst of a swing to the conservative side of its economic pendulum movements, was hell-bent for vigorous government deregulation in numerous economic sectors, including oil and gas. "Businessmen are not all that ideological," noted Brian Gilmer, a corporate finance officer for a major Canadian investment house. "A thirty-dollar barrel of oil found in the U.S. just looks a lot better than an eleven-dollar barrel in Canada."

Continuous federal-provincial bickering over energy prices creates considerable economic uncertainty in Canada, which Canadians take for granted but which foreigners see as disturbing, especially in the inevitable contrast with a stable, if somewhat rowdy, United States next door. In addition, Canadian government export restrictions and high export prices helped produce a surplus in some types of oil, which Canadians then began selling, not to their neighbor but to Japan. These government restrictions also helped feed a massive surplus of natural gas in Canada, an abundance that forced many new gas finds to be simply capped shut in the ground for years while the interest charges on those exploration expenses continued to accumulate.

"In Texas," added Mr. Gilmer, "a long shut-in is two weeks. I know one utility laid pipes right to the drill site. I couldn't even guess at the Canadian money that's flowed into Texas, the Rockies, and Michigan." Many of these investments were quiet, patient money, typically Canadian. Canadian companies with names like Ranger Oil, Texas Pacific, Asamera, Hudson's Bay Oil & Gas, Canadian Superior, and PanCanadian Petroleum (another finger of the CP empire) broadened their United States economic exposure.

Other Canadian moves like Dome Petroleum's nearly $2 billion bid for Conoco stock or the Nu-West Group's run on the Cities Service Company of Tulsa made larger splashes. Some astute attempts by Canadians to buy into American oil companies failed, and all they did was make a lot of money. For instance, the $525 million attempt by Denison Mines, Ltd., the Toronto uranium company, to take over the Reserve Oil and Gas Company of Denver came $100 million short of beating out the bid by the Getty Oil Company of Los Angeles. This may have been intentional; it certainly was lucrative because Denison made a handsome profit selling to Getty the Reserve shares it already owned and, in addition, earning a special $10 million fee from Getty "in consideration" for dropping its merger plans.

But the ramifications of some Canadian investments often spread across the United States far beyond the immediate target. Dome's $1.7 billion assault on Conoco, even though it was aimed at forcing the American company to sell off only its Canadian holdings of Hudson's Bay Oil and Gas, revealed Conoco's corporate vulnerability. That led a few weeks later in 1981 to its complete $7.67 billion takeover by E. I. du Pont de Nemours & Company, then the largest corporate merger in American business history, after a fierce multimillion-dollar struggle among Du Pont, Mobil Oil, and Joseph E. Seagram & Sons, yet another Canadian company on the hunt.

Similarly, the $600 million purchase by Toronto's Hiram Walker Consumer's Home Ltd. of some of the oil and gas properties of Denver's Davis Oil Company provided Marvin Davis with most of the money necessary, in turn, to win control of 20th Century-Fox six months later, turning that historic motion picture and entertainment giant into a privately held firm.

The shoe can go on the other foot, too. The unsuccessful $1 billion bid by Canada's Brascan Ltd. for Woolworth's in the United States added to the old Canadian company's image of vulnerability at home and led directly to its takeover by a branch of the Bronfman family, of Seagram's fame, whose fortune first began accumulating with sales to the Americans.

The Canadian interest in American oil and gas was so strong that Canadian investment firms like Mr. Gilmer's A. E. Ames & Company, which itself was to become a merger victim at home, began organizing investment seminars on oil prospects in the United States for its institutional investors. This often produced a string of Canadian oilmen enthusiastically addressing an attentive crowd of Canadian money managers on investment opportunities for Canadians—in Houston. Mr. Gilmer, for one, was so impressed that he quit Ames to start his own Canadian oil company with substantial American holdings.

Ironically, Mr. Gilmer's new company, among others, opened its headquarters in Toronto on a point of southern Ontario land that conveniently juts deep into the American heartland. Toronto, which had become Canada's premier city, owed much of its newfound economic prominence to the fact that American investors going north in recent decades had also liked its geographic proximity to the Midwest and selected it for their Canadian offices over scenic but troubled and more distant Montreal (Montreal was also hurt by the migration of many of its customers from its economic sphere of influence in the northeastern states toward the Sun Belt). Back in Ontario, though, now the investment flow was going into the States. But Toronto, clean, cultured, convenient, and eminently livable for a North American metropolis, had quietly arranged things to win either way.

The aggressive Charge of the Maple Leaf Brigade into the United States ignited some latent frictions on individual issues on both sides. There were smoldering resentments among some Americans over being bested at home by "foreigners," once they realized a new company was Canadian. And Canadians, who seem so similar to Americans during all those annual fall fishing expeditions to northern Ontario, were conveniently lumped in with other sneaky (i.e., successful) aliens like the Japanese and Arabs.

Among Canadians there was little apparent satisfaction at their economic successes abroad, nothing on the order of the Honda executives in Tokyo one day who exchanged nodding, knowing smiles at word that they had beaten yet another British motorcycle maker out of business. But if there was no exuding of glee in Canada, there was in many Canadian circles an eager anticipation of American resentment, especially in the Canadian media, which, like the press in most democratic societies, thrives on conflict, real or perceived. If an obscure state legislator in Oklahoma suggested to a wire service reporter that there ought to be some legal controls on Canadians and other foreigners buying up land there, that story received major attention in Canada (U.S. YELPS RING HOLLOW went one editorial headline). When the lawmaker's idea was thrown out of court, the story was worth only four paragraphs buried deep on an inside page. The former fitted what many Canadians were looking for; the latter did not.

This attitude was especially prevalent as the tide of American resistance rose to meet the tide of attempted Canadian takeovers. Many of the mergers were consummated quietly and efficiently and without rancor. Others evoked the full legal panoply of corporate resistance with batteries of lawyers filing lawsuits and antitrust allegations in scores of states, trying to raise the cost of the move beyond the price their opponents were willing to pay. The Canadians, accustomed to dealing on a national scale at home with few significant competitors and without significant fetters, professed shock at the rough American reactions and no-holds-barred tactics. It was a strange reaction from a people who wake their children for 5:00 A.M. Saturday hockey games to watch them slam each other into wooden walls in a move politely termed checking.

It didn't matter if Americans treated Americans the same way in similar intramural proxy struggles for supremacy. And it indicated that Canadians had been fooled by the same much criticized phenomenon that befell American investors in Canada long ago and still strikes American tourists on their summer visits. Superficially both peoples in both countries seemed so much the same—the same language, same culture, same cars, same books, same TV shows, music, and movies, even the same baseball, hockey, and soccer leagues.

But beneath this veneer of similarity lay entirely different grains with their own different strengths and fault lines, fears and prides, attitudes and assumptions. In short, they were completely different personalities from the same family. And as any police blotter, American or Canadian, will show, disputes within a family always carry the potential to become by far the most violent disagreements, a fact borne out, too, by any history of civil wars.

The economic changes afoot in both lands and the conflicts they led to in relations between the two always reminded me of two brothers growing up side by side, seeing the same things through two different sets of eyes. There is a long time when the world seems essentially the same to both. The younger boy, through a lack of his own experiences, accepts as gospel whatever his elder says and, in return, gets the right to lean on him for protection and guidance. The elder likes, perhaps even relishes, the sibling esteem and comes to expect a certain deference as part of the foundation of their relationship. It is comfortable and satisfying for both, and natural.

But there comes an unannounced time in their relationship when the rules of their games subtly change without warning. The younger brother was once content simply with his elder's attention and was willing inevitably to lose in any game they played, unless the big brother let him win when it didn't seem to matter too much. Now, however, that is not enough for the youngster. Tired of losing for so many years, he unilaterally starts changing their understanding by playing to win, gritting his teeth and perhaps tackling a little bit too hard by the standards that have existed up until then. At that point the shocked larger brother can react with hurt, anger, and animosity at the seemingly sudden and rude change in the game that could seem to threaten his superiority. And he might indignantly demand to know what he had done to deserve this (the answer, of course, being nothing except being witness to a normal evolution). Or the elder brother can smile knowingly and shake it off as natural growth, confident in the knowledge that nothing can ever undo the blood bonds between them and that they can, in fact, grow closer and stronger in mutual maturity.

It doesn't take a professional philosopher to realize that the five-year difference in age between two brothers thirty-five and forty is much less than the five years' difference when they were ten and fifteen, just as a century's difference in age and maturity between two countries is much less when they are a hundred and two hundred than when they were one and a hundred and one.

This raises serious questions about how the two countries are planning, or not planning, to shape together the second century of their continental coexistence economically. A steady string of frictions continues to erupt on both sides as Canadian and American interests clash and actually compete, many for the first time. The fact that the issues at hand appear petty in the overall framework of the North American economy does not reduce the strength of argument or of the emotion that sometimes bursts forth within individual sectors.

The significant American criticism has not focused so much on the Canadian expansion per se. Unlike many sectors of Canada's economy, rigorous competition is expected in the States. Or as Ron Graham, an editor of *Saturday Night*, put it in that magazine, "There are no slow lanes on the L.A. freeways." If you can take the heat, you can stay in the kitchen. "All companies in the U.S. market have to be aggressive to survive," said one marketing official of a prominent American life insurance company. "Canadian companies are welcome because the more competition, the better it is for all consumers and the life insurance business in general."

American objections—and they echoed even in the halls of Congress —centered, instead, on the alleged unfairness of Canadian concerns, grown large on cloistered markets at home, venturing forth to conquer American companies from their government-protected economic citadel to the north. "Should Congress permit American companies to stand vulnerable to the sort of raid now under way by Canadian Pacific Enterprises, reaching out from all the protections of Fortress Canada?" asked David Meeker, chief executive officer of the Hobart Corporation, as CP tried, unsuccessfully, to take it over. Mr. Meeker did not have to add what his opinion was.

When they looked north, American investors experiencing the Canadian expansion in the 1980's did not see a younger country coming of age economically, seeking to assert more control over its domestic economic future through legal means. They were looking to see predators in cahoots with a foreign government to change the way things had been done for so long, to hamper their own expansion, or, worse yet, to move into the Americans' own backyard and play hardball by a set of rules stacked to suit the visitors.

Canadians bringing investments into the United States could do so without much hindrance, save the normal hurdles and costs should a takeover be considered hostile. They might have had some problems if their target were a television station licensed by the Federal Communications Commission, for example, or a major defense contractor or a utility.

But with the United States energetically pursuing government deregulation in a broad range of areas, the economy was essentially open to penetration. In fact, in some instances Canadian banks were eligible to engage in multistate branch banking, as domestic American banks were not. Canadian companies for a long while did not even have to meet American federal domestic borrowing ceilings or margin requirements on loans. This meant that a Canadian company on the hunt could borrow 100 percent of the cost of a takeover while an American company pursuing the same takeover target was required to put up 50 percent of the price from its own funds before getting a loan for the remainder.

Americans bringing investments into Canada, on the other hand, confronted an essentially mature market dominated in most sectors by a few large, well-established firms. The Americans (or any foreigner) were required to demonstrate to the Canadian federal government's Foreign Investment Review Agency (FIRA) that their incorporation of a new business or purchase of an existing Canadian company was of some ill-defined "substantial benefit" to the Canadian economy. They might very well be required to sign a special agreement promising such things as set future sums of capital infusion, a minimum number of employees, specific programs to train Canadians for key management jobs, and quotas for future exports. All this required the hiring of Canadian lawyers and consultants. It could take a year of secret deliberation; at the end, the foreigners might be simply turned down.

Such a process was even required by Canada for an American takeover of an American company in the United States if the target had even a tiny exposure in the Canadian market. When, for instance, Coca-Cola of Atlanta bought out Columbia Pictures of Hollywood, Coke had to seek approval of the acquisition of Columbia's two small Canadian arms. And because Canada's communications minister was designing a detailed strategy paper on Canadian cultural industries to boost their strength and Canadian content and ownership, the review process became bogged down in politics.

As another arm of the same kind of domestic growth, the same Liberal government introduced the series of nationalist economic bills called the National Energy Program. Many were highly technical, but they were designed to chop foreign ownership in Canada's energy sector from 72 percent to 50 percent by the end of the century. They created a network of powerful tax and bidding incentives strongly favoring Canadian concerns with majority Canadian ownership and simultaneously discriminating against foreign-controlled companies, most of them American, long the energy industry's foundation. These rules often made it prohibitive for foreigners to compete, prompting loud cries of "Foul" and a chain of sellouts to Canadian-controlled energy companies by foreign firms interested in putting their money elsewhere, where a larger, quicker return was possible and the investment climate seemed more hospitable.

"Many investors have got the impression," said Richard J. Smith, a minister in the U.S. Embassy in Ottawa, "partly as a result of the way FIRA has operated, that they are less than warmly and cordially welcomed in Canada." And he noted that the agency's much cited approval rate of 90 percent did not accurately reflect FIRA's impact on Canada's economy since it did not reveal all the foreign investment proposals voluntarily withdrawn or not even submitted in the first place. An example would be the effort by the Great Basins Petroleum Company of Los Angeles to sell out to the Phillips Petroleum Company of Oklahoma for $250 million. The deal was in hand when FIRA decided that it would require the proposed new owner, Phillips, to sell off half of Great Basins' Canadian properties to Canadians. Phillips backed off. The deal fell through. And nothing showed up in FIRA's house statistics.

This coercive strategy may have made eminent political sense in any country seeking to emerge into its own, especially one so resentful of its economic dependence on decisions made outside its borders. As Canadians pointed out, would the United States have waited nearly a century to act if most of its oil and natural gas were controlled by foreigners? But this seemingly sudden change, packaged in its take-it-or-leave-it wrappings with virtually no voluntary effort to explain its reasoning outside Canada, handed opposing American businessmen and their vocal lobbies in Washington and state capitals elsewhere a powerfully persuasive weapon. (It also helped fulfill Canadian expectations that they would be attacked by foreigners for standing up to do what they thought best domestically.) And it handed American politicians a very hot potato. The outcome, given the relatively few American votes to be found in places like Ottawa and Regina, could be fairly safely predicted.

"I believe," thundered Governor David Treen of Louisiana, where Henry Wadsworth Longfellow's Evangeline and 6,000 other nonfiction

Acadians had finally settled (and become Cajuns) after being expelled from eastern Canada in the mid-1750's, "we should closely examine what appears to be an enormous, unfair advantage being granted to Canadian companies by the Canadian government, an advantage that markedly enhances their ability to do business in the United States. We in Louisiana have strong historical and cultural ties to Canada. But I believe that, as a matter of national policy, the apparent inequities in this situation should be fully explored."

House Democratic Majority Leader Jim Wright of Texas added, "Canadian companies, secure in their knowledge that government policy protects them by greatly limiting U.S. acquisition or operating opportunities in Canada, are becoming more aggressive in their acquisitions and takeovers of U.S. companies and resources." Senator Orrin Hatch of Utah, chairman of the Labor and Human Resources Committee, suggested the "preferable solution" would be mutual cooperation to establish bilateral ground rules and ensure general reciprocity in the treatment of Canadian and American companies in both lands. "It is apparent to me," the committee chairman warned, "that we cannot allow such a one-sided situation to continue." As part of their response, the Americans took their complaints about Canada outside the family to the international General Agreement on Tariffs and Trade.

Americans are not surprised to learn that these politicians, among many others who regularly join the verbal fray, are responding vociferously to complaints from constituent groups and their representatives stationed in Washington, D.C. Canadians may not be surprised either; they have come to expect almost anything from "the States." But they find this kind of special-interest lobbying to be impolite, somehow distasteful, not unlike submitting to elderly relatives a long, written list of Christmas presents that would be acceptable this year.

This is a strong reflection of the two countries' differing political systems and heritages. One land demanded its independence from a foreign country, fought seven long years to get it, and then forged a three-headed political apparatus of checks and balances based on distrust of authority and an ideal that for power to be legitimate, everybody has the right— indeed, the responsibility—to make himself or herself heard. The other country never even requested, let alone demanded, its independence, reached no national consensus on the need for a constitution of rights until 115 years after its founding, and thinks that three equal and independent branches of government create nothing but chaos. Government is there to build the country and to help the people. Why would it do anything else? If any real democratic check is necessary, it believes, it can be exercised every five years or so, when the government's majority party decides to call an election. People can then vote for their district's, or riding's, Member of Parliament, whose party affiliation, added to those of the other elected members, will determine who rules as prime minister for the next term.

To be sure, Canadians have their strongly held opinions on policies, issues, and political personalities. These have been voiced in private or in riding and committee meetings. Businessmen can get their point across to the government formally through their lawyers, called solicitors. But the tone and the volume have usually been more moderated than similar sessions to the south. It wasn't until recent years that the new mix of Canada's population could feel socially accepted after taking to the streets to chant and demonstrate for or against some cause, everything from American missile tests over isolated countryside areas to gay rights in Toronto. Even in the early 1980's there was some shock and indignation when crowds of demonstrators descended on Ottawa to picket against the government's anti-inflation program in front of a federal Cabinet minister's home.

So it fits in with the national personality that Canadian government and business executives would not instinctively turn to lobbyists to make their point in Ottawa, let alone down in Washington, where so many decisions affecting Canada are made and where there are so many times more lobbyists than there are elected representatives to be lobbied.

"There is a combination of gentlemanliness and fatalism that I sometimes find among Canadian companies," said Jerry Brady, whose Washington law firm client list includes a growing number of Canadian concerns. "Too few realize that they have a right to represent themselves just like any other interest." American lobbyists have noted a certain psychological resistance among Canadians, a feeling that they don't want to dirty their hands in such matters. Matt Abrams, who has founded a new firm called Canamco to lobby for Canadian clients, noted, "Often a Canadian company is represented once it sees a crisis looming. What one's objective should be is to prevent the crisis from coming up."

But as the persuasion activities by lobbyists and political action groups have intensified in Washington and the United States in recent times, most Canadian companies have stood idly by. This can prove costly, as, for example, when the U.S.-Canada fishing treaty died while few American voices outside the Carter administration were heard in its support. Or when a last-minute congressional amendment required use of American cement on roads financed by new fuel taxes, Canadians did not react quickly enough, and they lost a few million dollars in cement business.

When they do react, Canadians have preferred to rely on the "true friend" argument. "The best chance of influencing congressmen is not to say, 'Hey, we're Canadians, we're good guys,'" Mr. Abrams advised Canadians in a 1983 lobbying primer published by the *Globe and Mail*'s business section. "It is unusual when a congressman is swayed by the fact that Canada is a friend. There is a residue of good will, but on very specific industry issues, the good will disappears. Canadians have been polite too long."

This attitude is in marked contrast with efforts by the Americans' number two trading partner, Japan, which hires squads of Americans, some very prominent former policy makers, to make their trading points to American industrial allies to pressure and convince their elected representatives. Thus, the lobbyists for a Japanese manufacturer faced with possible import controls might meet with its American distributors and parts suppliers and urge them to make the "anti" case in Washington in their own best interest. The Canadians rarely thought of that. The distant Japanese did not need to be reminded of the different operating procedures in the United States. The nearby Canadians did.

For certain, Canadians did have their own set of economic grievances that grew out of American actions, inactions, or insensitivity to the fallout of some domestic policies. High on the list in recent times was so-called Buy American legislation, which required public agencies to purchase or to require their contractors to purchase for them only American-made goods and supplies. This was aimed primarily at overseas makers of such things as steel and vehicles, the aggressive manufacturers in Korea, Japan, and some Common Market countries that, politicians charged, exported their unemployment problems by underpricing their goods to keep their own mills rolling even if without much profit for the moment. As happened in the Buy American cement clause, Canada was basically an innocent bystander, but one increasingly resentful of always being over-looked or forgotten. The fact that it was inadvertent mattered less and less. The fact that it still happened mattered more and more.

Long a sore point was the question of extraterritorial application of American laws. Here the United States sought to force American compa-nies, no matter where they might be operating, to adhere to American laws and regulations against, for example, trade with Cuba or China. Canada, historically much more of a trading nation than its neighbor, saw no reason why an American Congress could tell an American toolmaker with an Ontario branch plant full of Canadian employees where he could or could not sell his Canadian-made goods, especially if such sales would help create more Canadian jobs, taxes, and investments. Both lands might expect such complications if either were dealing with a country of a different culture and language. But here once more Canada and the United States were caught in their intimate irony.

Then came the question of trucking, an important affair since half the vast volume of goods shipped between the two lands moves by truck. It is a characteristically knotty and potentially emotional issue that touches on sovereign prerogatives and retaliatory protectionism. To put the prob-lem simply, the American long-haul trucking industry, like several others in the States since President Reagan's inauguration was going through the adjustments of government deregulation, essentially reinstalling some free-market forces in the business.

These steps involved a liberalization of procedures for trucking firms to apply for routes. American truckers began to believe that the opening made it far easier for their Canadian competition to operate in the United States than for American truckers to obtain routes through cumbersome and, they felt, biased procedures before provincial governments in Can-ada. And the American truckers succeeded in getting a legislative rider attached to a Senate bill, setting a two-year moratorium on Canadian route applications.

The Canadians, who actually filed a formal diplomatic protest with Washington, claimed they were being discriminated against. They claimed that except for Quebec and Ontario, American trucking compa-nies dominated the business in Canada, that even in Quebec and Ontario, Canadian and American companies split the business about evenly, and that provincial governments approved 85 percent of American route requests. Bruce Maclaren of the Canadian Trucking Association saw a retaliatory "spillover implication" in American policy. "We are just a convenient target," he said, "for a lot of hurt and suspicious feelings generated by Canadian energy policy and the Foreign Investment Review Agency."

Even rain can link and divide the two countries' economic concerns when it carries pollution from the skies over both lands into the waters of both lands. The Americans, preoccupied with other issues and priorities, saw the precipitation carrying acidic pollutants into lakes and streams and the life-cycle of land as an environmental matter to be added to that lower-priority list. Much of the Americans' contribution to that two-way transborder pollution by acid rain comes from power plants that, seeking to reduce national dependence on foreign oil sources, switched to coal-fired generators with government encouragement.

Canadians, who rely less on foreign oil in the first place and generate much of their power from nonpolluting hydroelectric sources in the second place, tend to see a somewhat different agenda. Since none of them lives many miles from a wild lake or stream, they also tend to attach different priorities to halting the addition of such poisons to the landscape. This is especially true because of the substantial contribution to the economy from tourism. As the provincial governments and tourism industry association constantly point out in advertisements, 1 million Canadians, fully one out of every ten jobs, earn their living from tourism, and their patrons do not travel from other lands or provinces to look at dead fish floating in idle eddies.

The differing priorities also result from the fact that much of the Canadian identity is still tied up with the land. Canada may have 10 percent more area than the United States, but much less of that space is hospitable or affordably habitable because of extremes of climate and geography and distance. So Canadians have generally felt more careful about caring for the land and keeping it "nice," a trait confirmed by even the most casual comparison of an American urban street and the tidy thoroughfares, lined with tulips and unvandalized fountains, that characterize Canadian cities.

Canadians did not settle their land by moving across it in waves of migrating pioneers. Typically they arrived in one spot from overseas and then stayed there. Other bands from other lands came and settled farther west and so forth, isolated pocket after isolated pocket. So there has always been in Canada a greater sense of stability and staying power, which, I believe, prompted more caring for where you were because that was where you were going to stay. You had to protect what you had lest you lose it, with the emphasis on the chance of losing it. In their disposable society, gambling Americans always had another state, another mountain range, another region to move on to, and only when things were full—and dirty —did they start worrying about cleaning up. Canadians required deposits on all their beer bottles from the beginning.

But specific issues aside, the full-speed Canadian economic expansion to the south was not unanimously accepted as beneficial even at home. In opposition the Progressive Conservative party charged that the economic policies of the governing Liberals were chasing Canadian and foreign investments away from Canada, a charge no doubt inspired by political motivations but one that did carry some truth in some business circles. In power, Prime Minister Mulroney promised early steps to ease the concerns of foreign investors, and, not coincidentally, to attract new money to combat stubbornly high unemployment.

George Hartman, a financial analyst, said he found considerable skepticism about foreign investment adventures among Canadian institutional investors who displayed an "inherent inferiority complex about being successful outside of Canada." With the rapid growth in the labor force during the last ten to fifteen years, unions try to convince Canadian companies to make the same investments at home instead and save the jobs for their countrymen (or countrywomen since Canada has experienced the same massive return to the job market by women as the United States has). Some studies said Canada would need 3 million new jobs in the 1980's to absorb its young adults.

But among others, Northern Telecom, a 53 percent owned subsidiary of Bell Canada, which has become the largest manufacturer of communications equipment in Canada and second in North America only to AT&T's Western Electric unit, pointed out that much of its American sales would not have occurred without an American presence and that its foreign investments alone actually supported 1,000 Canadian jobs. Other union officials suggest that their government require that all corporate profits earned in Canada remain in Canada to create new jobs. This was because companies are free to move anywhere in the world, depending on how the economic pendulum swings, while Canadian workers are not. To many Canadians such ideas seem reasonable.

"The natural market forces are north-south," said Carl Beigie, former president of the respected C. D. Howe Research Institute, a Canadian think tank named for an American, "and until recently only the Americans have recognized this and benefited from it. Now the Canadians are forging north-south linkages and it's becoming a two-way street. As more companies in Canada find out they can cut the mustard internationally, they'll be expanding their horizons. It's only logical."

But resistance was stubborn. "If a Montreal supermarket is expanding into the United States," said Michel Belanger, president of the National Bank of Canada, "that is good. But if it is an activity that could be done in Canada, it is a net loss." To those who saw Canada as a declining industrial power with inadequate innovation, new investment, and research and development and with old-fashioned militant unions that made for more strikes and lockouts than any other developed country except Italy, the moves across the border were at best a mixed blessing and at worst a silent indictment. To some individual Canadians, of course, this is not threatening. One hot August afternoon on a curb in the Toronto borough of East York, Jim McCance, a street worker who had arrived in Canada in 1954 from Glasgow, told me a familiar story of opportunities elsewhere and weak links to Canada. "It's the same old story, you know, no work over there and lots of opportunities over here, at least then. No, I've had a good life, good work here. Raised two sons and a daughter and I've got a place in Florida. I go down there for five weeks every year and rent it out a lot to a lady from Long Island. My son's courting a woman from Minneapolis. I'm watching that. If he marries her, then he'll be a U.S. resident and he can bring me in and I can retire in Florida as long as I don't take nothing from the government."

Some Canadian companies, such as Cooper Canada Ltd., are simply trying to flee rapidly rising wage demands at home. They have already moved much labor-intensive work, such as manufacturing athletic equipment, to foreign plants in low-wage lands like Barbados, Taiwan, and South Korea. "If I put a Canadian-made and a Korean-made [hockey goaltender's] glove next to each other, you would see absolutely no difference," said Henry Nolting, president of the seventy-nine-year-old Toronto firm. The only difference is the price: $110 for the glove made in Canada and $71 for the one from Korea. Other experts suggest that Canadians seeking foreign investments might even be looking to the Soviet Union, using Canadian expertise, equipment, services, and foreign exchange to help build, for instance, a huge pulp and paper mill in Siberia or a liquefied natural gas plant, with repayments to be made in kind from the new factory's output.

One study at the University of Western Ontario, however, warned that tying up Canadian assets as collateral for United States loans may restrict a company's ability to expand at home later. Government figures seemed to confirm this by showing during the late 1970's that Canadian multinationals increased their employment abroad three and four times more than at home. Additionally, the sales of a United States subsidiary, especially one in, say, the Sun Belt, where energy and labor were cheaper, could easily start to replace vital Canadian exports, often the foundation of the home factory's success. Some might see this as an opportunity for the Canadian company to redirect its home office export efforts to another country, boosting sales even more. Other Canadians, however, would surely see it as a threat to what they already had.

The Bank of Montreal, which itself joined the southbound throng in 1983 by buying the Harris Bankcorp, Inc., Chicago's third-largest bank, noted that such moves would pay dividends in the long term. But it warned that even though some Canadian moves into the States were financed with American loans, in the short term the huge outflows of Canadian money, augmented by billion-dollar buyouts of foreign oil operations in Canada, served to reduce available credit at home, pushing interest rates there even higher for Canadians.

However, once again here the forces of economic integration proved too strong to resist the volatile continental flow of capital. Through just one purchase of around $544 million, the largest move yet into the United States by a Canadian bank, the Montreal-Toronto institution leaped from third into second place in Canadian bank rankings by assets. It strategically positioned itself to expand into the lucrative so-called middle market to serve medium-size businesses, and it better balanced its international loan portfolio. It was no coincidence either that the Bank of Montreal held $7.1 billion (Canadian) in United States assets, the largest of any Canadian bank. For this Canadian bank has a chairman, William Mulholland, who is American-born, a New Yorker who was first attracted to Canada by the latent investment opportunities in its wilderness hydroelectric projects in Labrador directly to the north.

But this massive move of money and resources from Canada into the United States did not come without cost. And at times it was a crippling cost because some of the moves came when interest rates were reaching their inflationary highs and just before cash flows were reaching their recessionary lows. This was particularly damaging for the Canadian real estate and energy companies that had shouldered so much debt with the not unrealistic expectation that land and energy values would continue to climb.

At first, around the turn of the decade, said one Canadian executive based in the United States, Canadian real estate companies in the states were "like babies in a candy store," buying up virtually anything they could lay their well-financed hands on. "It was pretty hard to make a mistake in those years," said Gordon Gray, chairman of A. E. LePage Ltd., a major realtor centered in Toronto. "Inflation kept us all on side and covered many errors in judgment."

The few big Canadian concerns, mostly publicly held, had grown large at home in the few scattered major markets and eagerly ambled south with their overpowering billion-dollar wad of assets as tempting collateral for any lender. Their expertise and experience with megaprojects and their easy access to financing through the close-knit fraternity of financiers in Canada made them instant heavyweights in the fragmented American markets.

And their energetic presence often prompted some strong criticisms from the smaller-scale American developers, many of them privately held. Because of the Canadians' close ties to Canadian banks, they said, the visitors could play by a different set of rules, and their burning desire to enter the American market bid up prices to a level where everyone would get hurt in tight times. "We moved in quickly," said Michael Prentiss, president of an American subsidiary of Cadillac Fairview. "If one company went into a market, the rest felt they had to follow." This led to a lot of overbuilding. With hindsight a number of Canadian developers decided they had relied too much on absentee management; not being an integral part of a community under investment study could lead a Canadian developer to make a costly misjudgment on a project's location, the kind of mistake Americans encountered when they first invested in that, oh, so seemingly similar place called Canada.

But the recession, high interest rates, increasingly difficult financing, and some of that overbuilding combined to trouble most North American real estate developers, including the expanding Canadians. And there followed a period of intense retrenchment, with companies like Cadillac Fairview, the Daon Development Corporation, and Nu-West Group Ltd. being forced to sell much valuable property in a soft market to meet or reduce their now crippling debts.

About one year after making a $21 million down payment to Citicorp for a 5,400-square-foot site on New York City's Lexington Avenue, Cadillac Fairview decided the project was no longer economically viable, and the Canadian company just walked away, saving on future expenses but embarrassedly forfeiting its initial payments. Faced with an overpowering $1.9 billion in debt, Vancouver's Daon ceased paying dividends and repurchasing preference shares and was forced into nearly two years of secret negotiations with its creditors, including Canada's five major banks. "Our properties are good properties," said William H. Levine, Daon's chief financial officer. "Our problem has been too much debt." The complex proposed solution, which involved issuing common shares to creditors in lieu of interest payments, also saw Daon sell off virtually all its residential properties at the bottom of the market, having bought many of them at the top of the market.

Canadian concerns about the price of its growth in foreign lands emerged most prominently in the case of Dome Petroleum and its affable and clever founder. "Smilin' Jack" Gallagher is a smooth-talking, hard-working multimillionaire who fashioned other people's money into Canada's largest non-government oil company. Decades past his youth, the sixty-eight-year-old Mr. Gallagher could still reap obvious satisfaction from recalling his skill at making tasty bannock, the chewy, durable breadlike substance that wilderness-wise Canadians stuff in their backpacks for backcountry treks.

Although Mr. Gallagher has now been eased out of his powerful executive position by the same kind of crushing debt burden that afflicted the real estate titans, his impact on his country and companies is far-reaching and typical of an emerging breed of Canadian entrepreneur who does not, automatically, limit his own vision by preemptive pessimistic predictions on any new ventures. More often than not, like Mr. Gallagher, these individuals were self-made men (women's liberation having just begun to penetrate the carpeted cloisters of commercial power). Often they had grown up on the Canadian prairies, tempered tough by the climatic and geographic extremes that do not tolerate weakness. Like the "Manitoba Mafia," the group of modern Manitoba-born executives who expanded and struggled to control the gigantic Canadian Pacific empire, these men carried into the boardrooms of the East and West a down-to-earth canniness and an innate savvy that enabled them to navigate successfully the corridors of power wherever they were.

They had worked on the trains and the oil rigs, or their fathers had. They knew how to make paper and money and a campfire when the wood was wet. They could talk with the brakemen and the drillers, and they often did on the frequent trips they seemed to have to make down into the dusty mines and noisy factories and the chilly outer reaches of their companies' realms. They thought it was a good idea if every employee owned a piece of the company. Makes 'em work harder, anyone knows that.

And because they seemed to know so much about so much so naturally over so many years, they could also tackle, as a linebacker might, the new brand of up-and-coming accountants and hothouse lawyers who, in their vests and, no doubt, carrying in a neatly labeled file folder somewhere their diplomas from the Harvard Business School or Queen's University, bustled around the halls back at headquarters en route to all their meetings.

The hardened veterans had diplomas from another school, and what they had to say to the new generation was not always couched to soothe, nor was it always considered couth by traditional standards.

There were, for instance, legions of stories—at times they seemed more like legends—about Ian Sinclair, whose tough-minded prairie vision built CP into a world-scale conglomerate. How flying cross-country with his wife on company passes on one of CP's orange and silver commercial airliners, he had Mrs. Sinclair bumped off the plane at Winnipeg when a last-minute paying passenger arrived at the gate. Or how he handled the group of suburban Montreal mayors who made the pilgrimage to CP's downtown Montreal headquarters to plead for a reversal of some cuts in rail passenger service to their communities. Mr. Sinclair greeted the men cordially and ushered them to the large table in his large office. "I hope you had a good trip in," said the hefty host in the deep voice that was known for plain speaking.

"Yes, indeed," replied one of the mayors. "The traffic was not too bad."

"I take it then," said Mr. Sinclair, arching his bushy eyebrows, "you did not take the train."

"Well, no," said a mayor, "we were in a hurry and—"

"This meeting," said Chairman Ian, "is adjourned." And it was.

"Sinc," said one financier and family friend, "is part of the old school. They work hard,. play hard, drink hard, and the deal is done about three A.M. over the second bottle of scotch. Today you've got a bunch of computer business school grads trying to fine-tune you for a hundredth of a point. Neither way is better. But one is a lot more fun."

John Patrick Gallagher, thin, carefully coiffed, neatly mustachioed, and favoring wrinkle-free shirts of thin stripes, packages his bluntness in a cellophane of suaveness. In his thirty-third-floor corner office, overlooking the snow-capped Rockies from the top of the black Dome office tower in bustling downtown Calgary, he greeted friends and strangers the same: a sincere smile, a long look right in the eyes, and a firm handshake, emphasized by cupping your elbow with his other hand. He spoke softly. He exuded confidence.

And if pressed, he would recall, modestly, his long career. It began in the 1930's, when he was a geology student from Winnipeg who earned $2.50 a day to wander through the muskeg bogs of Canada's northern wildernesses, mapping, studying, and fighting off the millions of tiny blackflies that swarm around anything living, burrowing under fur or collars to take tiny, stinging bites. "We looked ridiculous," recalled Mr. Gallagher, "slogging through the bush with our sleeves rolled down in the heat and wearing big hats covered with nets like a beekeeper. But it was great!"

He spent the next thirteen years in the Middle East, Africa, and South America for Shell and Standard Oil of New Jersey. During his World War II hunt for oil, Mr. Gallagher also found water for Allied desert troops, helped deactivate German acoustical mines air-dropped into the Suez Canal, and, in Ecuador, stumbled onto Japanese jungle supply caches set for an attack on the Panama Canal. "That was great, too," he said. "We made five trips across the Andes by foot, had to cut our own way. I spent twenty-three out of twenty-four months in the jungle in Ecuador. The area had good potential, but politically it wasn't ready. That's the problem with foreign work. It's okay for the majors to be in twenty or thirty countries, and maybe two of them pay off. But it's too big a risk for independents. That's why Dome has essentially stayed out of foreign work."

Ironically, it was only when Dome made an expansionist feint outside Canada that it fell into serious trouble. The company began in 1950 primarily with, not surprisingly, American money. Mr. Gallagher persuaded Harvard, Princeton, and the Massachusetts Institute of Technology each to put up $1 million from its endowment fund. The universities wanted good growth but, since this was endowment money, not terrible risks.

This led Mr. Gallagher to fashion his early management style: a steady string of bets on sure or almost sure things, spiced with regular flings at a long shot, always carefully hedged. Thus, for instance, many of Dome's efforts were step-out wells, safer drilling tries just a step beyond already confirmed wildcat discoveries. In 1951 Dome issued its first public shares priced at $11.22. They later fell to $3.80, and Mr. Gallagher says he bought all the way down, an investment that may account for his nickname of Smilin' Jack.

Gradually Dome moved into the gas plant business, producing propane, butane, and ethylene. It built and bought into pipelines to move the underground resources from where they were found to where they were needed, which never seemed to be the same place.

"You mix some of the high-risk plays with that sure cash flow," Mr. Gallagher said, leaning back in his high-backed chair, "and you end up with a company that can bust out all over if you're fortunate, and yet you're not going to break it."

A half century ago, while wandering around Canada's North in his own boots, Mr. Gallagher became convinced of its potential for rich petroleum finds. By 1958, when everyone else was looking for cheaper oil and gas in more hospitable climes, Dome was surveying Canada's Arctic islands. Over the years he set about acquiring the drilling rights to about one-third of the Canadian leased acreage in the Beaufort Sea, the frigid northern ocean just off the top of Alaska and western Canada. Then he quietly began developing the necessary drilling technology for the treacherous Arctic.

Mr. Gallagher would buy some acreage outright, as others did. But to maintain exploration rights, the government requires a minimum amount of development work each year. So as the deadlines approached for this costly work, other, more cautious companies with their own acres would turn to Dome and its drilling subsidiary to do the work. Payment often came in partial rights to whatever was found there, further broadening Dome's holdings. At the same time, to raise funds and hedge bets on their own land, Dome and Mr. Gallagher, the salesman, farmed out part interests in their holdings to investors and gas companies. This form of equity financing used plentiful land, which could turn out to be worthless, rather than shares, which could require dividends. For Dome, it resulted in maximum exposure to substantial discoveries at a minimum financial risk. Even if no oil had ever been found, Mr. Gallagher's losses would have been substantially shared, and he could always hire out his company's Arctic drilling expertise and technology to others with the money but not the foresight.

The overall idea was to find so much oil down Dome's wells that their native names, like Ukalerk, Koponoar, and Tingmiark, would become as synonymous with success as Bonanza and Klondike, both Yukon landmarks 600 miles to the south. Results have been promising if unspectacular so far, and the drilling continues in an effort to find enough oil and gas to bring it economically out of an icy environment that is frozen shut 300 days a year. Typically Dome simultaneously pursued development of a fleet of icebreaker-tankers to avoid the financial and environmental costs of building a disruptive pipeline across the fragile land and society of the North.

Dome's plans always seemed to have the additional, and certainly not coincidental, advantage of fitting in perfectly with the Canadian government's drives to develop the North, to reduce dependence on oil imports, and to push Canadian ownership in its domestic energy industry at least to the 50 percent level. This is the so-called Canadianization. Dome's ties to major political parties, especially the Liberals, who ruled for so long, have always been carefully tended, as, quietly, have its ties to the Conservatives. In 1977 the federal budget, dubbed the Dome budget, contained a super write-off, enabling investors in high tax brackets to write off any income anywhere from 167 to 200 percent of the money they actually invested in frontier oil wells costing more than $5 million. At the time Dome's $35 million holes were the only ones that qualified.

And when, in 1980, the Liberal government brought in its controversial and nationalistic National Energy Program with its generous tax and grant incentives for exploration by Canadian-owned companies, Dome was the first firm to reorganize itself to qualify, benefiting itself but also giving the government a needed note of compliance in a political storm.

Again to hedge its bets, Dome had been drawn into the energy rush on the United States in a modest way with an office in Denver and some properties primarily in the Rockies. But the United States did not seem very foreign to Mr. Gallagher and Dome's 1,500 employees, most of whom lived within a couple hundred miles of Montana and could watch the TV news from Spokane every night before they got the CBC's version from distant Toronto.

In the spring of 1981 Dome was to be drawn ever further into the American market, an ill-timed step in hindsight that would shake it and Canada's financial foundations for years to come. It was a time in a new cycle, sure to be repeated in coming years, when Canadian economic assertiveness was rising especially strongly in one sector, energy. With the NEP announced, many oil companies were reorganizing to push their Canadian elements up front prominently, while numerous others were thinking about putting their assets into a different locale where it could earn a better profit and also be free of the seeming cyclical schizophrenia that tainted Canada.

Much adverse publicity was garnered when Saskatchewan's socialist government had moved to force sellouts by foreign owners of its vital potash deposits and Quebec was to succeed in its forced sale of General Dynamics' Asbestos Corporation. The prime grievance, a potent political tool provincially, was that the foreign owners were mere resource extractors, taking the riches with minimal local labor and intentionally saving the job-creating processing of the resource for their home countries or other lands presumably less deserving of the wages and taxes than Canada. Some Canadian provincial governments determined they would change this, and Canada's federal government could only shrug and politely handle the protests.

But there was a quiet undocumented impact to all this, as Mr. Gilmer, the corporate finance officer, pointed out. "A lot of General Dynamics board members take these experiences back to their own companies. The bad reputation spreads—'I got stomped in Canada, why bother?'—and you can bet it'll be a while before they come piling back into Canada."

Belgium's Petrofina S.A. sold out to the government's Petro-Canada for $1.4 billion in early 1981. In the spring of that year the American St. Joe Minerals Corporation sold its Canadian oil and gas subsidiary, CanDel Oil Ltd., to a Canadian concern, Sulpetro Ltd., as part of its defense against a takeover by Canada's cash-rich distiller Seagram's. Union Oil of California, too, had put its Canadian holdings on the sales block.

The takeover activity by the government oil company, dubbed Petrocan, aroused its own debt controversy. Suggested by the socialist New Democrats and created by law in 1975 by their occasional coalition partners, the Liberals, Petrocan was to help build Canada's clout in energy from exploration to the gas pump. The company's symbol, of course, is a maple leaf.

Through a series of taxpayer-financed acquisitions, Petrocan's assets have grown from an initial $700 million to more than $7.5 billion today, becoming the country's fourth-largest gasoline merchant. Much of this was accomplished financially through the Canadian Ownership Special Charge, a tax surcharge of eight-tenths of a cent on each liter of gasoline sold anywhere in Canada.

This fee was hidden in the pump price of gas, but the debt it helped cover aroused considerable concerns. "When you see," said Harvie André, a Progressive Conservative parliamentary critic, "that the service station with the maple leaf charges no less than the service station with a scallop shell, you become disenchanted." There were also charges, at least in the West, of mismanagement and inefficiency sapping the sacred investments of Canadians in their own national oil company. Wrapped in patriotism and politics, Petrocan made eminent sense and likely will assure its existence into the foreseeable future. The government company placed its headquarters, dubbed Red Square for the building's color and its alleged philosophy, in a fifty-two-story skyscraper in Calgary that was the tallest in western Canada. Petrocan was to help stem the flow of some foreign oil profits abroad or into other sectors of Canada's economy, thereby increasing their foreign ownership.

But it also created a very heavy public debt and gave new foreign investors, historically the most adventurous entrepreneurs in Canada, considerable pause about leaping into the modern Canadian market. And economically the question of a government company (called Crown corporations) spending such huge sums without discovering or producing one more barrel of oil bothered many. "We have to satisfy our shareholders or we go down the tube," said Bud McDonald, president of the smaller Gold Lake Resources. "Petrocan is still not faced with that kind of discipline. It is a terrible waste of taxpayers' money."

Such activity also had the effect of flooding many foreign coffers with Canadian dollars, lowering even further their value and the attractiveness of earning more of them, and depressing stock prices for Canadian oil subsidiaries of foreign firms seen as potential targets. Some of the companies claimed they simply did not want to sell. Then Dome made its move.

Sending signals out from its new skyscraper in Calgary to the American stock markets, where Canadians sometimes take their proxy fights to win through the back door a fight for dominance at home, it put out a public tender offer for shares of Conoco. Not just any subsidiary, mind you, but the parent Connecticut company itself. Conoco resisted. But Dome persisted. And Conoco's executive chieftains were stunned to see the millions of shares willingly offered to the Canadian "interlopers."

Of course, Dome, given Chairman Gallagher's views on foreign entanglements for smaller independent companies, did not want control of all Conoco. It just wanted to force the sale of Conoco's 52.9 percent interest in Hudson's Bay Oil and Gas in Canada. It won that battle, but it was financially wounded in the process.

Dome paid $1.43 billion for 22 million shares of Conoco and then returned the shares plus an additional $245 million in cash to obtain control of Hudson's Bay Oil and Gas, a company with control of 13.6 million net acres in Canada and 8.9 million net acres elsewhere. Conoco's weakness caught the eye of a circling Du Pont Company, which won a struggle with Seagram's and moved Conoco down to Delaware.

But Dome was suddenly saddled with a near doubling of its long-term debt just as prices for its oil were weakening while interest rates were floating, and floating high. Dome started 1981 with a long-term debt of $2.6 billion (Canadian), or 58 percent of capital. By year's end the digits were transposed to $6.2 billion, or 70 percent of capital. That year Dome paid $724.4 million just in interest, up from the previous year's $291.8 million. And the loan total was to soar another $2 billion when the Ontario Securities Commission required Dome also to buy out the remaining minority interests in Hudson's Bay.

Playing on the government's discriminatory incentives plan, other Canadian companies sought to twist off the Canadian arms of foreign oil companies. The Nu-West Group Ltd. of Calgary started buying shares of the parent Cities Service Company just as Dome had assaulted Conoco. (That didn't work, and the following double play took place: The Cities Service Company was acquired by Occidental Petroleum Corporation, and Citgo's wholly owned subsidiary, Canada-Cities Service Ltd., was sold to Canadian Occidental Petroleum Ltd., another Occidental subsidiary but a Canadian one that could at least partially qualify for some of the government benefits.) Nu-West, meanwhile, sold its six million Citgo shares back to Citgo.

Later studies by the government's Petroleum Monitoring Agency were to show that the Canadian oil companies that went on the takeover binge to "Canadianize" their industry performed in a bad year far worse as a group than their less energetic energy competitors. For example, as a group, the "takeoverers" had 1982 losses of $600 million (Canadian) versus a profit of $500 million the year before. Meanwhile, the profits of foreign oil companies fell but by a much smaller margin (19 percent), and Canadian companies that did not eat up some competition saw profits decline even less (14 percent). "The acquiring companies really did suffer," said Ian Smythe of the Canadian Petroleum Association.

As one result of the complex financial snarl, Canada's inspector general of banks issued a "guideline" putting a recommended but nonbinding ceiling on loan totals by any one bank to any one borrower, a ceiling that, even if honored, still left Canada with one of the most liberal loan policies in the industrialized world. The United States limits a bank to lending 10 percent of its capital to any single borrower. Canada has no formal limit on its individual banks, many of them far larger than regional American banks, a rule that gave Canadian companies one leg up when seeking American takeover targets. But the Canadian government now recommends a 50 percent roof, still likely to raise cries of "unfair" among American businesses seeking to compete within a different set of rules.

But in the Dome matter there resulted more than a year of tense negotiations between bankers, who had been swept up in the flurry of Dome euphoria possibly to overextend themselves there, and Dome itself, which saw its glowing image plummet from the leading role of aggressive Canadian concern to one of a pleading, bleeding company requiring substantial debt restructuring just to stay alive. To raise cash, it also had to sell off a number of its pieces, including, ironically, much of its production and exploration properties in the United States, which Texaco Inc. agreed to buy.

Because the company had so closely identified itself with the nationalistic goals of the Canadian government and because the shock waves of a Dome collapse would surge out to engulf hundreds of the company's suppliers and allies, the federal government and some of its allied Crown corporations stepped in to help with the reorganization and to guarantee many millions of dollars in interim loans. Mr. Gallagher was given a hefty stipend to step aside. The Canadian oil company that had bought out many foreign oil companies in Canada turned to another foreign oil company (Royal Dutch/Shell Group) to find its new chairman and chief executive officer, John H. Macdonald, a chartered public accountant and not a Canadian. (He's British, the same nationality as Victor Rice, the chief executive who had been parachuted in to try to rescue Massey-Ferguson from its sagging sales and international loan troubles.) Millions of dollars in Dome subsidiaries were sold off. Dome stock fell back to around the $5 level. For a period at least the government steered the people's eight-tenths of a cent per liter gasoline surtax into a special Dome bailout fund. And as often happens in Canada, the handful of big banks, though still a little pale from their close call, came to loom even larger in the country's economic affairs as owners of oil companies and custodians of the Big Bucks.

Canadian banks are big and powerful. The lines of their power are not confined within individual state lines, as they have been in the United States. This means that a Canadian customer can walk into a branch of, say, the Royal Bank in Halifax, make a deposit, and enter another Royal branch in Vancouver the next day to make a withdrawal.

With upward of $400 billion in assets, Canada's twelve chartered national banks and their influence stretch across the country from coast to coast above- and belowground in seen and unseen ways. In fact, Canada's five large national banks are among the few truly national institutions the country has. Western Canadians may gripe about the Ontario Octopus, its financial tentacles reaching out from Toronto's Bay Street into every corner of the country. But each bank's network of hundreds of branch offices brings an array of assets and financial services to retail and commercial customers on a scale that boggles the minds of Americans. Going the other way, the battalions of branches provide their distant corporate chieftains with detailed economic and social intelligence from every level across the country every day, something which even the major political parties cannot do. The banks and their allied institutions also provide a respected social ladder for thousands of Canadians to climb, theoretically right on up to the carpeted and carefully curtained boardrooms, where executives escorting visitors whisper respectfully even when the chambers are empty.

Five banks sit atop the financial pinnacle of Canada, controlling fully 86 percent of the assets of all twelve national banks. The Big Five are, in descending order, the Royal Bank of Canada, the Bank of Montreal, the Canadian Imperial Bank of Commerce, the Bank of Nova Scotia, and the Toronto Dominion Bank. They fit the familiar pattern in Canadian institutions. Canada has far fewer than most other comparable countries; the geographically smaller United States, for instance, has about 15,000 banks, with every Grundy, Buffalo Ridge, Essex, and Tipton claiming its own First National Bank of Somewhere. In Canada there are fewer of just about everything. They are always far larger, and usually somewhere, somehow you will find the protective hand of the government still propping, pushing, molding, subsidizing, and/or encouraging the institution, whether it is a railroad, a movie or recording company, or a handful of powerful banks. (Such government efforts are not always successful, as evidenced by the $430 million dumped into the new Mirabel International Airport, which remains little used outside Montreal, or the $500 million spent on a Canadian supersonic jet fighter, which was abandoned, or the government's assumption of Canadair's $2 billion debt.)

Traditionally conservative and once run mainly by stolid Scots, Canada's banks have operated like a financial fraternity with a vast number of houses scattered across a large country with a small population, where it once was not hard for one man to know virtually all the decision makers who mattered. Peter C. Newman, the author of *The Canadian Establishment*, called Canada's banks "guardians of the temple" and once calculated that there were more bank branches in his adopted country than there were taverns.

Banking represents a calling for its careful conservative caretakers. For many the banks represent a ticket out of a small town and a hope for a better future, rising to live and deal on an equal basis with the country's moneyed aristocracy. W. Earle McLaughlin, former chairman of the Royal, once told Mr. Newman, "The old story in New Brunswick was that a young man could either cut wood, grow potatoes or join the Royal."

Although computers and modern business methods have blurred many distinctions, the big banks act socially much like independent duchies. Their boards of directors can number five or six dozen men, most of them ranking princes from client companies, and, unlike many Canadian institutions, are consciously drawn from across the country.

These boards, the greatest concentration of nongovernmental power in the land, meet regularly in regional clusters and then nationally at shifting sites across the country, where they are whisked about in chauffeured cars and wined and dined and briefed by private bank staffs long prepared for the dignitaries' state visit. The boards, which also provide a battalion of high-powered executive salesmen for their banks, serve as an informal and little-known but absolutely vital business intelligence network spanning a country with few other natural common bonds.

Board members more than likely attended the same private college preparatory school (Toronto's Upper Canada College, for example) and the same university (McGill, Queen's, or Toronto). And now, when they want to be seen, they frequent the same private downtown clubs, where waiters greet them by name and slowly usher them to favorite tables, allowing ample time for other diners to acknowledge with nods, small waves, handshakes, or soft whispers the arrival of the business celebrities. Because the world of Canadian business is clannish and always producing gossip at an efficient rate, the bankers and directors sometimes might not want to be seen together with a particular client or would-be client. Then they can invite their guest high above downtown Toronto to one of their banks' private dining rooms, decorated like an aristocrat's study with curtains, soft-glowing lamps, and glass-enclosed shelves of unread books. There the regular bank waiter is discreet, the service is impeccable, the view is spectacular, and the food is delicate and delicious. Regular dining room users (and the banks' annual reports) pretend not to notice the opulence. It is considered a necessary tool of business, something akin to the hidden buzzers and secret doors in some bank executives' chambers to thwart would-be kidnappers.

Canada's banks really represent whirling circles of corporate clans.

They are the powerful glue, the essential affiliation that links Canadian companies to allies and suppliers and bigger companies and to many sales and the necessary financing. The banks form the intelligence conduit for the domestic companies to move into the strange and, for Canadians, the once easily intimidating world overseas.

While here again distinctions have blurred in recent times, each bank is surrounded by a cadre of company clients whose allegiance to the bank and vice versa are first cemented in something as strong as the common alma mater of their two top executives a few decades ago. These carefully nurtured allegiances can shift if the personal chemistry of two executives is not right or if one borrower's new business objectives receive a cool reception from his usual bank just after the borrower has run into an old buddy at the symphony who said to give him a call at his bank someday because it was taking on some new clients. But by and large, the financial loyalties are sturdy links, forged on the hockey rinks of high school, on the golf courses of adulthood, and in the handshakes of friendships that seem to bind so much more strongly in manageable communities like Canada's, where almost everyone of consequence is known to almost everyone.

For many early years, sparsely populated Canada and its banks didn't even have a Canadian currency of their own. Government figures were given in British pounds, followed by parentheses with the equivalent in U.S. dollars. In the 1830's Canada debated creating its own currency; it was to be called the royal. Unfortunately that proposal lost. Canada created its own Candian dollar and fed its own comparative compulsion versus the United States. If, as has been the case at times, the Canadian dollar is stronger than its American equivalent, that is considered an achievement and a source of considerable Canadian pride. If, as is more often the case recently, the American dollar is worth more, that is a source of grumbling, one of the many kinds of artificial measuring rods Canadians reach for in their instinctive, compulsive comparing game. The comparison does have some basis in economic fact; more than two-thirds of Canada's imports and exports (not to mention the millions of Canadians who voyage to the American sun each winter, regardless of the cost) concern dealings with the Americans, whose financial situation thus easily overflows into Canada. But what other country in the world feels the nearly desperate need constantly to stack its currency, regardless of what it is called, up against another to judge its own efforts? Certainly not the Hong Kong or Australian dollar.

In this context Canadian banks have been fairly accurate reflections of their country, emphasizing in their traditionally conservative way resource and real estate development on a grand scale. In the United States both categories of endeavor have often been looked on by investors as slightly tarnished and a little too risky for reputable emphasis. Canada's national banks always operate nationally (that's the only way they could scrape together enough domestic customers to make it worthwhile). And there is nothing that there is more of in Canada than sheer real estate.

American banks by practice and law are far more local (what does a Pittsburgh bank want with a Nevada shopping mall as collateral anyway?). "United States banks tend to look at real estate as a rather high-risk business," Maxwell Field, a Briton running the Chicago office of Canadian Pacific's Marathon Realty, told a Chicago reporter, "while Canadian bankers see it as a first-class risk. Canadian banks will lend to developers at one-half a percentage point over the prime rate, while here it is two or three points over prime."

In addition, American tax laws on property depreciation encourage owners to sell off their properties after fifteen years. Canada's differing tax system lets developers hang on to projects for longer terms, enabling them to accumulate enormous assets, especially during inflationary times. This, not coincidentally, also gives them more collateral to borrow against for still other projects. And with the help of legislation, the powerful banks are the beneficiaries of Canadians' propensity to save. The first $1,000 of interest earned on individual savings accounts is tax-free, a step that also helps meet one of Canada's historic shortages, a lack of capital. As one result of such government encouragement, Canadians save about 14 percent of income, giving their economy large sums for new capital and investments, while Americans, who are encouraged by government policies to spend, save only around 5 percent. (The other shortage, a lack of people in view of its vast size, is combated by the federal government's baby bonus, a monthly cash stipend to parents that grows in size with the number of children, still in existence many long years after numerous other less developed lands are paying or forcing parents not to have children.)

With a well-developed, well-organized market at home, Canada's banks had drifted together into a smaller number of financial amalgamations, a pattern of economic power concentration that cuts across Canadian society—fewer, larger institutions. In search of growth and profits the banks began consciously to follow their Canadian clients to other countries, often even initiating such moves, rarely discouraging them. Quietly, without much notice the investments grew until about one-third of the banks' total assets are in other countries, a reflection of a looking out beyond Canada's borders. It is, too, a profitable development that allows Canada to ride along with a share of others' prosperity, although one that prompted a little grumbling at home about the good uses for money there and all the risks overseas. Much of the money went into the United States. "The banks have to go somewhere," said Henri-Paul Rousseau, a Quebec economist. "The obvious place is the U.S."

This was also in part an attempt to diversify their loan portfolios away from heavy concentration on resources and energy, one major reason behind the Bank of Montreal's purchase of Chicago's Harris Bankcorp, which overnight made that Canadian institution the sixth-largest foreign bank in the United States.

The United States was the favorite target of Canadian banks, although the homeland in Britain and the Commonwealth presented opportunities. Progress proved slower in Japan, where most foreign companies find progress slower. But for much the same reasons as it attracted other industries, the United States seemed to Canadian financial institutions to be an essentially familiar place where the language may have sounded a little funny but was basically understandable. There was less government hassle doing business. And because the American market was fragmented by this strange clutter of so many states, for once the Canadian institution was unquestionably the big boy on the block. "We want to be the largest foreign bank in the United States," said Rowland C. Frazee.

I remember, on one of those bright early-summer afternoons when the trees in Toronto's downtown skyscraper lobbies look even greener than they do in January, being formally ushered quietly and respectfully into the office of Mr. Frazee, the outspoken chief of the Royal Bank, Canada's largest and, as a result of its broad foreign moves, now North America's fourth-biggest bank. "We used to be a large Canadian bank with international operations," he said, "but now we are a large international bank with a strong Canadian base. There's a difference."

There certainly is. The Royal, which began in Halifax, Nova Scotia, in 1864 as the Merchants Bank with $729,000 and one branch, has grown to one with more than $86 billion in assets and some 35,000 employees at more than 1,500 branches across Canada and 82 overseas in forty-five countries. For the first time now the Royal's operations outside Canada produce more after-tax revenues than its operations at home.

The ability of one-third of the Royal's assets to produce 51 percent of its income is due to a number of factors, including Canada's recently anemic economy. But they underline the new importance for many Canadian companies seeking growth beyond the confines of Canada's home market. "Everything we do now," said Mr. Frazee, "we think globally no matter what type of business we're dealing with." Mr. Frazee, who had just returned from a week in Texas, several days in New Orleans and Chicago, and three weeks in the Far East, saw to the organization of global groups in energy, agriculture, and trade within his bank, which controls nearly a quarter of all Canadian bank assets.

We sat in his spacious office, filled with wood furnishings, in the Royal's golden glass tower so insulated from the outside world and so far above downtown Toronto's bustle that no other sounds invaded the room, save the soft whoosh of the air-conditioning system. "World trade," said the balding, bespectacled former football and hockey player, "is growing faster than domestic economies. And countries like Canada, where twenty-five percent of its gross national product is based on trade, highest in the industrialized world, are absolutely dependent on trade."

In recent years the Royal also moved its American headquarters from Montreal to New York, poured in more than $100 million in new capital, moved its Caribbean headquarters from Montreal to Florida, expanded operations in Asia (especially in China, where it positioned itself ideally for future business), started from scratch its own merchant bank in London, where it established a new European headquarters, and bought out a prominent West German bank (Burghardt & Nottebohm, later renamed Royal Bank of Canada AG) to use as its cutting edge for more purchases there. At the same time Mr. Frazee continued to roam his own country and the States, speaking out confidently and frankly on a wide variety of current issues (government economic policy, treatment of foreign investors, relations between Canada and the United States). It was not what Canadians had been accustomed to hearing from leading businessmen, who traditionally confined any public comments to their own narrow fields of endeavor.

The Royal was not alone in its interest in American expansion. The Bank of Montreal, which has maintained offices in New York City for 125 years, opened a divisional office there plus its new Chicago acquisition. The Bank of Nova Scotia maintains ten offices in United States cities and has elevated American expansion to what one executive calls "probably our single highest priority."

"The attractions of the United States are all so logical," said Charles Langston, an international vice-president for the Canadian Imperial Bank of Commerce, which has operations in 100 countries. He noted that many other countries have reached their borrowing limits within individual Canadian banks. And with the increasing risks and shrinking profit margins on large, long-term consortium loans to less developed nations, the United States appears increasingly attractive and, in fact, is usually treated by Canadian banks as a "domestic" loan, an internal category that makes an enormous difference when sorting loan approvals.

Richard M. Thomson, chairman of the Toronto Dominion Bank, sat in his headquarters office, just a couple of blocks from Mr. Frazee's, and decided to upgrade his bank's representative office in New York to the standing of a full division. "We see the United States as one of our major expansion areas in the years ahead," he said. "We are realizing that we are North Americans, not just Canadians. And this is a North American market, not just a Canadian and a United States market. We're not the fifty-first state. But the language, customs, heavy two-way trade, and investments between the two countries are shaping a new order of priorities." Then he shrugged. "We're seeing an integration of Canadian and United States corporate activities. And our management has to reflect these changes."

Thus, Canadian banks found themselves dealing, naturally, with Canadian companies in Canada, with Canadian companies operating outside the country, and then with foreign companies operating outside Canada (the Royal claims to be used outside the United States by a higher proportion of American multinational companies than any other non-American bank). Finally, Canadian banks got some business back home thanks to their foreign operations; they signed on as clients Canadian subsidiaries of foreign companies they had served in foreign lands, especially the United States. Synergism invades Canada. "The United States is the major economy of the world," said Alvin Flood, a vice-president of United States operations for the Bank of Commerce, which soon could be drawing half its foreign profits from the United States, "and it just happens to be at our back door. Now you're seeing more of a North American market developing."

This can, however, prove troublesome at times, as Canadian banks discovered. One prominent case involved the Bank of Commerce, which like other Canadian banks followed the federal government's guidance and sought new foreign customers abroad as well as followed its traditional Canadian clients in the same direction.

One of the foreign clients attracted by the Canadians' eagerness was the F. W. Woolworth Company, the giant American merchandising chain that at one time made the Commerce its largest single lending creditor worldwide. One of the bank's major Canadian customers was Brascan Ltd., the old holding company that had long been in the client circle of the Commerce. This relationship was cemented by a typically Canadian and complex network of interlocking directorships with Commerce executives serving on the boards of Brascan and its subsidiaries and Brascan executives doing likewise on the bank. Peter C. Newman, author of perceptive works on the Canadian establishment, estimates that Canada's 300 bank directors also hold an additional 3,000 directorships in companies with total assets exceeding $700 billion.

This was fine when the arena was just Canada, where everyone understands local conditions and rules. There have been few Canadian banks of sufficient size to handle the scale of financial needs of Canada's large modern corporations, so some banks do handle the business of competing concerns. To protect against conflict of interest, the banks wrote their own regulations for officers and directors, requiring total confidentiality for each account. Commerce directors must leave the room, for instance, whenever their companies or their competitors are discussed.

But then, one day, Brascan, long interested in foreign investments, decided to take a billion-dollar run at Woolworth's, emboldened in part by a $700 million line of credit from the Commerce. Part of Woolworth's defense was loud charges of conflict of interest against the Commerce, where the files included the most intimate financial details of both Woolworth's and Brascan. This was a natural enough charge in view of differing American regulations and banking relationships.

Commerce executives expressed shock. They said that only six officers knew of Brascan's bid and that its chairman did not participate in the line of credit's approval or in the initial takeover discussions by Brascan's board, of which he was also a member. Canadian banking authorities said there was considerable common law precedent requiring banks to protect records from outsiders. But there is very little statutory protection of confidentiality in Canada and nothing, save good faith, that legally prohibits bank employees from discussing accounts among themselves.

That Brascan takeover attempt failed. In fact, Brascan itself was soon taken over by investment arms of a branch of the Seagram's Bronfman family, which also directed its monetary attentions toward ownership of more American properties.

But the incident provided a revealing insight into the close personal relationships—and personal animosities—that characterize Canada's domestic economy. The Commerce, you see, had been run for years by a stolid and autocratic man of Scottish descent, Neil McKinnon. In 1973 Mr. McKinnon, since deceased, was ousted in a palace revolt that began within that institution as a methodical broadening of the management structure away from the one-man rule of past days, a theme that had moved through American banking ten years before.

One of the initial organizers of that successful boardroom uprising to oust Mr. McKinnon was a man named John H. "Jake" Moore. Jake Moore went on to become chairman of a company named Brascan Ltd., which sought that $700 million line of credit from the Bank of Commerce to swallow Woolworth's. A major beneficiary of that Commerce boardroom coup and management evolution was a man named Russell H. Harrison. He went on to become chairman of the Bank of Commerce, which gave Brascan the $700 million line of credit to try to swallow Woolworth's.

Banks are the hefty hinges of Canadian society. Without them, most deals could not be swung. With them, most any deal can be. And often there are angles to a deal that only the bank knows about, an obscure link or contact which an astute bank officer knows of from his schooldays or the like, a little detail that can swing the balance of power to his side and his client.

It is one significant mark of Canada's growing self-confidence and the interconnected rippling effects of that development that the country has now permitted foreign banks onto its home playing field in a meaningful way. At first the operating capital of the foreign banks, which are tiny by Canadian standards and grew to upward of six dozen, were confined by the government to 8 percent of the total assets of all Canadian banks. But within months the foreigners began petitioning for an increase in the ceiling, a move supported by a number of Canadian banks aware of the increasing importance of reciprocity in the world's tightening economic community. If Canada did not accord fair financial freedom to foreign banks there, then its banks would likely encounter some serious difficulties overseas soon.

So regulations were loosened even further. And competition in Canada's banking world increased, improving services and costs to customers, a development not always in the forefront of goals in the old inbred financial community. The foreign institutions were hungrier than the hometown hands, it seemed. Real competition was a bit painful for some to stomach; one newspaper business story whined that in order to offer attractive loan rates, "foreign banks are using every financing trick available." For instance, some raised money overseas to avoid reserve costs and then passed the savings on to loan customers to undercut the Canadian competition.

But Canadian customers seemed pleased. Not a few changed some business to the newcomers. "The Canadian banks are not being competitive in terms of price or service," A. H. C. Lewis, treasurer of Extendicare Ltd., told the *Globe and Mail.* That company transferred $100 million in loans from one Canadian banker to a string of foreign companies.

All this would have been unheard of not many years ago. Canadians would have instinctively turned to protection: the poor little guy just trying to survive in a mean and ugly world. But now, at least in banking, Canadians felt sure enough of themselves to go on the offensive and compete openly—abroad and at home. Although few Canadians realized it, the impact of this and numerous parallel developments in a growing number of sectors was slowly seeping through society. It was a healthy, natural development, if one that threatened comfortable old defeatist forms of thought that hung like last year's cobwebs in many corners of Canadian life.

One of the major reasons for this improving self-confidence was the sheer physical size of many Canadian institutions, and not just the banks either. They were big and muscular and crafty and less concerned now with others' toes. Samuel Belzberg, head of the Belzberg brothers' First City Financial Corporation of Vancouver, whose financial fingers crept down the coast to control Los Angeles banks, may not have wanted to buy all of the Bache Group, the New York securities firm, just as Dome Petroleum didn't really want all of Conoco. But Mr. Belzberg's purchase of a one-eighth block of Bache eventually earned him a substantial profit, and the American company was later bought up by Prudential as part of the financial blurring of institutions like banks, brokers, and insurance companies under way in the United States. It was not surprising, then, that when T. Boone Pickens, Jr., the Texas oilman (Mesa Petroleum Company of Amarillo) known for his bent for a similar profitable partial takeover strategy, drew up a new battle plan, one of his major financial backers would be Sam Belzberg. Together they took on the Gulf Oil Corporation, not just the Canadian subsidiary, mind you, but the entire international corporation, and cleared another substantial profit.

Of course, Canadians have always had some large institutions. The country was practically founded, certainly it was initially explored, by bearded representatives of the Hudson's Bay Company, the British concern that once owned nearly 40 percent of Canada's entire territory. The Bay's men and the wilderness buyers for its corporate antecedents and competitors, who often wandered down into what was to become the United States, were rounding up furs.

The classic of bigness, of course, is Canadian Pacific, a publicly held company, or rather 113 companies, which, like the Bay, are so tied up with history and with the country's development that its corporate distinctions are often lost in the Canadian mind, for better or worse. Like many Canadian institutions, CP owes its size, much of its success, and certainly its economic head start on every other major Canadian concern to the federal government.

It also owes much to a pattern of Canadian thinking radically different from the Americans. "Canadians have no automatic assumption that big business is evil," J. M. S. Careless, the noted historian, who has traced the development of large corporations through Canada's history, remarked in an interview. Unlike its richer, more populous, and traditionally more competitive cousin market to the south, Canada's national policies have actually encouraged monopolies. Efficiencies of scale seemed necessary for survival. And they also, by the way, helped keep prices up and

nettlesome competition down. Thus, while America's trust-busting movement sank roots deep into that land in the late 1800's, Canada's government was growing frantic for a transcontinental railroad to try to stitch
together its diverse regions against American expansionism. When my
great-grandfather Andrew, a cheesemaker from Ontario, decided to migrate out to western Canada in the late 1800's, he couldn't get there
through Canada. The wilderness Shield slicing Canada in half had not yet
been tamed by tracks. He had to take the train across Michigan to
Chicago and change trains and stations there for the long trek north to
take a barge down the scenic Red River to Winnipeg ("downriver" in
Canada usually meaning "north"). The hardships of those journeys and
family separations added to the border's nondenominational culture.

To get the railroad built, even tardily, the Canadian government offered the Canadian Pacific Railway $25 million, 25 million acres, tax-free
status on all railroad property in perpetuity, and a twenty-year guarantee
against competition, no doubt worth even more over time. To get railroad
terminals, small towns near the proposed route made their own sweet
offers to the company, which is a major reason, for example, why Selkirk,
Manitoba, is still a small town of 10,000 while nearby Winnipeg is the
capital of Manitoba and home to well over half the 1-million-plus residents in the province, which by itself is nearly three times the size of the
British Isles or a bit larger than Texas. The United States also offered
incentives to transcontinental railroads, but none so generous and none
so free of later skeptical scrutiny.

The incentives were part of a tricornered and, within Canada anyway,
much hallowed program of Canadian development proposed by Prime
Minister Sir John A. Macdonald and dubbed the National Policy.
Adopted by the federal government in 1879, the bold policy involved
building a transcontinental railroad, enabling broad settlement of the
Canadian West, and imposing strict protective tariffs to shape a national
market and give Canadian (read that, eastern) industry captive customers
at home to grow on. In a broad sense this plan, wedding protectionism
with deep government penetration of the economy, has shaped Canadian
economic thinking ever since. As Professor Careless has noted, "The
system begun in 1879 has become woven into the history and life of the
country."[2]

To be sure, the United States has had its occasional outbursts of protective tariffs (the first coming in 1816, like Canada's, but a few years after the country's creation), and the federal government has stepped into the economy to achieve specific ends (the financial salvaging through loan guarantees of Lockheed and Chrysler being but two recent examples). But such American moves have been more tentative, infrequent, often controversial, and even apologetically explained away as "one-shot" aid. In Canada, by contrast, the instinctive first response to a problem—at times it seems almost any problem—is, "What's the government going to do about it?" Canadians may argue over whether the government's aid did the maximum for an industry, a company, a town, a region. But you'll rarely hear anyone say the government shouldn't have been involved in the first place. The right, nay, the need, for such involvement is considered a given. The intentions are assumed to be good. And this trusting of government power forms one of the significant subterranean differences between the two peoples.

Canada's industrial system came to fruition only with the passage of many decades. As always, Canadians compare their efforts to the Americans, apples and oranges though they are. But former Progressive Conservative Prime Minister Joe Clark, a political descendant of Sir John A. Macdonald, made a very important point when he once noted, "The Americans talk, with pride, of being the new world, the cradle of accomplishment. But we Canadians settled the harsher half of the North American continent. It was easier to build Virginia than to build Ontario."

When Canada built its first railroad to the Pacific (completed in 1885), the young country had only 4 million citizens. When the geographically more hospitable United States built its first transcontinental railroad in the 1860's, it already had a market of 40 million, a population mass that Canada still falls short of by 15 million. And by the 1880's the American people, whose suspicions of distant authorities in Britain had ignited a revolution, were beginning to direct their skeptical attentions toward the distant powers of their own big business.

"Canadians are much more hierarchical and trusting of authority than Americans," said William T. Stanbury of Canada's Economic Council. "If businessmen say something is good, people believe it is so." When the proponents of larger-scale operations, perhaps 1,000 captains of the elite business clans that have traditionally run Canada's corporate world, speak out on the matter (it is not yet an issue), they talk of the need for jobs and for world-scale companies to compete in the big shadow of the United States in an increasingly competitive, international marketplace. This is especially important for a country that exports fully 25 percent of its gross national product, compared with around 10 or 11 percent for the United States.

Yet as the years pass, the march to consolidation continues, leading to one of the most perfectly appropriate lines I ever saw about Canada. It was written by Peter C. Newman, a dedicated Canadian nationalist who brought from Czechoslovakia to his new homeland the perceptive eye of a loving outsider, someone Canadians feel very uncomfortable with. Looking at the Canadian establishment, Mr. Newman wrote in *The Canadian Establishment:* "Power tends to connect; absolute power connects absolutely."

Consumer's Gas buys Home Oil and then merges with Hiram Walker. Hollinger Argus, which already controlled Dominion Stores, Standard Broadcasting, Massey-Ferguson, and Labrador Mining, bids for Norcen with the millions it received for its Noranda holdings from Brascan, which was seized by Edper Equities. Hudson's Bay, now a modern department store chain patriated from England to Winnipeg, buys discount Zellers before moving on Simpson's, another department store chain, and then being consumed itself in a $641 million struggle between the Weston family (160 companies, including Loblaw's supermarkets, National Tea, B. C. Packers, Weston Bakeries, Eddy Paper, and, in Pennsylvania, Stroehmann Bros. bakeries) and the Thomson family (100-plus mainly privately held companies, including North Sea oil holdings and more than 150 newspapers in Europe and North America). Even the telephone company, Bell Canada, got in on the act, buying up a substantial portion of Transcanada Pipelines Ltd. of Calgary.

No one, not even the Canadian government, can keep track of all the moves, let alone the score, in this continent-wide game of adult Monopoly that every day in many ways sees corporate power flowing into the hands of fewer and fewer individuals.

But because of the lack of strong public sentiment against bigness, accurately reflected in the complete weakness of Canada's antimonopoly laws, the Anti-Combines Branch of the Department of Consumer and Corporate Affairs is virtually powerless to do anything. And most Canadians are not in the habit of asking probing questions; Canadian reporters, for instance, enjoy little of the social status, public position, or legal protection of their colleagues in the American Fourth Estate. So the Canadian press does not play the prominent leadership role in setting the agenda for public discussion that its American peer group often does.

As one result, outside of an occasional outburst over some particularly blatant display of corporate power (e.g., competing newspaper chains each just happening to close one newspaper in different cities, freeing the chains from two costly competing operations and leaving each instead with one solid monopoly position), few Canadians these days are asking some vital questions. What forces—historic, political, and economic—are seizing the nation and turning its resources, manufacturing, and industrial might over to a dwindling number of corporate powers? How far will the merger movement go? The companies aside, is this good for their employees, for Canadians, and for Canada? What are its long-term effects within Canada and within Canada's economic and political relations with other countries as the outward forces spill over?

"What we will have, if this march of increased concentration continues," Robert Bertrand, director of the Anti-Combines Branch, told me one day, "is a national oligarchy in which a few dozen people will interact to bargain about the economic future of millions. The essence of a free society is choice. Fewer, larger economic units almost inevitably mean a narrower range of choices available."

Many might say that in certain sectors, such as steel, beer, cement, cigarettes, petroleum, newspapers, and aluminum, private oligopolies have already formed, often after costly and economically detrimental bidding wars that seemed to carry more elements of old boy gamesmanship than they did of economically judicious decision making. These battles have often left even the winners badly stricken, saddling them with crushing debts at floating interest rates that seemed to float up far more easily than down. Competition has been choked. Too much power has been concentrated in the hands of the few. The rights of minority shareholders have been reduced. And the scene has been set for market manipulations, which the government is virtually helpless to combat, even if it had the political will.

A few figures indicate the trend. At the time of Canadian Confederation in 1867, a total of 33 banks were open for business. Between 1820 and 1970, 157 bank charters were granted by the government. Mr. Newman has calculated that if Canada had as many banks today proportionately as the United States, there would be about 1,400 banks instead of 12. Additionally, the 100 largest Canadian companies now account for more than 45 percent of the value added to goods in that country compared with about 33 percent by the United States' 100 largest concerns.

There are powerful economic reasons for this continuing concentration. These include a standard push for growth and diversification, a run of robust profits that make many corporate treasuries attractive targets even without their factories, and the impact of inflation, which lingered longer in Canada than elsewhere. The last made it cheaper to buy undervalued stocks of existing companies than to build new ones, the prime reason, for example, behind Abitibi's purchase of Price to form the world's largest newsprint maker.

Donald Thompson, a business professor at Toronto's York University, points out the handsome cash flow of some companies in mature industries—like Genstar in cement, Imasco in tobacco, and Molson's in beer. Since increased dividend payouts are taxed more heavily than capital gains on stock values increased through takeovers, diversification from an older slow-growth field into an expanding new one is almost forced. Such developments also, not by chance, can open new avenues of professional achievement to hold and spur on ambitious executives. "There are huge forces pushing consolidation," said Mr. Stanbury, "and virtually none in its way. Increasing concentration will continue. No question." And in view of the attraction of U.S. ventures, this bigness portends serious consequences for American companies, which will be faced with an ever-expanding array of heavyweight competition, right there at home and abroad, from those old pussycats, the easily overlooked Canadians.

At the same time, because Canada's economic arena is smaller and most of the players are known to most of the players (and not always favorably), there is a sense of the hunt, of valued cunning and a real element of business sport here. It doesn't always come through in the columns of Canada's somber business press, the *Financial Post,* the *Financial Times,* and *Report on Business,* a self-contained business newspaper within the *Globe and Mail* that is the daily bible of corporate Canada.

Not until you talk with these intelligent men in their cars, clubs, offices, and favored restaurants do you get a feel for their excitement in the competition, the path-seeking and pathfinding and the skilled development and manipulation of business connections for offensive or defensive purposes. It is no coincidence, for instance, that Consumer's Gas and Hiram Walker, which merged to form one of Canada's newest diversified giants, both were linked in this Canadian network via the same bank, Toronto Dominion, where Hiram Walker's chairman, H. Clifford Hatch, was a director.

The jockeying to produce and avoid takeovers often seems in Canada like an intramural sport for those who can afford corporate chauffeurs, as if these back-seat riders were back on the hockey rinks of high school, swinging elbows, shoving each other into the boards, and perhaps hooking an opponent's leg with a stick if the ref wasn't looking. (At one meeting of high school parents I attended in a cavernous Toronto gym, the principal apologized to all of us, in a particularly sincere moment, because that year the school was fielding only *seven* hockey teams. He assured us they were trying to improve the situation. And he won a round of applause for his efforts.)

As for any expressed fear wth bigness, there is virtually none. That lack of concern was expressed to me one day by Kenneth R. Thomson, the press magnate who owns around 40 percent of Canada's daily newspapers. After passing through security and taking the private elevator, we sat high in his skyscraper office overlooking Toronto's curving City Hall and the ice rink and just inches away from his private museum of carvings and Krieghoff paintings. "There is a limit to how many papers one man, or company, should own," he said, "a point where going past it becomes ludicrous. But we haven't reached it. And I'm sure that we will know ourselves if and when we do."

At no time during their Machiavellian maneuverings, allegedly to maximize the benefits for their faceless mass of stockholders, do the corporate generals pay attention to the federal government. "We have a great concern over the size of these mergers," said Paul Mitchell of the Combines Branch, "but the law is toothless. Mergers are impossible to stop. We must prove an 'undue' loss of competition to the public's detriment before it happens." As one result, Canada has had one monopoly conviction since World War II. And that defendant pleaded guilty.

Several halfhearted efforts at change have failed. And neither major party seems likely to display a sudden enthusiasm for trust-busting. When the Progressive Conservatives were briefly in power in 1979–80, they proposed selling off some of the government-owned Crown corporations to become large shareholder-owned companies. And when Mr. Trudeau appointed one of his cosmetic commissions to investigate "corporate concentration," he appointed as its head Robert Bryce, who had written the legislation allowing companies tax deductions for interest on loans to finance takeovers.

That federal inquiry took three years and a few million dollars to decide that there was no undue concentration, which it called a "natural phenomenon" anyway. "We found no inherent evils in such concentration," Mr. Bryce told me, "other than on the whole they weren't as profitable. They tended to overpay in the heat of competition. But that won't slow the trend down."

Without effective government regulation the rules of Canada's continuing corporate consolidation are subtle and shifting with double standards not unheard of. They are gentlemanly rules, unwritten but understood, not unlike dueling with dollars as the weapons instead of pistols. It is the kind of *lèse majesté* attitude revealed at one point during complex negotiations involving bankrupt fisheries, the federal government, and one of the national banks in 1983. The parties were stalled some $70 million apart over compensation to be paid the bank. One of the officers then said, "It's too much to flip for, boys."

The unwritten rules of Canadian business are enforced from within. Valuable business links, for instance, can be denied some particularly aggressive outsider, say, someone like Peter Bronfman or Stephen Roman of Denison Mines, Ltd., who didn't attend the right school or who seems a little rough or unfinished by the standards of other alumni. Such folk might not get into the prestigious clubs like the Toronto or the National or invited to serve on a bank board with its helpful links to finances and intelligence. One investment executive explained the system to me. "It's just a way of saying, 'Hey, fella, we don't operate like that around here.' And it usually works." Of course, an outcast's ethnic or religious background would never be mentioned in such decisions. It doesn't have to be.

With some exceptions this kind of social stratification has worked fairly well in Canada's business community. And it still does within many circles. But the home arena isn't the same anymore. There are many more players with much more money in Canada today. And even if some routes are blocked at home for the Romans, the Skalbanias, the Belzbergs, and the Bronfmans, there is a much larger field of endeavor outside Canada, where membership in a Canadian club or on a particular bank board matters far less than some things called savvy and clout.

In recent years some winds of change began blowing through the corridors of Canada's establishment, the untitled aristocracy whose small numbers had made the major decisions affecting millions for so long. As picturesquely portrayed by Mr. Newman in his second volume on the Canadian establishment, the newcomers have divided the old power system into two camps. These include the Inheritors, the sons and grandsons of the moneyed elite—the Eatons, Westons, and Thomsons, et al.—who, perhaps unlike their patrician peers in other lands, do not fall into congenital, though affluent, profligacy. The newcomers he dubbed the Acquisitors, bravura entrepreneurs, mostly from the West, who by birth or behavior are strangers to the establishment, self-made, macho men who welcome risks and spend their money on extravagant life-styles of a dozen cars, gold-leaf bedroom ceilings, and cute women with long, flowing hair.

According to Mr. Newman, these newcomers, constantly changing, buying, selling, moving upward, consider themselves citizens of their age as much as of their country or province. The Acquisitors form a stark contrast with the old Inheritors, who "genuinely believed that the tumble of psychic catastrophes and raw emotions that agitate ordinary lives would always be visited upon people to whom one had not been properly introduced."[3] The clash of these two affluent generations, one savvy and comfortable, the other savvy and striving, was another sign of the new currents silently stirring across Canada.

Yet true to the Canadian spirit of compromise and their common search for profit, the two got along together, if not famously, at least pragmatically. New faces of new blood came on the scene; after the 1978 death of John Angus "Bud" McDougald, the Black brothers, Conrad and Montegu, cleverly won control of the giant Argus holding empire. The little personal touch, it seemed, still worked in the world of Canadian business; Conrad Black had thought to solicit the support of Mr. McDougald's widow in the voting. The brothers succeeded in ousting their internal Argus rival, Maxwell Meighen, a wealthy Toronto financier. The Blacks then began reorganizing and redirecting Argus's holdings, dumping their lackluster share in Massey-Ferguson, the farm implement manufacturer. These were aggressive steps which, as seemed to happen more often in recent times, spilled out of Canada into the United States with Hollinger Argus's controversial bid, through Norcen Resources, to take over Cleveland's Hanna Mining Company and its rich Canadian ore deposits.

Some of the jockeying provided revealing insights into Canada's old geographical fractures as well as its old and new power alignments. One time three companies vied to control each other. All backed off, however, in the face of opposition from a provincial government, but then another corporate giant moved in to close the deal.

The cast of the transcontinental struggle included Vancouver's Mac-Millan Bloedel Ltd., the largest forest products company in a land known for its forest products; Domtar Inc., a Quebec-based forest products company that was number three; and Argus, the Blacks' new bailiwick. Argus and its owners' fortunes had been built over the years on minority shareholdings in a number of companies, small holdings, often less than 20 percent, but large enough in those days in Canada to obtain effective financial control.

The thirty-four-year-old Conrad Black, an erudite man who wrote his own book on Quebec politics before entering the business wars, decided in 1978 that Argus should increase its holdings in companies with a future and get out of others. One of its expendable holdings, he decided, was a 17 percent share in Domtar. This had the added benefit of further cutting off his old Argus rival, Mr. Meighen, who sat on Domtar's board with other allies.

At first Domtar feared that Argus would sell its vital block of shares to Kruger Pulp and Paper, a small competitor or, worse yet, to the Power Corporation. But then, through its corporate intelligence network and business connections, Domtar learned that Argus was negotiating to sell its Domtar shares to MacMillan Bloedel. Even though such a merger would see number one swallow number three, forming a giant forest products concern with nearly $3 billion in sales, there was no antitrust problem with the government. (Number two, Abitibi-Price, was soon to be consumed by the Reichmann family, reclusive owners of Olympia & York, Canada's largest private real estate developers.)

So just before the sale of Domtar stock to MacBlo, as it's popularly called, was to be announced, Domtar made its own announcement: Number three would try to swallow number one. Then, as expected, MacBlo made its announcement: Number one would swallow number three; in fact, it already owned 20 percent of Domtar, having bought shares from Argus and its subsidiaries. Soon after, Canadian Pacific Investments, since renamed Canadian Pacific Enterprises, the nontransportation arm of the Canadian Pacific empire, announced that it too wanted MacMillan Bloedel.

While investors tried to balance the competing share offers, William Bennett, himself a former businessman-turned premier of British Columbia, announced that no high-powered eastern company was going to take away control of anything as sacred to British Columbia as its natural and human resources in MacMillan Bloedel. Such denunciations of carpetbagging from afar can still rouse considerable emotion in Canada's regions, especially if they hint darkly at secret financial machinations by large eastern Canadian powers.

Nobody mentioned that MacMillan had been run for some time by an American, Calvert Knudsen, or that Canadian Pacific, being one of the country's few national institutions, already had in British Columbia 19,000 employees, 13 percent of all its assets, and the corporate headquarters for two of its major subsidiaries (CP Air, Canada's largest private airline, and Cominco, the international mining giant).

After considerable shouting back and forth, some of it private, Premier Bennett forced the bidders to rescind their offers. His clout lay in the province's power to revoke the leases on Crown land logged by MacBlo. Without those forest tracts the company would be badly hurt. In a speech, Ian Sinclair, then CP's crusty chairman, could set off murmurs of agreement among his audience of Toronto financial analysts by grumbling about interfering western politicians. At that luncheon a Canadian reporter, a British Columbian by birth, could turn to me and, through gritted teeth, say, "That Sinclair is a true son of a bitch."

But the battle for British Columbia's largest company didn't end with the CP chairman's pullback in January 1979. Almost two years later, B.C. Resources Investment Corporation, a publicly traded company whose shares were widely held throughout the province but whose board was largely appointed by the B.C. government, acquired 20 percent of Mac-Blo's shares. Early in 1981 it offered $46 a share for a further 29 percent of the stock. Noranda, the diversified Toronto mining giant, jumped in with a cash-and-stock offer worth $56; B.C. Resources came back with $56, all cash, but Noranda won the day with a counter-bid equivalent to $62 a share. But first it agreed with the premier to dispose of its 28 percent of B.C. Forest Products, the province's second-largest forest operator, and not to seek a majority of directors on the MacBlo board, even though it controlled the company. So for $664 million and with cap in hand another major eastern conglomerate got what CP's Ian Sinclair had failed to get. He'd offered "only" $516 million.

The personal takeover battles with familiar casts of characters also saw what was popularly called Store Wars, a consolidation of department stores that had Simpson's, a 100-year-old Toronto chain that had twice rebuffed American takeover bids through the years, announce a merger with Simpson's Sears, a joint operation with Sears, Roebuck of Chicago. That was short-lived, however, because about twelve blocks away the board of directors of the Hudson's Bay Company gathered in a fourth-floor meeting room to sip coffee and Coca-Cola and vote into motion something it had first considered forty years before: the takeover of Simpson's.

Hudson's Bay, which had also just folded Zeller's, a discount retail chain, into its corporate balance sheets, has been a part of Canada's history since the issuance of its royal charter by King Charles II in 1670. Once strictly a British company, it had moved its corporate headquarters to Winnipeg and much of its ownership to Canadians, which was what attracted the second Lord Thomson of Fleet. For his father, the competitive Roy Thomson, Britain had provided the draw of the big leagues. He went there to build an international publishing empire ("It's a game," he said, "and I enjoy it"). And he won, not only ownership of the *Times* of London, among many other publications, but a seat in the House of Lords as well, something that most poor little boys from poor Ontario upbringings could only dream of. But that doesn't seem to matter so much anymore.

Now the press baron's son, who was to enlarge his company's publications holdings considerably, was in the midst of realigning his family's $10 billion in investments. Britain no longer held the prestige and glamour for this Canadian that it had for so many previous generations, a sense that was steadily creeping through much of Canada's moneyed aristocracy. In fact, back in Canada, where Kenneth Thomson spent more and more of his time, he disdained use of his British title. He collected Canadian art, not Renoirs. And he began shifting the weight of his company's investments away from their heavy British bent (even selling the *Times* to another outsider, Rupert Murdoch of Australia) and bringing the money and the attention and the benefits of investment back to North America, especially to Canada, where he felt the future was more promising.

So Mr. Thomson had two of his family's privately held companies bid for Hudson's Bay, which prompted a competing offer from the Weston family, another Canadian dynasty with British links. This pitted the wealthy son of Roy Thomson, who had once founded a rural radio station simply to spur sales of his radios, against W. Galen Weston, the wealthy son of Garfield Weston, who had turned a tiny Toronto bakery into Canada's largest merchandiser and a $7 billion multinational conglomerate (including Canada's Loblaws, the United States' National Tea Company, and Britain's Fortnum & Mason).

That time in the Hudson's Bay fray the baker's family of older money lost to the publisher's son of newer money. But they remained friends, of course. Galen reads Ken's newspapers, and his family's clothes most likely come from one of Ken's stores, while Ken's household help surely shops at Weston's stores. Marilyn Thomson, a graceful beauty who once modeled for Eaton's, the other major department store chain, might well serve Weston biscuits at tea. And when Ken Thomson sealed the deal to buy Canada's FP newspaper chain, the country's most prestigious and including Toronto's *Globe and Mail*, he drove home in his son's borrowed sports car and made himself a cheese sandwich, no doubt with Weston bread and Weston cheese. Without the Porsches, you'd hardly know the Thomsons were possibly Canada's only billionaires.

During our years in Toronto as nonbillionaires, as I continually tried to unweave the connections of Canada's societies, a new game developed in my family. I would ask, while driving of a Saturday afternoon, if anyone knew who really owned that company or store over there. Without raising his head from the sports pages, Christopher, our eldest, would inevitably pipe up, "Lord Thomson." It was the best guess. And he was right more often than wrong.

If it has been difficult for anyone in Canada to eat or read or ride something that is not controlled by a few famous families (or the government), it is also hard to avoid being touched somehow by one of the many arms of the Power Corporation. It is an aptly named collection of more than 150 companies assembled by Paul Desmarais, another aggressive entrepreneur tempered by the harsh elements of life in northern Ontario. Beginning with buses (later called the Voyageur line), the French-speaking Mr. Desmarais's interests spread into trucking, steamships, shipbuilding, forest products, publishing, trust companies, and insurance (Power's Great-West Life Assurance, with headquarters in Winnipeg and Denver, had numerous new American investments and was a major partner with Cincinnati's Taft family in Canada's Wonderland, the northern theme park cousin near Toronto of the Americans' Disneyland near Los Angeles).

In the early 1980's Mr. Desmarais sold off some of his oldest properties to finance the start of some new moves that show how things are still done in Canada. Back in college, some thirty-five years ago, Mr. Desmarais wrote a research paper on how someone could take over Canadian Pacific, the giant international corporate conglomerate so intimately tied to Canada's history. ("Canadian Pacific is Canada," David Schulman, a financial analyst in Montreal, explained to me one day, "and Canada is Canadian Pacific.")

Sometimes loved, sometimes hated, but never forgotten, CP (everyone in Canada knows what the initials stand for, though older Canadians would call it CPR) has become the country's largest nongovernmental company, criticized for much and loved for little. It is into everything from fine china to Arctic lead mines, from papermaking to steelmaking, from trains to planes, from hotels to insurance. Psychologically for Canadians CP equals bigness, strength, breadth. Historically its stock has been widely held, not as widely held perhaps as the old AT&T, but wide enough that no one owned more than 5 percent of its shares.

Both CP and Power have their headquarters in Montreal. Both companies' executives know each other. And both firms had no doubt heard the recurring rumors of a brewing takeover by one of the enlarged financial forces roaming Canada. The Nova Corporation, formerly Alberta Gas Trunk Line, the Hiram Walker-Consumer's Gas entity, the Alberta Heritage Savings Trust Fund, the multibillion-dollar repository of that province's growing oil royalties, Seagram's perhaps, or maybe even the British Columbia Resources Investment Corporation, the provincial government's resource-holding arm that bid for but lost MacMillan Bloedel to

Noranda. Wouldn't those people in B.C., including the premier, love to buy up the big eastern company that once controlled so much of their lives?

\A takeover of Canadian Pacific, especially by interests that might move its symbolic headquarters out of Montreal and Quebec wth their troubled linguistic and political histories, seems disastrous to many within and without Quebec. Not to mention among those generations of headstrong CP executives who had been left alone by fragmented shareholders to shape the future of the company and, by connection, their own careers.

Thus, it might be better to have someone friendly—not just anyone, mind you—well positioned to head off an unwelcome merger bid. His prominent, though enigmatic, presence might even prevent a bid in the first place. This person would have to inspire confidence, to understand how things are played, and to have big money of his own as well as access to even bigger money if necessary. A Quebecer would be good; he could ease the provincial sensitivities of a province where residents see "outsiders" behind every English word. But he'd have to be a Quebecer who opposed that province's political separation from Canada ("Can you imagine Canada's largest company, which was even named for the country, controlled by people who don't believe in a Canada?").

If this potential savior had his own companies, it would be good if they fit well in a corporate sense wth CP's varied interests. If there were any duplication, of course, that could be handled by simply selling them off. And things would have to be handled smoothly, no sharp turns spawning uncertainty.

Then at one point in 1981 large blocs of Canadian Pacific stock were traded, arousing suspicions and unease. Who was buying them up? "They'd buy around fifty dollars, back off when it rose to fifty-two or fifty-three," one broker told me, "and then they'd come back in like gangbusters when CP fell to forty-nine dollars." The purchaser of some 3.7 million CP shares was actually Cadillac Fairview Corporation Ltd., the real estate company controlled by something called Cemp Investments. Cemp is an investment arm of the Bronfman family, which also controls Seagram's. (The name comes from the first letter of the first names of the patriarch Sam Bronfman's four children—Charles, Edgar, Minda, and Phyllis.)

But the Bronfmans didn't want to control CP; they just wanted to make some money off someone who might. They had heard the rumors and jumped in first. "Without even talking to each other," said Mr. Schulman, the Montreal financial analyst, "these business families all think alike. They know the rules, the rumors, the goals of others. Cemp read the signals. They had some spare cash to fool with. So they assembled the bloc and went to Paul and made a deal. That's the way these things get started."

Mr. Desmarais, of course, claimed that he was simply making an attractive $174 million investment for 4.4 percent of CP. But he then just happened to sell off for $195 million his transportation subsidiaries (shipping, busing, and trucking), which might seem to conflict with parallel CP activities. And then through a gradual process he began to accumulate more CP stock. Today the Power Corporation or its chief, who has close family ties in the top ranks of the Liberal party (one of his sons married the daughter of Jean Chrétien, a party elder, chief Trudeau aide, and fervent opponent of separatist Quebec, not to mention a likely Liberal party leader and prime minister someday when it was, once again, the turn of a Francophone), owns more than 10 percent of CP, the giant. And Mr. Desmarais, a native of northern Ontario who made his national fortune by linking himself with Canada's other giant province and language group, has been appointed to CP's twenty-three-member board of directors, along with, later, a second Power Corporation representative. It is almost a parable of national unity.

Mr. Desmarais also executed a special protective agreement with both sides. He would not seek to own more than 15 percent of CP's shares so long as no one else owned more than 10 percent. The next largest CP shareholder is the Caisse de Dépôt et Placement du Québec, another example of new financial forces rising within Canada, which just happens to own 9.776 percent of CP. Once the Caisse was just a sleepy manager of the provincial government's pension funds. But under the persistent prodding of that government's nationalistic Parti Québecois, which first assumed power in 1976, the Caisse has expanded its vision and ambitions to become a major player in Canadian stocks.

It is a secretive organization that controls in excess of $16 billion, including the money of the province's social security system. Its managers, who are overseen by the provincial government, maintain they are just investors seeking to maximize the funds' gains for that day in the fast-approaching future when they must begin liquidating some holdings because the drain on its resources by the retired will exceed the gain of contributions from the still-working.

But Caisse critics—and in Canada there is always an ample supply of people voicing criticism—see the silent hand of the Parti Québécois behind the scenes, seeking control of assets and changing the direction of companies it controls to suit one province better than the country as a whole. This struggle is typical of many disputes that corrode Canadian unity, pitting province against province, province against federal government, and French-speaking against English-speaking. Canadians (along with Belgians, Nigerians, and other linguistically divided peoples) have found no final solution to such splits, other than to back off and let some steam escape at the boiling point. (This assumes a common sensitivity to just when that point is approaching.) Nonetheless, these splits remain spotted about the countryside of Canadian life like some wild animal traps, their fragile coverings of camouflage over the deep pits ready to give way at the slightest misstep.

The Caisse was banned from trading on the Toronto Stock Exchange because it refused to file insider-trading reports. So it took to dealing on American exchanges and at home on the faded Montreal Stock Exchange, which was only too happy for the business and where on some days the Caisse could account for two-thirds of total trades. The Caisse fast became the largest single player in the Canadian stock market. And it began demanding, with considerable success, board representation in its holdings such as Domtar, Alcan Aluminium, and Brascade, a Brascan-Caisse joint venture that owns much of Noranda, the mining giant.

"The Caisse represents the state," Mr. Desmarais charged at one point. "They are nationalizing companies, that's what they are doing, by the back door." He and CP turned for help, instinctively, to the federal government, which introduced legislation banning a province or any of its agencies from holding more than 10 percent of the voting stock in any company engaged in transportation between the provinces or outside Canada. The justification was the federal jurisdiction over interstate, or, rather, interprovincial, transportation, which in Canadian as well as American history has been seen as a major tool for nation building.

But another underlying reason is the guardianship of natural resources. Psychologically Canadians have always felt themselves abundantly endowed with natural resources, and with very good reason. The energy crises of the 1970's showed the world the increased value of a barrel of oil. But in Canada the people, investors and consumers alike, also saw an increase in awareness of the increased value of natural resources, all kinds of them from oil and gas to fish and uranium and coal and lead and even pure water.

Natural resources are the thing of legend in resource-rich Canada. "Once there was a little boy lost in the wilderness," the old Indian named Snowbird told me and my son Spencer around a wood stove fire in a tent one blustery March evening in northern Alberta. "The little boy was found by a she-wolf. She raised him, took care of him, and taught him the ways of the land. One day she knew it was time for the young man to return to his people. She took him walking far across the land. They came to a hill. She told him there was a large bush by a hole in the ground. She told him to put his hand in the hole. He did. And when he pulled it out, his hand was glowing in the dark. On that spot, the she-wolf told him, would come a city."

Even that old tale, handed down with countless others by countless elders in the long, cold nights of Canada's long, cold winters, knew of the glowing importance of at least one resource. For on that spot was erected a city named Uranium City, Saskatchewan, an aptly named frontier town that embodied so much of a part of Canada tied up in the rugged and expensive business of extracting resources for a resource-hungry world.

For centuries Canadians had toiled in their seas or in their vast wilderness areas to provide God's goods for the voracious markets of the world. With its vast distances and minuscule markets at home, Canada had always to rely heavily on foreign trade. Today, still, Canada must sell much abroad to survive economically; more than a quarter of its economic activity is based on international trade—61 percent of the country's zinc goes abroad, 85 percent of its wheat, and 88 percent of its newsprint.

And what Canada had to trade were natural resources, providing the raw materials for skilled craftsmen or industrialists or canny traders to use elsewhere. The first actual settlers, in fact, came not in flight from religious or political persecution. They came for Canada's fish first and stayed briefly in Newfoundland, not because of the country's richness but only because they could lengthen their fishing season by saving sailing time from Europe the following year.

Later, the British came to what would become the Maritime Provinces of Nova Scotia, New Brunswick, and later the Ottawa Valley not to bring civilized government or ways to the savage world of North American natives but to fell the tall, straight trees that held aloft the sails of the Royal Navy for so many generations.

Even later English and French merchants jockeyed for the rich furs of the Canadian wilderness, the beavers, minks, wolves, otters, and seals, whose pelts were so fashionable in so many lands for so long. They canoed and portaged thousands of miles inland, establishing trading posts at choice geographic locations that later led to cities on the same spot. Almost incidentally these hardy frontiersmen launched an exploration of Canada's raw real estate that remains vast and raw in most places today.

Resources have been the key to unlocking Canada and any understanding of that huge, unfinished place. Canadians don't have all that many common heroes to put on postage stamps, but they do have their resources. So there are beautiful stamps honoring such things as nickel. Without resources, there seemed little good reason to enter Canada's hostile immensity. Without resources or a strong profitable market for them, many isolated Canadian communities have shriveled up and died, crumbling monuments to that resource and the scars it left on the land and the people. And if the promise of gold in the streets has failed to materialize time after time after time throughout Canada's history, that only fed an innate national cynicism and a deep suspicion that every apparent opportunity was also laden with the certain specter of failure. According to an apt routine by the Royal Canadian Air Farce comedy group, "Some people look at things as they are and say, 'Why?' A Canadian looks at things as they might be and says, 'No way!' " No way has seemed a safer way.

Canada, for example, never paid any attention to its Yukon (and modern-day Yukoners would claim it still doesn't) until the shiny prospect of some yellow metal in its ground and streams ignited a historic stampede of 100,000 souls that became the great Klondike, actually an American gold rush on Canadian territory. To this day Americans still constitute 80 percent of those visiting Canada's Yukon.

In later years Canada's economic resource attractions have included cheap land, lumber and pulp, zinc, silver, lead, asbestos, low-cost electricity for such energy-thirsty industries as aluminum, whales, oil, natural gas, and the helpless little baby seals with the big eyes whose annual harvest by club-wielding men on eastern Canadian ice floes earned Canada so much adverse international publicity each spring. And there is also the recreational isolation of Canada's huge, unspoiled emptiness that millions of modern-day American tourists find essential to their annual rejuvenation known as the vacation. They are helped to this revenue-raising conclusion by all those expensive, glossy, colored government advertisements in American magazines showing a breathtaking Canadian panorama titled "Shangri-La" with its own toll-free telephone number. As Americans quickly discover there, that is about all that is toll-free about Canadian prices.

Canadians too have drawn on the resource of their sheer size for their psychic well-being. Living in Canada near the American border looking south, always south, to the noisy bustle of the United States, the Canadian can appear like some middle-aged, affluent homeowner leaning on his front fence on a busy street in a clean residential neighborhood, knowing that his comfortable home just behind him is safe and secure and that behind that structure lies the second-largest backyard in the world. He may not ever hike back into that geographic resource more than a few steps a few times a year. But the knowledge that it exists lets him feel like a part of a larger whole, which Canadians relish. And inside, it provides a warm feeling like donning dry boots next to a radiator on one of those wan winter mornings that make February seem like the longest month of the year.

In Canada there is simply so much more space where nobody is than where anybody is that there has seemed no end to the bounties of nature that sit there free for the taking. As one result, Canadians remained in the 1980's the industrialized world's largest per capita consumers of energy (conservation not being a crucial matter, the highway speed limit remains at 62.5 miles an hour, or 100 kilometers per hour). The only gasoline lines in Canada had been those of Americans crossing the border for the cheaper, plentiful fuel at a currency discount. Near major border crossings a line of cars with New York license plates waiting to fill their tanks with Canadian gas could be aggravating for some. But deep down, the sight of Americans having to come to Canada for something they want makes many Canadians feel very good. It is not unlike the good-natured but homely girl who remembers well those years as a wallflower at all the parties. Upon turning sixteen, however, she finds herself the beautiful young lady whose company is in demand by all those who once benignly ignored her. She never quite forgets the years that came before, but she can become annoyingly picky with her newfound power.

The ample fuel also lets Canadians indulge themselves in one of their few national luxuries: their love of large cars. Automobile executives, rubbing the fingers of one hand together against their thumb to indicate a watchful eye on the pennies, told me that Canadians may not go much for the luxury models, and they generally prefer the plainer budget styles without many optional gadgets. But they do like the large, plain cars that can glide along the immaculate city expressways which often turn into two-lane thoroughfares a few dozen miles out of town.

One of the more popular auto options (in the northern United States as well) is the engine-block heater, a coil denoted by its telltale cord hanging through the grille or beneath the front bumper. When connected to an electrical outlet, the coil warms the oil and engine block, easing the starting burden on frozen car batteries. One bitter Toronto morning, before I got such a heater, my car would not start, and I left the hood raised to retire to my warm kitchen and phone for help with fingers still stinging from the cold. Upon hanging up, I went back outside to discover a tow truck driver already hooking up his equipment to start my car. I remarked on the speed of his arrival. "Oh, did you phone someone?" he asked. It turned out he was from another garage, had been on another call, and, seeing my raised hood, just decided to stop and help someone else trying to cope with the climate. Adversity seems to breed these kinds of bonds in Canada, within or without the never-ending hunt for resources.

The search goes on day and night from one end of the country to the other and way beyond into the three surrounding seas. From afar, the romance of resource hunting is more apparent than up close. It is a dirty, dangerous life dominated by men in coveralls and full of hardships and hardhats and hard decisions that directly affect the lives and careers of hundreds of thousands of Canadians and, indirectly, millions more. One figure I saw estimated that more than 1 million Canadians still reside in one-industry communities that live and die with the fortunes or misfortunes of one resource or one-resource companies. These towns' sole reason for being has been to extract something and send it somewhere, it is hoped at a profit.

These are little, self-contained places like Wawa, Uranium City,

Hemlo, Polaris, LG2, and movable communities, like Sedco 709, the semisubmersible offshore drilling rig. They can often be reached only by helicopter or supply ships in tossing seas or for a few weeks a year in semitrailers that creak across frozen lakes turned into ice roads. Some of these places live for a time only to disappear for good, or bad, when the construction is done or the ore vein runs out or the price dips too far. In inhospitable places some communities like Sudbury grow into substantial hospitable cities that are too large to die when nickel times are tough and too small to do much else.

One constant in all these settings is the precariousness of life, the boom and bust, the peaks and valleys, that shape the existence and thinking of generations. If the muskrats or fish are plentiful this year, they may not be next. If they are plentiful, prices could go down. If the last two wells discovered black riches far below, the next forty might be dry holes. Sure, there's a lot of ore down there, but if there's no demand for it somewhere, the riches are worthless. Never expect too high a peak, and never underestimate the depth of a valley. Optimism and thoughtful, long-range planning do not sprout in a hand-to-mouth existence. Nor do good feelings about the absentee corporate parents, especially foreign ones, who become the bearers of bad news so often in such capital-intensive industries in an era of expensive capital.

The original Yukon gold rush was ignited one summer day back in 1898 by a single paragraph in the *Seattle Post-Intelligencer* reporting the steamer *Portland*'s arrival with Yukon miners and a ton of gold. Modern-day Klondikers, who can still take out a ton or two of those fabled yellow flakes in some years, look more to the London gold market than to Seattle today. The Yukon, a wild territory of awesome beauty on the east side of Alaska and in many wonderful ways still on the other side of the twentieth century, is fortunate because its 400-million-year-old rocks were never disturbed by glaciers. Natural erosion washed some of the gold-bearing rocks into creeks, where grizzled panners sifted the specks from the icy water rattling over the rocks. But many gold veins were left intact on top of bedrock, where modern miners, at times no less grizzled but far more efficient, can aim an unnatural stream of erosion at the most profitable points.

Many of today's claims, which cost $10 to stake and require $200 of work annually to retain, are leased by their individual holders to prospecting companies, which have the expensive equipment necessary and, in return, pay the claimants 10 percent of all the gold found. The companies bring in gangling front-end loaders, their mammoth hoses and pumps, and their bright yellow D-9 Caterpillar tractors. Their scarred blades, with a single shove, can push more dirt than two men with shovels in an entire day a century ago. "When the Guggenheims mined this area around 1910," Pat Scoretz, a mining foreman, told me one rainy afternoon while we stood in ankle-deep mud at one claim near Dawson, "they moved four and a half million cubic yards of dirt in ten years. We move a million yards every fifty days."

With the modern mushroomed price of gold, some new miners can make money by simply sifting through the old debris, or tailings, which line many valley bottoms in snaking rows of man-made minimountains as far as the eye can see, even from a hovering helicopter. Others, such as Gus Heitmann, go after the gold in new deposits. Mr. Heitmann, a truck driver, had a hunch about a piece of land called the Jackson claim. When a previous holder inadvertently let his claim lapse in 1969, Mr. Heitmann jumped in with his own claim. He worked it a little by himself and then, about ten years later, leased it to Universal Explorations Ltd., a Calgary oil company looking for a hedge against inflation for some of its assets. It began a full-fledged hydraulic mining operation.

Although the scale of gold mining has changed, the basic techniques have not. The idea is to break up dirt and rocks in a huge flow of water, which then tumbles through long wooden boxes called sluices. The box bottoms are lined with various barriers to create turbulence, making the moving water drop the heavier gold while carrying away the lighter dirt, much the same principle as snow fences along a highway.

On Mr. Heitmann's claim it was necessary to remove 18 inches of moss, which had kept the ground permanently frozen for centuries. Then, just to get near the 20-foot pay zone, 280 feet of dirt and gravel had to be taken away. Under Mr. Scoretz's direction, huge hoses loft high-powered streams of water against the mountainside twenty-four hours a day seven days a week eight months a year. The water thaws the mountain and carves out canyons, carrying everything down the slope. Then bulldozers shove the loosened material toward the sluices, which rumble and shake under the pounding and weight.

Every twelve to twenty-four hours, the water flow is diverted to a second sluice. Then, if all has gone well, as the last puddles of muddy water drip away, the closely monitored work crews will find tucked in against the wet wood several thousand minute pieces of prehistoric yellow, each ounce worth several hundred dollars in a faraway market. Exactly how much profit the Yukon's frozen ground is yielding is a secret as closely guarded today as it was nearly nine decades ago. Miners estimate that only half the gold found is actually reported. This is because Canadian law requires a report only when the metal leaves the Yukon. That is when it collects its ridiculous royalty of 22.5 cents an ounce, an assessment still based on the old gold's old value of $35 an ounce.

But while one area enjoys a peak, others suffer a valley, possibly for good. Corner Brook, Newfoundland, for instance, has enjoyed the employment provided by Bowater Newfoundland, a unit of a British multinational that for forty-five years has produced paper and a local economic boost of $200 million a year. That may have spawned some complacency over the years; Corner Brook and its 25,000 residents were one of the province's few pockets of prosperity, and people always need paper, right? But the mill grew old and the economics grew as sour as the sulfurous stench of papermaking; the company can grow trees faster and harvest them cheaper in the American Sun Belt than it can on a gloomy North Atlantic isle. So Bowater decided to sell out or close out, dumping nearly 2,000 workers and loggers out of work in an area where unemployment already stands near 1 in 4.

Two time zones to the west, unemployment is often higher (nearing 30 percent) in Sudbury, a hardworking city that lives and withers with the fortunes of Inco Ltd. and Falconbridge Ltd., whose nickel operations once shipped 85 percent of the entire world's production from the desolate surrounding Shield (in fact, American astronauts traveled to Sudbury to train because the barren terrain is so much like the moon's). Just after local employees are called back to work and begin to get their debts paid off from the last nickel layoff or strike, another layoff or strike comes along. In the early 1970's Inco had more than 18,700 workers in Sudbury, which is sometimes jokingly called Sludgebury for its reputation for industrial ugliness (until recent replanting efforts, the fumes from its smelting had killed wide areas of the city's surrounding trees and vegetation). Today there are fewer than 8,000 union members. And Inco plans to drop permanently one worker every day over the next four years at a time when, on the average, three young workers join the city's labor market every day. "There is less employment," said Mel Soucie, a federal economist there, "and nothing is coming in to replace it."

Of course, some of the resources hunted by Canadians are alive and wild. Furs, an original attraction for the northern half of North America, have clothed Canadians and still form the focus of a rugged life for thousands of trappers, traders, and workers. And nothing has played as important a role in Canadian furs over the centuries as Lord Thomson's Hudson's Bay Company. It was founded nearly 320 years ago, so long ago that many isolated Canadians joke that the company's initials really stand for Here Before Christ, which in a way is true since the trappers and traders preceded even the missionaries.

For most Canadians, the Bay, as it is called, is an aggressive, trendy department store chain in malls and bustling downtowns. But half of its nearly 250 outlets are so-called inland stores, isolated and rural modern-day trading posts that sell groceries, rifles, magazines, eggs, televisions, nails, and carved wooden elephants holding up table lamps. And their operations provide a revealing insight into some Canadian communities' organization.

The stores still play a unique and often dominant economic and social role in Canada's vast northern areas. They not only sell goods but also buy them. Mainly their local manager is interested in furs, but he also pays for the magnificent crude soapstone carvings by some northern natives. Bay stores, often the reason a community developed where it did, are an important place for socializing. Their doorsteps become the "downtown" taxi stand. Their walls and loudspeakers become community bulletin boards. Their quality and prices become area standard setters. And because the Bay often is the town's sole retail outlet, the stores can become the focus of accumulated native grievances over prices and other problems blamed on outsiders.

Through its store training the Bay helps construct a continental cadre of native clerks and junior managers, who often move on to found or staff other businesses, while it also provides a rare source of nongovernmental employment in many areas. More important, though, the Bay store pumps money into the local economy by its purchases of furs. In the Northwest Territories, in Rae, 900 dirt-and-gravel-road miles north of Edmonton and 1,300 more miles north of Denver, the Bay pays local trappers more than $100,000 a year for pelts caught in a 150-mile radius. In fact, the Bay's traditional fur-buying times of year determined the dates of most native holidays and weddings. That's when everyone was in town.

And the local Bay manager, like Rae's Dan Marion, plays a very prominent and influential role. "In these monopoly situations," said Mr. Marion, "local opinion of the Bay is precisely the same as local opinion of the Bay manager. You've got to mix well, be fair and honest."

The store manager, who was 38 when I first met him, must also be a mechanic, a shipping expert, a social worker, a banker, an engineer, a teacher, a community leader and accountant, a heating technician, and a trilingual public relations officer as well as a savvy fur buyer. "It's a tough job," he told me one 35-degree-below-zero afternoon as we plugged my rented car's engine-block heater into a line of electrical sockets on the wall outside his store, "but I don't think I could survive anywhere else."

For his managerial and diplomatic skills and his fifty-five-hour workweeks, Mr. Marion, a veteran Bay employee, was paid nearly $20,000 a year plus food discounts, inexpensive housing, and a bonus of up to 25 percent of salary based on his store's overall performance. He told me that his store, which first opened in 1829 to buy dried caribou for company trappers, made about $85,000 profit a year on total sales of $1.1 million —60 percent of it food. If he is lucky, he will have three inventory turnovers a year, but distance and local society make for some unusual economic rules.

With the cost of airfreight so high (it easily exceeds $1 per pound), Mr. Marion organizes almost everything into 40,000-pound truck shipments, when the roads to the Edmonton warehouse are passable. Mistakes in orders can take months to correct. Goods for one Christmas must be ordered well before the previous Christmas. Half the eggs trucked in are broken. And frequent power and heating failures can freeze everything solid in hours. In Rae, named for a company doctor and explorer, Mr. Marion must stock fine china and boots as well as dog harnesses and steel traps.

Petty thefts totaling $8,500 a year are a minor problem. But credit is something else. "If you expect all bills to be paid on time," he said, "then we have a problem here. Here you have to make more allowances for individual family problems and for seasonal incomes. The unpaid bills, with no interest charges, really add to my costs. But that's reality up here."

Just then in our conversation Big John Robuska arrived at the store after a four-day snowmobile trip from touring his traplines. While they chatted in English, French, and Dogrib, a fading Indian language, Mr. Marion inspected Mr. Robuska's batch of lynx, fox, marten, and mink pelts. The manager calculated his offering price on a torn envelope. The offer was $1,140. Mr. Robuska hesitated. Mr. Marion spoke: "I'll add an extra sixty dollars—you're a good supplier—and you can pick out a new shirt, too." Mr. Robuska nodded. The deal was consummated.

The Indian put $300 toward his running $500 bill and added the rest to his share of the $20,000 that local trappers leave on deposit with the Rae Bay. "You can't cause anyone to lose face," Mr. Marion said as he carried the furs to a frigid storeroom for packing and shipping to auctions in cities many miles away, "so you buy everything everybody offers. You just pay less if it's poor." He must also meet regularly with chiefs of the Dogrib bands to sip tea and to chat about the weather and their needs, such as a new kind of animal trap. He must give them free shirts at holidays as a sign of respect. And each year he chips in $150 of the store's money toward the tribe's New Year's feast dance, an all-night affair that leaves them all feeling very warm as they trod home in the snow that is so beautifully noisy at those deeply sub-zero temperatures.

When I left Mr. Marion one night after midnight under the eerie green light curtains of the Northern Lights, he was frantically draining toilets and water pipes in Bay buildings and moving a portable propane heater between rooms. The power had gone off again that December night. It would remain off for two days this time, sufficient to freeze everything on his shelves colder than the meats in his store's freezer room. In fact, with the power off, Mr. Marion did the only logical thing: He opened the freezer doors wide to let in the Canadian air and keep the foods frozen very solid.

"Yeah, it's demanding," he added. "You've got to socialize and be tough, stay up all night fixing the furnace and do the books in the morning, to satisfy the people right here and the big bosses many miles away. But you know, I couldn't live down South anymore."

Down South at the same time a number of lesser-known private companies were busy harvesting another natural resource in demand in distant markets. They were chopping down Christmas trees to decorate the living rooms, dens, and basements of millions of American homes. All over Nova

Scotia, New Brunswick, and Quebec, the brattling sound of chain saws echoes through the woods from the last ten days of October through the first ten days of December. Their harvest, mostly ten- to twelve-year-old balsam trees, is bundled, 6 to 8 to a bale, and trucked, 1,600 to the truck, on round-the-clock routes often 2,000 miles away. It is a grueling time: On Monday one truck will load in Nova Scotia, one time zone into the Atlantic east of New York City, for Milwaukee and be back in Nova Scotia on Friday. Sometimes six-truck convoys will drive the entire American East Coast to deliver some 10,000 trees to a freighter waiting in Miami and bound for South America. "For us," said Pat Septon, a Christmas tree worker who might have been speaking for many in Canada's resource economy, "you make it when you can."

Such intense seasonal, or cyclical, work tied to demand among consumers far away is typical of many of Canada's local economies. Also typical is a growing sophistication. There was a time when fallers simply walked through the woods and cut down any tree. Now the trees and their land are carefully managed. Near Halifax, Nova Scotia, Kirk Ltd., the largest tree exporter in the largest tree-exporting province, owns 30,000 acres. As its woodlands are cleared of larger trees for timber and pulp, it plants Christmas trees behind. They are ready for harvest as Christmas trees in less than one-quarter the time a good timber tree takes to develop in that climate.

Modern Christmas trees get much more loving care, too, and year-round. Kirk, for instance, now employs 50 Christmas tree workers all year and hires an extra 150 come fall. Beginning at age three or four, the trees are individually cultivated, fertilized according to their soil's needs for fast, full growth, and annually trimmed to stimulate buds and the bushy shape Canadians know Americans like.

But with prices rising along with the costs of long-haul transportation, Canadian exporters are experiencing more competition from American growers expanding their production in the Midwest and upstate New York, all areas closer to major population centers. Timing is also crucial in the holiday tree business, where there is no opportunity for post-Christmas sales. So Canadian exporters must cut as many as they think they can sell. But no more. "It's like playing blackjack," said Mr. Septon. "Do you think you can cut it a little closer and win bigger or maybe blow it all?"

United States retailers want most of the trees on their vacant sales lots by Thanksgiving. That means a very hectic time for Mr. Septon, a part-time fisherman who has cut Christmas trees for Americans for thirty years and finds his Christmas spirit running very short come early December. By December 9, when many people are just starting to think about their Christmas tree, Mr. Septon's Christmas tree business is over. All the Christmas trees will have been shipped south. And Mr. Septon will be realizing, as he does every holiday, that he has processed more than a quarter million Christmas trees and forgotten to save one for himself. "But you know," he said, "after handling all those trees for all those years, I'm not too fussy about having one of my own."

The exploitation of Canada's little-known Christmas tree business is a decent example of two historic problems in that country's economic history. There are few major markets with enough people to support by themselves such an industry, and there were, at least initially, few Canadians with the idea or the money or both to develop the industry. To this day many of the Canadian companies exporting Canadian trees to American customers are really controlled by Americans.

There have been two vital resources in short supply throughout Canadian history: people and capital. So, more often than not, those who organized the taking of the country's resources were foreigners with enough money and enough gall to risk a bundle for a profit.

British merchants financed the first planned visits to Canada's Arctic North, which was actually explored before the more habitable South. They were looking for a route to somewhere else, the fabled Northwest Passage to the riches of the Orient. But they stumbled onto the fertile fishing grounds that drew the French and Irish and Scots. And as time went on, British money and ways came to dominate the land and still pervade many habits. More than a century after their independence, diners at Toronto's Canadian Club meetings still begin each luncheon with a toast to Her Majesty the Queen. As a Canadian friend said upon reading these lines, "Why not? She's Queen of Canada." There are also few dry eyes when the royal yacht sails into a Canadian harbor for yet another visit. And even modern-day immigrants from Britain still talk about "when I came across . . ." as if the Atlantic Ocean were a mere lane.

British money, it is said in Canada, comes, makes a profit, and goes.

But American money comes and stays, although overall foreign investment has been decreasing from one-third of net Canadian capital stock
in 1961 to 27 percent in 1971 and 20 percent in 1981. Americans,
according to Mordecai Richler, the Canadian novelist, have been builders,
investors, chance takers. Canadians, he added, have not. Americans have
invested themselves and their money in Canada for generations. Faced
with the overflowing frontier in the American West near the turn of the
century, 1 million American settlers headed north to help populate and
tame the Canadian land. American settlers could have the land, break it
to the plow, and then take their earnings back to Illinois or wherever a
few years later, assuming there were earnings on the farmland that was
not quite as good with not quite as long a growing season and nowhere
near the market. One standard American attitude was said to have been
expressed by J. P. Morgan, the New York financier not known for being
tuned to others' sensitivities. "Canada," he is said to have said, "is a very
nice place. And we intend to keep it that way."

On both sides of the border there has been regular advocacy of and
resistance to the kind of continental economy that has inexorably developed anyway, the result of fierce forces far beyond the rhetoric of any
Canadian leader playing the strings of nationalism or of any ignorant
American leader deleting the word "overseas" from a speech and referring
to Japan as the United States' largest trading partner.[4] The nineteenth
and twentieth centuries saw official steps closer and official recoils back,
depending on the usually conflicting political expediencies of the day in
each land. Two relatively rare examples of merged economic interests
were the construction of the St. Lawrence Seaway and the creation of the
Auto Pact, which let new cars flow back and forth tariff-free with specific
American company promises to build set numbers in Canada. But if
settlement of the Canadian West was more a factor of an American
overflow, then development of the Canadian mining industry was a result
of demand from American markets and a good deal of Canada's manufacturing development came out of the now much criticized branch plants.

They are often portrayed in Canada today somewhat like leeches,
sucking sales from the Canadian market, sending profits and new jobs to
distant ogres, who do the valuable research and development there and
purposely deny Canada its due share of the future. Often it seems the only
things these branch plants do is provide jobs for thousands of Canadians

where such a company did not exist before, give the Canadian economy access to foreign technology, and pay their taxes to provincial and federal governments to help finance a far more vast array of social welfare services than in their homeland. A Canadian could hardly care more that his washing machine was made in Indiana; an average American could hardly care less that his car was assembled in Windsor or Quebec.

American money poured into Canada after World War II in the glow of wartime camaraderie and cooperation when Canadians began to implement their decision to reduce foreign financial influences. Previously Canada had sought capital predominantly from foreign loans. Those payments abroad had to be made in good times and bad. It was better, Canada decided after considerable debate, to invite foreign investors to share the risks through equity investments. In good times they would also share the profits. In bad times they would share the hardships.

No investors were more eager to put up their bucks than the corporate finance officers of American companies that emerged from the war unscathed, strong, and ready to forge secure investments for an assured supply of resources to fuel their factories. And in those first ten postwar years, no Canadian official of the governments of Mackenzie King or Louis St. Laurent was more ready to encourage such growth than the most powerful economic policy minister in Canada, C. D. Howe, a former engineer and businessman who was born an American. The decisions made by the Canadian governments of those days brought the country rapid economic growth through infusion of branch plants, mostly American. But they were also forever to change the face of Canada—for instance, thrusting Toronto into new national prominence as the Americans' favorite capital of capital. But despite the affluence that came, these Canadian decisions also carried the certain seeds of bitter future nationalistic resentments and conflicts. The full scope of these has yet to be gauged.

The arrangement proved beneficial to both sides. To the Americans it offered ready access to convenient resources next door. To the Canadians, who had seen their Depression last right up until the war, it offered new jobs and growth and a special relationship with the most powerful nation on earth. It was, in effect, replacing a colonial mother with a colonial big brother. "We moved from British influence to American influence," Prime Minister Lester Bowles Pearson once noted, "without much feeling of purely national identity in between."

But the relationship was not a little flattering for a "new" country that had no foreign policy and no foreign missions of its own until 1927. The American economic link promised a road out of the quiet backwater that Canada has always felt it inhabited and sometimes says it prefers. It turned Canada, with fewer people now than California, into the world's sixth-largest manufacturing and trading nation. And it brought with it a standard of living far higher than the country could ever have financed or achieved by itself so quickly. "By pursuing their particular comparative advantages within the broader North American context, Canadians came to enjoy a standard of living only slightly below that of their southern neighbor with but a fraction of some of the costs such as defense, but the price they paid was integration within a wider continental economic system."[5]

The phenomenon has seen Americans invest more than $50 billion in Canada, by far the most they have entrusted to any foreign land. That has been three-quarters of all foreign investment in Canada. It has founded and built up many Canadian industries from scratch. But it also allowed American companies to hammer unto themselves control of most major economic sectors, so much so that Canada's economy is the most heavily dominated by foreigners of any major industrialized country. In recent times Americans controlled 72 percent of Canada's oil and gas industry, half its manufacturing, many of its unions, bought 70 percent of Canada's total exports, and most of its natural gas exports. In Sandwich, Ontario, a former French farm site now incorporated into a city called Windsor, which, despite its location in Canada, is on the same latitude as Rome, Italy, there actually once were competing Canadian car makers with names like Regal Motor and Two-in-One Auto Company (it was part truck and part car). But now American companies control the country's entire automobile industry, which is the largest single employer in Ontario, Canada's industrial heartland.

Those numbers have declined somewhat more recently. In 1982, for example, Americans bought only 47 percent of the natural gas that their Canadian suppliers were authorized to export to them. The reasons for these declines in American control are varied and complex. They include higher prices in Canada and lower costs elsewhere as well as the Canadian government's drive to reduce foreign influence in certain sectors and a resulting bad image that grew in many foreign minds at the mention of economic involvement in Canada. Not to mention the perceived political uncertainties in other areas such as Quebec and a widespread series of quiet individual decisions to diversify Canada's buyers; in natural gas, to take one commodity, there was no shortage of buyers, and Japan, the number two trading partner for both Canada and the United States, gleefully was prepared to buy up the Americans' unwanted tankerfuls. But the slip in American economic influence went largely unnoticed; it didn't fit the popular cliché. And anyway, if it's such a good deal for Canadians, how could Canadians work it out?

This American control, though weakening, created a wide range of problems. As things developed, the price for Canada's foreign-created jobs and affluence was forfeiture of a good deal of economic independence. When the American automobile industry stumbled over the energy crisis and Japanese competition, for instance, what clout or levers did Canadian officials have over the impact of layoffs? When the time came to close down a plant, which would go first: the one next to headquarters at home or a branch plant in Canada? And where would the research so vital for the future and future jobs be conducted? The Americans could finance the good times, but that also linked Canada to the throes of difficult days.

Critics also blamed foreign investment for Canada's poor economic performance, saying foreigners fragmented domestic industry for their own profits, and for Canada's low investments in research and development (1.2 percent of gross national product versus 2.5 percent in the United States). And little of that investment was by foreign concerns, they charged. "If foreign ownership is so beneficial," asked Lorne Nystrom, a Member of Parliament for the socialist New Democratic party, "why are some of our Latin American neighbors counted among the most wretchedly poor countries of the world, despite mind-boggling investments by scores of multinationals?"

There were few cheers in Canada when an American company decided to move into or expand within Canada; in fact, the firm often had to run a gantlet of suspicion. But there were many very loud boos and "I-told-you-so's" when someone left. The widespread defensive assumption, sometimes unspoken, has been that everyone who could would leave at some point. The fact that most people could understand such moves rationally did not stop them from resenting them emotionally.

This kind of one-sided relationship also fomented the fires of nationalism. In Canada, economic nationalism dies down when things are going well. But it flares up again when times are tough or uncertain and when scapegoats—in other provinces, in other lands—are needed. It is such smoldering resentments that drain the color from the United States' image as benefactor.

Canadian leaders and politicians still make the familiar trek to United States centers of financial power, mainly New York City. They must, in view of the massive needs for capital at home and the even larger need for public relations work among many Americans who think Canada is somehow still part of Great Britain. Thus, at times Premier René Lévesque of Quebec made weeklong "campaign" forays to cities across the United States carrying his message of calm reasonableness and ethnic pride and talking about how deeply rooted French-speaking Quebecers are in the North American way of life. Among potential lenders in the United States, this can help the Parti Québecois and Mr. Lévesque, a skilled speaker and broadcaster who worked on propaganda for the American government during World War II. His reception by friendly American audiences free of the emotional, linguistic splinters in English-speaking Canadian provinces is televised back home and could elevate his own image and help legitimize his controversial cause among hesitant Quebecers. And as it does with touring American Presidents, a foreign trip can help those at home forget at least for a moment things like high unemployment. "Quebec is not going down the drain," Mr. Lévesque tells Americans possibly concerned with a new unknown, independent political entity on their unguarded northern border, "and the sky is not falling in Montreal." But so great are the North-South ties between Canada and the United States and so weak are the East-West ones within Canada that this is the kind of full-fledged political and public relations effort which Mr. Lévesque never duplicated in his own country.

But there can no longer be even the slightest tinge of hat in hand to these trips. When William Bennett, the powerful premier of British Columbia, visits an American city like New York, he checks into a suite in the Waldorf-Astoria with his five-man delegation for two or three hectic days of well-orchestrated financial briefings, discussions, luncheons, and a speech or two. The message for the Americans concerns his own province's economic growth and potential. But should a visiting premier want to make headlines back home, he will sharply criticize his own country's prime minister to a foreign audience. This is everyday stuff at home, but the same words pronounced outside Canada and inside the United States somehow carry far greater impact. "New York is a stimulating place," said Kenneth Taylor, Canada's consul general, "and there's a certain local legitimizing factor in Canada to being taken seriously abroad."

Most of the stops on these Gotham visits are arranged by Canada's consul general in New York, a major posting for its importance and exposure. That is the reason why one recent consul general was Mr. Taylor, the bespectacled, curly-haired former Canadian ambassador to Iran who smuggled out some Americans during the 1980 hostage crisis. His act and his name gave Mr. Taylor—and Canada—priceless entrée to the corridors of American power, financial and otherwise, although his success annoyed the hell out of some foreign service peers.

Mr. Bennett and his entourage meet together and separately with credit-rating agencies, making sure to shore up the rating that determines the interest they must pay on loans. They meet with industrial leaders who might want to invest in their province and with executives whose firms are already doing business there. Sometimes the questions concern wonderment over some national Canadian policy, and Mr. Bennett, whose Social Credit party leans to the conservative side of the political spectrum, will shake his head over the misguided policies of the federal government, especially if it is run by the Liberals at the time.

Always, though, the talk is of growth and investments, and usually that concerns natural resources of some kind. Mr. Bennett, thanks to his family's successful furniture store, was at one time the only former businessman among Canada's ten provincial premiers. (The others sometimes frowned on business. "If I had a choice between believing in free enterprise and Santa Claus," said New Brunswick's Premier Richard Hatfield, a Conservative, "I would believe in Santa Claus.") Mr. Bennett points out how his province alone is seven and a half times larger than New York State with but one-sixth the population. He'll talk about the oil and gas there and the proposed pipelines that could carry the black gold south. He'll describe all the untapped hydroelectric potential so near ocean waters for cheap transport and so suitable for aluminum smelting. And no doubt, the subject of the new deepwater port and B.C.'s rich coal deposits will come up. "At 30 million tons a year," Mr. Bennett told one audience, "there's enough coal in the northeast [of B.C.] alone for 3,000 years." And he will surely point out how much American investment is already in British Columbia, where fully 20 percent of the nearly half million member labor force works for American employers. "I'm not afraid of equity ownership from other countries in our province," Mr. Bennett said. "I just don't want it to be dominant." All this sounds eminently reasonable to his attentive Americans and can seem as if business as usual was under way.

But there are growing indications of change "up there," and its effects have been spilling over into the United States and elsewhere. Lynn Williams, a soft-spoken Canadian, worked his way up to become president of the United Steelworkers of America, all 720,000 of them on both sides of the U.S.-Canada border. Then just as Chrysler, the American automaker, was getting back on its financial feet in 1982, it was hit with a crippling five-week strike by 10,000 militant union members, not in Detroit or Ohio but in Ontario. The Canadians were not about to wait for an improved contract. They wanted more pay now. The Canadian walkout, which could have silenced all Chrysler facilities for lack of parts, did shut down production of some of the company's most profitable models and, according to Chrysler chairman Lee A. Iacocca, cost the company about $100 million. A settlement was reached, and the Canadians got their raises and their salaries equivalent to the Americans', always a touchy issue in Canada. But for the first time in the history of the United Automobile Workers union, a Canadian agreement provided the foundation for a contract settlement in the United States as well.

Elsewhere in the Midwest, American farmers were struck by the crushing effects of low commodity prices and high interest rates that prompted mounting farm foreclosures. Some potato farmers in New England were severely affected by cheap Canadian imports. But many of their financially troubled midwestern colleagues turned not to American aid groups but to militant Canadian farm organizations that had enjoyed some success with imaginative tactics against forced farm sales. The Canadians traveled about the American Farm Belt, speaking and giving seminars on direct action. (One favorite Canadian tactic was to disperse among sympathetic neighbors a farmer's expensive equipment about to be repossessed. Thus, there was no direct confrontation. The financier could not get at the equipment. But the farmer could.)

Even the American underworld felt the effects of aggressive Canadians moving out from their own land. Canadian gangsters, who had long coexisted with their American cohorts during their winter vacations in the South, began clashing openly in parts of North Miami and Hollywood, which became known not as Little Italy but as Little Montreal. In one eighteen-month stretch Florida police arrested half of Canada's ten most wanted fugitives.

The Canadian mobsters were attracted by the climate, the greater ease of obtaining arms, the larger potential for illegal moneymaking, and the considerable impunity. If they victimized Canadians living illegally in Florida, the victims were unlikely to run to authorities, fearing deportation back home, to where the Canadian gangs had a vicious reputation for tortures and reprisal killings. Some American police, who were hampered by a lack of French-speaking officers and by the distance necessary to coordinate activities with Canadian authorities, said the Canadian criminals seemed to have established an annual routine. They would commit a major crime in Canada in late fall, flee to Florida or Arizona for the winter to avoid the legal heat at home and to enjoy the American Sun Belt, then commit a crime there come spring and run home for the summer to avoid Florida's seasonal heat.

In Great Britain one aspect of the Canadian invasion took the very audible form of Canadians making investments in more than half of all the country's private radio stations and broadcasting what many English heard as a bland blend of North American music and entertainment rather than developing distinctive local programming.

And when Canadian institutions ran into trouble, the impact spread beyond Canada. Now there were Canadian-based multinationals, such as Massey-Ferguson, the farm implement giant, which, when times were tough, were ordering foreign factory closures and employee layoffs in Britain, France, West Germany, and a string of plants in the United States. When Canadian authorities developed a new international air terminal called Mirabel near Montreal, they found Canadians reluctant to make the long trek from the city to the underutilized field, which became a fiscal and physical embarrassment. So they began pushing the airport as a handy travel alternative for residents of New England and upstate New York, who were closer to that major Canadian airport than they were to similar American facilities.

Some of the legions of Canada's small businesses latched onto one imaginative idea and sent the down business up. Despite recessions and record-high prices for the little puffs of feathers, the making and selling of down-filled clothing became a $100 million-a-year industry plus lucrative international sales. Once down had been something worn only by geese, ducks, and a few hunters in reversible red and green vests. Then, with more imaginative uses and more fashionable designs and clever marketing, the down business exploded in North America and even in Asia, where other countries, such as China, began harboring supplies of feathers to compete internationally with their cheaper labor.

Down, whose tiny, resilient filaments number 2 million to the ounce, has long been popular as a pillow filler and, in Europe, for bed comforters. It was warm and lightweight. But its bulk and perceived image as masculine, "outdoorsy," and unfashionable confined sales to the sporting goods sections of most North American stores. There is considerable dispute, as there often is in Canada, about which one of Canada's many private clothing companies first combined new colors, better design, and a stylish stitching pattern to make the first down coat for women. But there is no dispute that it happened in the late 1970's in Winnipeg, the old prairie riverboat town that has the lowest mean temperature of any major Canadian city. "You don't care what you look like in Winnipeg in winter," said Russill H. Morin, president of the Canadian Down and Feather Products Association. "You just want to be warm."

Now there is a complete line of manufactured down products—coats, mittens, parkas, comforters, slippers, skiwear, sleeping bags. The basic quality of down, however, owes nothing to humans. Its many water-resistant filaments, naturally arrayed in clusters like a ripe dandelion pod, trap warm air next to the body yet allow the garments to "breathe." The best down comes from the breasts of geese. While one mature ten-pound goose might produce eight ounces of feathers, that includes only two ounces of down. So the down can cost more than $54 a pound, which is a lot more than the entire rest of the bird is worth.

The problem is that feathers and down are a by-product of the meat industry, and there has never been that overwhelming a demand for goose and duck in North America. So, according to Mr. Morin, a number of Canadian farmers are raising geese, selling the meat frozen to European outlets at little more than cost, and making their profit from the by-product. The feathers arrive at Canadian processors in burlap-wrapped bales in 40,000-pound container loads. They are washed, blown dry, and blown sorted for shipment to Canadian clothiers, who are doing their own scrambling to arrange the down in the best designed, most fashionable fabric wrapping.

The problem is that Canadian farmers can't find enough feathers to pluck to satisfy even a quarter of the country's down business. The rest, some 2 million pounds a year, has to be imported, primarily from China. But the Canadian sales success prompted the Chinese to slap a lid on feather exports and launch their own down clothing industry, followed by the Koreans, both of whom pay wages far below North American standards. That means a Chinese down coat can sell for almost half what a Canadian-made coat can. "Our challenge is to make our coats look that much more expensive than the imports," said Murray Waldman of the Canadian Garments Company, which changes its name to Miami Fashions Ltd. when it does business in the United States.

The Canadian downwear manufacturers cite many reasons for down's sudden success without any large-scale advertising. They include inflation, which places greater value on quality, changing tastes toward more outdoor activities, acceptance of more pragmatic clothing, down's impressive insulating power, and the strength of a fad that first introduced many to the comfort, practicality, light weight, and warmth of some slightly used feathers. But no one I talked with ever mentioned another major reason —the Canadians' ingenuity for taking one of their natural resources and processing it into an internationally popular and profitable product.

This growing desire among Canadians to do more than simply harvest a resource also emerged in the potash and asbestos industries, where provincial governments took it upon themselves to organize more job-creating, resource-processing activities by taking over some foreign companies. These always were legal and always involved large sums of money, but they also involved in some cases years of angry public wrangling over the need and the price. In Quebec the nationalist Parti Québecois decided to buy, under the threat of expropriation, the Asbestos Corporation, a subsidiary of St. Louis's General Dynamics Corporation. Elsewhere the sight of a government's wanting to become involved for millions upon millions of dollars in an industry where the main component was linked to a fatal disease may have seemed strange. But in Quebec, the world's largest producer of asbestos, the drive to harness further the value of a natural resource was not strange at all. The government even formed a company to design new uses for the inert subterranean fuzzy fibers that somehow came from volcanic action to underlie much of that province. Yet 97 percent of Quebec's asbestos production was hauled elsewhere for processing, a telling statistic to virtually all Canadians.

The lengths to which Canadian governments will go to help build new kinds of jobs was graphically illustrated in Nova Scotia, one of Canada's most spectacularly scenic areas but also one of its most chronically depressed. There a major labor confrontation erupted involving the provincial government, a French tiremaker, and the United Rubber, Cork, Linoleum and Plastic Workers union, based in the United States.

The issue was an amendment to the province's labor laws that required a union seeking to organize one plant of a manufacturing company to win certification at all the company's facilities within that province if the plants were "interdependent." This creates single provincewide bargaining units for each company and, the Conservative government maintained, promotes labor stability and economic development in an area always plagued with high unemployment. But the Nova Scotia Federation of Labor and the rubber workers' union claimed the measure, in effect, would dilute prounion sentiment at some plants so severely and compound union organizing activities so greatly as to become virtually a denial of democratic rights. And, labor noted, the law was worded to benefit only one Nova Scotia manufacturer, Michelin Tires (Canada) Ltd., whose French corporate parent is scarcely known for its union sympathies. After the bill had been introduced, Michelin announced plans for a third plant in the same province.

Michelin first moved to underdeveloped Nova Scotia back in 1971. Eager to have the employment and the taxes, both Liberal and Conservative governments took special account of Michelin's needs. They gave the company a $50 million loan at 6 percent, a $10 million grant, and a three-year remission of the 17.5 percent import duty on tires from France. Then, when labor strife threatened construction work at the new plants, the province passed legislation banning wildcat strikes and picketing and effectively restricting craft union organizing. With its several thousand workers, Michelin, the target of labor organizers at its nonunion American facilities, quickly became one of Nova Scotia's largest employers.

The confrontation set a potentially powerful precedent for foreign investors in their dealings with provincial governments, which were under considerable political pressures from job-hungry Canadians stung by the painful economic transitions that afflicted most modern industrial countries in the 1980's. "How far do you go to satisfy a multinational?" asked Gerald Yetman, a carpenter and part-time president of Nova Scotia's labor federation. Kenneth Streatch, the provincial labor minister, replied, "You've got to till the soil of legislative policy to get jobs."

Canada went basically from a frontier society, which it remains in some areas, to a modern welfare state without an intervening period of digestion and fundamental growth. One of the reasons it was able to do this, beyond so much foreign investment, was that Canadians expect their governments on all levels to till the soil of the economy to a far greater extent than their American continental peers do. This was true even before the Yanks started down the painful road of deregulation that weaned industry after industry—airlines, oil, trucking, banking—from the coddling world of government regulation. Canadians perceived a need for deep government economic penetration because of the scale of building such an immense country and the often equally immense scale of defending it from the energetic, overreaching, overpowering competitive individualism of American life.

In Canada a smaller number of economic buccaneers helped build the land along with the government instead of despite it. This hidden disparity was one very natural thing when Canada was building itself. Many projects needed government help to have any hope of success or, often, to have any hope of even getting started, let alone being successful. Because Canada's market has been so small historically, it has had to turn to trading to survive. But what was previously acceptable, politically and morally, within a backwater country trying to build a nation is fast becoming unacceptable behavior to others in a world of trade reciprocity for a country that has become so well developed, so sophisticated, and so aggressive as to pursue much of its economic future abroad.

It is hard, for example, to argue convincingly that Canada's powerful banking system still requires stiff legislative protection from the government against the wily ways of predatory foreign banks when the Canadian institutions have been able to place easily around $120 billion in investments in other lands where the economic rules for foreigners are far less strict than those at home.

Canada has not been the kind of basically closed market for foreigners that, for example, Japan remains in many ways, economically and racially. But when Canadian goods venture out now to compete with those of many other lands, they go with a vast underpinning of government support and subsidy, much of it hidden but all of it helpful in the increasingly competitive and important international marketplace. And as times become more uncertain economically in an era of declining smokestack industries and rising high technology, Canadians instinctively turn more and more to their governments for solutions. Why not? It has worked well in the past.

This demand for government services is natural but expensive. Canada's deficits can seem small compared to, say, the Americans'. But the resulting myriad of taxes and levies can create over time serious disincentives for future growth, especially among the foreign investors who have been so important as that country's economic turbines. This is typically true in Quebec, where a bloated civil service and social welfare programs, including government-subsidized dental care, has pushed provincial taxes 15 percent above the also high level of Ontario, its economic competitor next door.

And nowhere does government involvement in the economy pose as potentially serious a friction as in Canada's relations with the United States, which accounts for more than two-thirds of Canada's exports and imports. Even for the Americans, Canadian trade has grown in significance to nearly 20 percent of exports and imports.

Once that trade was largely raw resources moving south and finished goods heading north. But with the ongoing changes within Canada's economy and psyche, all eagerly encouraged by virtually all forms of government, the scene is set for significant competitive problems in the future. As Robert B. Reich, the author of *The Next American Frontier*, has pointed out with one telling statistic, "By 1980 more than 70 percent of all the goods produced in the United States were actively competing with foreign-made goods. America has become part of the world market."[6] So, too, has Canada, competing with Americans as both buyer and seller in a frenzied rush to create jobs for the future that can no longer be contained within the geographical bounds of any single country. Trade is so important to Canada that it involves one out of every three jobs. Managing this emerging new relationship would be difficult enough to handle even were these two neighbor countries not dangerously comfortable in their old-fashioned accustomed roles as simple supplier to each. And again the image of the two maturing brothers comes to mind.

Under a variety of government programs, Canadian employers can get much of a new employee's wages back, especially if they are in an area designated for economic development. Research is subsidized. The government also helps with association meetings; the Society of Forensic Toxicologists, the chemical detectives of modern police forces, always holds its conventions in Canada with their colleagues there as hosts because the Canadians get much more government money to fund such activities than the American groups.

The government seeks to develop exports in all ways, including government loans and a little-known government company called the Canadian Commercial Corporation, established in 1946 to act as a reassuring middleman between foreign buyers and Canadian suppliers. The government even handles the export billing through its company, which has over the years facilitated more than $11 billion in sales, including production of the long cargo arm aboard the American space shuttles.

When Massey-Ferguson Ltd., the long-beleaguered tractor maker, fell on hard economic times in the late 1970's, the federal and Ontario governments (along with, ultimately, the British and French governments) stepped in with cash and credit infusions to prop up the company. The plan gave about 65 percent of Massey's equity to governments, making the Toronto-based firm one of the world's first state-controlled multinationals and a continuing challenger to American equipment manufacturers going through their own financial traumas without such aid. Even when the government pulls out of financial backing, as it did when it withdrew its loan guarantees for White Farm Equipment Ltd., the shudders go beyond Canada. White went into receivership owing at least one American supplier more than $30 million.

When the Canadian government decided to keep its infant aerospace industry alive, it spent hundreds of millions of dollars (and, later, $1.4 billion in loan guarantees) to acquire De Havilland Aircraft of Canada Ltd. and Canadair Ltd. and keep them in international competition. The federal and Quebec provincial governments joined to contribute $275 million toward a $514 million Bell Helicopter project to develop and market three models of light twin-engine helicopters near Montreal. The federal government also promised to give $468 million over ten years to

Pratt & Whitney Aircraft of Canada Ltd., an American-owned firm, to make engines for the helicopters. The key attraction for Canada: 2,800 new jobs.

To help hard-hit Sudbury, the second largest city in northern Ontario (population 97,000), the provincial government set up the Ontario Centre for Resource Machinery to back and develop manufacturers of forestry and mining equipment, something the area and its workers are experts in. The organization offers venture capital to companies that want to develop existing or new machinery for international or other national markets. It was yet another sign of Canadians looking, or being forced by economics to look, outward beyond the immediate mine or town or province at hand. And it boded for new competition for the likes of the United States' Caterpillar Tractor Company and others. "I could never understand when I worked in the mining industry," James Wade, the center's president, told the *Globe and Mail*, "why every time I picked up a piece of equipment, it didn't have 'Made in Canada' stamped on it. Maybe we haven't grabbed the opportunities. Maybe we've been shy."

When the depression in world iron ore markets shut down mining operations in northern Quebec, many workers for the Iron Ore Company of Canada got an average $9,000 in severance pay plus a special relocation allowance up to $9,200, three-quarters of it paid by federal and provincial governments. In this case, however, Americans benefited. The company, which had to pay only 25 percent of the relocation expenses, is controlled by the Hanna Mining Company of Cleveland, although the Black brothers of Toronto now own part of Hanna. One recent president of the Iron Ore Company of Canada: Brian Mulroney, a Progressive Conservative, who became Canada's eighteenth prime minister in September 1984.

Under provisions of the National Energy Program, the federal government will cover up to 80 percent of the costs of drilling for oil and gas in "frontier" areas such as the Arctic and off the coasts of Nova Scotia and Newfoundland, if the company meets the criteria for majority Canadian ownership. In 1982 alone the federal government gave oil companies $501 million to drill just in the Beaufort Sea north of the Yukon near Alaska.

Canadian governments even own hundreds of regular companies operating in the marketplace like any other entrepreneur, except that they carry the full weight of the government behind them and they are not answerable to demanding shareholders as other firms are. The federal government didn't know for sure until recently exactly how many companies it did own. But one recent tally by the Treasury Board, the government's financial guide and monitor, put the number at 186 companies fully owned by the federal government, and 72 of these firms own 114 other subsidiaries. They include the post office, but also an arts center, a wheat marketing board, medical research council, Air Canada, and a barge company. It all totals, according to the government, corporations with 263,000 employees and recorded assets of $67 billion.

All the provinces also control their own range of companies, including airlines, research facilities, oil and mining operations, electric power utilities, and even auto insurance. When the city of Chicago bought 580 diesel buses and San Francisco ordered 110 from Winnipeg's Flyer Industries Ltd., it was actually buying them from the Manitoba provincial government, the sole owner of the company, which was founded in 1930. "The Canadian market alone is not large enough to support a company of our size," said Flyer chairman Hugh Jones.

Just Saskatchewan itself owns twenty-one corporations employing 14,000 workers and controlling in excess of $5.8 billion in assets right on down to fur marketing. All levels of the government use the companies to appoint political pals to powerful positions. Supporters of such government companies, called Crown corporations, say they help protect against the problems of competition running amok, a common phrase in Canada that invariably brings knowing nods of agreement.

But there are signs of some change here, too. For one thing the governments seemed to be recognizing that their vast megaprojects—for example, multibillion-dollar trials to melt heavy oil far beneath the ground's surface and pump it up to an energy-thirsty world—were not becoming the major engines of economic stimulation that their country's history had led them to expect. Canada and its vast nation-building projects could remain self-contained Canadian when they were railroads. But today the grand plans had to do more with such things as oil, which had a world price and a world demand, and Canadian companies, tied as they are now to the world beyond the drill site, had other profitable options to choose from. Canada, like it or not, had quietly become part of the world now, part of the interdependent economics that undermine so many old-fashioned political borders. And Canadians began to realize that perhaps the grandiose expectations of another time were rubbing up against the cost realities of the present.

Quebec, for instance, considered selling its 360 provincially owned liquor stores to private interests. "It is not necessary," said Finance Minister Jacques Parizeau, "for governments to be in the retail business." Returning government-owned enterprises to private hands has often been cited, in advance, as an eventual goal, the government claiming it was getting involved just to put the company back on its feet. But a government's actually divesting itself, or even talking about divesting itself of one of its enterprises, could be seen as heresy, De Havilland's continued government ownership being but one example. In fact, unholy storms erupted as late as 1980, when Prime Minister Joe Clark suggested selling off some federally owned operations, a weakening of his public support that helped give that government a very short life-span of just nine months.

Premier Bennett aroused another storm in 1983 by proposing that his province of British Columbia actually reduce the number of government employees, matching the outgo more realistically to the province's income. In British Columbia 15 out of every 1,000 citizens were employed by the government. In Ontario the number was 13.8, the same as Quebec, where public employees were guaranteed their jobs for life. Mr. Bennett's proposals, backed by his legislative majority, brought mass demonstrations and threats of a general strike. "It's a sign," wrote Peter C. Newman, the author and part-time B.C. resident, "of how far we have come in assimilating the ethic that governments must underwrite our basic needs that Bennett's objective of balancing his treasury revenues and expenditures is seen as a radical act."[7]

Another government decision that arrived quietly but grew to seem radical was the imposition by Mr. Trudeau's Liberal government of the metric system on a people who still think fondly of Britain as the motherland, where they even call their money pounds. The metric controversy is an instructive nonmetric measuring stick itself because it shows the power of government and authority in Canada while it also shows how some more democratic rumblings are rising from below to affect official policy.

In 1970, with an official federal government white paper, Canada began the move away from the imperial measurement system of ounces, pounds, inches, feet, miles, and Fahrenheit degrees toward the metric system of grams, kilograms, centimeters, meters, kilometers, and Celsius degrees. The original thinking was to join the global movement to the metric system, which, unlike imperial, is based on easily handled units of ten, in order to guard Canada's vital international trading position.

According to Mr. Trudeau's government, one yard (the distance between Henry I's nose and fingertips) and an inch (the width of three barleycorns laid side by side) must give way to thoroughly modern millimeters. There was no referendum, no parliamentary debate, not even any public debate. It simply became policy, like it or lump it.

More than 100 Industrial Sector Committees were appointed to work out methods and schedules for a phased conversion. No national cost estimates were released. "We knew better than to give the political opposition that kind of ammunition," I was told by a member of the Metric Commission, official metric overseer. The dollar sum, however, certainly ran into the hundreds of millions of dollars, most of it absorbed initially by industry but later by consumers.

In 1975 Canadian weather went metric, but Canadians could still drive to work in miles. In 1977, however, they had to drive kilometers to work. No official deadline was set for complete metrification, but the goal was for Canada to be "predominantly metric" by 1980. The goal was missed by a mile (the distance a Roman legion marched in 1,000 double steps).

There was some antimetric grumbling along the way, and a few antimetric clubs were formed. In 1979 the grumbling grew louder as the country moved toward imposition of metrics on retail sales. Children had grown up in school with metrics, and their parents had developed their own private conversion tables (reversing the figures for 16 degrees Celsius and 28 degrees Celsius, for instance, happens to provide their Fahrenheit equivalents). But few people knew what a kilopascal was (it measures air pressure like pounds per square inch), and others found themselves mistakenly asking for "five kilometers of hamburger." Then, just as gasoline approached the psychological barrier of $1 a gallon, the prices suddenly changed to 25 cents a liter.

The Conservative government of Joe Clark, saying that Canada had gotten too far ahead of its chief trading partner in changing measurements, delayed further metrification a year in 1980, a recognition of its mounting political potency. The issue was apparently so sensitive within the government's vast bureaucracy that at one point Paul Boire, who was assigned to smooth the country's transition to metrics as executive director of the Metric Commission, declined to discuss the matter with me or even to confirm the existence of the white paper written a decade before. He told his secretary to say that he was "unavailable for comment for the foreseeable future," a long time to be indisposed. But measured in pounds per square inch or in kilopascals, the pressure continued to build, especially after a transcontinental Air Canada 767 Jet Liner was forced into an emergency landing in 1983 as the result of a faulty conversion of fuel loads from liters to pounds, instead of liters to kilograms, that left the craft with only half the necessary kerosene to complete its trip.

And open defiance began breaking out, with many people charging that their basic liberties were being violated under the new Charter of Rights and Freedoms that Mr. Trudeau had fought so long to pass. A Montreal carpet store that advertised its wares in yards was charged by the federal government with violating the Weights and Measures Act and fined $1,700. Officials warned grocers they faced possible jail terms for noncompliance. Then Jack Halpert and Raymond Christiansen, the two owners of the Toronto Car Café, began openly selling gasoline in gallons. The federal government charged them, too, with serious violation of the Act. But something unusual happened this time. Ontario Provincial Court Judge William Ross ruled for the defendants, saying the Weights Act was "draconian" and "so devoid of any semblance of decency, fairness and natural justice as to be completely abhorrent to the mind of this court." He also noted that the poorly drafted federal regulations did not specifically prohibit sales in imperial units.

The ruling applied only in Ontario, but it cast a long legal shadow across the country, feeding antimetric and anti-Trudeau sentiments. And the Liberal government, which faced an upcoming uphill election struggle against a revived Progressive Conservative party, decided that 28.349 grams of prevention are worth 0.453 kilogram of cure. Consumer and Corporate Affairs Minister Judy Erola, who herself admits to having difficulty learning the new system, announced indefinite suspension of the metric system imposition until the legal air was cleared. (In the September 4, 1984, election Canadian voters cleared the air themselves in one of the largest landslides in Canadian history, dumping Mrs. Erola and more than one dozen other Liberal Cabinet ministers and installing a new Progressive

Conservative government with a huge majority.) The metric issue, however it is measured, may not be earthshaking. But such successful defiance of authority, matched at other times in large turbulent demonstrations against government economic or defense policies, told veteran Canada observers that something different was happening within that now only sometimes silent land.

Canada is not alone in its concern over the future and the uncertainties of how best (or least worst) to get there. But it is uniquely ill-equipped to make the kinds of national policy decisions that seem necessary to cope with the kind of wrenching changes facing modern industrialized societies trying to cope with reality while easing the pain and social cost of such adjustments. There has been, as we've seen, no enduring national political party to take the lead and to consistently bridge the old gaps, let alone the new ones. And this is unlikely to change in any way other than cosmetically. In part, this will take a very long time because Canada's federal and provincial political parties are really different political parties, though they may carry the same Liberal or Progressive Conservative names. No provincial premier in Canadian history has ever gone on to become prime minister. So there is a provincial political system representing narrow provincial needs and priorities. And there is a federal political system with its different focus. The two levels' leaders meet in occasional summits, and they routinely argue over money—how much is the federals' share of rising health insurance costs, for example. But there is not the constant interplay of local and national ideas and perspectives that there is all along the interconnected political career ladder in the American system, even with all its own faults.

And nothing can ever change the separating geographic realities of the land or of the powerful tugs to the south. Interestingly, everyone but Canadians is forced to admit that Canadians have shown a most impressive ability to succeed when they themselves set aside their limiting regionalisms to move out beyond their confining colossus of a country. They just can't seem to think the same way at home. H. C. Rynard, the president of a Canadian consulting firm that began doing business in the United States, too, noted that Americans do not allow themselves to be held so tightly in the grip of biased regionalism. "Generally," he said with amazement in one interview, "American clients are more interested in competence and price than they are in where you come from."

Nowhere is this regionalism more apparent and more strictly applied by both sides than in Quebec, the beautiful French-speaking province that contains one-quarter of the country's population, one-third of its unemployed, and four-tenths of its bankruptcies. For one thing, the provincial economy is liberally spotted with the "soft" kind of industries, such as textiles, furniture, and shoemaking, that have a lot of workers (and, therefore, a lot of votes to prompt government support) but not a lot of future outside countries like Korea, newly industrialized and still much lower in labor costs. Quebec's asbestos industry confronts a bad health image among consumers, while the Quebec paper industry confronts competition from the southern United States, which once also sought secession. The American South's sun and longer growing season make for better wood-growing economics, as does its proximity to major markets. Many northeastern American companies, traditional Quebec customers, have also decamped for the Sun Belt. Then, too, the Parti Québecois (PQ) provincial government has consistently used its legislative majority to enact North America's highest minimum wage law.

The same government also enacted controversial language laws that sought to free French speakers from the demeaning linguistic discrimination of the minority English speakers, or Anglophones, who dominated decision making there for two centuries. That is one kind of adjustment for a French-speaking cobbler or computer programmer, say, to make. But it is quite another for the headquarters of a major industrial company that is accustomed to running its research, its meetings and memos, and its global empire in English. The linguistic policy decisions, which reached right down to changing "Stop" signs to read "Arrêt," made sense on a PQ priority list. These are the Francophones, who until recent times could be rudely ordered by Anglophones to "Speak white" if they tried to converse in French on a Toronto streetcar. But the Quebec party has not had to try to convince an English-speaking couple in Calgary that the husband's proposed assignment to Montreal is, in fact, a promotion when for several years it meant that their children had to start, cold turkey, in French in a Quebec school (a provision later invalidated by Canada's Supreme Court) and when his salary rises but his take-home pay decreases and when, for the first time in their lives, both husband and wife will have that unsettled, surrounded feeling of being a member of an obvious but silent minority.

Such recruiting problems and fears combined with the general westward drift of population within North America to draw away from Montreal dozens of companies ("Where accounts go," said one company vice-president, "account managers must surely follow") and thousands of workers and citizens. First Diane Giddings left when her husband's employer moved its computer operations to Calgary. Then Jennifer Giddings left for Vancouver to avoid the kinds of language frictions she encountered when she tried to speak English in a Montreal department store. Then Philip Giddings left for Toronto when he lost a promotion to someone whose French was a little better. "You can't blame them," said their mother, Judy Giddings, a French-Canadian and lifelong Montrealer. The trend, as one government report noted, was turning that graceful Old and New World-style city into little more than a big Milwaukee, important only regionally. Statistics abound: Toronto, the city Montrealers love to hate as gauche, now has more than 22 percent of Canada's labor force; Montreal, 11. In building permits, Toronto's run 22 percent of the country's total; Montreal's, 10. In head offices, Toronto has more than 33 percent; Montreal, under 18.

It is the kind of change from national to regional prominence that Boston and St. Louis and other fine cities have had to endure throughout history, which does not show that angry residents left behind then launched costly product boycotts of the departing firms. For some Francophones it has been an exciting, heady era as they move into positions of increased responsibility and opportunity in Montreal's business world, once synonymous with "English elite." But it is also a painful era for the region, which is further complicated by the deep, often irrational but always potent, emotions tied to all language disputes. In a series of violent antiprovincial government demonstrations over recent years, the people in several rural Quebec towns—Amqui, Matane, Grande Vallée—erupted into flag burnings and road blockades, symbols of frustration for people who wanted back the old ways, when there was work and their children, no longer children really, didn't have to leave their hometowns to find work.

The imminence of such change strikes many Canadians within and without Quebec as a sad realization. "None of us now thinks our kids will easily find jobs in the industry," said Nick Bos, a vice-president of the International Woodworkers of America in British Columbia. But though painful, such change may hold great promise for the country. For Canada seems to be undergoing a fundamental change, a little-noticed broad-scale mixing of the population, where some regions are up and some are down for now, where people come and go and marry while they're there and have children there and here and parents back there and friends from several moves over there and vacation travels there and there and over there. When I traveled to Manitoba once, I looked up some cousins. They were delightful people, hardworking, good company, hospitable, and full of interesting tales about all their long family camper trips—*across the United States.* They told me all about California, both north and south, Washington State, Arizona, Las Vegas. And then, they said, someday they hoped to get to southern Ontario, the bottom of the province next door. Well, they got there sooner than they anticipated. That fall the family was transferred to Ottawa for two years, and they have moved elsewhere again since.

But this is becoming a natural phenomenon. Another relative in Toronto once bemoaned my many moves. He is now divorced and gone to another region to find work. The *Globe and Mail* of Toronto had a big party back in 1980 to celebrate opening its first news bureau in Alberta, where an American publication, *Time* magazine, based reporters years ago. Now that paper, Canada's best, is available via satellite transmission and satellite printing plants all across the country on the same day of publication in a professionally packaged product that is another new example of surmounting the old regional mentality.

Many nationalities take for granted a somewhat detailed acquaintance-ship with their country's regions from a collection of family vacations, visits to relatives, or senior class types of trips. This is relatively new in Canada. Even my son's French class in Toronto planned a trip to Quebec City to practice the country's second language. This kind of thing is dangerous to a stubbornly fragmented country. It could promote understanding and provide the kind of glue and cultural and geographical bridges that the country historically has lacked.

How can you seriously make fun of Saskatchewan hicks if your brother lives there? Worse yet, how can you ignore that place when you get letters and phone calls from there every couple of weeks now and you're visiting there come Christmas? The brother wouldn't have lived there years ago. The largest city, Regina, has only 160,000 residents. I have family photos of the second-largest city, Saskatoon (with 155,000 people), taken when my grandparents were married there, and you can still see log cabins and dirt streets.

But now that the Canadian economy is maturing, the brother's Toronto employer has opened a Saskatchewan office or two. And the brother is on a management training course that will see him assigned to many other regional operations, including, no doubt, some in the States. One federal minister of employment and immigration has said that Canada faces a period of internal migration as people move in search of jobs. "A major part of our economic problem," the then minister Lloyd Axworthy said, "is that we have the wrong people in the wrong places doing the wrong jobs, and we need to get things in synchronization."

In the old simple resource days a Newfoundland fisherman could not survive in Ontario. A British Columbia logger would have had very little to do in Prince Edward Island. Canadians' jobs defined their living location, and their geography defined their jobs. But this is an age of technology now, and the career horizons of that B.C. woodworker's child need not be defined or confined by his father's. Computer technicians are needed everywhere.

Canada's modern job skills are far more portable than its old ones. And the government is changing the focus of its job-creating efforts. "Canadians have looked to the huge megaprojects to help them," Mr. Axworthy noted in an interview, "but now we see that these approaches have failed, and what we want is to encourage the formation of hundreds of smaller, locally based activities."

Federal officials have also suggested that jobs can no longer be defined by the traditional forty-hour workweek, that a new approach, involving more flexible and more rapidly adjustable job training as well as more job sharing, is necessary. The latter is designed to help spread the benefits of employment among the million-plus unemployed now, the 1.3 million new workers expected in the next five years, and the 1.7 million new jobs now estimated to be created in that same period.

Fear for future work, of course, is not a problem confined to Canada. The adjacent American Midwest, too, is undergoing the same convulsions in cities built around smokestacks. "The Canada we grew up in—the land of unending promise, a place where betterment of the human condition was certain—is no more," said Tom d'Aquino, president of the Business

Council on National Issues. "No longer can we count on our vast material resources to give us a privileged position among economic powers. We have built one of the most advanced and comprehensive social systems in the world, yet we can no longer afford it."

These new realities have prompted serious thinking among some Canadians, few of them politicians. It is a feeling that change need not always be a depressing threat to moan over, although it will be if its opportunities are not seized and shaped. There is the same old tired talk about developing an "industrial strategy" that will point the way everyone ought to go to assure a prosperous future,[8] as if a government commission could aim 25 million people. Strategy talk is great for speeches on the political stump to commerce associations and the like. But this approach has not worked too well in polyglot democracies where everyone is free to feel he has his own plan for success and can, freely, ignore others. The Canadian government took ten years from the report of one industrial strategy commission to talking about drafting some of its ideas into legislation.

This debate or, rather, discussion on the future has just begun in Canada. Much of it still focuses on trying to blame other peoples or governments for Canada's troubles. But, warned Donald Daly, a York University economics professor, "We can no longer pretend that the difficulties we have are occurring because of problems in the rest of the world." Too many Canadians have taken charge in too many ways in too many places for that to wash.

The discussion is broad and unfocused as yet, requiring, as one official put it, "some hand holding." It is at times narrow and self-serving to a particular area or industry. It often sounds like grumbling as some seek to find scapegoats from yesterday for the uncertainties of today. "Many Canadians," David Slater, chairman of the Economic Council of Canada, wrote in a recent Council annual report, "have forgotten the dimensions of Canada's true economic potential and are willing to settle for second- or third-rate solutions." Calls for idealism and excellence, like those for militant flag-waving patriotism, make Canadians squirm.

However, much of the discussion and the action so far have centered on two broad areas: the use of imagination and research and development (R&D), and changing the country's ties with the United States. To boost R&D, the vital spark for future jobs and investments in new products, the federal government has given generous tax breaks to companies ranging from 100 to 150 percent of the actual research spending. It has helped spawn a kind of high-technology Silicon Valley North with a number of rapidly growing companies like Mitel established near Ottawa. The reason is that there simply is a lot of money to be made, and now some Canadians are no longer waiting to ride the safer second wave. They are in the forefront. "North America is a single market," said Mark Stirling, an industry analyst. "For Canadian firms the key to success is to pick a specialty and be very good at it." Added John Roberts, one firm's marketing director, "High-tech is potentially bigger than crude oil. By 1995 worldwide markets are expected to exceed $95 billion a year."

Northern Telecom, for one, has poured more than $1 billion into R&D in recent years, which has built the firm into one with 34,500 employees in fifty plants around the world. With Bell Canada, Northern's major stockholder, it has even opened its own large research laboratory, Bell-Northern Research, and has forged a unified telecommunications company with a major push into sophisticated integrated office systems just as its main North American competitor, AT&T, with its own research lab, was broken up under government and federal court order.

But new R&D investment and new imaginations are also being applied in other areas, too. Three mining companies—Inco, Falconbridge, and Kidd Creek Mines Ltd.—have formed an equally owned company to undertake joint research programs that would benefit all three competitors and boost efficiency for stiff international competition, a mutually beneficial step that might not be approved by other governments more interested in potential antitrust problems. Canadian oil companies are taking their frontier expertise overseas to get their feet in the door of many lands. Around the world such names as Ranger Oil, Asamera, Inverness Petroleum, Bow Valley Industries, Sulpetro, Sceptre Resources, United Canso Oil & Gas, and PanCanadian Petroleum are appearing as minority partners in vast exploration projects that can offer potential bonanzas for relatively small risks. There, Canadian expertise carries inordinate weight for the dollars invested. These Canadian companies can operate free of the idealistic political weights attached by other countries' governments. As outlined to *Maclean's* magazine by a senior prime ministerial aide on one of his trips through Asia, Canada is not going to "increase unemployment in Sudbury to free a nun in the Philippines." With the emphasis on trade and not on global police actions, the aide added, "Quite a long time ago we decided that if we started applying the individual criteria of Canadian good behavior to all our trading partners, we're not going to be trading with anyone."[9]

In finance and business there are new developments, too. Canada's powerful insurance industry, in cooperation with the Ontario provincial government, is designing establishment of a billion-dollar insurance exchange in Toronto. This exchange, in effect a market for insurance companies to become insured to spread the risk of large projects, would attract considerable foreign money as well as help stem the flow of hundreds of millions of dollars out of Canada to offshore reinsurance markets such as Lloyd's of London and the New York Insurance Exchange.

The Toronto Dominion Bank took the lead in Canada in introducing a cut-rate stock brokerage service for its customers. This step blurred the traditional distinction between banks and brokers and threatens to add even more financial clout to the already powerful banking system. The Toronto Dominion's assets alone are many times larger than those of all Canada's brokers. With this service the TD offers its customers anywhere in Canada the ability to buy and sell stocks through discount brokerage houses that offer rates as much as 85 percent less than those of their full-service competition.

In an attempt to offer a new full range of financial services, Brascan, among others, has invented a new kind of company to center its variety of financial expertise intensely on customers. Called the Trilon Financial Corporation, it became in just ten months the country's sixth-largest financial institution. Into this new concept, Brascan transferred its holdings in London Life, Canada's fourth-largest insurance company, and Royal Trustco, Canada's largest trust company. To sell its financial services, the new parent company will be able to draw on the records and established business connections of its subsidiaries with their thousands of salesmen and corporate clients as well as its hundreds of thousands of individual customers. "I visualize the day," Allen Lambert, Trilon's chairman and former chairman of the Toronto Dominion Bank, told the inquiring Peter Newman one day in 1983, "when a family's entire financial services will be handled by one company. Theoretically, Canada is small enough that we should be able to have all the family units on our computers so that we know precisely how old everybody is—when each son and daughter gets out of university and is old enough to buy his or her first insurance policy, for example."

The second major area of serious, though as yet ill-defined, discussion among Canadians is the need for substantial changes in their economic relationship with the United States. Canadians being Canadians, they will not soon agree among themselves on any specific plans. But they must— and soon—since any set of proposals from the United States is doomed to defeat by a Canadian people whose instinctive defensive stance has often seemed justified. As Dean Rusk, the former U.S. secretary of state, said to his Canadian counterpart, Paul Martin, at one public appearance, "You speak first, my friend, because if you speak first, I might be able to agree with you. But if I speak first, you would be compelled to disagree."

The Americans, for now, need only to accept their close economic ties with Canada and to work harder and more attentively at nurturing them (I say, "need only," though that is a formidable enough task for the Yanks, given their habits and traditional priorities elsewhere). But the Canadians must face up to their economic reality and to their new hard-earned stature. They have tried in recent times to dodge the issue ("Poor old Canada, at once so big and yet so small," what Peter Newman once called "the Gulliver of the North with no visible means of enforcing its will"). They have sought a Third Option, close ties with the Common Market and Asia. That was politically palatable (and profitable) but a complete flop in terms of altering Canada's basic ties. Nothing can change them, not even the New Democrats.

This immediate mental readjustment toward equanimous equality on both sides, I believe, is absolutely imperative, and quickly. As the University of Toronto's Professor Stephen Clarkson described the countries' national interests to a Chicago audience in 1983, "I think they are diverging. I don't think it is any longer true that what is good for the United States is automatically good for Canada. What is good for Canada isn't necessarily good for the U.S." He focused on the Canadian side, its attempts to right the nationalistic economic balance within and the Americans' indignant reactions. And he warned his American audience, "More radical politicians will get responses to their voices. It is worth asking whether you would prefer to have a Papandreou or an Olof Palme to a Trudeau or a Clark running your northern ally's political system. Would you prefer to have Canada run on the principles of a capitalist mixed economy or that of a socialist system? . . . I am asking, in short, whether the United States can be broad-minded enough to let its weaker neighbor be different and seek its own solutions to its own problems. I am not asking whether the United States can give Canada charity. None is wanted; none has ever been given. . . . But if a $20 million problem is given a $10 billion response, then the issue between us will become one of nationalism after all."

It simply requires both sides to recognize that trade has been the fastest-growing element of the world's economy in recent years and that no two lands anywhere trade any more than Canada and the United States. A little self-interest, not altruism, could rule handsomely here. Although governments cannot control this immense relationship, they can color its environment—darkly bitter and suspicious ("There they go again") or warm and glowing ("Our two countries . . . great neighbors . . . peaceful border"). It has always amazed me how the American memory can reach so far back to Revolutionary War days ("Thank you, Lafayette") when it deals with the cantankerous French, but when it comes to Canada, the memory stalls at a week ago last Wednesday. Likewise, Canadians prefer to overlook the economic affluence they have gained and the largely free military defense they enjoy next door to the Soviet Union ("Well, who'd want this place anyway?"). The problem as well as the solution is tied tightly to proximity. It is what the late prime minister and Nobel Prize winner Lester Pearson once called Canada's "national schizophrenia," its deep desire for material well-being, guaranteed, and its own political and cultural independence, two perfectly natural desires that do not easily fit the economic realities of Canada's physical and political location.

Both the American and Canadian sides have shown glimmers of recognition recently. The Americans have stayed so wisely mum about the potential for Quebec separatism that neither side there can find any Yank-beating ammunition. The Americans have elevated Canadian affairs within the State Department's hierarchy. And Jean Chrétien, then energy minister, told a New York audience, "We have not forgotten that a great deal of our petroleum industry exists because of the investment, know-how and frontier spirit of American entrepreneurs." Now if he'd just say that at home, too.

But at times this inexorable independence, which Canadians are painstakingly assembling day by day, may not seem to matter quite so much once it has been achieved, especially when it seems to threaten an intimate trading relationship with a next-door country that regularly buys around $7 billion more from Canada than it sells there. So what Americans and Canadians are likely to see in coming years are periods of flourishing Canadian economic activities, at home and abroad, alternating with other periods of seeming lesser activity. These will be times (also tied to economic conditions, interest rates, and the quality of political leaders onstage) when Canadians are aggressively seeking to seize control of more resources and facilities at home and in other lands, followed by times when they pause, apparently wondering if this is really the right thing to do or the right way to go about it or what awful thing will happen if they keep it up. It is a classic Canadian lurch rather than a continuous surge, a halting advance tempered by an inborn deep, though diluting, uncertainty and the need to balance and rebalance all the many contending and muttering forces at home. It is rather like all those exhausting obstacle courses that military trainers seem to favor. Sure, they build physical strength, but of equal importance is that the activity spawns self-confidence; after each stage, participants can stop and look at themselves ("My God, I did it").

For their own good, Americans can aid and abet this inevitable growth with large doses of understanding and patience, not patronizing permissiveness but a confidence, like that of the elder brother, that with the underlying blood ties, Canadians will make the right democratic decisions for themselves. And in the long run that will prove far more advantageous for the United States than any immediate victories that short-term and shortsighted interference might gain.

Overall, Canadians are likely to look first, not necessarily last anymore, to the safest road through this unexplored territory of economic maturity. Canada, the smallest of all the major industrialized nations, has been forced to stake its economic future on trade. "Sales abroad mean jobs at home," declares one advertisement for Alcan, which sells 70 percent of its Canadian production outside Canada. Although the importance of trade is increasing in the United States, trade still plays a far greater role in the Canadian mind. This makes Canada and Canadians unusually sensitive to talk of protectionism, which may at times make eminent political sense domestically in the United States and which is usually aimed at other alleged trade offenders. But it creates in the minds of Canadians yet another dramatic example of how Canadians are often adversely affected by American policies that overlook or ignore the trader closest to home. It no longer matters that this is benign ignorance. Americans might do well to realize that proximity aside, the most natural trading partner for Canada—that is, the country that has the greatest shortage of energy, food, and resources with the greatest abundance of quality goods to trade for them—is not the United States. It is Japan, which has now passed Great Britain as Canada's second-largest trading partner. Others have not missed the emerging country atop North America.

Canadians, for their part, would do well to remember, thoughtfully not instinctively, how vital their relationship with the United States is on all levels and to work actively at molding it instead of simply reacting when a grievance seems to erupt. Unbeknownst to many Canadians, their relationship with the United States has an important impact on their relationships with many other countries. This is because for many foreign buyers and investors, Canada is seen through an American prism—the international business grapevine, the news agencies, the newspapers and television coverage that is often based, mentally and physically, in the United States and has covered Canada at times only coincidentally. The maple leaf on the postage stamp or the hiking backpack is just not sufficient to dispel the Canadian-American similarity that so many elsewhere perceive. Thus, their image of Canada is the same as their image of the Canada-U.S. economic relationship. And if Americans are sour on Canada for the moment, for whatever reason, then others tend to become sour, too.

In addition, both countries would do well to face a hard fact: With the import of trade rising in most domestic economies, magnifying the already intimate relationship of Canada and the United States, scarcely anything is purely domestic anymore. Virtually everything has an impact somehow on the other country, whether it is a winter frost in Florida that hikes the price of Canadian salads or a government drilling policy that boosts the costs of Canadian natural gas piped in to heat midwestern American homes.

There has been much informed talk within Canada over new directions in economic policy. There is support, for instance, for formation of national trading corporations, a government version of the private trading conglomerates that dominate Japanese buying and selling abroad. To eliminate what is viewed as costly competition among several Canadian firms, some Canadian government officials favor forming officially endorsed export consortia to win major projects abroad.

But the dominant current theme, consciously for the Canadians and unconsciously for most Americans, is to forge even closer economic links. Thanks to the Canadian-United States Defense Production Sharing Arrangement of 1946, the formal border between the two countries has been virtually eliminated in terms of military products. Thanks to the Canadian-United States Automotive Trade Agreement twenty years later, the formal border between the two countries has been virtually eliminated in terms of automotive products. That may not have been the pact's initial goal; originally the idea was to overcome the deficit in the Canadians' massive automotive trade with the United States. But when everything from salaries and fringe benefits down to the length and shape of the smallest dashboard screw must match each other in both lands, then the lasting result is a tighter integration.

Without much detailed planning, for instance, the Yukon territorial and Alaskan state governments have gone together to advertise their distant tourism attractions jointly in both countries. But more significantly, after the Canadians had issued a major policy paper tying their economic future to trade, both governments began quietly exploring different lists of new areas to construct sectoral free trade, a continuation of the old step-by-step integration. Separate agreements might be crafted in any number of fields, including petrochemicals, specialty steels, textiles, surface transportation, furniture, forest products, heavy electrical or telecommunications equipment, and chemicals. For the Canadians alone this could mean important increases in sales to Americans that already stand around $60 billion each year.

The long-term results may be the same as the kind of grand-scale union occasionally proposed by Americans, most recently in 1980 by Ronald Reagan, then a presidential candidate. But such goliath proposals are inevitably received by stiff opposition within Canada now. They smack too much of being swallowed; Canadians today seek a series of separate agreements on an equal footing.

But no one is yet seriously studying one area of potentially great economic—and emotional—concern. That is water, the ultimate natural resource. People may be able to mine iron ore elsewhere, to develop an environmentally acceptable alternative to asbestos, to grow trees for wood and paper in another climate, or to buy oil from secondary sellers. But everybody and everything need water. And nobody can yet manufacture that pure, fresh substance that is so much a part of both countries' lives and of Canada's psyche. I have often thought that if Canadians could ever agree on a national crest of some kind, it would certainly have to include fresh water somehow, tumbling over rocks, roaring through power turbines, sitting sedately in pocket-size ponds or vast inland lakes stretching to the horizon.

In fact, the word that Canadians most often use to refer to electricity, "hydro," has to do with water because so much of their electrical power is generated by falling water. Every weekend every summer affluent Canadians migrate by the thousands to "the lake," as if there were only one in the whole country, or to "the cottage," the unspoken assumption being that it is on or near fresh water of some kind. The water can vary from the murky shallows of Manitoba's Dauphin Lake, where my father spent many summer swim days kicking his feet free of grasping grasses growing in the mud, to the shiny pristine coves of Georgian Bay way north of Toronto.

There thousands of Canadians, including Ontario's premier and a declining number of wealthy Americans, own summer homes lining the shore or perched atop the merest outcropping of primeval rock. (The wife of Premier Davis, for so long the most powerful politician in Canada's most powerful province, has posted a sign for her husband by the bathroom door: "Please don't walk on the water.") Surrounded by crystal-clear water, these houses that march to the horizon in leisurely disarray are marked by a handful of struggling trees and a bevy of stiff flagpoles, their colored hangings flapping in the steady, chill winds out of the northwest. These restful locales, where Canadians can escape the pressures of their pleasant lives in their tidy cities, are linked to the nearby shore by battalions of pleasure boats and a goodly fleet of seaplanes. A number of inland lakes are even linked to each other by canals and locks.

This is called Cottage Country, an ill-defined area that appears on no Canadian maps and implies rural villages inundated on warm weekends by large numbers of station wagons, boat trailers, and little children in bare feet and drooping swimsuit bottoms. Thanks to favorable tax rules on second homes, their local geography and affluence, Cottage or Cabin Country for all kinds of Canadians is not so much a place as a way of life. Workers talk about it all week long over lunch with colleagues. It comes up at cocktail parties. The Friday afternoon helicopter pilot on the radio, hovering over the rush-hour jam on expressways, is guiding drivers not to their homes but to Cottage Country somewhere to the north.

There is no precise count on the number of Canadians with cottages, on the number of cottages, or even on the number of lakes that attract Canadians so. One survey involving just Toronto found nearly a half million vehicles heading north on an average summer Friday afternoon and another 50,000 going early Saturday morning. Figuring roughly two persons per car, a conservative estimate, that means that fully one-third of Canada's largest city moved north to its Cottage Country and the lakes each weekend, not counting those who traveled east or west before turning north.

There is no real definition of what a cottage is in Canada—an unheated hut in the woods inhabited by humans only on summer weekends; a converted chicken coop on a farm pond rented by some office group; a luxurious cabin or a man-made lakeside condominium with weeklong time slots "owned" by different families. In some areas, especially in the Arctic on federal land, there are even waterfront cabins owned by no one but used by anyone with enough money to charter a floatplane for an hour.

Canadians like Pat and Robert Varty and their cottage on the water play an important economic role in these areas. It is a 120-mile, 150-minute drive from their Toronto home to "their" lake, if they avoid the rush hour to leisure land. Like many cottage owners, or cottagers, including retired couples, the Vartys now use their cottage year-round, putting an increasing burden on the fragile tax and ecological bases of the rural areas.

Dozens of times every year Mrs. Varty, a fifty-year-old substitute teacher, makes the migration from the city, where she has studied plumbing and carpentry at night, to fix up "the cottage." Five years ago she went shopping for this hobby with a real estate agent. She saw many different pieces of wilderness and crumbling cabins before settling on a twenty-five-acre tree-covered lot with a leaking three-bedroom cabin that was home to a number of mice, chipmunks, and bats. The owner sought $23,500.

They agreed on $16,000, some $12,000 of it easily borrowed from the bank back in the city. The Vartys put over $7,000 more, including $4,500 for a well, into the property.

The first task was to build an outhouse, using a Styrofoam life preserver as the seat because it gets warm quickly in winter. Countless hours have been invested in laying new shingles, putting in living-room ceiling beams, filling dozens of mouse holes, cutting out picture windows, making screens, nailing up paneling, and building a wraparound bench for the kitchen table. A skylight went in, along with a floating dock and, of course, a large stack of firewood.

The Vartys' dirt road is closed in winter, so family members ski in the three miles and find their cottage sitting silently in the drifting snow by the frozen lake, where they skate and fish. "We get a fire going and bake in the old stove and walk in the woods," said Mrs. Varty. In the summer there are fishing and hiking and swimming and campfires and picnics down by the water. "My favorite time," said Mrs. Varty, "is early morning. You paddle the canoe slowly across the water without a sound. Up ahead there's a little ripple from a beaver chugging along. You only get so close and then, wham, he slaps his tail and is gone."

The Vartys are not at all unusual Canadians. Their attachment to water is felt as a part of the Canadian character, something to be treasured and protected, something else to feel threatened over. So their strong emotional reaction to the subject of acid rain or the subject of selling water should come as no surprise. Acid rain is the problem of airborne pollutants from both lands being washed out by rains and snows and precipitation to fall onto the soil and into streams and rivers, there to fester chemically through the various life systems. The American government has dragged its feet on studying the problem and, thus, has inadvertently come to shoulder in the Canadian public's mind much of the blame for its impact. Official American government encouragement to utilities to switch from expensive oil-fueled to coal-fired generators has raised the specter of increasing air pollution and provided one more case of how perfectly justified economic decisions on one side of the border inevitably have an impact on the other side somehow. It might be called the Sideswipe Effect.

All this sets the scene for some serious future water problems. Canadians and Americans have always been dimly aware of water as a common bond between them. The waterways formed the highways for much of the continent's initial exploration by canoe and barge. They formed the battleground for Canadians and Americans to kill each other during first the Revolution and later the War of 1812. More than a century ago Walt Whitman wrote, "The Saint Lawrence and lakes are not a frontier line, but a grand interior or mid-channel." In the early 1900's there was a serious international dispute when Chicago decided to reverse the flow of a river to carry its sewage inland toward the Mississippi and away from the city's supply of drinking water in Lake Michigan. Canadians felt this threatened the level of the common resource of the Great Lakes, the world's largest collection of fresh water.

In addition, Canadians, who make up 1/172,000,000ths of the world's population, have somewhere around one-quarter to one-third of the world's fresh water within their boundaries, with much more flowing unseen and uncalculated through subterranean caverns far below. But fully 60 percent of the flow of Canada's rivers drains northward, where fewer than 10 percent of the people are, eventually flowing "uselessly" into saltwater oceans. There is lots of water; it's just in the wrong place most of the time (or perhaps the people are in the wrong place).

In contrast, there is next door the United States, a wanton water user with supplies that are fast slimming in many regions. Houston is sinking as its groundwater reservoirs are drained upward. Huge sinkholes have opened in Florida. New York City must regularly urge water rationing. California and the Southwest compete for limited supplies, a competition that has seen the once mighty Colorado River reduced to a salty trickle by the time it reaches its would-be Mexican users. "We live in an oasis civilization," said Colorado Governor Richard Lamm, "in which one out of five people gets water from more than 100 miles away."

Already separate states are scrapping over mammoth water diversion schemes, involving movements of vast quantities of water from the Great Lakes to dry areas elsewhere. The Great Lakes states, which see their water reserves as a means to counter the flow of economic opportunity to the burgeoning Sun Belt states, may or may not have control over the resource that washes the shores of so many states at once. But they have promised not to divert any lake water without the agreement of their Canadian counterpart, Ontario. And there are other older agreements between the two countries governing the use of common water bodies for wildernesses, for navigation, or for electric-power generating.

One exporter has been licensed to ship bottled British Columbia water to Asia and California. And there has been another proposal to ship 300,000 gallons a day in supertankers from western Canada to the parched Middle East. Water, as one scientist put it, tends to flow toward money. But two other particularly grand multibillion-dollar water schemes have also emerged. One, proposed by Ralph Parsons, the late California construction company chief, involved pulling to the south the powerful waters of two Alaskan rivers, the Yukon and the Tanana, to flow through Canada and form a 500-mile-long reservoir in the Rocky Mountain Trench. From there western states and provinces could draw on the immense supply.

The other "megafix," proposed by Thomas Kierans, a Canadian engineering consultant, involves constructing a ninety-mile-long dike across the mouth of James Bay above Ontario and Quebec. This would halt the drainage of all of James Bay's freshwater rivers into the larger Hudson Bay and eventually the surrounding salty oceans. And it would create a vast reservoir of fresh water to be steered southward into the Great Lakes for use there or transshipment elsewhere to the prairies or even Mexico.

Very little has been studied yet on the impact of such projects. There is, for one thing, the environmental aspect, the long-range effects on the world's climate, for instance, from the diversion of such huge quantities of warmer, tempering waters from their current Arctic destinations. And there is, too, as usual, the lack of political preparation on such a vital issue between the two countries, which are, it sometimes seems, drawing closer to each other despite themselves. Both sides are ready to fall, instinctively, into their accustomed roles; the United States feeling it has a right to such an important resource because it needs it, its politicians of the moment basically unaware of the new political and economic currents flowing to the north, mumbling—off the record, of course—about not wanting to have to get tough and, by the way, look at all the things America does for Canada; Canada feeling ever more possessive about its resources and rights, sitting up straight and proud, its righteous politicians of the day playing to and on the old Canadian fears about their poor little land in the dangerous shadows of this big bully next door.

It would all seem so preposterously petty and most of all tiresomely ignorant if the consequences for the future of both lands and their peoples were not so dire and not so unnecessary.

"We can't move Canada out of North America, and the Americans cannot move us out either. So we have to agree to live here together."

—Gerard Pelletier, Canadian diplomat and Cabinet minister

FIVE

❧❧❧

My Canada

❧❧❧

To me, Canada has always been a very special place. As an only child growing up in the forties and fifties in both the United States and Canada, I linked that northern land with warm, very personal symbols. They were, like the country, simple and basic, yet like familiar objects in a home, quietly important. People need stability and some sameness, to come home to a familiar place with familiar objects in familiar places, right where you remember leaving them. It is comforting. To return every day to a rearranged living room would be disconcerting, disorienting. The positive description is dynamic; the negative is restless. It seemed to me as a child that things were always changing in the United States at a speed that has increased over the years. It was exciting and stimulating, at times also destructive. So what became familiar and comforting about my United States life was that change wasn't change anymore; it was normal. My parents would take me to a dentist, and on the next visit a new building occupied the downtown parking lot. A two-lane road suddenly became three or four or more. Family friends were in one house for one birthday party and in another neighborhood for the next. After Eisenhower, Americans changed Presidents more often. These days they even change mates more.

But in the Canada of my youth things didn't change. Period. Or if they did, it was imperceptible. Nobody honked or yelled there. Canadians, it seemed, were always waiting for the bus, it'll be along; Americans always looked for it, where the hell is it? Canada was the only place I saw relatives beyond my parents and sensed somehow that warm "included" feeling of acceptance that comes in larger family groupings, even if those adults did talk with a little inflection instantly foreign to an Ohio ear. Canada meant crawling up in the lap of a bosomy grandmother in a wicker rocker that creaked beautifully on a screened front porch during those warm summer evenings when even the crickets clicked slowly.

Canada was swarthy Indians living just down the dusty, curbless road, chickens clucking by an asparagus field, pictures of funny little crowns on mailboxes, stamps and road signs and dollar bills carrying a woman's image. It was different brands of candy bars and soda pop, nickels with flat sides, and butterscotch ice cream from Weaver's General Store. Canada had doorbells you twisted instead of pushed and elderly men who wore gloves to drive automobiles, who carried linen handkerchiefs, and who dressed up for Sunday dinner and lit large cigars afterward on the veranda, where they didn't watch television; they talked with each other. People didn't seem to kiss so much in Canada, not when they met, not when they parted, and not in my presence even when they knew each other quite well.

Canada was also a place that grew relatives, lots of them. They were old and strong, like hard oaks. The men worked hard all week and Saturday, and then on Sunday they sat around and rested. The women, on the other hand, worked hard all week and Saturday, and then on Sunday they worked hard, too. They seemed drawn to silver-colored pressure cookers (I figured it was because the color matched their hair). And they stood around kitchen tables to talk and peel the most immense piles of fresh vegetables that left a little film of sandy dust on the enameled metal. The men drank beer; the women drank tea or water, maybe sherry if it was a special occasion. The women were more attentive to a little redheaded boy's comments. It was an automatic acceptance. But when the men talked to a little boy, it was a bigger deal, more of a recognition granted. The women were the teachers, frequently correcting my speech or syntax, especially Grandma Malcolm, a retired schoolteacher who had taken my father out of high school to tutor him two years in one for college. In Canada I could pronounce the letter Z the Canadian way or the American way. In school in the States to say "zed" was to draw puzzled looks or chuckles. It was an early substantive lesson that the two peoples were different and that Americans didn't know it. Canadians seemed more receptive to different.

In Canada people sat on big chairs and couches without once knocking off those funny little doilies perched on the arm. They were there for no reason I could tell except to be knocked off and to get a little boy in Dutch. Canada had grandfathers with exciting adventure stories of their youth in the oil fields or on the western frontier, where they had hunted wild animals (I didn't know then they had killed them, too). They had herded cattle through blizzards that forced people—Grandpa, that tall man right there—to seek shelter under cattle for a couple of days. Canada had streetcars and huge steam engine trains that chanted in puffs and railroad crossing guards who let little boys pump the gates down by hand and adorn them with oil lanterns at the end of long summer evenings. Canada had a newfangled electric toaster that didn't pop the bread slice up; it cooked one side at a time and you could open a little door and flip the piece yourself to cook on the other side. Canada had telephones with handles and cranks, and every caller was named "Hello, Central." Canada seemed older somehow, or newer maybe, I didn't know which way things naturally progressed. Did diesel engines come first and then steam, or the other way around? All I knew was that Canada was a part of me. And it was different. Very familiar, very friendly, and very nice, but different.

A generation later I returned to live in Canada, full of my American friends' envy and my own eager anticipation of adventure to discover the rest of this land from my past. I was looking for something in every corner, some things about Canada, about my past, about me. I found Canada very different, but very familiar, very friendly, and very nice. Canada was thoroughly modern, of course, and a pioneer in health care and sensible urban planning. The Queen's picture was still on the stamps and the money, but the railroad crossing gate had an automatic clanger now. The trains were double-decker commuting caravans in shiny silver with no wooden-framed windows that slid up to let in the air and smell of smoke and with that thundering clickety-clack that implied such weight and strength and power. Mr. Weaver's store belonged to a merchandising chain now. The asparagus patch was a mall parking lot, and the nickel's edges were rounded. But stuffy old Toronto, where my grandmother and I went to eat honeydew melon at Eaton's and watch Jerry Lewis movies, had turned left somewhere on the way to obscurity to discover diversity. The city had kept its streetcars—how sensibly Canadian! And somehow it had navigated the threatening narrows of development to build a bright, exciting, engaging collection of new and old, familiar and foreign. It was safe and clean and far less smug than it had been. To many Americans, Toronto had become what every American city wanted to be. "America borders on the magnificent," said the Canadian ads. And they seemed right.

Elsewhere, I discovered over the years, Canadians were still struggling peacefully with their linguistic differences, erecting essentially new cities in Calgary and Edmonton, building new economic empires to harness vast resources, pioneering new technologies in the frigid Arctic, and launching an aggressive economic invasion of the United States. In childhood I would tell my American friends about Canadian things, and they had never heard of them. Now they've heard of them, but they don't know they are Canadian.

After living in New York City and urban Asia, I thought Canadians had the cleanest air in the world, the most abundant pure fresh water, the largest woods, the cleanest, safest, most attractive cities, the cheapest gasoline, the most reliable, convenient city services, the most imaginative museum and park systems, the greatest array of towering mountains, the most exciting, untamed frontier in their Far North, and the most varied selection of outdoor activities within a very few miles of the cities.

Canadians reading those lines will feel a sharp sense of unease and start to think of all the "buts" to qualify the praise. It is instinctive. The only way to get a Canadian to praise his or her country is to announce you are American and then to criticize Canada unmercifully. Inevitably the first remark of new friends in Canada was: "Whatever did you say when your boss said you had to go to Canada?" It was an inkling of a major theme I was to encounter time after time after time in my long travels throughout the country. At times I found myself, an American, according to my passport, trying to convince Canadians they have a great country. They listened quietly at times and then put it down to a guest's natural politeness. It puzzled me for a long while. Canadians, it seemed, did not think much of their country, of each other, of their future together, or, thus, of themselves. Americans didn't know much about this newer country, but what they did know, they thought more of than Canadians themselves.

Nobody in Canada bragged about Canada. That is well and good, I suppose. One Texas in North America is sufficient. But it seemed that few in Canada publicly and openly appreciated Canada either, not until someone attacked or mocked it. Praising the country was rarely done. Canadians always seemed to be apologizing for something. It was so ingrained. And looking around at that special place, I couldn't figure out what there was to apologize for. When I subscribed to *Maclean's* magazine there, I got a standard "Dear Subscriber" letter from some executive. "I'm delighted you will read Maclean's in months to come," he said, "and think it's a wise move on your part! Do I sound brash? Forgive me, but it is really a good idea for Canadians . . ." etc. Brash? Forgive me? What the hell for?

I asked Peter C. Newman, then *Maclean's* editor, about that one day. He told me of a contest the magazine ran once. It challenged readers to complete the phrase "As Canadian as . . ." The winner was: "As Canadian as possible under the circumstances." Canadians have been so conditioned by their geography, their history, their teachers, and their parents to temper their expectations that they limit themselves, even when conditions scream they could do far more. For many years *Maclean's,* then a monthly magazine, was to Canada what the *Saturday Evening Post* was to the United States, a regular reaffirmation of traditional values for a people sensing baffling and sometimes frightening social changes. One by one these general-interest magazines—the *Post, Collier's, Look, Life*— died off in the States. Some were reincarnated in a new infrequent form years later. But *Maclean's,* the Canadian publication, became the only such general-interest publication in North America to change its personality completely while continuously publishing and to make a success of it —no small accomplishment in magazine publishing annals. *Maclean's* became a financially successful weekly newsmagazine looking at Canada and looking out at the world. Yet it wouldn't have happened, according to Mr. Newman, without Americans. When he went to Canadian advertising agencies, they hedged, looking at the failure of so many other magazines and surely expecting a flop in the relatively tiny Canadian market. American agencies, on the other hand, urged *Maclean's* to take the plunge, give it a try—why not?—and promised advertising support. It was another example of how closely linked the two lands are. But it also showed how others can sometimes see, or are willing to see, Canadians' potential better than Canadians can. And others do not see the limits that Canadians are sure are there.

It seemed for so long that Canadians were content to settle. To survive comfortably was enough for many. And, given the formidable obstacles of the early days, there was a definite element of grace to that. Canadians were not in a hurry for anything. That is swell in a vacation place but can be awfully deadening year-round without some juices flowing. Ernest Hemingway, who wrote as a foreign correspondent for the *Toronto Star*, noticed this in 1922 and asked a Swiss hotelkeeper what difference he saw between Canadians and Americans. "Monsieur," the hotelkeeper replied, "Canadians speak English and always stay two days longer at any place than Americans do."[1]

Compromise has always been an integral part of the Canadian character, a tempering of extremes that wander back and forth across the land, a meeting of extremes somewhere closer to a middle. At a certain unspoken point in internal disputes Canadians sense a need for consensus, a backing off to get by, some give, some take, something to let things move on for a while until the next time. Historically Canadian confrontations have tended more toward the verbal than the violent. "I sometimes think," Marc Lalonde, a former Liberal Cabinet minister, observed, "a Canadian's idea of heaven is an eternal panel discussion." But such conflicts have also tended to become more frequent and louder, raising concerns that the constant tugging back and forth will one day rend the fragile fabric of Canadian unity or, more likely, compromise it into impotence in a more competitive world that requires boldness to succeed. It is a subject always at hand in that land. Shortly before my return to Canada, Robert Stanfield, the former Progressive Conservative party leader, said in a Toronto speech, "I suppose there are times when we ask ourselves whether we deserve to survive as a country. But I believe we will survive somehow, if only from habit."

This complex country's complex may have been realistic at one time. Mavor Moore, the theater professor and former chairman of the Canada Council (the government body established to encourage arts, humanities, and the social sciences), once listed his countrymen's favorite convenient excuses. There was the Myth of Our Preoccupied Forefathers (too busy on the frontier to create culture). There was the Small Market Myth (no matter how great a Canadian product, it will fail because the market is small and the ingenuity pool is minuscule). There was also the Myth of Others' Guilt (it's all the fault of the imperial British, the neglectful French, or the pushy Americans. Or maybe—say it softly—it was the fault of Almighty God Himself, who, it is said, created Canada on the seventh day when He was tired). When Jeremy Brown, a radio commentator, sought to define the difference between a Canadian ánd an American, he found part of the answer: "One component is the Canadian's need to bite his own hand." This might have made sense for a baby country, an artificial political creation really that is not even defined by discernible geographic lines. But today, in view of Canada's obvious accomplishments, it is so self-limiting at a time of increasing national strains when Canadian unity faces repeated tests. It is one thing if an aging, self-satisfied dowager Canada lacking in confidence, drive, and national verve is forced to remain an awkward nobody in the comfortable shadow of a big brother it hates to love. But it is quite another if that same comfortable Canada chooses to remain in that supine colonial position blaming it on whatever excuse suits the audience at hand—the United States is so big, we're so small, and the climate is so harsh, and foreigners control so much of the power, and we don't want to be like them anyway. Such a decision —and it can be a tacit one—condemns uncounted future generations to limited horizons with no alternatives but to acquiesce or leave the land of their birth, as hundreds of thousands of Canadians have done in the past, for more challenge or opportunities elsewhere. "I just wish," Pierre La Marche, a former Canadian Davis Cup tennis player, told Connie Rennick of *Racquets Canada*, "someone had told me that it was o.k. to think I could be the greatest—not just in Canada, but the world."[2]

The domestic impact aside, what do the United States and indeed the world lose in artistic, business, cultural, athletic, medical, and even government creativity when such a potentially excellent people lazily opt out for fear of failure? And beyond that, what impact does this have on the world and Canada's democratic neighbor if that failure to live up to a potential of its own design presages a slow internal decay and federal fragmentation? It would not be only Canadians then who paid a very steep price. So Americans have a vital stake, even a self-interest, in helping or at least not hindering through narrow-minded reactions the economic and psychological development of Canada.

Such an attitude long permeated the Canadian existence. There was the slightly surprised page one headline about a Canadian political leader's visit to Cuba: CASTRO HAS TIME FOR BROADBENT. John Gray, a Canadian writer and composer, once called his country "a kind of Woody Allen of nations." Then there's the joke that Adam must have been from Canada because only a Canadian would stand in a perfect tropical garden next to a perfect naked lady and get excited about an apple.

Looking at Canada's impressive accomplishments in any number of fields, other countries and a growing number of Canadians themselves grow impatient with its lack of impatience. And they seek to understand this spiritual frostbite by comparing Canada and the States. "Why should Canada, wild and unsettled as it is," wondered Henry David Thoreau as long ago as 1851, "impress one as an older country than the States, except that her institutions are old? All things seem to contend there with a certain rust of antiquity, such as forms on old armor and iron guns, the rust of conventions and formalities. If the rust was not on the tinned roofs and spires, it was on the inhabitants."

"Americans like to make money: Canadians like to audit it," said Northrop Frye, part of the Canadian conscience. "I know of no country where accountants have a higher social and moral status."[4] Sometimes to the uninformed, including a goodly number of Canadians, their country can seem somewhat dull, the kind of land that would name its professional football trophy the Grey Cup.[4] Or authoritarian. Alan Borovoy of the Canadian Civil Liberties Association described the Canadian style as "autocracy with decency." Larry Le Blanc, a free-lance writer, examined the Canadian mind from another angle in *Saturday Night*: "If you close your eyes and think of a naked Anne Murray, parts of her always come up airbrushed."

"One side of the border has a policeman for a hero, a red-coated Mountie," June Callwood wrote in her *Portrait of Canada*. "The other celebrates mavericks. One country believes father is always right; the other may put a bullet in father's head. In the United States the entrepreneur, the person who stands out from the crowd, becomes immortal; the Canadian ideal is the one who emerges from a snowdrift with the toes intact—a survivor."

At another point Miss Callwood noted, "Good behavior, while laudatory, makes people yawn." I've never yawned over Canada, but I do remember all the emphasis on good behavior, proper form, the right thing to do. Although such niceties are more often seen now as old-fashioned cobwebs from another time, there is something to be said for enforced observance of proper form. All the "How-do-you-do's" on first meeting and how the older folks would quietly stand back and wait to see how the young one performed. All the time good, firm handshakes. My father and I practiced them I don't know how many times. He had been born in Calgary, then a cowtown, now a symbol of the New West, and reared on a farm in Manitoba northwest of Winnipeg, where his morning chores included breaking the ice on the washbasin.

My mother was reared a proper young lady in Toronto, symbol of the Old East, the economic octopus that controlled so much of so many Canadian lives all over. When they met, it was at a proper Sunday dinner at the home of a family friend who may have had more matchmaking in mind that day than Yorkshire pudding. That evening my father escorted my mother home on the streetcar. He waited a decent interval, twenty-four to forty-eight hours, before having flowers delivered and phoning shortly afterward to request a dinner date, coyly accepted, according to custom. They had a not unusual engagement for the time—two years—during which they exchanged frequent letters, as my father had gone to work in the States, the only place hiring in the late 1930's. From thence, in a sense, comes this book. Their only son becomes the first American in the family, reared as a Yank-Canuck.

This background was to give me a special perspective on both lands, a part of each but not all of one. We traveled back and forth all the time in daylong drives that now take under six hours. In fact, the first expressway I remember was the Queen Elizabeth outside Toronto. Those were the days when a speed of fifty miles an hour was pretty fast, when some rear car doors still opened toward the front, when windshield wipers stopped at red lights, and when the sight of a license plate from your home state required a beep of hello on the car horn. In those times one radio speaker per car seemed sufficient.

There was much excitement about these trips to Canada: the rising before daylight in Ohio to beat the traffic; the grunge of Pennsylvania; a late-morning picnic in a lakefront park in New York somewhere from a flowered metal picnic basket I still have; rush hour in Buffalo near a steel mill where the city buses had such huge windshields I dubbed them "bright-eyes buses." There was a pattern to these car trips. I would sit in the back seat with my legs straddling that funny hump on the floor and my chin on the front seat right in the middle crack. This gave me an unobstructed view of the front seat and through the windshield to the highway where I could "aim" the hood ornament at passing objects. My mother sat in the woman's place, the right-hand seat where all women seemed to sit (except grandmothers, who sat in the back with grandsons). My father, of course, did the driving. From my midseat vantage point I also had an unobstructed view into my mother's purse whence sprang all Life Savers. My father got the first one—no fair because it was always cherry. If I opened a roll of Life Savers, the first one was always lemon or something. If my mother opened it to offer the first one to Dad, it was always cherry. Cherry was the most important flavor, and my Dad always got it. (Being a dad means never having to do without cherry Life Savers.) Not that the color mattered to him; he'd take any flavor, even, ugh, orange, crunch it up, and have his hand out begging for another one before I even got the first little round circle in my mouth (would you believe it, orange again). I would always complain that he was eating all the Life Savers, which he thought was funny. I could tell this even from the back seat because when he smiled, his right ear moved up a little. (To test this ear theory on one long car trip, I made the same observation out loud, and sure enough, there went the right ear up just a little.)

By dusk we'd be moving through Ontario's sandy wine country until the familiar turnoff near Oakville and the slow ride down a shady, curbless, very familiar street, across the bumpy railroad tracks, and into the dirt driveway with grass growing down the middle and small cedars along both sides. Grandma and Grandpa would be there: she in her apron; he in white shirt and stiff but open collar with suspenders on each shoulder. There would be excitement all around, and then out would come the newfangled toaster to produce unlimited slices of toast smothered with homemade jams. The radio might still be on (CFRB, of course) and that afternoon's *Toronto Telegram* would be on a rocker on the porch (Grandma's was the only place I could ever find "Mandrake the Magician" comic strips).

Life seemed a lot slower then and there. I didn't wear a watch. There were chores to do, but they seemed exciting then. Like feeding chickens. They always seemed happy to see me or at least my hand chucking out the grain. And some of those silly birds, I swear, I conversed with, crouching down in my little-boy shorts and T-shirt with the horizontal stripes to imitate their sounds and the movements of their heads. There were big barns and musty sheds to explore, scything to be done, real Indians to watch in the field, and sometimes, every week or two, Bert would appear.

Bert was a hobo, a tall, filthy man who wore an old two-piece suit. He would offer to do some chores for a meal, but he always wanted glasses of water. So Grandma left a little glass in a wire holder outside by the storm cellar door. I was never to use that glass.

Sometimes I was admitted to the adult male world. I could help my grandfather take the chickens to the train station in Port Credit for shipment. We'd take the trunk lid off his 1932 Ford, stick some of the cages in there, and climb into the two-seat cab, where the doors were clamped shut by a sliding door bolt. The front windshield cranked out from the bottom for air conditioning. And the horn ran off a little switch on the steering hub. We'd talk over the putt-putt-putter of the motor as we eased down Highway 2. Neither of my grandpas talked much. They liked to hear little boys talk, it seemed, but they tended more to nods and short questions than long discourses.

Sunday afternoon was the time to hear the big men talk. They would start arriving after lunch. Because neither of my parents had any siblings, my relatives were older. It wasn't until many years later that I learned an uncle and aunt are your parents' brothers or sisters. I thought they had to be your grandparents' brothers and sisters. That's all I had. The first arrivals would be Uncle George and Aunt Bea, he with a bald pate ringed by snowy white hair, she tall and magisterial with the wonderful strong laugh and voice of the classical singer she once had been. Next would come the Malcolm grandparents, he unfolding from his pale green Studebaker to rise to his height over six feet. She was short and stout with her hair in a bun. Because of her bad eye, she usually carried her head turned to the side a little. I don't remember ever seeing her laugh, but she played a crucial role in shaping my father and his toughness and Calvinist view of self-discipline.

The last to arrive, from the shortest distance, were Aunt Flossie and Uncle Jim, one of Grandpa Bowles's brothers, the successful one. It was a special occasion for me, and I would stand there in wonder, just outside the front gate, watching this frail man go through his arrival ritual. You see, Uncle Jim was an old man of the Old World. He had a fifteen- or twenty-year-old Packard, which he eased carefully out of his narrow garage every few weeks, whenever the occasion seemed to warrant it. As one result, he had but a few thousand miles on the ancient vehicle. As another, it looked like a showroom model still, shiny, gleaming, with a spotless interior that screamed to little boys, "Don't put your feet up here, or you're in some kind of trouble."

The car would glide up the road to the old house silently on the sandy soil, and I would emerge from my waiting post in the bushes, the ones with the big, squishy white berries you should never eat because they could kill you just like that. Aunt Flossie, a large woman (that seemed to be the style in those days) who, I recall, always wore dresses with large ·floral patterns, would quickly get out of the passenger's side, give me a smothering squeeze, and rush into the house to see someone named Jennie. I often wondered who that was since I had been watching the front for a long while and the only women I knew in the house were called Grandma, Grandma Malcolm, and Mom (it turned out to be a name other people called my grandma).

But Uncle Jim was a man of particular deliberation, frail but stylish. He would step from his motorcar onto the running board and then onto the ground, being ever so careful not to raise any dust that might settle on his shiny black shoes. Slowly, he would remove his gray leather gloves and place them just so on the seat to be donned later for the return home. He would remove a cap, too. And then came the long white driving coat he wore even on the hottest summer days. Although it was midcentury by then, and cars were closed in from the elements, Uncle Jim still wore a long driving coat to keep road soil off his gray suit. The coat would be placed on the seat, too. The door was closed, but the window left open. Uncle Jim would straighten his suit and pull down the vest with its gold watch chain across his stomach. We would shake hands. "How do you do, young man?"

"Fine, thank you, Uncle Jim."

And into the house he would go at his own careful speed. It was a different way of doing things. A special way. And it seemed to happen only in Canada.

After a first glass of cold ginger ale there was nothing really going on right away at these affairs. So I would wander up the street to Weaver's General Store. Sometimes Mr. Weaver, the old man, would be sitting in a rocker at the top of the stairs. People seemed afraid he would snap at them for anything, but we would have long talks together through the railing. And in 1949 Mr. Weaver gave me my first pet (not counting a pack of sex-crazed hamsters). He was a gentle cat I named Rusty for his color and because the name Orange seemed dumb. Rusty, a Canadian, was to become an American and to confirm one of my father's favorite theories: that a young person, and an occasional old one, too, needs another living soul around to teach both sides of dependence and to exchange love even if it is between two different worlds.

Across the road was a gasoline station (they were called service stations in those days). I loved the place. It was dirty and smelled unusual, and the men did mysterious things to motors inside the hood, which I couldn't see. They used a lot of strange-shaped tools to do this mysterious work. And the tools got dirty. One day I got my first job for money. The boss there asked me to clean up all the tools and he'd pay me a whole quarter. I did the job eagerly and waited around until after closing for my pay. The next day I wandered by several times, but the man said he was too busy still. The next day he said he'd changed his mind. At dinner one night everybody asked me how I was going to spend my wages, and when I said there weren't any because the man had changed his mind, the women had to restrain Grandpa from charging out the door toward the gas station. That night Grandpa paid me a quarter. If it hadn't been such a huge sum of money, capable of financing five boxes of Mackintosh's butterscotch toffee, I think I would have kept it as a souvenir. Years later I returned to the same, enlarged, store and bought another red plaid box of Mackintosh's toffee. It somehow gave me a feeling of completeness and continuity.

But the candy boxes went away when the countdown to dinner came within two hours. These meals were immense affairs—meat, baked goods, vegetables from everybody's gardens. But you could never say they were from your garden. Somebody else had to point out that the yellow beans came from the Malcolms' garden, and the asparagus from the Bowleses', and the corn from Aunt Bea's. And the ham from just up the road. And Grandma made the pies. Wonderful pies, everybody agreed. But to maintain her modesty, she'd have to deny the compliments. She'd point out something wrong with her crust. And everybody but me would contradict her (children weren't supposed to contradict grown-ups; a contradiction license is mysteriously conferred sometime later in adulthood).

Another thing that came somehow with adulthood was mustaches. More Canadian men seemed to have them in those days; I figured Canada invented them. They were wonderful, I thought, long and distinguished or short and clipped. My great-grandfather Andrew had one. Uncle Jim had one. And I never did see my father without one. Neither did my mother. So when my university days drew near a close, I, too, had to have a mustache. My children have never seen me without it. Neither has my wife.

After Sunday dinner the men would adjourn to the front porch. And out would come the cigars, long brown things that produced great clouds of smoke to drift slowly off through the screening and the hollyhocks. Each man would snip off one end of the cigar with a little pair of clippers from his vest pocket. Then they'd produce long wooden matches. And it would make them all talk about the past. It seemed a wonderfully romantic time, the early 1900's. I pictured a lot of mist in those days, rather like a curtain that would open and close on each one of these tales about life in the old oil fields around Petrolia, growing up in the same neighborhood with the MacDonald brothers, or riding the prairies on real horses.

The mists have closed around most of these stories over the years. I remember talk of the great flu epidemic that killed so many people right after World War I, the friends who returned disfigured from gas, the hard times of the Depression. While the details fade, the impressions remain of thoughtful men made rough to survive, the last generation to know the frontier in southern Canada.

Thanks in part to an unpublished autobiography he left behind, "I Took to The Road," I remember Grandpa Malcolm's tales of old Canada best. His father, a cheesemaker born in Scotland, had migrated west from Ontario the only way he could: through Chicago on the train and up, or, rather, down the Red River to Winnipeg and thence in wagons to a place called Minnedosa. A drought in the 1880's financially wiped out their operation there, so the family migrated in midwinter over the Riding Mountains to Dauphin. My great-grandfather lost his toes to the cold during that trip, but the family found rich land free for the homesteading, and each one of the eight boys staked his own place. Grandpa talked about growing up in rural Manitoba without book learning, his fascination in Winnipeg with an invention called the chain flush toilet, the luxury of having sugar on his porridge in good times, travelers thawing their long beards over the stove before dinner in the cabin, moose tallow candles, hay for bedding, and three brothers in one bed. Then there was that awful day when John, the eldest, announced he was leaving to start his own life.

His father went to a box in the kitchen and got all his money: $2.60. "I'm sorry, John," said his father. "That's all I have."

Not until he was an older teenager did Grandpa learn to read and write at a grade school. He had difficulty fitting his gangly frame into the little desks then, but he was determined to "get away from the smell of the stable." He did learn enough to get into college and earn enough during summer circuit riding to Presbyterian churches to help finance his college education. Sometimes on these long, lonely journeys he would accidentally wander across the unmarked border into the United States for prayers with Americans. At other times farther west in Alberta, he hunted and trapped to live and clothe himself.

"We had learned," he wrote later, "that necessity has no rules and calls for no embarrassment. The richness of natural beauty around us left no room for coveting more material pleasures. Everyone was happy and content. It was not like today, when the more people want what they haven't got, the less they want what they have."

Philosophies of life like this seemed to seep out all the time at times like this in Canada, sayings such as "Life is a little like shooting; foresight helps your aim." Then Uncle George, Uncle Jim, Grandpa Bowles, and Dad would nod and agree, and another cloud of cigar smoke would rise and drift off through the screen. By then the cigars had become mere stubs and the women would join the group from the cooling kitchen. Someone would walk around the porch, pumping a spray gun of insecticide at something out there in the dark, and at times I got to help.

Then I would crawl up into the lap of Grandma Bowles to cuddle, something I felt Canadians were very good at. At some point then I would begin to tell, under my breath, a long, complicated story about being on a train in New York State, about seeing something shiny under the radiator in the observation car, about sticking my hand in to get it, about my mother telling me to get my hand out of that dirty place, and about my proudly pulling out a dime. Finders keepers. It had all the elements of a child's favorite tale: buried treasure; seeing something adults didn't; being right when they thought you were wrong. But this story was a hallowed game, too. Because as soon as she began hearing the all too familiar unfolding details, Grandma would say in mock outrage, "I have heard this story too many times." And she would begin tickling me in the ribs. The idea was for me to finish the tale in complete sentences before

335

erupting into gales of giggles. If I did, I won. If I didn't, she won, but only for a few minutes because soon she would hear the familiar muttering, even over the surrounding conversations. And the game was on again. Years later, her body all frail and pale from the cancer within, Grandma lay on a hospital bed, too weak to sit. But I leaned down by her ear anyway and whispered a story about a little boy who found a dime on a railroad train in New York State. I know she heard it; she tickled my hand. It was the last time we talked.

Other Sundays we would go to other relatives' houses. Grandpa Malcolm's was on the outer fringes of Toronto. He had an immense garden with a path that led down to a creek where I practiced dam building and learned that there is more to engineering than the naked eye can measure. I also got in some trouble there one hot afternoon. You see, I was hiding in the ditch by the stop sign, ambushing cars with my squirt gun, and I'd jump up and squirt the car when it stopped and then dive back down to hide, you know, and all it was was water, but this one car came along and stopped, and well, I squirted it, just a little bit of water, and, um, well, the car window was open, and the man kind of got a little wet, but I didn't mean to, really.

Aunt Bea's house was in a scenic little town called Galt, later renamed Cambridge. She and Uncle George lived across the street from a large park that had live deer to feed, and on Sundays lots of men in white suits ran around with wooden paddles, hitting a big wooden ball and then running from one little post to another. It was a game named for one of my favorite insects, cricket, and I thought for sure it would be fun. I watched that game so much. I applauded when everyone else applauded. Next to the 13 million hours I spent in algebra, I thought cricket the most boring thing I had ever seen.

Uncle Jim and Aunt Flossie had a gloomy little house somewhere in Toronto, one of those disconnected images that float around in a child's memory or an adult's memory of childhood. I didn't remember where it was or getting there, but I remember being there. She always served little cookies, about a third of a bite big. I figured old ladies must have about the smallest mouths in the world if that's all they could fit in. At their house, Uncle Jim would let me pretend-drive his Packard in the garage. But the big attraction about Aunt Flossie's house was that it came equipped with its own anthill. Right in the front yard. In the city. It was great! While everyone sipped tea indoors in the dark living room, I could

poke around that hill for hours (some of those little critters had wings!)
and I could look down the quiet street three doors to the big road, where
the red-and-cream-colored streetcars clanged by, so eloquently implying
a larger world out there somewhere. After all, I thought, those big electric
cars must be going to and coming from somewhere other than Aunt
Flossie's, as natural as that seemed to be.

Years later, after exploring good portions of part of the world, I was
narrowly to avert an auto accident as I drove down Toronto's Mount
Pleasant Road. There was a slight bend in the street, nothing remarkable
then, but it jarred my memory strangely. I pulled over to look around. It
was a déjà vu that I really had seen before, from a shorter height perhaps.
The streetcars were gone. But over there, right where it should have been,
was a very familiar corner. So down that street, let's see, right about there,
should be, yes, there it was, Aunt Flossie's house. The ants had moved.
But another piece of my past was put in place.

It was a sense of growth, of fulfillment that I was to experience many
times in many places in Canada—even when I had never been to that spot
before, never met those people before. Most of the time I was not
consciously aware of this search. A few times I was.

It was gray, overcast, and cold with a wind-driven drizzle that coats
coats with moisture in seconds. Faces winced. Hands and feet chilled. It
was a perfect day for sitting by the fireplace, sipping something hot and
reading a newspaper. But there on the deck of the *St. Barnabe* as it cruised
in the St. Lawrence River that Sunday were forty humans huddled together, periodically stamping their feet like primitive dancers and peering
relentlessly out over the chill, broad waters with the same common determination that salmon share on their upstream swim to spawn. What
drives these people to such unlikely places to endure such discomfort—
and to pay money for the privilege?

"There's one!" came the joyous cry. And up from the depths, dark,
lumbering, and incredibly immense even at a distance, came a giant blue
whale, 80 tons of seagoing mammal gasping for air. Oblivious of onlook-
ers, the animal moved slowly ahead, filling its muscles and tissues with
oxygen for perhaps forty-five seconds—no one thought to check. Then
with a gentle surge the creature arched, still revealing no more than half
its bulky length, and dived down for more food.

"My God," said one man. And there was silence.

For centuries such a sight would have prompted but one response: the hurling of a harpoon. But on that special weekend I had taken Spencer, then six and fascinated with the idea of whales, out on a Canadian whale-watching boat, a benign expedition to see the world's largest mammals at home in the sea. Essentially such trips provide the suspense of the hunt and the thrill of the find without the guilt of the kill. To maintain a kind of intimacy, the Zoological Society of Montreal takes only about forty people per trip. We had ridden for a silent five hours by bus from Montreal to Rivière du Loup, Quebec, for a whale lecture and two days' cruising the river.

Our fellow whale watchers, all unknown to us, included a seventy-two-year-old widow who had always wanted to see a whale, a doctor and his wife, a sociology professor, a nursing home administrator, a lawyer, a housewife, and Spencer, who remembered the whale in *Pinocchio*. None of us knew fully yet how sharing an awe and exhilaration over whales would affect us.

The Friday night lecture was to have lasted thirty minutes. But two hours after it had begun, many participants were still lingering to chat about the creatures they had never seen. "Whales are like cats," said Michael Kozicki, an expert from Canada's Department of the Environment. "You can have a six-pound house cat and a two-hundred-pound Siberian tiger. But they are all cats." Whales, which have not been hunted off eastern Canada since 1972, routinely move up and down the East Coast from the Bahamas to Baffin Island. Large numbers wander up the St. Lawrence in May or June and stay until the freeze-up starts in November.

There are several theories on why whales like the river, where they have been protected since World War I. One is that they come to see the humans, who appear on the river around May or June to gaze out over the water, holding strange black glasses to their eyes. The people seem to migrate elsewhere when the freeze-up starts in November. Another reason, possibly more accurate, is that the whales are following their food, which must be consumed in prodigious amounts—about 5 percent of body weight per day. We were told that one whale, feeding off the bottom, was found entangled in a telephone cable at 4,500 feet. Others, tracked by sonar, have risen 3,000 feet to the surface in one minute.

Coming on top of such intriguing information, the 6:30 A.M. wake-up call didn't seem too bad the next day. We donned far warmer clothing than the August calendar would seem to suggest and boarded the 125-foot ship to journey where the deep, cold Saguenay River hits the shallower St. Lawrence, flushing up plankton and other marine life. The first few hours were uneventful. Bird watchers logged numerous sightings, and a few seals swam by. The water was calm, a hopeful sign since whales linger longer on smooth surfaces. Some people dozed in the pale sun. But the first sighting ended such reverie. "It's a minke," said Mr. Kozicki. Perhaps 22 feet in length, the whale bobbed up straight ahead and coursed slowly to the right for half a minute before diving out of sight. Six minutes later it popped up behind the drifting ship, prompting a furious scramble to the stern.

Whales, like humans, can be very curious, and a drifting, quiet ship can be an intriguing object, a trick Norwegian whalers used profitably for years. Whales in the busy St. Lawrence, however, are generally accustomed to ship traffic. And as the day's first sighting dived out of view, the ship chugged on its way. It was the only time everyone was certain how many whales had been seen. There followed in rapid succession a series of sightings that sent the whale watchers from side to side and stem to stern. Minkes. Fin whales. Bunches of belugas. Some were in a hurry. Some lolled. Others dived in a distinct circular pattern, herding frightened fish into the crowded center before diving there themselves for maximum fish per pass. There was no way to photograph them all or even to keep count, just to revel in their company. "Isn't this exciting?" said Vera Smith, one passenger.

Suddenly someone saw a spout. Or thought he did. It was far away. Maybe some mist. Or fog. No, came a cry from behind; someone else had seen it, too, or thought so. Slowly the ship crept ahead. Ten minutes. Fifteen minutes. Twenty. Eyes turned elsewhere. There it was again. Over there this time. Are you sure? Yes, positive. Then a chorus: "I see it."

"It could be a blue," said Mr. Kozicki.

It wasn't. It was two blues. From a distance they could have been logs. But from 300 or 400 yards, there was no doubt. They were living. They eased through the water. "Lumbering" is not a graceful enough word. Each was perhaps 75 feet long. First, the spout's 20-foot spray came from apparently nowhere. An instant later the sound reached the ship, a rushing blast as about 600 quarts tore out of the silver dollar-size blowhole in less than a second. Then under the falling spray appeared a dark dome like a basketball, which grew and grew to perhaps the size of a couch. And then a car. And a truck. More and more of the glistening broad body continued through its gentle arch between the waves. It just kept coming. Then a tiny fin. Or at least it looked tiny after all the rest. More body. And then down.

The pair of whales did this perhaps a half dozen times. No one was counting. Many even forgot to take pictures. Then the whales dived for perhaps fifteen minutes. And surfaced to do it again. "They're bigger than big," said Harold Plaskett near me, "and we only saw their backs." The views of those two creatures lasted for only a few minutes. But they provided fodder for hours of excited conversation during dinner on the ship and on the ride back to the motel. There were more sightings the next day, which dawned cold and drizzly and frequently sent even the hardiest watchers inside to warm up. As the novelty began to wear off, some passengers broke out Scrabble games or watched television. And a shipboard romance even flourished.

But inevitably Mr. Plaskett's energetic shout of "Whale ho!" brought everyone running. One whale appeared for a second right off the bow, close enough, some wet witnesses swore, to see its mouth. That ignited even more conversations among these people who were nameless strangers on Friday and first-name friends by Sunday. Everyone agreed that the specialized nature of the trip eliminated the more annoying characteristics of group tours. There were no complainers and no perpetually tardy participants holding up the rest. The whales, it seemed, had united the humans.

This spontaneous camaraderie carried over to the animated return bus trip to Montreal, which certainly did not seem like five hours. There was much talking. And jokes. And a happy birthday song. And some whistles and shouts of "Take it all off" as passengers peeled off layers of warm outdoor clothing no longer needed. There were also numerous unsolicited suggestions as to what I should write about the trip someday. "Tell everybody," said one woman, "that we saw sixty-seven whales."

We saw sixty-seven whales.

On another journey I retraced the Manitoba migration route of my great-grandfather from Minnedosa north to Dauphin, where my father had grown up on a farm. It was no big deal by car a century or so after the fact—seventy-five miles perhaps—but I drove slowly and tried to imagine times when the mail came through once or twice a month, when unbridged streams could carry away wagonloads of supplies and earnings, when nomadic Indians dropped by to trade their skin-tanning skills for milk. I had heard many stories about life there from Grandpa and my dad. I invited my father to accompany me on that sentimental journey, but he would not. The place was laden with too many unspoken memories, I guess. "The reason the prairies look lonely," he once told me, "is because they are."

I found a distant relative in Dauphin, Bob Malcolm, a playmate of my father's long ago. He couldn't understand why any Malcolm would become a "goddamned Yank," but he was hospitable, housed me, called over a few other distant relatives with the same name, and we fumbled for common ground. That night I bought a long extension cord to plug my car heater into his porch for the minus 35-degree temperature. We ate a hearty meal with a friend, Marian Campbell, and she played some hymns on the organ. In the morning I prevailed on the old man to ride out in the cold with me, along the still-dirt roads where horse-drawn sleighs once slid with their passengers bundled in blankets and their booted feet resting on heated bricks. I wanted desperately to see the old homestead. Despite the vicious winds and blowing snow, he guided me through the drifts and along the property lines that run straight as an arrow in rural America.

"There it is," he said. "Your poppa grew up there." It was exciting, but it was not on a hill. The road was in the right place, but I had always pictured the house on a little knoll with the barn over there. I left my friend in the car with the heater and radio on; he couldn't believe anyone would go out on a day like that to return to a place his relatives had worked so hard to leave. The wind blew the parka hood over my head before I could don it. The snow was hip-deep. And I was puffing when I reached the crumbling buildings 100 yards away.

The squat house or cabin was made of logs. They were caulked with a decaying mud. The roof was gone. And the door. The land was large. It was very large. But the yard was small. Over there, I figured from my dad's old story, was where that farmer and his son had loaded all the hay on a wagon to haul home across the lake that winter day; no one ever saw them again. There was the milking shed back by the trees. There were no wires running into it. That's where Dad had loaded up the milk to take to town. His other chores had included calling on milk customers behind in payments. His face always got hard when he talked of that. The stones in those shed walls I knew had been hauled, one by one, from the surrounding fields; Grandpa always said he grew the best stones for miles around.

I'd like to go back in the spring sometime, when the blackbirds are chirruping and the landscape is less monochrome, when the blatant power of natural forces seems less lethal and softer, when man puts his mark on the land in neat rows. On the way back to the car I noted that the buffeting wind had already erased my tracks, as if I'd never been there. "Well," said Bob, "what did ya find? Just a lot of snow, right?"

"Yes," I said, "and all the stones."

"Of course," he said, nodding, "the stones would be left."

One of the regular features of my childhood was a teasing game with my mother. At every opportunity, to her predictable exasperation, my father and I would recite an American's cliché description of Canada as a frozen Arctic tundra peopled only by Eskimos and Mounties (and a British queen, of course, although the only monarch who really lived in Canada was Dutch; she was hiding out from the Nazis at the time). This ignorant image lives on today, one could swear by Canadian design. Not long ago a Wisconsin TV station weatherman, a transplanted Canadian, as it happens, ran a name-the-snowstorm contest for his American viewers so accustomed to forecasts containing cold Canadian air masses. The prize was an all-expense-paid winter weekend fling in Flin Flon, Manitoba, or a $500 snowblower. David and Mary Collin, harassed by sniggering reporters, opted for the snowblower. This was perfect for prolonging clichés because it let the Canadian Press news agency write about Americans' picking a common machine over a visit to Canada. It could provide hours of anxiety for Flin Flon's mayor in northern Manitoba: "Naturally, I hope they haven't heard something bad about our community." And it made Canada seem the originator of all things wintry, which Canadians could then complain about as a cliché. But the whole incident, completely ignored in the land where it was happening, was Canadian-created.

One of the major contributors to this limited vision of Canada in my childhood was, of course, Sergeant Preston of the Yukon and his trusty dog King, fictional figments of a radio writer's imagination whose snowy afternoon adventures never really left a radio studio in downtown Detroit (actually Sergeant Preston's Michigan home city is one of the few United States sites where you go south to get to Canada).

So one of my required personal journeys in Canada was to track down Sergeant Preston and at least one of his myths. I made a horrible discovery: despite all those boxes of Quaker Puffed Wheat (the Puffed Rice tasted like eating air), I didn't really own a square inch of the Yukon.

Once upon a time, I discovered, there was an advertising executive in a city called Chicago. His job was to make children yell, "Mommy, I want Quaker Puffed Wheat!" For many years this man told the children his cereal was shot from guns. This helped his sales. But other cereals had talking tigers and gave away prizes in every box. This hurt his sales. What could the poor businessman do? He needed a new idea. Or soon he would need a new job. The idea had to be something catchy and simple and it had to do with the cereal's radio show about a scarlet-coated good guy who ran around in the woods saying things like "On, King, on, you big huskies."

As Bruce Baker, the adman, recounted the tale to a friend before his death, he was in the smallest room in his house the night before his ad presentation was due. Sitting there, near panic, he was suddenly inspired. In each box of Quaker cereal he would give away a square inch of land in the romantic Yukon right by Dawson, where the sergeant and King had their adventures every week. He could almost see the ads before his eyes on the back of the door: "You'll actually own one square inch of Yukon land in the famous gold country!" The deeds would have lots of small print and a decorative border, a blank for the owner's name, maybe a drawing of a miner panning gold, a corporate seal, of course, and lots of legal terms like "conveyance," "grantee," and "hereinabove mentioned." Kids would love it.

Quaker Oats hated the idea.

Too many potential legal problems, the lawyers said. It would cost far too much to register every deed to every little cereal eater out there. Right. Well, then, Mr. Baker suggested, just don't register the deeds. And he found a Yukon lawyer who thought it was legal. Mr. Baker flew to the northern Yukon, as one had to do in those days of the early fifties because there was no road to Dawson yet. And after his own Yukon winter adventures in a boat, including an accident that was to cost him part of his leg, Mr. Baker saw the land and bought it for $1,000. Thus was launched the Great Klondike Big Inch Land Caper, one of the most successful sales promotions in North American business history. I mean I sent away for more than my share of secret signal guns, jet launcher rings, and baking soda-propelled plastic submarines. But I wanted a square inch of the Yukon so bad I could taste it, and I was willing to eat Puffed Wheat to prove it.

Twenty-one million numbered deeds were printed up. And on January 27, 1955, the promotion was begun on the Sergeant Preston show. The response was far beyond Mr. Baker's wildest dreams. Quaker Oats had struck a gold mine, so to speak. Special store displays went up to handle mobs of mothers dispatched to turn their tots into Yukon land barons. The shelves were stripped daily. Quaker's puffed cereal plant in Cedar Rapids, Iowa, could hardly stuff the deeds in fast enough. Within weeks every box was sold.

And it seemed there were now suddenly millions of Americans with a small stake in Canada. The land, I discovered by poking through the files of Dawson's dusty land claims office, was Lot 2 in Group 243, a 19.11-acre plot on the west bank of the Yukon River about 3 miles upstream from town where Malcolm McLaren first homesteaded back in 1911. The land, a quick helicopter hop showed, is flat, bordered with firs and poplars and, like much of the area that gold prospectors combed for so long, is strewn with wagon wheels and homes and bits of cabins.

But cereal promotions, like their own products, grow stale quickly. Mr. Baker and Quaker Oats went on to other business, including a twenty-five cent offer for a pouch of "genuine Yukon dirt," an offer that involved shoveling and sifting four tons of the stuff from a riverbed near Dawson and trucking it to post offices in Alaska because of Canadian customs regulations. As time went on, Quaker redirected its cereal sales, eliminating promotion and going more for a different, diet-conscious market.

But this cereal sales saga refuses to die. For long after all the rocket sets and codebooks and all the other cereal prizes had been lost, millions of those official-looking, legal-sounding, gold-embossed deeds to a square inch of Yukon land remain in drawers, albums, safe-deposit boxes, scrapbooks, vaults, and, more important, the memory of a generation of men and women not so young anymore. And given the ravages of the years and the economy, a steadily mounting stream of these former children, their attorneys, their widows, and their executors is writing the Yukon to inquire after their property, which they assume has increased in value over all these years.

Thousands of people have written. "Please tell them to stop," pleaded Cheryl Lefevre, a land office clerk who stores the Yukon's files on the matter, files now nearing a thickness of two feet. Owners complain they are not receiving tax statements. Others ask if anyone wants to lease a square inch or buy some out for real small-scale real estate speculation. One youngster even enclosed four toothpicks so officials could fence in his square inch spread. Steven Spoerl wrote the prime minister that he was formally declaring the independence of his four square inches. Genevieve Burg of Wisconsin, like many Americans generally confused about Canadian geography, asked the governor of Alaska about her Yukon land. She got a reply: "Alaska does not maintain records on Canadian lands." In a charitable mood Ralph Chamberlain of Michigan offered to donate his three square inches to become the world's smallest national park.

But alas, the replies carry sad news. Not only do these people not own the land now, but they never did. Each individual deed was never registered. The Klondike Big Inch Land Company, an Illinois subsidiary of Quaker's, has gone out of business. Anyway, the Canadian government repossessed all the land back in 1965 for nonpayment of property taxes totaling $37.20. "The deeds were not meant to have any intrinsic value," a Quaker spokesman told me in Chicago, "but rather to give the consumer the romantic appeal of being the owner of a square inch of land in the Yukon." Each writer is informed that the deeds are actually worthless. Ironically, however, there were also unconfirmed reports that Mr. Baker's late-night bathroom brainstorm, those seven- by five-inch deeds that were thirty-five times larger than the piece of land they represented, have brought $40 in some antique and memorabilia shops (no, I don't know which ones). This means that a worthless piece of paper from a cereal box some thirty years ago has at times fetched more than each real share of the Quaker Oats Company.

Indians were long a part of my image of Canada, as they have been of the States. I had only seem them in American movies, but they lived just down the road from Grandpa Bowles in Canada. And they worked for him. Being less violent than their American cousins, Canadians, it is said, handled the problem of their aboriginal settlers with more humanity and less massacre.

On the surface, the midwinter gathering of the Dogrib Indian tribe looked the same as it has for uncounted generations around the Arctic Circle in the Northwest Territories in a wonderfully wild area that Robert Service, the poet, so aptly called the Great Alone. Midwinter to the Dogribs means fur trading, visiting relatives, weddings at the Roman Catholic mission, dancing to drums, and feasting on boiled caribou and lard chunks. But beneath the surface are markers of the powerful change that is creeping through the tiny bands of Indians, 8,500 in all, who are scattered through the scrub forests of Canada's Far North. It is a change that only the old-timers and Arctic veterans notice, but it threatens the fragile fabric of Indian society as well as the very existence of some tribes. "Young people," said Herbert Zimmerman, "don't want to go fur trapping anymore because they don't have oranges and TV out in the bush."

Herb Zimmerman *Nohtsi enitl'e-cho dok'e wots'ikw'o ha tlichoyati k'alaiwo*. Or to put it another way, Herb Zimmerman is translating the Bible into an Indian language, Dogrib. Translating the Bible into another tongue is a difficult assignment in itself. But Mr. Zimmerman must also translate the Bible into another culture, one in which, among other things, kings and ceremonial foot washings and even shepherds are utterly foreign. Beyond that even, Dogrib is an irregular language that was never written before Mr. Zimmerman and his wife, Judy, tackled it. So to keep his tongue in shape even after more than two decades living among the Indians as a missionary, Mr. Zimmerman and I got in a car in Yellowknife one night around New Year's and drove into the wilderness on a frozen dirt road that ran about sixty-five miles to Rae. The temperature was minus 43. We had been invited to the feast.

It is a joyous affair, a celebration of tradition, of free eats and of life, albeit a changing one. It included four weddings, which usually just legalize existing living arrangements. They are not grand ceremonies followed by long honeymoons. Six of the new husbands and wives had to be back at work first thing Monday morning. "There's a change right there," said the Reverend Jean Amours, a Catholic missionary who arrived in Rae from France in 1951, when I was still chasing chickens as a Grandpa's helper outside Toronto. "Twelve years ago," said the priest, "none of these couples would have had full-time wage jobs, and they wouldn't have worn suits to the altar either."

For centuries the nomadic Dogribs, believed to have been pushed north by more warlike tribes, have wandered the hostile north woods—first hunting, later trapping to meet the demand for fur far away. At times they might venture beyond the tree line into the barren Arctic, but that was usually left to the Inuit. Three times a year the Indians would gather in Rae—at midwinter, Easter, and summer—to celebrate the anniversary of their treaty with Britain. They would trade and socialize and marry and eat and dance and receive their government payments. Then they would return to the bush, where the rules of survival were harsh but familiar. Some of the 2,500 surviving Dogribs still live that way. For instance, Jimmy, who claimed no last name, left town in October to run his traplines. At year's end he had just returned with his dog team.

But the ranks of these men are diminishing, and their children are not always learning the old ways of survival on the land. "One man can still live off the land," said Peter Andersen, a town official, "but an entire family can't make a living off the land. There's a difference." For complex and interlocking reasons, the old ways have been undermined, usually inadvertently. Father Amours traces this in part to government attempts to improve health care, which has reduced infant mortality. But it has also led to larger families, which hinder nomadic movements and require higher family income to survive. The children begin learning more in formal schools than from their traditional teacher, their father.

Better health care has also increased life expectancy, which means young families' care of elderly parents, a traditional responsibility, lasts much longer and costs much more. In addition, the cash-and-wage economy has chipped away at the concepts of community needs and community sharing, although wages, which are larger than income from trapping, are necessary to support the new needs and wants introduced by formal education and television.

Political and business systems are also evolving. But none of these changes crossed anyone's mind that night as 500 Indians and 2 visitors, one of them speaking fluent Dogrib, gathered for the feast on the floor of the community center—chiefs in front, men on the right, women and scores of well-behaved children on the left.

In the old days the food would have been mostly meat. This time,

347

however, the men assigned to wait on the diners sitting cross-legged on the floor moved among them dishing out mounds of store-bought and store-donated foods. First came a couple of scoops of mushy rice. Then came a man with a large bucket to ladle frozen raspberries onto the rice. One or two hard-boiled eggs were added to the mounds, which were then surrounded by two or three raw hot dogs. On the side were chunks of dried caribou to chew with some bread, butter, jam, and a slab of lard gouged from a pail by a man with a large hunting knife. Peaches, oranges, apples, apricots, and cups of cold tea were also distributed. Then almost everyone dug in. There was considerable trading of foods—the older men would give their portions of cookies to the youngsters in exchange for their hard-boiled eggs, which had turned purple in the raspberry juices.

As the dinner wore on, Chief Joe Miquie, speaking only in Dogrib, welcomed his visitors, to an enthusiastic round of applause. The chief was elected for his ability to encourage a sense of community. His was the first of many brief and not so brief discourses by men, all elders who felt the momentary urge to address the tribe and to hail its labors in the past year. There were some jokes told. And the chief also thanked God for His bounty of food and furs and for keeping the trappers and their families safe for this year anyway.

By 11:00 P.M. the newlyweds had greeted everyone. The leftover food had been carted home. And the men had cleaned the hall. With the chiefs and elders watching from under their quilted, peaked caps, seven men began rhythmically beating hand drums resembling large tambourines. At first no one moved. The chief told us it takes some time for the spirits to rise. But within twenty minutes a handful of dancers began hopping and shuffling and chanting in rhythm, one behind the other in long, curving lines around the hall. Suddenly there were 60 people on the floor for the ten- to fifteen-minute dances. Then 100. Then 200 and more, in circles. Hour after hour they danced, with short breaks to try to gulp cola drinks that had frozen solid outdoors during the evening. The community's white members—the police, the store manager, a priest or two— made brief, polite appearances to chat, watch the dancing, and down a soft drink (the Northwest Territories being officially "dry" of liquor, there was no alcohol in sight; the Mounties had stopped my car on the highway outside town and thoroughly searched it for any illegal beverage I might be smuggling in).

Gradually the tempo quickened. Parkas came off, and the fringe on decorative jackets bounced faster and faster and faster. There were broad smiles and cheers and whoops of joy. Children too small for the dance floor caught the spirit and began running about through the crowd. Even the elderly joined in. The floor shook, and the temperature indoors climbed. On it went for hour after hour, until about 5:00 A.M. Then, reluctantly, the revelers donned their parkas and went out into the cold to their shiny snowmobiles or their powerful pickup trucks or cars for the forty-five-second drive to oil-heated homes, where the ubiquitous television was still on and a new day of programs was falling from satellites far above.

"It's a challenge," said Mr. Zimmerman. He was speaking of translating the Bible, but he could have included the thought of work the morning after such a party. He was a native of Moline, Illinois, age fifty when I first met him. The Zimmermans, both members of the Evangelical Free Church of America, consider the Bible translating a divine mission. They arrived in the Northwest Territories in February 1964 with the thermometer at 35 below zero and Mrs. Zimmerman six months pregnant. For fourteen months they lived in an isolated camp of tents and huts. They had to squeeze in many part-time jobs to make ends meet; they are responsible for raising their own support money, about $25,000 a year, which is channeled through Wycliffe Bible Translators in Huntington Beach, California. When the job is done, a Bible society will handle the publishing. Each day for years the two struggled to learn the guttural consonant sounds and tones of Dogrib, which appears related to Navajo and is so named because the people who speak it believe God made the first Indian from a dog's rib. Once learned, the oral language had to be written, and somehow rules formulated. When I visited their living room office, seventeen years into their project, they had finished the Book of Mark and 10 percent of Luke and John. Mr. Zimmerman calculated he would need another eight years to complete the New Testament and parts of the Old. "It's like a roller coaster," he said. "It's slow getting up that ramp learning the language and preparing to translate. But then, coming down, things pick up considerably." The couple was unperturbed that fewer than 3,000 people in the world speak Dogrib and that half of them have already learned English. "You see," said Mr. Zimmerman, "pastors spend their whole life with a congregation of two hundred. Maybe having the Bible in their language will provide a reason for the Dogribs to keep their tongue. And just because the King James Version has been around three hundred years doesn't mean every translation has to live that long. I know I'm not writing the King Herb version."

Besides the vocabulary (eight words for "ice") and the grammar (pronouns go in the middle of the verb), the Zimmermans had to learn Indian manners. It is rude, they discovered, for a newcomer to wait for an invitation to a neighbor's house. You must immediately make a "walk around" to every home, starting with the chief and the elderly, to pay your respects. They spent countless hours socializing and working with the Indians to earn their trust and to practice new phrases. Cross-cultural communication, they learned, is rife with traps for misunderstanding. A draft translation of the Easter story drew guffaws when it included a word for simply inserting the cross in the sand instead of one for formally erecting the cross. "I spend days on four hundred words," said Mr. Zimmerman, "and then I go over it with several people. You know, 'Does this say what I want it to say?' "

Some terms, "public baths," for example, require explanatory footnotes, baths, even private ones, not being a part of everyone's daily ritual. Other ideas can simply be adjusted. The Three Wise Men become three chiefs. And instead of some kind of weird animal like a camel, they ride horses, which are still exotic enough; at least there's a word for horse. But since there is no neutral word in Dogrib for "brother" in a spiritual sense —there are only brothers who are older, younger, or twins, and anyone outside the family cannot possibly be a brother—an explanation plus considerable research into biblical families was required.

With the Indians' strong sense of community property, possessives can apply only to the body and to relatives ("my arm," "my father"). Inanimate objects belong in prepositional phrases ("this sled is to me"). One of Mr. Zimmerman's major problems involved the word and concept of "shepherd" with its spiritual connotation of caring for a dependent flock. Being nomads, the Indians had no domesticated herds, and any mountain sheep encountered would be slain immediately and eaten. So Mr. Zimmerman settled on the word *gikedi* ("one who cares for people"), although it usually describes a communal baby-sitter.

The Zimmermans showed me a biblical passage in English, Mark 6:34:

"And Jesus, when he came out, saw much people, and was moved with compassion toward them, because they were as sheep not having a shepherd: and He began to teach them many things."

Then he showed me the Dogrib version:

Zezi ka-atla ko do hlo ni-ideh goai
("Jesus came out when people many they were there he saw them")

etege-et'i gonihwo
("they are pitiful is how he felt toward them")

sahzoa gikedi hwile lagit'e t'a
("sheep one who cares for them was missing that is how they were since")

Hani niwo t'a t'asi hlo t'a hoghagoreto
("That way he felt since things many he taught them").

In the Indian vocabulary there are also several kinds of white man: *qwheti* ("stone-house people"), *molah* ("people with many buttons on their clothes"—that is, the French Canadian trappers who wandered through), and then there is *beicho* ("the big knife people," or the Americans with the oversize Bowie knives). I learned a few easy words. *Nohtsi* is God, or the "Creator." *Enitl'e-cho* is the Bible, or "Big Book." And *lanecha* is what Mr. Zimmerman has: "a big job."

Although all Dogribs live within 200 miles of one another, the Zimmermans must reckon with regional dialects. In Yellowknife an "airplane" is *tseta*. Sixty-five miles away in Rae it is *enitl'ek'et'a* or "paper plane," recalling early canvas-covered craft. It is an exaggerated example of the kind of lingering regional myopia that to me helps define the word "provincial." Even in the one area that Canadians have in common, their northern climate, they have cut themselves off from each other. When Reggie Bouffard, a Quebec miner, traveled outside his home province, even just next door into Ontario, he watched in vain for detailed weather reports on the doings back home in eastern Quebec. But he noticed, whenever he watched American television, he saw temperatures and details there from all over that country. It was a lesson that the new Canadian owners and editors of the *Houston Post* had to learn for themselves.

One of the first things they did upon taking possession of that metropolitan American newspaper was to substitute a new restyled regional weather map, emphasizing the state over the rest of the country, just as they would do back home. Local protests erupted, and the next thing the new owners had to do was replace their Canadian-style regional map with an American-style national one.

And this kind of entrenched estrangement runs right up to the top of the country. When Pierre Elliott Trudeau, then prime minister, went out to visit voters in British Columbia on one trip, he started off by telling his dinner hosts, who had paid $150 each for the privilege of dining with the country's leader, "You are terribly unaware of what is happening in this country, terribly unaware. You know, very often those who live at the foot of great mountains are the last ones to climb those mountains just because they're there."

"You're insulting us" came a cry from the audience.

"Well," replied the prime minister, "I'm sorry if I insult you. I really was giving you more credit for your intelligence than I know you deserve."

Such fractious feelings, such constant petty pushings, what some publications call the Canadian disease, continue despite ever-increasing development of a single national economy, a distinctive national culture, and certainly a singularly aggressive economic drive outside Canada. "We seem to have lost sight of the fact that, in large measure, the problems we are squabbling about," noted Rowland C. Frazee, chairman of the Royal Bank of Canada, "are actually problems of plenty. We are arguing about the distribution of our substantial wealth."[5] There are long governmental fights over dividing oil revenues and, in eight courts, over federal constitutional moves. Newfoundland sues Quebec over power rates. Quebec issues its own maps claiming part of Newfoundland. There were fights over Canada's two-language policies, over the design of the national flag, over one province's blocking workers from another, over how to divide health and welfare costs, even over the wording of the national anthem. Segments of the government argued long over a memorial for Canadians killed in World War II and Korea. Opponents feared it would cheapen an existing memorial to World War I dead. The typically Canadian solution: Inscribe the later wars' dates on the side of the earlier war's monument and then have a rededication ceremony. Of course, all free countries have jurisdictional and policy and even silly emotional disputes.

But Canada's constant squabblings often seem more like a married couple that has grown so comfortable with their steady stream of bickerings that it no longer seems strange. Always arguing has come to seem normal. It is a bad habit that seems bad only from outside. Some kind of settlement, often temporary, is usually reached over time, but not until bitter exchanges and political posturings have added a bit more venom to modern memories.

Many Canadians, Stratford director John Hirsch said, like to clutch vipers to their bosom. "Maybe what we need," Walter Sicinski, a Toronto worker, suggested one morning, "is a good depression to teach all these young workers what it is to have something and then not have it."

John W. Holmes, the author and former diplomat, has written that "Canadians are perversely loath to face up to any good news."[6] And Douglas Morris, a Canadian businessman, suggested one day that Canadians perhaps suffer from excess expectations, that their economic achievements had outpaced their mental ability to accept them while their expectations of a better life had leaped so far ahead of fiscal reality they had doomed themselves forever to disappointment. It leaves Canada sometimes with the visage of a shrinking violet on the outsize stalk of an aggressive sunflower.

Some Canadians have noted this themselves. My grandfather Malcolm would talk sometimes of his later career days in government service as Canada's immigration officer in Scotland, rounding up and screening candidates to emigrate to Canada and become new citizens. He'd talk of how hard they had worked for this chance at a dream for a new future in an unseen land whose name they pronounced gently with reverence. And he told of a visit one evening to the well-scrubbed Scottish house of one Jimmy Muir, whose wife and children were lined up in their best clothes to impress the officer from Canada. After the interview Mr. Muir looked up at my grandfather and said, "Do ye think, Mr. Malcolm, they be goud enough for Canada?"

"I hesitated," Grandpa wrote later, "because I wondered if Canada was good enough for them."[7]

The immigrants over the years spread a certain wanderlust flavor that has often been lacking in Canada, in part at least because it is simply so much more expensive to explore that land than it is to go to, say, Europe. One day when airlines were offering round trip tickets from Toronto to

Britain for $350, I paid $1,050 to fly about the same length of time, only straight north to the Canadian Arctic. It helped explain why few travelers encountered up there were on the luxury tour. I met, instead, wanderers like Buzz Kuhns, who spent his twenty-third birthday cycling across the Arctic Circle, four and a half months and several thousand miles out of his Connecticut home. He had wanted to see cross-country North America from close up, so he was bicycling from Staffordville, Connecticut, to Anchorage, Alaska. To cover a stretch that took me twenty hours of comfortable, if rugged, driving, Buzz had to undergo nine days of cold food, flat tires, and riding. "I figure," he said with a smile, "I'm getting about five miles to the peanut butter sandwich. And when I get to Alaska, I'm going to sit for a very long time on something I don't have to pedal."

He was heading down the Dempster Highway, the 460-mile-long dirt road from Inuvik in the Northwest Territories to Dawson in the Yukon Territory. And he had stopped on the roadside to chat with two upbound cyclists in their twenties, Mike Wyllie from British Columbia and his friend Ron Deffenbaugh from Montana. He warned them about road and weather conditions ahead and then passed on the most important news of the day: There were two American girls, Cindy Beyer and Janet Ellis, about 100 miles ahead. The two young men looked at each other silently, made their friendly farewells, and got back on their bikes.

Also wandering the area then were three motorcyclists—Lance Hill from Perth, Australia, and Frosty and Rex Woolridge, two brothers in their thirties from Lansing, Michigan. Every other year the brothers work six months in Michigan, bartending, dance teaching, truck driving, Christmas tree farming, to earn enough money to wander somewhere for eighteen months. Frosty got off his huge bike with the homemade stone shield on the front and the tall pile of camping gear on the back. He unzipped his black leather jacket to reveal the sturdy chest of a former Michigan State defensive end. He lifted off his bright, shiny helmet, scratched his beard, and said, with a bright twinkle in his eye, "I want to explore life's total multiplicities."

The brothers got the idea for their odysseys from a biker they once met who said he was seven years into his lifelong dream, a lifetime odyssey wherever he wanted to go. They talked with me that August Arctic morning about how cool the rain was, then how warm the sun felt through their clothes, how funny even many flat tires can be among friends, and how good a hot shower was going to feel later that day. They also said how much they had come to love Canada by just enjoying it. They had heard Canadian advertisements to discover Canada, but they hadn't found many Canadians doing that. "I feel like a kite in this country," Rex said, "zipping along the roads with the dust rising behind me and the sun up ahead and the world so clean and fresh. You take in all these days of joy on a motorcycle here, and then you can handle the few bad ones somewhere else."

There was no warm sun as soon as the elevator door slammed shut. And the loud, whining grind of the electric motor sent us plunging deep beneath the earth's surface. I had wandered around all over the surface of Canada, I figured. Now it was time to see some life under it. For Quebec's asbestos miners, who spend a third of their lives 1,000 feet beneath their homes, the trip begins like any office worker's—in front of an elevator. Except that in their line of work, the elevator goes down at the start of the day and up at the end. The vertical commute takes more than two minutes, and the men, clad in coveralls, steel-rubber boots, safety belts, and battery-powered light helmets, emerge into an intricate network of tunnels and rail lines requiring subterranean road maps.

A journey into a modern asbestos mine is a trip into an eerie, noisy world of dark, muck, and dust, where fierce winds blow and the lights and sounds of an oncoming train appear in the shaft ahead only to disappear suddenly moments later. In the Bell Asbestos Mines, around 100 men were on duty at any one time. They work one week of nights, one week of days, and one week of evenings in a never-ending rotation that miners claim is more dangerous and disruptive to their health and personal lives than the seemingly distant dangers of disease or tunnel collapse.

Some men labor at the 1,500-foot level, blasting and carving out the shafts and ramps that will be mined in coming years. Others maintain the eight- by nine-foot horizontal drifts or tend to the huge heavy-duty machinery that must be lowered from the surface in pieces. Still others gouge out the side alcoves that let gravity do much of the miners' work. There are long dark stretches of tunnel laced with steel rails, a bright clean lunchroom with hot plates and refrigerators, and even a cavernous subterranean "garage" for machinery repairs.

But no one room can be too large, or the soft surrounding serpentine rock carrying the fuzzy asbestos fibers will collapse. Tunnels, some of them six inches deep in muck, are lined with steel reinforcing mesh and several inches of concrete to support the walls. Strong fans blast winds through most shafts, improving ventilation but capable of knocking over the unwary or ripping a steel door from their hands. Alcoves about the size of a large living room are blasted and gouged out of both sides along main shafts. There wait squat front-end loaders driven by men wearing space age Darth Vader helmets and masks that circulate fresh air from backpacks to their faces. These husky machines scoop up the dark gray rock and haul it perhaps 200 yards to breakers, large hydraulic drills that punch the boulder-size rocks through metal gratings to start reducing their size.

Simple gravity carries the debris fifty feet down to the next lower drift, where a chute funnels seven tons into each narrow-gauge railcar. In twelve-car trains that twist and screech their way around sharp turns, the rock is carried to elevators and the surface for further crushing, sorting, and bagging of the off-white fibers—all done automatically by machines that constantly monitor themselves and report their status to lights in a closed control room. The leftover rocks, or tailings, are hauled to the man-made mountain ranges encircling the mine site to add weight to the mine below to help collapse it for more mining.

Underground, each eight-hour shift ends with a thundering thud as explosives experts carefully place and ignite the fifty-three sequential charges that create the rubble for the next shift to mine. The deep, rumbling whumpf of the blasts, which consume a half ton of explosives daily, are timed for when the men are off in the crowded, muddy elevators, the rush hour up to home. Their brief absence allows the dust and dangerous nitroglycerine mist, similar to the medicine used by doctors to stimulate faltering hearts, to settle in the shafts. "You have to be careful," said Gerald Verret, an engineer, as he reached the sunlight once again. "You can get a headache down there."

Then, more than likely, it is time for a good solid meal, perhaps some tender Canadian bacon. But, I discovered, there is one country in the world where you can't get any Canadian bacon. Canada, of course.

In fact, Americans asking for Canadian bacon in Canada are likely to get (1) a blank look, (2) an Egg McMuffin, (3) some wisecrack on the gastronomic irrelevance of a hog's nationality, or (4) all the above. This might be called the chow mein or pizza syndrome, in which all-knowing American diners come to consider a particular food as indigenous to a particular country, much to the surprise of that country's particular citizens.

Canada does have those funny little round slices of pink meat that look like ham but don't taste like bacon. However, in Canada it is called back bacon. In the United States it may be growing in popularity as a breakfast snack, perhaps for a leisurely weekend brunch, or as a minor dinner item to perk up a pile of leftovers. But in Canada the supplies of Canadian bacon are steadily declining (but that's Japan's fault). No one knows for sure precisely how or where the name Canadian bacon originated. "I don't have any idea," Larry Campbell of the Meat Packers Council of Canada told me. Charles Lindsay of Canada Packers Inc., Canada's largest meat processors, suggests it might be Britain's fault. "I think," he said, "it was the name American colonists gave to the kind of bacon that came down from England's other North American colony."

Although North America is increasingly becoming a single market for some products like automobiles, considerable culinary confusion can exist in other areas among those who speak American or Canadian, two languages that can seem the same until a discussion of bacon begins. In the United States bacon is bacon, those long, thin strips of pork neatly arranged in plastic packs to hide all the fat they contain and to emphasize the thin layer of meat. To a Canadian, however, American bacon is side bacon because it comes from the side of a hog or breakfast bacon because it is often eaten then.

To an American, Canadian bacon, which does not come from Canada, is a special bacon, a luxury item that seems imported. To avoid any geographical misunderstandings, American labeling laws require such bacon be called Canadian-style bacon. In Canada, American Canadian-style bacon doesn't exist. It's called back bacon. That's because it comes from the hog's back. Got it? And it's not all that popular anyway.

At one time Ontario and Quebec, Canada's biggest hog-producing areas, shipped a lot of back bacon south to the United States, where it became Canadian bacon. The Canadians felt they had a better, leaner breed of pig. And since the loins, a hog's most expensive cut, aren't frozen, something profitable had to be done with them. With very little sales effort, Americans, especially those on the eastern seaboard, ate them up.

Now, however, there are more government regulations to comply with. There are better American pigs to become Canadian bacon. As Mr. Lindsay put it, "It would be pretty dumb to ship hogs to Iowa or Illinois." Also, today there are more American companies turning out Canadian bacon, some of which may even return to Canada as American Canadian bacon. So nowadays many of Canada's leftover loins are being turned into the onetime British food that Americans call Canadian bacon and shipped to Japan, where consumers may be confused over just what to call it, other than expensive.

A member of any other nationality might be confused if he arrived in Vancouver or Toronto or Montreal on a certain Sunday in November, the annual climax of a nationwide frenzy that once a year gives vast Canada a sense of unity and belies all that tripe about Canadians' being such a sedate people. For this is the day, or rather the week, of the Grey Cup, which is really silver. That is the prize for the Canadian professional football champion. This is the longest weekend of the year, the time when, Canadians believe, it is okay for Canadians to dance, drink, sing, drink, party, drink, yell, blow horns, drink, eat, and drink in a wild manner usually associated with another North American nationality. Somehow amid all the festivities in the streets, the bars, the hotels, the restaurants, and the living rooms, some Canadians even find time to watch the game itself. The game, in fact, is deemed so important to the country that a law requires free distribution of television coverage to any Canadian network that wants it.

Most of the year Canadians seem divided by their economic, linguistic, and geographic diversities and adversities. On Grey Cup Day they are still divided by their athletic antipathies and loyalties, but they are united in one thing: to have a grand old time in what Canadian newspapers call the Grand National Drunk. The cup is named for Earl Grey, a former governor-general (representative of the queen or king) who donated it, and the game site shifts among cities to share the profits and the damage.

A week before kickoff downtown hotels begin storing all movable furniture, sand ashtrays, and other things that might break if, say, they were thrown against a wall. Liquor deliveries are tripled. To handle milling mobs of good-natured boozers in downtown streets, extra police are called in, including some mounted on horses with rows of red reflectors strapped to their flanks. Officially celebrations usually begin on Wednesday, but unofficially television sets begin flying out of windows the previous Sunday, when the top two teams are determined.

Newspaper editors huddle to call for a thorough media blitz—special sections and special shows—and to determine the year's theme: one team's revenge for a midseason drubbing; another's hunger for victory after a quarter century's absence from the championship game. American players on the Canadian teams, who are called imports, are interviewed. Politely they say it is the biggest thing in their lives. Canadian players, who are called nonimports for reasons that seem sensible only to Canadians, are interviewed, too. They are calm and polite and deeply honored.

Then come all the Grey Cup luncheons, Grey Cup press conferences, Grey Cup photo sessions, Grey Cup awards ceremonies, and bevies of shivering beauties posing in skimpy skirts for, of course, the Miss Grey Cup contest. More recently Vancouver's new domed stadium has taken some of the shivering, the snow and rain, and most of the fog out of the game. The night before the contest thousands of cheering fans roam downtown streets, drinking, yelling, cheering, and rocking cars caught in the gleeful traffic jams. By then the movers are done rearranging the furniture in thousands of apartments like Dorothy Archer's so that the television set is more centrally located for any Grey Cup party guests who can find time to watch some of the game.

The festivities have a certain Mardi Gras flavor to them, coming as they do at the end of autumn just before the long festival fast of Canada's winter. The parties begin before game time Sunday with drinks and then snacks and later home-delivered Chinese or chicken or pizza dinners. Most takeout places advertise Grey Cup delivery specials. Guests choose up sides. But by game time the week-long nationwide party is past its peak. That night Canadians begin their fifty-one-week-long recovery. Monday morning, as usual, worker absenteeism will be unusually high. But those who can focus their eyes will be able to find the victor's identity in the newspaper.

Winter in Canada is not so much an interruption of normal life as it is an integral part of normal life. I found Canadian winters where I was could become depressing in their length but never in their features: the beautiful snow, soft and drifting or hard and driven; the resolute ice with its steel grip on all things; the wonderful winds and wan sun; the invigoration of brisk fall days of warning; the exciting release come spring. The elements there belong there, and there's a beauty and a wisdom in that and them. Canadians always grouse about their winters. But I notice that even the millions who annually flee to warmer climes never leave until winter is well established and always return before it is over. The climate is something of a psychic touchstone. When Christopher and I traveled up the narrow Baffin Island fjord from Pangnirtung to the Arctic Circle, the austere beauty and immensity were silencing. The clouds, thin that one October day, were impaled on the mountain peaks, which glowed pink through the mist in the waning sun. The wind was biting, but at the Arctic Circle we picked up some rocks for souvenirs. We talked about how far away anyone else was and wondered if any creature's eyes watched us right then. We looked at the rich emptiness whose stillness seemed as fragile as the finest glass. And we held hands. We didn't talk much on the way back, just watching the dark blue and black waters and the thin sheets of new ice creeping across the bay. And when we had safely returned to town, our local friends wanted to hear nothing of the scenery or the beauty. They demanded to know how far along was the ice. And when they heard it was just starting to form in mid-bay, they all nodded, reassured that things naturally were progressing as they should.

Months after the Grey Cup comes another special day that appears on no calendar. Many Canadian towns celebrate the end of winter with a festival and a lottery. In St. Georges, Quebec, the townsfolk chain an old car in mid-river and then sell tickets to guess the exact date, hour, and minute when the vehicular carcass will plunge through the spring-weakened ice to signify the end of winter. J.M.S. Careless, a history professor at the University of Toronto has a private theory on when spring arrives in Canada in general and in that special North American city in particular. According to him, every year around mid or late May there is one very long night when city crews in silent trucks work their way up and down the many miles of well-kept streets methodically replacing the tall, barren trees that have stood there so starkly since fall. ·

The next morning, when residents glance out their bedroom windows, they find regiments of bushy green trees billowing in warm, gentle breezes. The professor has not yet completed his theory to explain why, come September, these same city crews spread tons of dry old leaves on every yard for residents to rake into the streets for cruising city bulldozers to remove. But his theory must be correct. Spring didn't come to me in

Toronto; it erupted, well after it had been established to the south. And a special kind of happy spirit of appreciation seems to infect the place.

Canadian winters can be snowy or dry or both, sunny or drizzly or both, cold or mild or both. But in most places they are always long, very long. Often there is a teasing false spring in March just to get people thinking of nice, coatless weather, chatting hopefully at the bus stop, and planning to store away the boots with the telltale white salt lines around the soles. The tall, broad snowdrifts, a dirty gray by then, start to shrink. They may even disappear, but the knowing ground remains rock-hard. And sure enough, winter always returns for many more, seemingly longer weeks.

But then, without warning, comes that welcome May day. The streets are shady again. The lawns on the north side of streets quickly green up, to be followed a few weeks later by those on the south side, as the sun climbs farther north in the sky. Bedroom windows, taped shut against sneaky drafts, are cracked open once again, letting in the pad-pad-pad sounds of late-night joggers sweating by and the clop-clop-clop of the city's mounted horse police on their neighborhood dawn patrols, the horses now free of their heavy blankets and the officers without their cossack-style winter caps. Even the motorcycle corps changes that day; their sidecars, added for extra stability on icy roads, are stored away for four or five months. Suddenly the tulips explode in the broad median strips of avenues where cone-shaped fountains of cascading water give the air a fresh, moist smell. Sidewalk cafés blossom. And every noon thousands of office workers stroll and sun themselves and look at each other again on the wide office plazas.

Residential areas are dominated by the fragrance of fresh-cut lawns, where battalions of dandelions and garage sales spring up every weekend. Elderly men patrol the side street sidewalks with their handbells and their little carts with the stone wheel, summoning residents to have kitchen knives spring-sharpened for a negotiable price that may or may not be reported to tax authorities.

Even in the chill evenings, children are back at their ubiquitous street hockey games free of officials and penalties and interrupted only by carefully cruising cars. Canada's very old and very young also seem to emerge with the flowers in the short spring-summer. It is a time when icy walkways do not threaten to break hips and the only time parents are not seen hustling little bundles of pink and blue blankets from well-heated cars into well-heated buildings.

Of course, not everything spring brings is good. It is the time for city property tax bills. And one spring day my basement water meter sprang a spring leak. I telephoned the Public Works Department at 12:10 P.M., reaching a jolly city worker who apologized; it being lunch hour, you know, and such a beautiful day, he explained, for the first time in months the crews were eating their sandwiches outside their trucks and away from their radios. So there would be some delay in the meter's repair.

He was right, of course. The little leak was not repaired until 1:15 P.M., a whole sixty-five minutes after I had notified officials in that city of 3 million. But that is the kind of awful inconvenience one must expect when spring strikes Canada.

I was thinking about things like this one day on the train returning from New York City through Buffalo and Hamilton to Toronto. Trains are great places to think; planes are not. Instead of the roaring whoosh inside an aluminum cocoon seven miles high, trains have that semimonotonous clickety-clack that lulls and assures me of progress toward a destination while erasing other nearby sounds. It was near the end of a day near the end of my time in Canada this time. I was staring idly out the window at the passing countryside. The trackside phone poles were passing blurs. But out in the fields a few hundred feet I could focus on objects: a dog silently barking at this passing object; a parked farm truck; a gnarled tree; a barn; rural operations preparing for another dusk. Eastern Canada, with its tidy fields and fences, its paved roads, its history, doesn't feel as expansive to me as the West with its skyscrapers, its newness, its immense fields, its broad, uncluttered horizons, physical and mental. The West is a New Canada aborning within an old one. The East for me is full of history and memories.

I thought about little things really, human things that make Canada for me a special place. I thought about Janice Le Sarge. I never met her, but when she sent through a ticket refund on one of my credit cards because of my impending departure, she added a little note at the bottom: "Good luck on your move." I thought about Sam Luciani, who spent most of his life above Canada's Arctic Circle. "It's not a bad country really," he said. I thought about Terry Fox, the one-legged Canadian cancer victim who overcame his disease in a run across much of his country before the disease overcame him. "I believe in miracles," he had said, "I have to." I thought about old Gus Heitmann, the Yukon prospector who still keeps a horseshoe over his house trailer door and still pats it every time he leaves.

And I thought about my grandparents, who could have used a horseshoe sometimes. They were gone now, buried together in a plot near the same railroad tracks that ran by their old home where everyone would gather on those Sunday afternoons so very long ago. After everyone else had gone home in those days, my grandparents and I would walk down their sandy driveway, hand in hand, and stroll the 500 or 600 feet to the local railroad station. It was a pilgrimage, I am told, I made even as a toddler in a stroller, demanding stones to play with en route.

The station was just a shed really. But I had an inexplicable fascination with those trains. I'd look and look so hard down the tracks and see nothing. Then the moment I'd turn away for a second to chase a frog or something and then look back, wow, there was the white-hot dot of an engine headlight. I couldn't hear it yet, not even if I put my ear down by the steel tracks. But I knew something was coming, something very big, very fast, very strong. Some evenings there were two or three trains, freights mostly by that time of night. Some nights there was just one train: "Oh, Grandpa, five more minutes, please. I just know one will be along soon."

And then the light would grow larger and brighter and even larger and brighter. From the side of the tracks I was transfixed. It looked as if it surely would run me over, and I wanted to run away. But I couldn't. I would miss seeing it. I was so awed by these machines sometimes that I wouldn't notice the butterscotch ice cream melting down my hand and dripping into the sand. Which, to anyone knowing how I felt about butterscotch ice cream, would say a good deal about my state of mind at those moments.

Then, at last, I could hear it coming, sometimes a bell, sometimes, joy of joys, that beautiful mournful whistle. Sometimes I'd hear only the massive rumble of so much weight moving so quickly, and that was all right, too. Without speaking, Grandpa and Grandma would pull me back a few steps. We all knew something special was about to happen. But each time it was a wondrous mystery again. My eyes never left that powerful oncoming engine. Suddenly it seemed to gain speed, so much speed. It was coming right at us! Right at us! And then, with a terrifying roar, that hot, steaming engine would blast past. And the air all around would swirl about in vicious gusts. The ground would shake. And the steel rails would bow down with each set of wheels passing over. My ears would be so full of noise and steel thunder that I couldn't hear myself yelling for joy at Grandma. It was hard to believe there was a man inside that engine. Sometimes he would wave. And I would frantically wave back for the passing instant that I could see him way up there looking down.

With their Canadian National and Canadian Pacific names emblazoned by their rippled steel doors, all the boxcars going by were good and noisy, too. But nothing could top the engine. Somehow, when the caboose went by with the red lantern swinging on the back, it seemed to be going so much more slowly than the front. And that made sense at the time since it was farther behind, right? If I hadn't finished my ice-cream cone by then, it would be covered with soot. But that was a small price to pay. And as my grandfather and my grandmother and I slowly walked home, sometimes I'd hear that same mournful whistle down the line at the next crossing. I figured it was moaning me good-bye.

Late on those hot summer nights I would lie in my bed up on the second floor of Grandma's house. Some nights I would wait in vain and drift off to sleep to the sounds of moths and big june bugs buzzing at the screen. But most nights my patience was rewarded. I would hear that whistle coming. And I would get ready. I couldn't see it. But if I moved over against the cool green plaster wall, when the train got close, I could feel in my back the rumbling power of that thing. The house would shake. The glass lamp would rattle. Sometimes, if I was very lucky and had been very good, two trains passed Grandma's house at the same time, doubling the rumble. You could hear each approaching through a different window. I'd picture the two steaming, steel behemoths rushing headlong toward each other. I'd picture the windy confusion of their mingling maelstroms. And I'd picture the rails bending and the trackside bushes blowing about and the reddish brown cars obediently following along and then going away into the distance with their secret cargoes and the little red lanterns silently swinging on the back.

Suddenly, an adult's idle dreaming of childhood days gone by was jolted by what I saw through the modern train's window. My God! That was my grandmother's house out there in the dusk. I sat bolt upright and turned my head to follow as we quickly passed. It couldn't be. But it was!

There was the front porch. The cigars. The men. The rockers. Some trees were gone. But the driveway remained. And the shutters. And the old lightning rod with the ceramic ball. And behind that same second-floor wall a little boy had lain so many nights and dreamed about the trains and Canada. He always wondered where they were going.

NOTES

Chapter I. Geography

1. J. M. S. Careless, *Canada—A Story of Challenge* (Toronto: Macmillan of Canada, 1965), p. 3

2. Northrop Frye, "Thoughts of a Great Scholar," *Maclean's* (April 5, 1982), p. 43.

3. Cole Harris, "The Emotional Structure of Canadian Regionalism," a lecture at McGill University, Montreal, March 17, 1981.

Chapter II. The People

1. Northrop Frye, "Canada's Emerging Identity," *Toronto Star*, June 28, 1980, pp. B1 and B4.

2. Ibid.

3. Charles Gordon, "How Canadians Mistreat Heroes," *Maclean's* (December 5, 1983), p. 17.

4. Nora McCabe, "Give This Man a Chance and He'll Produce a Champion," *Racquets Canada* (March 1978), p. 21.

5. The British created the province of Canada in 1841 by joining Upper and Lower Canada (a reference to their location on the St. Lawrence River). In 1867 the Dominion of Canada was created by joining the provinces of Nova Scotia, New Brunswick, and Canada, by then divided into Canada West, which became Ontario, and Canada East, which became Quebec.

6. Without the fort victory to cheer in hindsight, American students learn perhaps a bit more about another part of the same campaign, the Battle of Lake Erie, which is more famous to Americans for what was said than for what was shot. "Don't give up the ship!" U.S. Captain James Lawrence cried with his dying breath after his engagement with a British frigate. Oliver Hazard Perry later added, "We have met the enemy and they are ours."

7. "God Bless America," *The Royal Bank of Canada Monthly Letter*, Vol. 60, No. 8 (August 1979), p. 2.

8. "Hated the Film; Loved the T-shirt," *Saturday Night* (December 1979), p. 4.

9. "A Vision That Transcends Borders," *Maclean's* (May 24, 1982), p. 6.

10. "Williams Battles Theatre Clichés," *Globe and Mail*, January 1, 1984, p. 10.

11. "Nationalism Hurts Culture, Author Says," *Toronto Star*, October 25, 1978, p. A4.

12. "The Joys of a Bountiful Season," *Maclean's* (December 19, 1983), p. 46.

13. As in many areas of Canadian life, a government has indelibly left its imprint. In 1939 the federal government created the National Film Board (NFB) to initiate and promote films "in the national interest" and "to interpret Canada to Canadians and to other countries." Besides training hundreds of Canadians and pioneering in such technical areas as animation, sound recording, and cinéma vérité documentaries, the NFB has won more than 2,000 awards, including 6 Oscars, and produced thirty-two feature films, including the acclaimed *Mon Oncle Antoine*. It was a far cry from the early days, when the board opened in a converted sawmill and dispatched squads of projectionists on regular routes to hundreds of small communities like cinematic circuit riders. There, for the first time, Canadians, until then exposed mostly to United States films, could see the wonders of their own country and their own lives through the labors of their own homegrown talent.

Chapter III. The United States and Canada

1. David A. Baldwin, "Canadian-American Relations: Myth and Reality," *International Studies Quarterly*, Vol. XII, No. 2 (June 1968), p. 128.

2. Marie-Josée Drouin and Harald B. Malmgren, "Canada, the United States and the World Economy," *Foreign Affairs* (Winter 1981–82), p. 393.

Chapter IV. The Economy

1. Northrop Frye, "Thoughts of a Great Scholar," *Maclean's* (April 5, 1982), p. 43.

2. J. M. S. Careless, *Canada—A Story of Challenge* (Toronto: Macmillan of Canada, 1965), p. 278.

3. Peter C. Newman, *The Acquisitors: The Canadian Establishment*, Vol. II (Toronto: McClelland wart, 1981), p. 5.

4. Both Presidents Nixon and Reagan made such statements in public talks during their administrations.

5. Crawford D. Goodwin, "Canadian-American Relations in Perspective," *Current History*, Vol. 62, No. 369 (April 1972), p. 178.

6. Robert B. Reich, "The Next American Frontier," *The Atlantic* (March 1983), p. 44.

7. Peter C. Newman, "Rewriting the Social Contract," *Maclean's* (October 17, 1983), p. 52.

8. One interesting proposal for the government involves a new kind of job voucher. A worker accumulates job entitlement points during his or her working life. If the worker becomes unemployed, he or she could offer these points to a potential employer, who could cash them in for money from the government, the idea being to give older workers in the job market some recognition and a better chance in the tightening competitran for work.

9. Mary Janigan, "The Price of Salesmanship," *Maclean's* (January 24, 1983), pp. 10–11.

Chapter V. My Canada

1. Ernest Hemingway, "The Hotels in Switzerland," *Toronto Star Weekly* (March 4, 1922).

2. Connie Rennick, "Building for the Future," *Racquets Canada* (May 1977), p. 4A.

3. Northrop Frye, "Thoughts of a Great Scholar," *Maclean's* (April 5, 1982), p. 43.

4. Actually it is named for a man, Earl Grey, who donated the prize.

5. Rowland C. Frazee, "Getting Our Act Together," *The Royal Bank of Canada, a Message to Shareholders* (January 8, 1981), p. 1.

6. John W. Holmes, *Life with Uncle* (Toronto: University of Toronto Press, 1981), p. 112.

7. Another immigrant, Robert Haas, wrote me a letter in 1943, when I was five months old. "My dear little friend," he began. He had heard of my birth from my grandfather, his immigration case officer. "This uncle," Mr. Haas wrote to me, "probably will not be alife [sic] anymore when you read these lines." He went on to describe the travails and discomfort and awkwardness of being an immi-

grant. "Of course, we had more faults than merits," he said, "being strange here, uprooted homeless people." But he wanted me to know of the many kindnesses of Canadians like my grandfather and of how valuable and warming they had been at a difficult time. I knew Mr. Haas only through this letter. But he was right. He was gone when I read it.

INDEX

ⒼⒼⒼ

Index

Igloolik, N.W.T., 31
igloos, 33
Imasco Inc., 203, 257
immigration, 64–66, 147
  from American colonies, 13, 65, 134
  to Australia vs. Canada, 57
  motives for, 58–59
  regional settlement patterns and, 12, 227–228
  from U.S., 106–107, 110
  to U.S. vs. Canada, 66
Imperial Life Assurance Company of Canada, 210
Imperial Oil, 18, 162
Inco Ltd., 275–276, 306
income, personal, 78
  of men vs. women, 77
India, immigrants from, 59, 67
Industrial Sector Committees, 298
inertial navigation systems, 42
infant mortality, 76
inflation, 164, 214
insulin, 132, 163
insurance industry, 191, 210
interest rates, 157, 245
International Thomson Organisation, 212
Inuit, 30, 31–33, 35, 46–47, 49, 67, 72–75, 134
  art of, 141–142
  as Canada's first settlers, 64–65
Inuktitut languages, 7, 36, 50, 71, 134
Inuvik, N.W.T., 22, 23
Inverness Petroleum, 306
Investment Funds Institute of Canada, 211
ionamut, 7
Iranian hostage crisis, xii, 60–61
Ireland, immigrants from, 59
Iron Ore Company of Canada, 295

Jacobi, Lou, 126
James Bay, Que., 44, 119–120, 317
Japan:
  immigration from, 72
  trade with, 20, 175, 185, 196, 197, 198, 215, 225, 293, 311, 312
Jenkins, Ferguson, 130
Jennings, Peter, 127, 201
Jess, Peter, 37, 39
Jewett, Audrey, 115–116
Jewison, Norman, 127
Johns, Johnny, 98
Johnson, Lyndon B., 154
Johnson, William, 144
Johnston, David L., 124, 173, 183

Jones, Hugh, 296
Jonsson, Rangar, 49
Joshua Then and Now (Richler), 69
juvenile delinquency, 93

kanata, 63
Karsh, Yousuf, 126
Keeler, Ruby, 127
Kennedy, Edward M., 164
Kennedy, John F., 171, 191
Kennedy, Leo, 145
Kent, Peter, 127
Kerouac, Jack, 123
Kidd Creek Mines Ltd., 306
Kidder, Margot, 126, 191
Kierans, Thomas, 317
King, Mackenzie, 282
King, Martin Luther, Jr., 154
Kirk Ltd., 279
kisiskatchewan, 16
Kives, Philip, 211
Klondike Big Inch Land Company, 345
Klondike gold rush, 20, 273
Klondike Highway, 107
Knox, Alexander, 126
Knudsen, Calvert, 262
Koffler Stores, 202, 203
Koponoar oil well, 236
Kozicki, Michael, 338, 339
Kruger Pulp and Paper, 261
K-tel, 211
Kuhns, Buzz, 354

Labatt's, 206, 207, 209
Labrador, 9
Labrador Mining, 255
La Grande River, 119
Lake Erie, Battle of, 154
Lalonde, Marc, 326
La Marche, Pierre, 327
Lamarre, Bernard, 195
Lambert, Allen, 307–308
Lamm, Richard, 316
Landed Immigrant status, 66
"Landless Man and Manless Land, The," 29
Lane, Virgil, 151
Langston, Charles, 248
languages, Canadian, 134–137
Lavalin Inc., 195
law enforcement, in Yukon, 95–100, 115–116
Layton, Irving, 145–146
Leacock, Stephen, 145
lead resources, 20, 43, 44, 270

Index

ABOUT THE AUTHOR

ANDREW H. MALCOLM served as Toronto Bureau Chief of *The New York Times* for four years and is currently Chicago Bureau Chief. He has also reported for *The Times* from Indochina, Japan, Korea, New York, and San Francisco, and has won four major awards for national reporting. He and his wife, Connie, have three children.